Real World Microsoft Access Database Protection and Security

GARRY ROBINSON

Real World Microsoft Access Database Protection and Security
Copyright © 2004 by Garry Robinson

ISBN (pbk): 1-59059-126-7

Printed and bound in the United States of America 12345678910

Appendix C reprinted with permission from *From Access to SQL Server*, ISBN: 1-893115-24-0, published by Apress. Copyright © 2000 by Russell Sinclair.

Trademarked names may appear in this book. Rather than use a trademark symbol with every occurrence of a trademarked name, we use the names only in an editorial fashion and to the benefit of the trademark owner, with no intention of infringement of the trademark.

Technical Reviewer: Frank Rice

Editorial Board: Dan Appleman, Craig Berry, Gary Cornell, Tony Davis, Steven Rycroft, Julian Skinner, Martin Streicher, Jim Sumser, Karen Watterson, Gavin Wray, John Zukowski

Assistant Publisher: Grace Wong

Project Manager: Sofia Marchant

Development Editor: Tracy Brown Collins

Copy Editor: Kristen Imler

Production Manager: Kari Brooks

Production Editor: Janet Vail

Proofreader: Linda Seifert

Compositor: Susan Glinert Stevens

Indexer: Kevin Broccoli, Broccoli Information Services

Cover Designer: Kurt Krames

Manufacturing Manager: Tom Debolski

Distributed to the book trade in the United States by Springer-Verlag New York, Inc., 175 Fifth Avenue, New York, NY 10010 and outside the United States by Springer-Verlag GmbH & Co. KG, Tiergartenstr. 17, 69112 Heidelberg, Germany.

In the United States: phone 1-800-SPRINGER, email orders@springer-ny.com, or visit http://www.springer-ny.com. Outside the United States: fax +49 6221 345229, email orders@springer.de, or visit http://www.springer.de.

For information on translations, please contact Apress directly at 2560 Ninth Street, Suite 219, Berkeley, CA 94710. Phone 510-549-5930, fax 510-549-5939, email info@apress.com, or visit http://www.apress.com.

The source code for this book is available to readers at http://www.apress.com in the Downloads section.

To my father, Keith, I hope that I will be as inspirational to my sons, Sean and James, as you have been to me.

Contents at a Glance

Contents

Chapter 12 Protecting and Securing Your Database with the Operating System 403

Appendix A Specific Access Security Information 453

Appendix B Registering the Access Workbench 459

Appendix C Why Migrate from Access to SQL Server? 461

Index 475

Foreword

Security and Garry Robinson

RIGHT NOW, for software developers, it would be hard to imagine a more important topic than security. If you're reading this book, then you are one of those people who know that Access is a great tool for building database applications. In this book, Garry Robinson brings these two topics together to show you how to create secure Access applications. If you're an Access developer, a database administrator, or an IT manager responsible for Access application development, you probably need this book. If you're a consultant who's creating Access applications for paying clients, then you definitely need this book.

I first "met" Garry through the pages of *Smart Access*. Garry was this working consultant over in Australia who was building great applications in Access and sending me proposals for articles. Garry's first proposal described a data mining package he had built for some clients that he was marketing (ironically enough, many of Garry's clients at that time were in the mining industry). Over the years, I continued to get more article proposals from Garry. They were all great, and they all found their way into *Smart Access*.

Why were Garry's proposals so great? Three reasons:

1. They described genuinely useful techniques for Access developers.

2. Garry frequently packaged the tools so that other Access developers could use them as utilities.

3. All the code reflected an understanding of what it takes to create great software in the real world.

So, now, Garry is a contributing editor for Smart Access, and we communicate frequently by email. I even managed to make it over to Australia once and met Garry in the flesh. Garry and his wife squired my wife and me around Sydney for a day. It was great. I thought we bonded.

But Garry has never written an article for *Smart Access* on security, a subject that he, unbeknown to me, knows a great deal about. Now I find out why—he was saving up all that material for this book. You can't trust anybody. Which, I guess, is the point of this book.

And Garry knows a lot about security. Normally, discussions of Access security start and end with workgroup security. It turns out that there's a lot more to consider. Garry begins, for instance, by discussing the security issues around common Access practices that you've already been using (for example, in Chapter 4, where Garry discusses splitting databases and using the AutoExec macro). In Chapter 8, where Garry discusses workgroup security, he begins by telling you why it's important and where it fits among all the security-related actions that you must take. Garry also goes into workgroup security in depth, discussing security for topics that others ignore: Data Access Pages, user surveillance, and menus. Even with workgroup security completely covered, Garry isn't done—I've been using Access for more than a decade now, and I had never even thought about integrating Windows security with my Access applications in the way that Garry shows in this book. This book is for the real Access programmer: Though Garry covers material relevant to Access Data Projects, the focus remains on Access itself and the Access developer's main tool—the Jet database.

What I really appreciated about this book is that Garry covers these issues from the point of view of the real-world Access developer, the database administrator, and the IT manager. Throughout the book, Garry provides the sample code and the step-by-step instructions that you need to implement these techniques, along with the perspective to understand what's important to you.

If you apply all the techniques described in this book, you may never know whether they work. That's the problem with security: No news is good news. But if you ever have a security breach and one of Garry's techniques would have prevented the problem—well, try explaining that to your boss/client/customer.

I'm going to keep this book near at hand. You should, too.

Peter Vogel
Editor of *Smart Access* newsletter from Pinnacle Publishing

About the Author

Garry Robinson got started in software development two decades ago, after completing a Masters Degree in Three-Dimensional Mapping. From there, he ran a small team of programmers that developed customized software for a mining company by using programming tools such as Fortran, Informix, and Microsoft Access. For the past eight years, he's headed his own software consultancy business, GR-FX Pty Limited,  and has been involved in developing and supporting more than 100 Access applications for more than 30 organizations. Garry's clients include mining, insurance, and transport businesses, and quite a number of his jobs are assisting other Access programmers who are working for their own clients. Garry is a contributing editor to Pinnacle Publishing's monthly *Smart Access* newsletter and is an editor of the popular programming Web site vb123.com. He develops and sells Access database shareware software for database administration, graphical data mining, and toolkits for developers. When Garry isn't sitting at the keyboard, he can be found playing golf or swimming with the sharks at the beaches of Sydney, Australia.

About the
Technical Reviewer

Frank Rice is a programmer/writer for the Office Developer Center at Microsoft. Before that, he was support engineer and application developer specializing in Microsoft Access. He enjoys working with and writing about databases, especially those in Access.

About the Foreword Author

Peter Vogel (MBA, MCSD) is a principal in PH&V Information Services. PH&V provides consulting services in client/server and intranet development. PH&V clients include Volvo, Christie Digital, the Canadian Imperial Bank of Commerce, and Microsoft. Peter's white papers appeared in the Visual Studio.NET and Microsoft Office 2003 release package. He also did extensive work on XML in Office 2003.

Peter is the editor of the *Smart Access* newsletter from Pinnacle Publishing (www.pinpub.com) and wrote *The Visual Basic Object and Component Handbook* (Prentice Hall), which has been called "The definitive guide to 'thinking with objects.'" Peter was the founding editor of the *XML Developer* newsletter, now *Hardcore Web Services Developer*. In addition to teaching for Learning Tree International, Peter wrote their ASP.NET and technical writing courses. His articles have appeared in every major magazine devoted to VB-based development and can be found in the Microsoft Developer Network libraries. Peter lives in Goderich, Ontario, Canada, but presents at conferences all over the world.

Acknowledgments

OVER THE LAST NINE MONTHS, I have learned that a technical book like this one comes about not because of one supposedly smart developer typing words into a notepad computer on Bondi Beach, but because of the teamwork and structure provided by a professional publishing company like Apress. So thanks to those at Apress who were involved in my book, including Karen Watterson and Gary Cornell, who both said I could do it; Sofia Marchant; Tracy Brown Collins; Julian Skinner; Janet Vail; and finally to Kristen Imler, whose writing skills were the icing on the cake. I hope to meet you all in person one day.

My special thanks go to Frank Rice, the technical editor for the book, who had to wade through all my first drafts and was successful in steering the ship back on course on many occasions. To Peter Vogel, who kindly wrote the foreword, I must thank you for plucking me from obscurity in 1998 to write for the *Smart Access* magazine and for your guidance on good technical writing. To Russell Sinclair, thank you for allowing the readers to benefit from your knowledge on Access to SQL Server migration, which I have included in an appendix to this book.

Thanks to Bob Weiss from Password Crackers, Inc. and Dmitry Konevnik from Passware for their insights into what the smart people actually do know about Microsoft Access security.

Back home in Australia, I would like to thank Scott McManus and Doug Thatcher, whose counsel is always welcome; my clients, whose projects have helped fine-tune the real world samples in this book; and the guys at the Art Lounge in Coogee, whose wonderful coffee kept me going on many occasions. I need especially to single out John Reidy, whose system administration skills led me quickly to some useful operating system security solutions.

Finally, to my lovely wife, Fran, who endured my obsessive drive to grind out the book (and sneak off to golf) while bringing James, our latest software project, into the world just a few weeks before the book was finished. Thanks also go to my family, Mandy, Keith, and Margaret, and Fran's family, who helped out Team Robinson during this busy year.

The Access Protection and Security Driving Instructions

WELCOME TO MY FIRST BOOK on my favorite topic, Microsoft Access. I hope you enjoy reading the book and that it will add yet more luster to the desktop/network database that keeps coming up trumps for millions of users around the world.

In this chapter, I summarize what you will learn about Microsoft Access database protection and security from this book. I also include some "driving instructions" that you can use to identify and locate the information that is relevant to you. This chapter includes an explanation of how to use the demonstration material that comes with the book; and, for those of you who want to get started right away, I outline two simple security measures that you can deploy without too much complication. To complete the chapter, I discuss whether upgrading software will improve your security and, as you will find at the end of every chapter, I have included a list of Web pages and help material that you can follow up on to read more about the topics raised in the chapter.

What's This Book Going to Do for You?

Microsoft Access is the most popular desktop database in the world today, which means that many people have investigated its security measures and some have worked out ways to get around them. Coupled with that, Access is a versatile database designed for both developers and users. When you first set up a database, it comes with all its security turned off and all the developer tools turned on. This book tells you how to turn on the security properly and also shows you how to protect the investment that you have made in the database.

This book also describes the issues and demonstrates best practice protection and security for Access. I will discuss internal Access security and protection and folder permissions of modern operating systems. Where possible, I will show you strategies to combine both of these security measures to create a number of layers of defense for your database. If you properly adopt and use the protection methods outlined in this book, you should be able to thwart all but the most determined and skilled users and hackers. So what is it that you are trying to secure? I'll discuss that now.

Learn What It Is that We Are Trying to Secure

From the outset, I must inform you that good Access security will require you to set up many roadblocks of different types to keep your database villain at bay. Among the many things that you need to do to secure your database:

- Hide the important Access menu commands that expose the objects in your database.

- Stop people from importing your objects into another database.

- Stop people from getting to your treasured code and objects.

- Make sure that people use the user interface that you create for the database.

- Keep the workgroup file that maintains your internal security from your database users.

Unfortunately, if you implement each of these measures on its own, you will be able to lay claim to having only good quality protection and, arguably, some security. To make any security fail-safe, you need to combine different internal protection measures and touch that up with operating system security, all that while understanding the flaws of an old and popular product such as Access.

Setting the Record Straight on Access Security

This book tells you what Access security is, how you apply it, and how to determine whether it works. The book is very pragmatic because in most cases, Access security isn't very secure anymore, and labeling it that way is misleading, because it is only really offers protection. It is only when you set it up in a certain way and then combine different Access security and protection techniques that you end up with best-practice security for your database. If you then store your databases in operating system-protected folders and open the databases by using secured shortcut techniques, you can lay claim to a secure system because people will have great difficult copying the database; and then when they do, they will be unlikely to unravel your internal security.

If you are a seasoned Access programmer and feel that you have security covered, let this book be the wake-up call that makes you re-assess the database security that you have been involved in. If there is one message that you take from this book, be it that you need to schedule regular reviews of your database security because no matter how good your skills, things can change over time, especially where humans are involved. This means that many Access users and developers are aware of its vulnerabilities and therefore may be able to use those on your database. Worse still, some companies have developed password-cracking software that decodes the built-in Access security. As a result, Access developers have to be extra diligent when it comes to protecting their databases, and this book shows you how to shore up your defenses.

 NOTE   As many publications for enterprise issues such as secure Internet sites and big company operating system security will tell you, security works best when there are multiple layers of defense. Because the files that form the Access system are just that—files—Access database security relies not only on the techniques that I have outlined in this book but many other security systems such as firewalls, operating systems, networks, physical security, and of course, the biggest issue of them all, people.

Find Out How to Protect Your Investment

This book aims to achieve a lot more than helping you keep people from stealing your database or code. It's all about doing things that will protect the investment that you made in your database. To help achieve this, this book has extensive coverage on issues such as

- Appropriate database options.

- Good programming practices, such as splitting databases and error handling.

- Backing up and recovering databases, tables, and objects.

- User surveillance.

- Setting up, implementing, and protecting your menus.

But Will It Take a Long Time?

Most databases can be secured in less than a week, and quite a lot of techniques that I will illustrate can be done in less that a day or so, especially with some of the tools that I have provided. So read the book that I am happy to have written for you, and good luck. In the meantime, you are probably already wondering how much work this is going to mean for you, so I have prepared driving instructions so that you can quickly find the material that is relevant to your situation.

The Overall Road Map

Before I provide you with the individual directions, I will explain how the book is organized and give you a brief rundown on what you can expect to find in each chapter. Essentially, I have split the book into four chapter threads that deal with different aspects of protecting and securing your Access database. Introductions to the chapter threads and the chapters follow.

The Options and Attributes Chapters

Access is a very versatile product, and you can vary the way that it works and what people see by changing the startup and database options and the attributes of objects in Database window.

Chapter 2: Protecting Your Database with Startup Options

Startup options will make it difficult for users to modify your database objects and data. They will also direct the user to employ the user interface that you intended for them to use and, as you will find out later, you will want to be aware of a number of issues if you want to protect the database options. Even though they seem easy to use, you have to be careful about how you set them up if you want users to continue using them.

Chapter 3: Using Database Options and Attributes to Protect Data and Objects

Find out which of the 50 or so database options will protect or expose your database. You will also learn how to hide objects in the Database window so that users, who are exploring the objects through the Database window or the importing interface, are less likely to stumble on your important data and objects.

The Protect and Improve Your Database Chapters

There is more to protection and security of an Access database than just stopping people from doing or seeing things. These chapters explain why you have to set up your database in a certain way, how you can recover from object changes or unintentional deletions, user surveillance, and specific improvements offered by changes to toolbars and menus.

Chapter 4: Providing a Solid Foundation with Good Programming Practices

This chapter will show you how to launch your Access software, how to split your database into software and data, and how to set up error handing. These issues are necessary background topics when you are setting up Access protection and security.

Chapter 5: Backing Up and Recovering Your Databases

It goes without saying that backups are important. This chapter shows you how to make additional copies of your database and back up the data and objects in them. More importantly, it shows you how to recover them.

Chapter 6: User and Object Surveillance

Find out who is using your database and how they are using it. This important surveillance information can help you with administration issues such as asking users to log off the database for maintenance and upgrades of the database or the network. It can also assist you in targeting security for your database. Auditing user activities is an important part of the protection process.

Chapter 7: Protecting Your Database with Menus and Toolbars

Find out the tricks of the trade for building menus and toolbars, and then how you can apply those toolbars to your database by using either form and report properties or the Access startup options. By setting up menus and toolbars correctly, your database will be easier to use and harder for most users to crack.

The Internal Database Security Chapters

If you want to lay claim to having security in an Access database, you really have to implement some form of workgroup (user-level) security. These chapters detail how to set up a more secure workgroup environment, the bigger security issues, and the specifics of securing the different types of objects in the database. Included in the chapters are strategies that allow you to avoid the pitfalls of password-cracking software, Access importing options, and solutions to the most illusive issue of all, data protection.

Chapter 8: Developing Workgroup Security

First up, you will learn how to set up a developer's workgroup file and why it is an important tool for every Access developer. You will also find out how to achieve a lot of security and protection without producing too complex a security design and how to create a database that is not susceptible to password-cracking software. In this chapter, you will also find a complete list of all the driving instructions relating to workgroup security that covers all the internal database security chapters.

Chapter 9: Security Concerns, Encryption, and Database Passwords

Find out about the tools and Access menu options that can readily punch holes in your supposedly secure Access database. In the process, learn why you need to set up your workgroup security in a certain way and understand why database encryption and database passwords are more applicable as a spoiler rather than a security defense mechanism in their own right.

Chapter 10: Securing Data with Workgroup Security

This chapter takes you through the conventional ways of protecting your data with workgroup security and then outlines how you can set up your workgroup files so that password-cracking software will not be very effective. Get instructions on incorporating Windows 2000/XP security so that your users simulate logging on to the database by using Windows user accounts. Finally, if you contemplate distributing important Access data outside the company network, be wary.

Chapter 11: Object Protections and Security Measures

Learn the intricacies of the all-important MDE database format, as well as many other ways to protect the queries, forms, reports, macros, and modules in your database. Specifically, get instructions for hiding linked tables, using remote queries, opening your forms and reports so your users cannot edit them, and how to use data access pages with workgroup files.

Chapter 12: Protecting and Securing Your Database with the Operating System

No matter what internal protection and security measures you add to your Access database, you can improve your protection substantially by using a modern operating system with a file server or peer-to-peer server. This chapter details how you can set up a group of Windows users that has permission to open the folder that your database resides in. If you really want to improve this protection to a secure level, use the detailed instructions in this chapter or show them to your network administrator so that no one can browse the folder and subfolders where the databases are stored. This process also makes it very difficult to copy the databases from these folders. You'll also get a brief review of many other issues, like external security, personnel, and other related computer security topics.

The Appendices

Appendix A has a list of all the workgroup security information used in the chapter. Appendix B details the instructions for registering Access Workbench 1.3, a program I wrote. Appendix C is a free bonus chapter from Russell Sinclair's Apress book, *Access to SQL Server*. This chapter discusses the reasons for and against migrating an Access database to SQL Server and the difference between Access and SQL Server.

Your Personal Driving Instructions

This book is like any knowledge-based tool: there is a lot of material to sift through and not all of it is going to apply to you now. For some readers, the amount of material won't matter because you may have the time to read the book from cover to cover. For others, like me, computer books are for skimming and absorbing what is appropriate at the time and then, hopefully, for returning to later to read completely. For these types of readers, I have assembled a number of different sets of driving instructions to help you find what suits your situation most quickly.

No matter what happens, you are going to have to slice and dice the ideas, examples, and samples to fit your own situation, and I hope that the chapter introductions and book-driving instructions that follow help you to get the most out of the book.

 NOTE   Throughout this section, you may come across terminology that you may not be familiar with. I have deliberately not elaborated on the terminology at this stage, but I will do so at the appropriate times in the chapters referenced immediately following the terminology.

This book aims more at providing a comprehensive review of the protection and security topic than catering precisely to a particular reader skill level. As a result, the book has to cater to different audiences and cover a variety of topics. To help you digest the information relevant to you, I have prepared brief driving instructions for different topics or reader types, as follows.

Protecting Your Data Locally

First, you will need to turn off the all the startup options (Chapter 2), split your database (Chapter 4), protect your menus (Chapter 7), use workgroup security to protect startup options and your user interface (Chapter 8), and add workgroup security for your data (Chapter 10). To support your internal Access security, you can restrict the people who use your database by using operating system security (Chapter 12).

Securing Your Data Locally

Securing data is not easy and will require you first to follow the instructions in the previous "Protect Your Data Locally" section. Once you have all those elements working, you will need to implement the protected Access folder strategy (Chapter 12), look carefully at how you manage your workgroups (Chapter 10), and build a secure shortcut to open the database (Chapter 10).

Securing Software and Code

Making an MDE-format database will secure your forms, reports, and VBA code (Chapters 1 and 11). If you find that you have to stick with the MDB database format, you will need to read about developer workgroup security (Chapter 8) and securing your objects (Chapter 11). No matter what, you will need to split your database and add error handling to your database (Chapter 4).

Managers' Top Issues

Once a manager has identified his or her important databases (and for big companies, this process may involve sifting through a large number of them), there are some important issues to get on top of. Probably most important is ascertaining whether important data that may seriously damage your company if it is lost or ends up in the wrong hands is stored in the Access databases. To protect this data, you will need to verify that you are backing up and can recover the databases (Chapter 5), to protect your database properly by using internal security (Chapter 10), and to protect the databases by using the operating system (Chapter 12). On the software side, if you have any internally secured databases, you need to ensure that you have backups of the passwords and workgroup identifiers used to secure the databases (Chapter 8) and that you have access to the source code that is legally yours (Chapter 11). Finally, when your developers or DBA say that the Access database needs upgrading to another programming language or a server database, you can verify the value of that advice of that by collecting user statistics (Chapter 6).

Backing Up Your Database

A very important part of protecting your database is having backups that you can recover (Chapter 5). To assist you with that process, you are going to need to find out who is using your database so that you can ask those users to log off (Chapter 6). Finally, if you are trying to secure your database, you will need to ensure that your users cannot prowl around the backup folders by using the Access protected folder strategy (Chapter 12).

Options for the Procrastinator

Procrastination is not an advised option when it comes to security, so let me suggest some easy habits. First, you should turn off the nonmenu startup options (Chapter 2). Next, you should identify the important objects in your database and hide them (Chapter 3). Now, turn off the nonmenu startup options (Chapter 7) and add some simpler menus and toolbars to make your database look more like a user interface than a developer interface. Put a note in your diary to review all the other options in two months.

Apologies to All Ye Hackers

In this book, I have been open about the issues caused by password-cracking software and quiet about some of the little issues that cause a threat. In some cases, I crafted the information to help you avoid a particular threat without actually discussing how you could take advantage of that threat to exploit a particular vulnerability of Access. So if you are thinking of using this book as a guide to help you pilfer someone's database asset, you will be a little disappointed.

Protecting and Building a Better Interface

One side benefit of introducing protection and security measures is that you can improve the interface. To do so, look at the startup options (Chapter 2), better error messages (Chapter 4), and protecting menus (Chapter 7). Sometimes when you're working on a software database that has many forms and reports, you just cannot decide what the best thing to improve next is. For those times, I recommend user object logging (Chapter 6), which will help you ascertain what objects are being used the most.

The Server Database Option

If you have determined that you want to transfer your database to SQL Server or some other server-based database (Appendix C) for performance, stability, or enterprise-level security, first ensure that you have split your database (Chapter 4) and then ascertain user levels and which objects are being used the most (Chapter 6). For the bigger conversion, it would be a good idea tto freeze the design of all the tables and objects by using workgroup security (Chapters 8 and 10) at the same time that you start setting up the test projects for migration.

The Author's Highlights from the Book

While I am protecting a database, I always like to set up the secure menus (Chapter 7). I really enjoyed when I found out that you can actually set up an Access group account in your default workgroup file. If you combine that with a secure Windows XP/2000 local directory, you can open a workgroup-secured database by using operating system security (Chapter 8). My favorite discovery came near the end when my good friend John Reidy and I worked out how to establish protected folders so that users could not copy the database (Chapter 12). At that stage, I realized that we now had a way to make Access databases pretty secure again.

About the Book and the Demonstration Material

The goal of the material in this book is to improve Access protection and security, and, as a result, the material in the book does not target a particular skill level, such as developer or DBA. More than half of the book is at a level that a competent Access DBA could manage, and, where possible, I have set up the more complex demonstration examples as plug-and-play forms. In other words, you can use the forms in your database with only a few modifications to some constants at the top of the VBA code. Naturally, because I regularly write for developers' magazines, there are some examples that will keep the very skilled end of town happy.

Another design criteria of this book was to help you protect and secure any Access database created with Access 97 through to Access 2003 and beyond. In addition, the download samples, where possible, will work unchanged with the different versions of Access. If you are wondering how I managed to put together an Access book suited to four versions, you'll be interested to know that it's because I wrote a lot of this material by using Access 97. Looking back on that decision, I am glad that I did because the help relating to many of the protection and security issues was more forthcoming in Access 97 than in the later versions. In the book, I always refer to Access XP as Access 2002, and that terminology decision was vindicated with the new name for Access 2003.

Now I will describe how I have structured the chapters, and then I will tell how you can find and work with the download material.

How the Chapters Are Structured

While writing this book, I tried to keep to the following structure:

- An introduction describes what you can expect to find in the chapter.

- A separate overview for the IT manager, the DBA, and the developer discusses issues and includes download examples relevant to each group.

- Where possible, the easy material appears near the beginning of the chapter.

- Where the material is relevant to the DBA or is difficult to describe in words, graphics accompany the material.

- At the end of each chapter is a list of all the relevant Internet or help material. You will need to visit a Web page for the actual links to the pages. I have set it up this way in case the location of the material changes.

- Each chapter closes with a summary of discussions throughout the chapter and an introduction to the next chapter.

As I have mentioned earlier, the book covers material for different versions of Access. In the book, I have used the following icons to tell you to which version of Access the particular section applies. In most cases, the material is compatible from that version of Access to the newer versions:

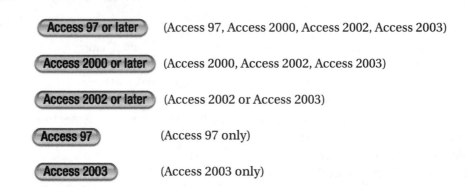

Access 97 or later   (Access 97, Access 2000, Access 2002, Access 2003)

Access 2000 or later   (Access 2000, Access 2002, Access 2003)

Access 2002 or later   (Access 2002 or Access 2003)

Access 97   (Access 97 only)

Access 2003   (Access 2003 only)

If you happen to be reading this book in 2007, you will probably be able to use any material that's applicable for Access 2003, and if this book is still selling well at that time, you had better have a look at the Apress Web site, which may offer a newer and even more relevant version of this book.

How to Download the Demonstration Databases

This book is accompanied by a single download from the Web site http://www.apress.com/. When you get to the Web site, click the Downloads button on the left side and find this book in the list.

In the download .ZIP file, you will find a separate database for Access 97 called grMap97.mdb, one for Access 2000 called grMap2000.mdb, and one for Access 2002/2003 called grMap2002.mdb. Then follow these steps to use the demonstration databases:

1. Open the database suited to your version of Access.

2. Select the chapter number from the drop-down list at the top of the form (shown in Figure 1-1).

3. Select the object that you want to review and click the View Object/Code button at the bottom of the window.

The demonstration database holds approximately 40 different objects. Some of these modules are re-used for different demonstrations. Some of the modules and form class modules require references to other common Microsoft libraries. If this is the case, I have mentioned the library reference in the header of the module. After you have downloaded the database, you should keep a copy of the demonstration database in its original form in the .ZIP just in case you need to return the demonstration database to its original state. Because Access has improved since 1997, some of the demonstrations apply only to the later versions. You may want to see my discussions on versions in the section "Does Upgrading Assist in Security?" later in this chapter.

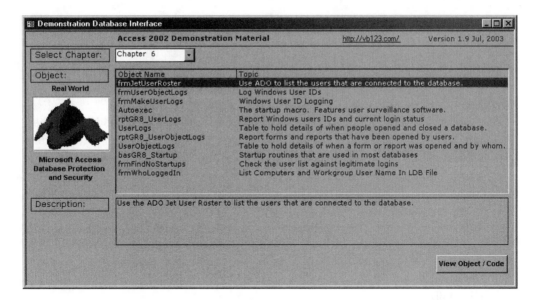

Figure 1-1. The demonstration database for Access 2002.

The Testing Database

Throughout the book, I have referred to the Northwind database as the database that you need to use for testing. I do so because we needed a database with a good variety of objects, and I needed a database that most of the readers would be familiar with. Don't worry too much if you don't think that you understand the Northwind database, because understanding it isn't necessary. Another reason I choose this database becuase it will be familiar to most readers and because it has a good variety of objects. If you want to use your own database for testing, that will be okay for almost all the examples in the book, as there is little that is very specific to Northwind.

CAUTION No matter whether you use Northwind or your own database, the important thing is that you experiment with a copy of the database in an experimental directory.

You should find a copy of the Northwind database in a subdirectory called samples in the folder where Microsoft Office or Access was installed. The likely locations of Northwind will be something like these:

- C:\Program Files\Microsoft Office\Office\samples for Access 97 and 2000.

- C:\Program Files\Microsoft Office\Office 10\samples for Access 2002.

- C:\Program Files\Microsoft Office\Office 11\samples for Access 2003.

Another way of tracking down the location of the sample database is to open any Access database and press CTRL+G. This action opens the Immediate window, where you can type the following expression to find the folder where your computer administrator installed Access:

```
? Application.SysCmd(acSysCmdAccessDir)
```

If you do not have a copy of Northwind.mdb on your computer, you will need to open the Access installation CD and make sure that Northwind is one of the options selected. If you really get stuck, send me email, and I will return one by email.

Further Instructions and Issues

Because some issues will probably crop up on some computers, I will maintain a Web page that discusses what the latest versions of the demonstration databases are and what changes, if any, have been made. You will find this list at the following address, along with my email address: http://www.vb123.com/map/dem.htm.

Any bug fixes required for the demonstration database will be posted to the Apress Web site when they are identified.

Secure Things that You Can Do Now

To get the ball rolling, two relatively simple things that you can consider now will provide some good security without any complications. All the other security procedures that I discuss in the book start off as being protection against an ordinary user. It is only when you combine a number of different protection techniques and set them up in a certain way that you have security for your database. Here is an overview of the straightforward secure things that you can easily do and descriptions of where they are applicable.

MDE Format: Gold Standard Security for Objects

If you want to secure the forms, reports, and modules in your database, there is no better and quicker way to do so than to convert your database to the compiled format, called the MDE format. Before you do that, you need to

- Split your database into two databases. The first will hold all your software (queries, forms, reports, macros, and modules) and the second will hold all your data and relationships. Many of this book's readers will no doubt know this structure, but if you don't understand it, you should read the section on splitting your database in Chapter 4.

- Make sure that development is not happening to the live front-end database. You will need to have well-established control over who develops the front-end database and where that development takes place before you embark on using the MDE format.

- Ensure that development takes place on a computer drive to which the database users do not have access.

To make an MDE-format database, all you have to do is choose Tools ➤ Database Utilities ➤ Make MDE, and you will have your MDE-format database.

If you are unsure whether the MDE format database will suit your needs, use it yourself as your production version. Once you have completed your test, direct a small number of users to try the MDE version. Generally, switching over to the MDE format is quite simple as long as you have good control of front-end database development. For further description of MDE databases, read Chapter 11.

 CAUTION The MDE format will not provide any security for your tables, queries, or macros.

Use the Operating System to Restrict Who Uses the Database

To preclude some of your fellow network users from opening your database, your best option is to use the operating system to restrict the people who will actually have access to the database. To give you some understanding of how this process works, I will give you a brief rundown here:

1. Place your database and related files in the specific database folder.

2. Create a new group of users (which I call "Access Editors") by using a Windows Server or Windows Peer-to-Peer computer.

3. Make any Windows user whom you want to open the database a member of this new group.

4. Remove all permissions for users and groups that currently have operating system permissions to open and use the files in the special database folder.

5. Grant permissions to the new user group (Access Editors) so that they can create, modify, and delete any files in that special database folder (as shown in Figure 1-2).

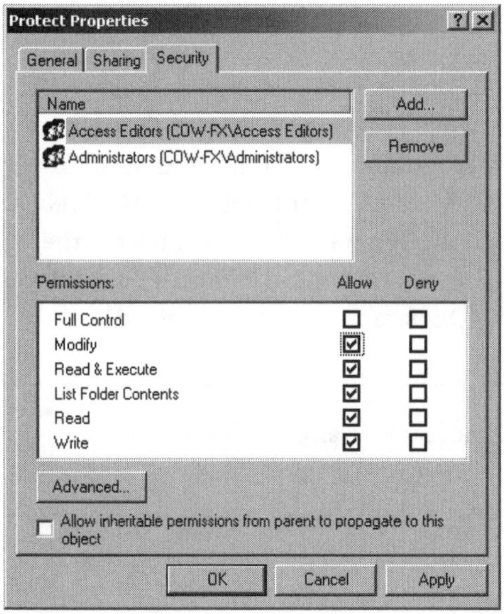

Figure 1-2. The permissions on a folder that a normal Access database uses.

Although this sample is not complete, I thought it was important enough to demonstrate the permissions in the Windows professional and server operating systems. Using this method to reduce the number of people using the database is very important because the Windows operating system's security is the result of much past and ongoing research for Microsoft. You can find out more about the operating system permissions in Chapter 12, particularly how to set up folders so that users cannot browse the folder contents. To supplement this security, this book discusses how you can combine using the Windows operating system with the Access internal security tools whenever it can.

In the next section, I will outline one of the more interesting bylines to the book—the topic of upgrading software. At this juncture, let me tell you that my normal counsel to clients is to bide their time when it comes to software upgrades. Unusually though, while writing this book, I came to realize that I was impressed by the subtle but useful changes that the newer versions of Access and Windows offered to protect the database.

Does Upgrading Assist in Security?

One interesting conclusion that I reached while researching for this book was that Microsoft made a number of small but worthwhile improvements to Access since the 97 version that would make the 2002 and 2003 versions more appealing. The following sections describe some of these improvements.

Access 2002 or Later

I have been using Access 2002 to develop both Access 2000 and 2002 databases ever since the version became available, and I have enjoyed the 2002 interface more than the 2000 interface. Included in that environment were these new security and protection related improvements.

- You can switch workgroups from within Access, which is a good time saver if you decide not to use shortcut files when swapping workgroups (Chapter 8).

- The inclusion of XML makes saving and retrieving tables from text files more effective. This feature will improve your backups (Chapter 5).

- The default workgroup file is saved in the secure \documents and settings\ path used by Windows 2000 and Windows XP. This feature is useful if you adopt the anonymous windows authentication strategy that I discuss in Chapter 10.

- You can open a password-protected database from another Access database. This feature makes the password more valuable as a protection mechanism, especially in environments where the majority of the users know the password.

- The `FileDialog` object is included as part of the supported libraries. This feature allows developers to support a file browser from within the Access-supported libraries, as shown in the linked table demonstration example in Chapter 4.

- You can create a workgroup file directly from VBA code. I use this feature in a demonstration on creating a developer workgroup file with user names and passwords in Chapter 8.

Access 2000 or Later

Included with Access 2000 was the ADO library, which offered some subtle changes, such as the following.

- The ability to find out who was using the database and to stop new users from opening the database. This technology can be combined with the surveillance techniques provided in the download database to work out whether anyone was using the database without using the startup procedures (all discussed in Chapter 6).

- SQL query enhancements in this version offered a more readable way of changing workgroup security in code (Chapter 8).

Another big change was a new approach for VBA code management. This change unfortunately included the removal of protection for modules in the Database window. You can find a good solution to this change in Chapter 8. To replace this protection, the VBA project now has password protection (Chapter 11), a protection mechanism that is not without its weaknesses (Chapter 9).

Upgrading or Fine-Tuning Your Operating Systems

When I started planning this book, I attached very little significance to using the operating system as part of Access security. Now that I have concluded this research, I was surprised by how much importance I now attach to the operating system as a way of protecting and securing the database. Therefore, I suggest that you consider how you use the latest operating systems and upgrade to them if you haven't already. As for developers, consider this tip.

TIP   Developers really should understand and experiment with Windows XP and 2000 folder permissions and become proactive with your clients to ensure that they are protecting databases in the best possible way.

Further Reading

As you might expect, there is never enough information when it comes to powerful products like Access. To assist you with further investigations in every chapter, I have put together a Web page with links to Web sites and articles on the issues that relate to the material in every chapter. In this chapter, I will simply discuss the resources that I used regularly for this book and Access in general:

- The help files from all the versions of Access used in the book. For Access 2000 or later, don't forget to widen your search by also trying the help within the VBA Environment.

- I must say that I resolved most of the complicated and open-ended issues by using http://www.google.com. Of particular value with google.com was its Groups tab at the top of the page (shown in Figure 1-3). Another important thing with google.com that I am sure applies to other search engines was to include very particular words in the search. Searching usually means looking twice to find the topic of information. In some cases, when I searched for particular errors, I would simply type the error description exactly as it appeared in Access. No doubt, there will be other search engines in the future that will work as well.

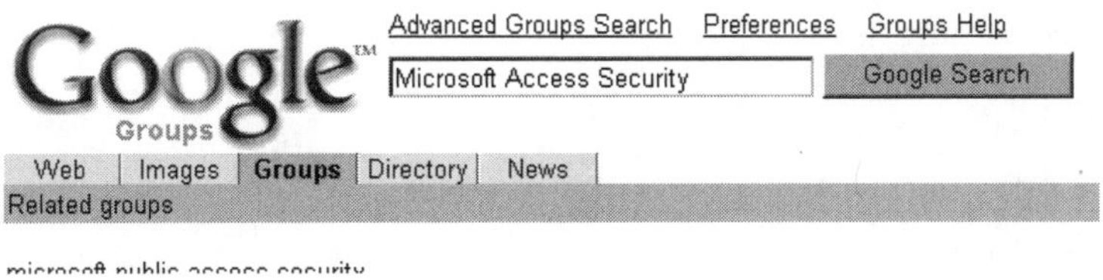

Google™
Groups

| Advanced Groups Search   Preferences   Groups Help |
| Microsoft Access Security   Google Search |

Web | Images | **Groups** | Directory | News

Related groups

microsoft.public.access.security

Figure 1-3. The invaluable Google Groups tab.

- For insight into programming workgroup security, I turned to the *Access Developers Handbook, Enterprise Edition*, written by Litwin, Getz, and Gilbert and one of my favorite authors, Mike Gunderloy, who wrote a couple of chapters in the book. You may notice later on that my book really doesn't include much of the detailed programming of workgroup security demonstrated in the *Access Developers Handbook* because that seemed not to be as important as keeping the password crackers at bay.

- As ever, my source of inspiration for Access programming is the *Smart Access* magazine, and I have certainly learned my trade by reading that magazine from cover to cover every time the convict cargo ship arrives in Australia with the mail.

- Many of the discussions in the book were supported by the many hundreds of accurate articles, white papers, and Web pages that Microsoft posts on its Web site about Microsoft Access. Surprisingly, though, as I wrote the book, I generally had better luck finding the articles by using google.com and restricting my search to use only the Microsoft Web site.

- This list would not be complete without providing links to newsgroups, where people might actually answer your Access questions.

Just one final word on the Internet that I noticed while compiling this book. Many people in the newsgroups seem to be under the impression that they can learn a computing skill such as Access security through the results of a search engine or by asking members of user groups to answer a question. This sort of advice is generally most suited for the completion of a major task. It is always important that you get your facts straight before starting on a task like adding security to a database. For that task, you need to turn to thoroughly researched and tested material, such as a book or a developer's computer magazine.

You can find the further reading Web page for this chapter in the Downloads section of the Apress Web site (`http://www.apress.com`) or at the following address: `http://www.vb123.com/map/dri.htm`.

Security: The Journey Never Ends

I like Microsoft Access because my company's clients are happy with Access before they call us in and even happier after we have set up the database and user interface. It is a fun and challenging environment to work in, and it generally is versatile enough to adapt to most situations. So, having mastered most of the skills necessary to work with the product, I was left with the choice to learn a new product and tout that skill to my clients or find a new Access skill that I can market to my clients. As you can guess, I decided on the latter, and now I like to emphasize the benefits of protection and security for their existing and new Access databases. One example of the value of this approach is when my company was selected to manage and protect the exploration databases for a mining company based in the Gobi Desert (as shown in Figure 1-4). As readers of this book, you too can reap the benefits of this approach and become skilled in protecting and securing your own Access databases. An interesting twist to that additional skill is that once you conquer the protection and security issues relevant to your databases, you will always find more to do because with computer security, the journey never ends.

Figure 1-4. Garry's security journey found him working on databases in the Gobi Desert.

Now, before you start to explore the rest of the book, feel free to join me in my Access adventures by visiting my Web site at http://www.vb123.com/ and joining my popular newsletter, *Access Unlimited*. This magazine comes out every month or so and has survived to nearly 50 editions by the middle of 2003. To conclude this chapter, I have an invitation for the readers of this book: If you have any suggestions or comments about the contents of the book, email me at access@gr-fx.com, and I will do my best to get the content out there in the real world, be it through a magazine, vb123.com, or even an update to this book at some time in the future.

What's Next?

In the next chapter, we will kick off with the relatively easy and important startup options. These options are the key to ensuring that your users open the database and use it the way that you intended. Of course, as is always the case with security, you will encounter problems of who is allowed to manipulate this security and what you have to do to get on with the job once the security is in place.

Nonetheless, enjoy the journey.

Protecting Your Database with Startup Options

IF THERE'S ONE CHAPTER in this book that will help you protect your database, this is it. The startup options are simple and important safeguards that will hide the Database Window and Access programming commands and disable special keys used to access the developer's environment. These options apply to the current database and apply the next time the database is opened.

The low-risk steps required to modify the database startup options with menus are quick and easy. Once you've turned off the options, the data and application objects are less accessible to the average user. For the user, some of these changes provide a less-cluttered interface that should make your application easier to use.

The demonstration material for this chapter includes the following:

- An Access form that allows you to change the startup options. This form is very useful when the menu item to display the Startup dialog is disabled.

- Visual Basic for Applications (VBA) code within that Access form that will show you how to change the startup options.

- VBA code within that Access form that will disable the AllowBypassKey property, an option that is not available from the menus. This code ensures that the user cannot change the startup options.

- Accelerator keys that you can use when the developer menus and toolbars are disabled.

 NOTE   To find the demonstration material, open the download database for your version of Microsoft Access—for example, grMAP97.mdb—and select Chapter 2.

I'll begin the chapter with an overview of the startup options.

Do I Need to Read this Chapter?

In this and the following chapters, I'm going to give three separate overviews—one for developers, one for database administrators (DBAs), and one for IT managers because the people in each of these categories will approach the chapter in a different way. Developers will want to find ways to use the startup options to protect the database, DBAs need to understand how startup options will affect the database, and IT managers should be aware of how the startup options might affect their companies' business.

Overview for the Developer

It's difficult enough for a programmer to provide a system that works according to users' requirements. When the end users take it on themselves to alter the database, however, certain issues arise:

- Who has the latest version of the database?

- What has changed?

- How do we integrate those changes with our latest modifications?

Turning off the startup options manually or with VBA code will assist in reducing these development issues. If you also set the AllowBypassKey property to False with VBA code, users will find it difficult to view the database container, change toolbars, or skip the startup display form and the AutoExec macro.

Because the impact of changing these settings will change the way that you work with your database, you should become conversant with how to turn these options on and off manually and with VBA code.

For those programmers who are looking for something simple that will add value to their databases, you can import a demonstration form into your database that will immediately allow you to view and switch all the startup options. This form is very helpful, as some startup options will remove the menu options that allow you to undo your changes.

Overview for the Database Administrator

Understanding the startup options is vital if you're to administer Microsoft Access databases. At some stage you, the developer, or your users are going to change the startup options. Once that happens, you'll need to work out how to navigate to all the objects in the database with those new options in place. More importantly, you can easily change the options manually or by using the startup options demonstration form. This form will help you make appropriate changes to the startup options so that users will be hard-pressed to use the customization features that are available to the developer.

Overview for the IT Manager

If you have any concerns about users modifying your database objects and data or avoiding the user interface that you intended them to use, then this chapter is important. You should discuss the startup options with your developer and even adopt a standard group of startup options that you apply to all your databases. When you are considering if there is any risk with your developers providing you with software that has unwanted and undocumented security, the only risky startup option is if the developer has set the AllowBypassKey property to False by using VBA code. In this case, you may have difficulty opening and editing the database objects. This problem may arise if the relationship between your developer and your company goes sour.

Manually Changing Startup Options · Access 97 or later

To change the startup options in your database manually, choose Tools ➤ Startup, as shown in Figure 2-1, and you will see the options form, shown in Figure 2-2.

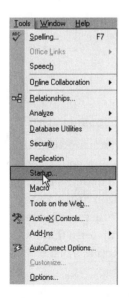

Figure 2-1. Opening the startup options on the Tools menu.

Figure 2-2 shows all the startup options in Access 97 (with the Advanced button selected). In Access 2000 and later, this Advanced button does not appear. If you want to experiment with these options for the first time, then I suggest you experiment with a copy of the demonstration database for this chapter.

 CAUTION   If you're going to experiment on your own database, *please* be sure to make a full backup first, as options like the AllowBypassKey require a little practice to undo.

Startup			? X
Application Title:	Display Form:		OK
Modifying the startup properties of a	frmStartupProperties	▼	Cancel
Application Icon:	☐ Display Database Window		Advanced >>
	...	✓ Display Status Bar	
Menu Bar:	Shortcut Menu Bar:		
(default) ▼	(default) ▼		
✓ Allow Full Menus	✓ Allow Built-in Toolbars		
✓ Allow Default Shortcut Menus	☐ Allow Toolbar/Menu Changes		
✓ Allow Viewing Code After Error	☐ Use Access Special Keys		
	(Show Database Window, Show Debug Window, and Pause Execution)		

Figure 2-2. The startup options available for Access 97.

Now I will tell you to add a startup form to your database, something that you more than likely did on the first day that you started developing your database.

Defining Your Startup Display Form

When users open your database, they should be greeted with a form that helps them to navigate to your database. If the database doesn't have a startup form, the first thing users will see is the database window. Clearly, this window could overwhelm some users, as it is similar to driving in a foreign city with no road map. Subsequently, if you are intent on hiding the database window from users, the users will be in a desert with no map. Therefore, let us add a startup form to the database. One form that you will probably recognize is the startup form that has welcomed users to the Northwind sample database ever since Access 97 (see Figure 2-3).

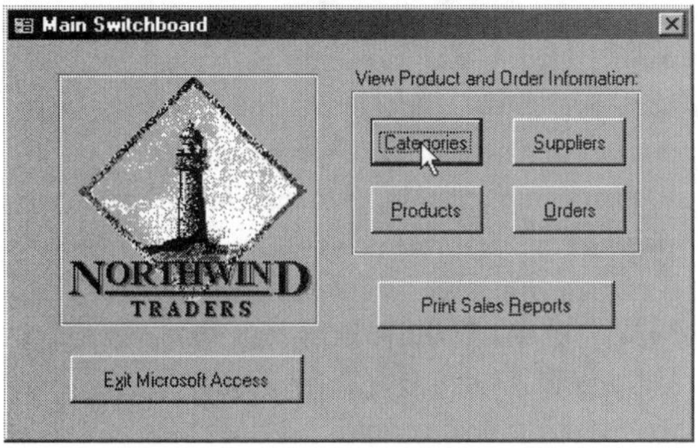

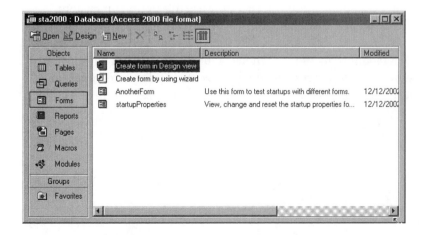

Figure 2-3. The Main Switchboard startup form in the Northwind sample database.

When looking at the design of the Northwind startup form, it's clear what options the user can use to interact with the database. One thing that we aim to achieve with the protection and security discussed in this book is to put in place a framework that ensures that users will interact with the database in the way that *we* intended.

Displaying the Database Window

If you select the Display Database Window check box in the startup options, the database window (shown in Figure 2-4) will be available to all users. If the users are meant to use only the user interface, exposing the Database window will probably confuse them or, worse, may allow them to modify or delete any object in the database without authority. It is good to know that if you disable this option, you can display the Database window by pressing the F11 key.

Figure 2-4. The Database window makes the data and objects easily accessible to everyone.

User Story *I personally have sent at least 50 databases to clients with just the Show Database Window option cleared. In all that time, I have yet to run into any users who have maliciously tampered with the database. Occasionally, some users have modified objects while I was developing, but that is rarer than you think. That said, in a number of the database applications that I have delivered, if it was important that the users didn't change anything, we modified a number of the startup options as the first line of protection. The main person these changes seemed to affect was the developer (me). I quickly learned how to change the startup properties in code so that I wasn't inconvenienced too much.*

Options that Require Custom Menu and Toolbar Development

In Chapter 7, you can read in detail about how menus are an important part of protecting your Access interface. In this chapter, however, I will give a summary of the following menu-related startup options:

- Menu Bar: Display your own menu when Access starts.

- Shortcut Menu Bar: Display your own default shortcut (right-click) menu on all the forms and reports.

- Allow Full Menus: When you select this option, users will see all the developer-related menu items. When it's disabled, users will see a simpler menu.

- Allow Built-In Menus: When disabled, the user will not see the Microsoft Access built-in toolbars. You will generally use this option for custom toolbars that you need to allocate to each form and report in your database.

- Allow Default Shortcut Menus: When disabled, the user will not see the built-in Access shortcut menus. You will use this option sometimes for custom shortcut menus that you need to allocate to each form and report in your database.

As a part of this discussion, you will learn that custom menus are an important protection and user interface topic because the alternative, standard menus, provide the user with access to the same tools to change the database that are available to the developer.

Allowing Toolbar and Menu Changes

Selecting this startup option will allow the users to make changes to all the toolbars, menu bars, and shortcut menus. As a consequence of selecting this startup option, users will have easy access to the full repertoire of Access menu options, as shown in Figure 2-5.

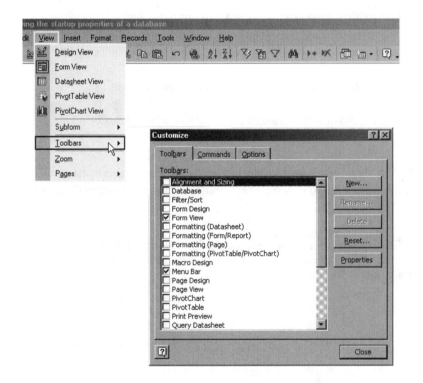

Figure 2-5. Selecting the AllowToolbarChanges option will give your users access to most options.

Clearing this option anchors your toolbars, disables the right-click modifications to toolbars, stops the closing of toolbars, and removes the menu option (View ➤ Toolbars). In summary, turning this feature off should not affect users, and it will make it easier for you to maintain a standard interface for all users.

Using Access Special Keys

The Use Access Special Keys option is important because it allows users to use all the special key sequences that enable them to get to your normal programming environment. By clearing this option, you and your users will not be able to use the following special key sequences:

- F11   To bring the database window to the front (see Figure 2-4).

- ALT+F11   To open the Visual Basic Editor (VBE) (Access 2000 or later).

- CTRL+F11   To toggle between custom and normal toolbars.

- CTRL+BREAK   To show the current point of execution of the VBA software or stop retrieving records from a slow query.

- CTRL+G   To view the debugger window. In fact, clearing this option will stop anyone from using the Debugger, a point discussed further in Chapter 4.

 CAUTION   If you are thinking of clearing this option, remember that this option has significance only if you have also cleared the Display Database Window option.

Now we will find out how we can program the startup options by using VBA code.

Programming the Startup Options

Selecting and clearing the startup options manually will suffice for a good percentage of Access databases. However, there are occasions when you will want to check and change the options by using a customized form or with VBA code, such as:

- When you want secret and faster ways to select the startup options again.

- When the Startup dialog is not available from the menus.

- When you have disabled the bypass key (discussed later in this chapter) and you need to enable it again.

NOTE   The Access help guide switches terminology from referring to "startup options" as "startup properties" in the VBE help guide. The Access guide makes this change because when you deal with a startup option through VBA, you are actually dealing with a property of the database. This chapter adopts the same convention.

To manipulate and interrogate the startup properties of the database by using VBA code, I've prepared two easy-to-use functions called StartUpProps and DeleteStartupProps. These functions are stored within a simple wizard-like form called frmStartupProperties. You will find this form in the download database.

User Story   *Since I put this form together, I have found it quite useful to include in databases in which I am constantly changing the startup options. I like it because it provides a safe and simple way to return the options back to normal. After including the form, I have also found it useful to retrieve this form by using accelerator keys. You can read about this in detail at the end of the chapter.*

The Startup Options Demonstration Form

The frmStartupProperties demonstration form is shown in Figure 2-6. When this form opens, it first checks the status of the database startup options and displays the results in a series of check boxes. If a check box is not available (appears gray) like the Allow Bypass Key check box in Figure 2-6, then you or your users have not set the property, and Access will use its default value for the property. If you are interested in protecting your database, you will be disappointed because the startup options are enabled by default.

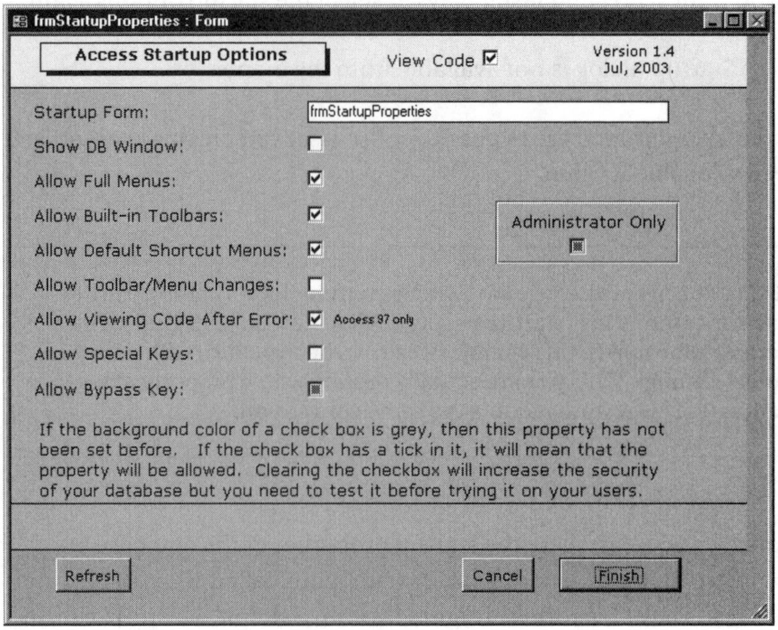

Figure 2-6. The frmStartupProperties *enables you to change the startup settings in code.*

This full list of startup properties are relevant to Access protection:

- Display Form

- Display Database Window

- Menu Bar

- Shortcut Menu Bar

- Allow Full Menus

- Allow Built-In Toolbars

- Allow Default Shortcut Menus

- Allow Toolbar/Menu Changes

- Allow Viewing Code after Error

- Use Access Special Keys

- Allow Bypass Key

These properties are not illustrated in the demonstration form:

- Application Title

- Application Icon

- Display Status Bar

- Menu Bar

- Shortcut Menu Bar

If you want to work through the examples in the demonstration form, open the form and you will find that these buttons on the form execute the following actions. If you want fast access to the VBA code behind the button, select the View Code check box at the top of the form before you click the button. Remember that when you have finished testing the startup options, return to this form in the demonstration database, select all the check boxes, and click the Finish button.

The Refresh Button

The code in the Refresh button's onClick event looks at the status of the database startup properties and changes all the check boxes to match. To change onClick event, we use the function called StartupProps that you will find in the demonstration form. The following code snippet illustrates the VBA code that retrieves the current value of the StartupShowDBWindow property and displays it in the appropriate check box:

```
Me!chkShowDBWindow = StartUpProps("StartupShowDBWindow")
```

The Finish Button

The code in the Finish button's onClick event takes the values from the check boxes in the body of the form and modifies the database startup properties to these new values. When this process is complete, the form closes and the Startup dialog box appears, which allows you to see if your changes were successful.

The following code illustrates the VBA code that sets the `StartupShowDBWindow` `Startup` property to the value in the appropriate check box:

```
StartUpProps "StartupShowDBWindow", Me!chkShowDBWindow
```

If you look carefully at the two ways that I have called the `StartUpProps` function, you will see that it allows us both to retrieve and to change the values of a startup property, depending on whether we include the new value in the second argument of the function call.

The Cancel Button

The Cancel button ignores any changes that you made and closes the form.

 TIP   To display the VBA code under the button, open the form in Form view, select the View Code check box (shown in Figure 2-6), and click the button. To look at the contents of a subroutine or function (like `StartUpProps`), right-click its name in the VBE and choose Definition from the menu or press SHIFT+F2.

Now I will show you the VBA subroutines that make this form tick.

Manipulating the Startup Properties by Using VBA Code

The procedures that are required to view and change the database's startup properties are a little involved. Their relative complexity arises from the fact that you need to assemble some code that manipulates database properties. This involves code to

- Change the value.

- Add the property if it doesn't exist.

- Delete the property.

- Handle subtleties due to the different data types of different properties.

To satisfy these programming requirements, you are required to put together subroutines, something that I have already done for you. After you have them running to your satisfaction, you should not have to look at them again for a long time. So let's look at the code to find the startup properties. I simplified this code from a sample included in the Access 97 help file by making the arguments call the subroutine specific to the data types found in startup properties.

NOTE   Access 97 help is much more thorough on this topic than the later versions of help due to its emphasis on the Data Access Objects (DAO) library. Access 2003 help seems to redress this issue to some extent.

You will find the relevant code by exploring the VBA code from the Refresh and Finish buttons' onClick events on the frmStartupProperties form. This programming example uses the DAO library, which is the only way to modify these Access Jet engine-specific properties.

NOTE   To add a reference to DAO while programming a form, open the form in Design view, choose View ➤ Code, and you will now be in VBE. Now choose Tools ➤ References and select the check box next to either Microsoft Access DAO 3.5 or 3.6 Object Library.

```
Function StartUpProps(strPropName As String, Optional varPropValue As Variant, _
         Optional ddlRequired As Boolean) As Variant
' This function requires a reference to DAO library.
' This function will both return and set the value of startup properties
' in your database. It can also be used for other database properties
' with some slight modification.

Dim dbs As DAO.Database, prp As DAO.Property, varPropType As Variant
Const conPropNotFoundError = 3270

If IsMissing(ddlRequired) Then
  ddlRequired = False
End If


' Because this code is specific to the startup properties, we assume that the
' data type of the property is Boolean unless stated otherwise.
```

```
varPropType = dbBoolean
Select Case strPropName
  Case "StartupForm"
    varPropType = dbText
End Select

Set dbs = CurrentDb

' This function will either set the value of the property or try to
' return it. It knows which mode it is in by the existence of the
' property value in the procedure that called the function.

If Not IsMissing(varPropValue) Then

' As we change the value of the startup property, we will first try to
' assign that value. If the property does not exist, it will be
' added to the database object by using the following error handling code.

  On Error GoTo AddProps_Err
  dbs.Properties(strPropName) = varPropValue
  StartUpProps = True
Else

' If we find out the value of the startup property, we first see if
' that value exists. If the property does not exist, we will return a null string.

  On Error GoTo NotFound_Err
  StartUpProps = dbs.Properties(strPropName)
End If

StartupProps_End:
  On Error Resume Next
  Set dbs = Nothing
  Set prp = Nothing
  Exit Function
```

When a property doesn't exist in the database, you must use the CreateProperty method to add the property to the database. The error handling section of the subroutine handles this method as follows:

```
AddProps_Err:

  If Err = conPropNotFoundError Then
    ' Property not found when adding a property value.
    Set prp = dbs.CreateProperty(strPropName, varPropType, _
             varPropValue, ddlRequired)
    dbs.Properties.Append prp
    Resume Next
  Else
    ' Unknown error.
    StartUpProps = False
    Resume StartupProps_End
  End If
```

The final section of error handling handles instances where the function is searching for an existing property value and none exists. In this case, the StartupProps function will return a null value as this makes it simpler to set the value of a check box.

```
NotFound_Err:
    If Err = conPropNotFoundError Then
      ' Property not found when returning a property value.
      StartUpProps = Null
      Resume Next
    Else
      ' Unknown error.
      StartUpProps = False
      Resume StartupProps_End
    End If


End Function
```

If you were looking at the detail of this subroutine, you would have seen a mysterious variable called ddlRequired. In the next section, I will explain why and how you can use this variable to make your startup properties extremely hard for your smart users to change.

Preventing End Users from Changing the Startup Properties

Access offers an additional safeguard for the startup options for those databases that are protected through workgroup (user-level) security. This protection is provided by an oddly named protection mechanism called Data Definition Language (DDL). In a nutshell, this DDL protection will stop any person who doesn't have Administrator permissions for the database itself from changing the startup options by the menu or by VBA code.

Therefore, if you are thinking that this sounds interesting and you might like a piece of this additional security, then you first must complete the following:

1. Secure your database by using workgroup security (discussed in Chapter 8) or run the User-Level Security wizard.

2. Users must not have Administrator database permission for their workgroup user account or any group account of which they are a member. Figure 2-7 illustrates how the database permissions should look for the users group.

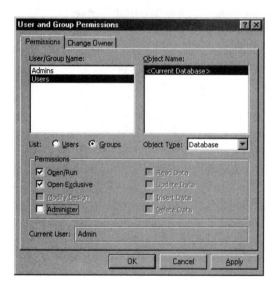

Figure 2-7. The users group does not have Administrator permission for the database.

NOTE If you don't understand steps 1 and 2 or you haven't secured your database as yet, it is probably best that you skip through the chapter until you get to the section "The AllowBypassKey Property." I will remind you in Chapter 8, when I have discussed workgroup security, that you should to return to this point.

Now I will discuss one last reason not to get too involved in DDL protection before I describe how the frmStartupProperties form will apply the DDL protection for you.

DDL Protection for Startup Options for Workgroup-Secured Databases

Before we head to the technical discussions on DDL protection, there is just one last thing to discuss before you make up your mind that you really need some of this DDL security. Surprisingly, DDL security is one of the few Access protection mechanisms that is turned on by default. So, before you even worry about DDL security for your database, you should test it by logging on to your database by using an end user's workgroup account. If you find that the user account can actually modify the startup options by using the menu Tools ➤ Security, then you will need to use the DDL property protection. Conversely, you may actually want people who do not have administrator permission for the database to change the startup options. If that is the case, you need to remove the DDL protection.

To add or remove DDL protection for the startup options, I have setup an Administrator Only check box on the frmStartupProperties demonstration form. To use it, follow these steps:

1. Open the frmStartupProperties form.

2. Select or clear the startup options as appropriate.

3. Select the Administer Only check box and click Yes to confirm that you want to protect the options.

4. To remove DDL protection, clear the Administer Only check box and click Yes to confirm once again.

5. Click the Finish button to change the startup options. You only have to do this procedure once as long as you select or clear all the options.

Now if you are a hard-nosed programmer, I have included for you in the next section the technical details on the code that will allow you to apply and remove DDL protection for the startup options.

The Software Used For DDL Protection for Startup Options

Whenever you change any of the startup (and other database) properties by using VBA code, you can prevent users from changing the database startup properties by themselves. This security restriction even applies when the Tools Startup menu is available to users. When you apply DDL protection, only workgroup accounts that have administrator permission for the database (obtained through workgroup security) will be able to change the value of the property.

In the following code, you will see how to stop workgroup users from making toolbar changes in the database. To accomplish this change, I have used the StartUpProps function that I discussed earlier in the chapter. In the example, you will notice that there is now an additional fourth argument (called ddlRequired) that is set to True.

```
StartUpProps "AllowToolbarChanges", False, True
```

To demonstrate how this change works in the StartUpProps subroutine, I repeat the lines of code that use the CreateProperty method, as follows. Note that I have used the optional ddlRequired argument in this instance.

```
Set prp = dbs.CreateProperty(strPropName, varPropType, _
        varPropValue, ddlRequired)
dbs.Properties.Append prp
```

NOTE In Access 97 help, this optional Data Definition Language (DDL) argument is described as "A Variant (Boolean subtype) that indicates whether or not the Property is a DDL object. The default is False. If DDL is True, users can't change or delete this Property object unless they have dbSecWriteDef permission." This argument is not described in the any of the help files in Access 2000 and later because DAO information was removed from the help files.

There is a trick when using VBA code to add the DDL argument to the startup properties. First, you must delete the property before you add it with the new security setting, which you do in the demonstration form by calling the deleteStartupProps subroutine:

```
deleteStartupProps "StartupShowDBWindow"
```

Now I will show you the deleteStartupProps subroutine so that you can see how a database property is deleted. This process is complicated by the fact that the property may not exist in the first place and therefore this needs to be handled by error-trapping code.

```
Function deleteStartupProps(strPropName As String) As Boolean
' Function requires a reference to DAO library.

Dim dbs As DAO.Database, prp As DAO.Property
Const conPropNotFoundError = 3270

deleteStartupProps = False

On Error GoTo deleteStartupProps_Err
CurrentDb.Properties.Delete (strPropName)
deleteStartupProps = True

deleteStartupProps_End:
  On Error Resume Next
  Set dbs = Nothing
  Set prp = Nothing
  Exit Function

deleteStartupProps_Err:
  If Err = conPropNotFoundError Then
    ' Property not found.
    deleteStartupProps = False
    Resume Next
  Else
    ' Unknown error.
    Resume deleteStartupProps_End
  End If

End Function
```

That ends the technical coverage of the DDL protection for startup options. To summarize, remember that workgroup security, when properly applied, will more than likely provide this protection. Once it is in place, test your workgroup user accounts to ensure that they cannot change the options. If they can change the options, select the Administrator Only check box in the frmStartupProperties form before modifying the options. Most users will never get this far anyway!

Now I will describe how to stop people from using the bypass key, commonly known as the SHIFT key, to sneak into your database. I can guarantee that a few users will be up to speed on this trick.

The AllowBypassKey Property

The bypass key (SHIFT key) sequence is a sneaky little Access trick that has been around since Noah kept a database of animals on his ark. Once you know the SHIFT key sequence, you will be able to use it for all versions of Access. Though it's disappointing that anyone can sidestep security so easily by using the SHIFT key, once I have demonstrated how it actually works, I will show you how to disable it.

The Access help guide describes the bypass key as follows: "You can use the AllowBypassKey property to specify whether or not the SHIFT key is enabled for bypassing the startup properties and the AutoExec macro. For example, you can set the AllowBypassKey property to False to prevent a user from bypassing the startup properties and the AutoExec macro."

The best way to illustrate what effect the bypass key will have on your database is to walk through an example, using the Northwind sample database.

1. Open Microsoft Access.

2. Choose File ➤ Open.

3. Navigate to Northwind.mdb in the samples subdirectory of your Access installation directory (see Figure 2-8).

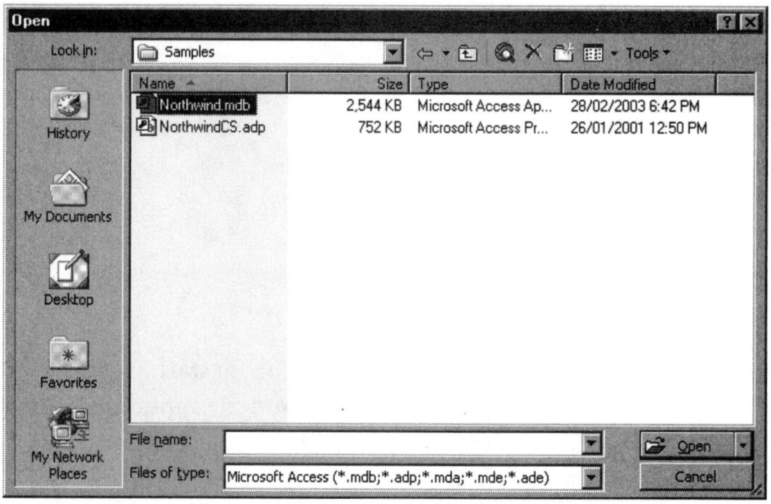

Figure 2-8. Opening the Northwind database.

4. Select the Northwind.mdb file, and click the Open button, and you will find yourself using the Main Switchboard form.

5. Exit Access.

6. Open Access.

7. Choose File ➤ Open. Now navigate back to Northwind.mdb.

8. Select the file name.

9. Press SHIFT and click the Open button.

This time the database will open a lot faster, the database window will be visible, and the Main Switchboard form will not open at all. In addition, the AutoExec macro will not run either, so any special startup sequences that you have built into your database will not be triggered. You can repeat this trick by pressing SHIFT when using Windows Explorer or even in the Most Recent Used List on the Access menus to open a database.

NOTE   Unless the AllowBypassKey property has been set to False, you can bypass the startup options in any Access database by pressing SHIFT in Windows Explorer and then double-clicking the database file. This is a good way to view the hidden database window, turning on the special keys and avoiding customized menus. Your users can also do this, so you may want to think about invoking this extra bypass key protection just before you deliver your software.

CAUTION   It's now time to back up your database, because it can be a bit tricky if you do not leave the VBA code somewhere accessible in your database so that you can change the AllowBypassKey property back to True.

Let's look at how we can use the frmStartupProperties form to set the AllowBypassKey property to False.

1. Open this book's demonstration database for your version of Access.

2. Select Chapter 2 and select frmStartupProperties.

3. Because we are testing the process, select the Display Database Window check box just in case we have to return to frmStartupProperties from the Database Window. This form provides a safety net because it will allow us to reset the AllowBypassKey property back to True.

4. Clear the Allow Bypass Key check box.

5. Click Finish.

6. Check the startup options, which won't show the AllowBypassKey property.

7. Close the database and then try to open it while pressing SHIFT. You will find that you won't be able to—you have turned it off.

Now there is one last step for those who just must have the best protection for their startup properties.

Applying DDL Protection

Finally, if you consider that one of your users may understand how to enable the AllowBypassKey option by using VBA code and you have used workgroup security, you can use the DDL protection to limit this modification to database administrators only. This limitation is possible by using the optional fourth argument (ddlRequired) of the StartUpProps subroutine. Remember that before we set the DDL property, we first must delete the current setting of the property, as demonstrated by the following code:

```
DeleteStartupProps "AllowBypassKey"
StartUpProps "AllowBypassKey", False, True
```

What this code means in real words is to test whether a workgroup user can use the frmStartupProperties form to turn off the AllowBypassKey property. If they can, then use the Administrator Only check box on the form to lock it.

The Bypass Key Wrap Up

If your database relies only on the startup properties to protect the data and the objects, then you probably want to make sure it is as safe as possible. A user who knows how to press SHIFT (the bypass key) when opening a database can easily modify or delete any object in the database, copy those hidden tables that the developer tried to hide, or simply enter the data directly into the tables and avoid all the form-based data rules. If you think that your users will never find out about the SHIFT key, try typing "Startup" into your Access help and the instructions for "Ignore startup options" will figure very prominently. So, do you want to trust your database protection to a SHIFT key?

The final word on this topic is that you may want to look to the end of Chapter 6, where I show you a tool that will locate people who have connected to your database without using your required startup form. Now I will show you how special keys can make using the startup options a little easier for the developer.

Using Homemade Accelerator Keys in Restricted Environments

Now that you've gone to all the trouble of disabling a combination of the database window, menus, toolbars, shortcut menus, and the special keys from the database, you'll probably find that it's difficult to develop and administer your database. To assist you with these tasks, I have deliberately set up the frmStartupProperties form in such a manner that you can easily use it to modify the startup properties in your database (and modify them back again). You can augment this form by allocating your own accelerator key sequences to open this form. Another accelerator key sequence that is described below will allow you to open any form or report in the database in design view without having a design view menu or toolbar option. To do this, build a macro that stores all your database accelerator keys:

1. Open the database window.

2. Select Macros.

3. Create a new macro (unless you already have an Autokeys macro).

4. Choose View ➤ Macro Names.

5. In the macro name column, enter ^ Q (see Figure 2-9).

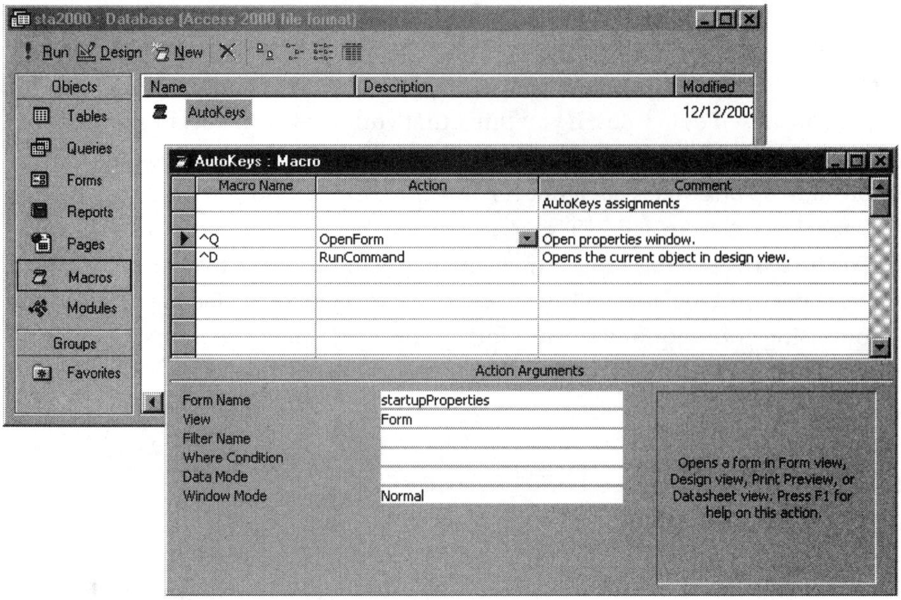

Figure 2-9. Setting up the Autokeys macro to make getting around Access a little easier.

6. In the Action column, select OpenForm.

7. Select the frmStartupProperties form in the Action Arguments pane (near the bottom).

8. Now start a new line and enter ^ D into the Macro Name column.

9. Enter RunCommand in the Action column.

10. Select DesignView in the Action Arguments pane.

11. Now save the macro and call it Autokeys.

NOTE   Accelerator keys are stored in the database in a macro that is always called Autokeys. From now on, you can type the following two key sequences: CTRL+Q to open the frmStartupProperties demonstration form and CTRL+D to open any object in design view. You can even add triple key sequences like CTRL+SHIFT+X if you want extra security on these key sequences.

Now if you want to use accelerator keys to open the frmStartupProperties demonstration form in your database, all you need to do is import the form and the Autokeys macro into your database. If you set the AllowBypassKey property to False, you can still open the frmStartupProperties startup options form by using the CTRL+Q key sequence. Test the accelerator keys and demonstration form before setting the AllowBypassKey property to False.

Further Reading

As you might expect, there is never enough information when it comes to powerful products like Microsoft Access. To assist you with further investigations, I have put together a Web page with hyperlinks to Web sites and articles on the issues relating to the material in this chapter. This page includes

- A Microsoft page that shows how to use startup options.

- Discussion group comments on the AllowBypassKey property.

- Alternative approaches to disable the important special key sequences.

- Discussions on accelerator keys.

You can find the further reading Web page for this chapter in the Downloads section of the Apress Web site (http://www.apress.com) or at the following address: http://www.vb123.com/map/sta.htm.

Reflecting on this Chapter

First, you have seen how easy it is to change the startup options in your database by using Access menus. If you do use the menus, you will make it reasonably hard for the majority of users to get up to much mischief in your database. Unfortunately, every time you change a startup option, you make it harder for the developer to make changes to the software and objects in the database, which means that the additional security starts to add to the development costs. Therefore, I suggest that you experiment with each of the properties one at a time and see what effect it has on both your application and your development productivity.

Now that you know how to change the startup properties by using VBA code, you will find that you can enable the options for development and disable them for end users. In addition, another benefit of using VBA code is that you can disable that (not so clever) bypass key that allows people to use the database as they see fit. You can also combine workgroup security and VBA code to make sure that only users who have administration privileges in your database can change the startup options.

Finally, if you find that you would like the additional protection for your database and really haven't the time to research these issues in detail, you can import the demonstration form and Autokeys macro into your database. These tools give you a way to change the startup options all the time, regardless of the changes that you make. This approach provides secrecy, flexibility, and a good safeguard with little of the programming effort. That's my idea of low-cost security.

What's Next?

In the next chapter, I will take you through many of the database options that affect your databases' security and stability. Once again in the chapter, I will demonstrate how to make changes manually and then how to make the changes programmatically. In addition to these database options, I also expand on the manual and VBA code techniques that will allow you to hide objects from your users. Though these subtle vanishing tricks, coupled with the startup options described in this chapter, are not foolproof, they certainly can keep the casual software saboteur or data nomad from wandering into places in your database that they shouldn't.

And, as a smart computer systems manager told me once, you can achieve 80 percent of the gain with 20 percent of the effort. He always left the office on time and drove a good company car, so I guess he knew what he was talking about! The same principle applies to database startup properties and options because these two chapters show you techniques that take very little time and achieve quite a good deal of protection for your database.

Using Database Options and Attributes to Protect Data and Objects

MICROSOFT ACCESS IS a flexible product that allows database users to open and view a database in many ways. It is this very same flexibility that can also put your database at risk. In this chapter, you'll find out which of the 50 or so database options will protect or expose your database. You will also learn how to hide objects in the database window so that users who are exploring the database window are less likely to stumble on your important data and objects. In particular, you will find out:

- Why the Compact on Close option leaves copies of your database lying around.

- Where personal information is stored.

- Why the most recently used file list exposes the location of your databases.

- Why its best to turn on confirmation messages to stop inadvertent deletions and changes in your database.

- How you can stop people from opening your database in exclusive mode.

- How to hide objects in the Database window.

As we review the options and attributes that control these issues, you will learn what values are advised and how you can manually change them. In some cases, I recommend that you experiment with the changes because they may not apply in your situation. Finally, if you are a developer, you will see some Visual Basic code for Applications (VBA) that allows you to control these options and attributes more effectively and even undertake some additional protection measures that just aren't available through the Access menus.

To help you better understand the techniques outlined in the chapter, the demonstration material for this chapter includes:

- A number of forms to display and change protection-related database options.

- VBA code that hides objects.

- VBA code that gives tables the same attributes as system tables, which means that they can be opened only in read-only mode from the Database window.

- VBA code that lists all hidden and system objects.

 NOTE   To find the demonstration material, open the download database for your version of Access—for example, `grMAP2000.mdb`—and select Chapter 3.

How Will This Chapter Help Me?

Once again, I am going to provide separate overviews: one for the database administrator (DBA) and the developer and one for the IT manager. I do this because people in each of these categories will approach the chapter in a different way. The DBA and the developer need to understand how to change the database options (as shown in Figure 3-1) and attributes and what effect those changes will have on their databases. On the other hand, the IT manager should be aware of how changes to those options and attributes might affect databases that are important to his or her company's business.

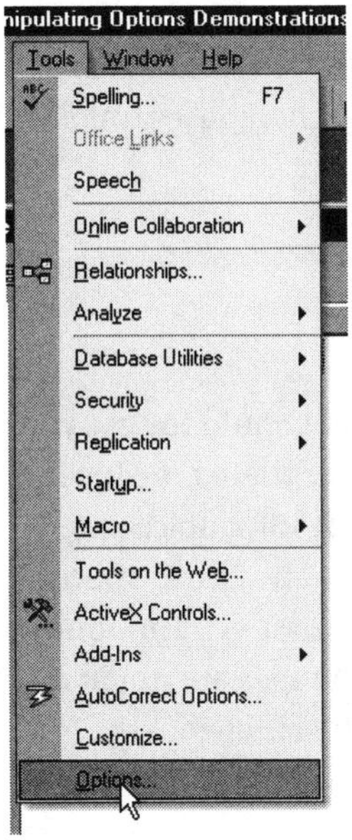

Figure 3-1. Choose the database options from the Tools menu.

Overview for the Database Administrator and the Developer

This chapter illustrates the database options most pertinent to a DBA or developer who is trying to protect an Access database. The DBA and the developer should be aware that any user who can choose Options from the Tools menu can change all these settings manually. In situations where the number of users is small, manually reviewing the options on each workstation is possible. For larger groups of users and databases where some management issues are being encountered, I recommend that you enforce these security-related options by using VBA code for when users open the database. Finally, you should consider hiding the important tables, queries, forms, and modules by using the manual process demonstrated. You should also consider using VBA code techniques to hide objects and even add the system tables attribute to a normal table so that it is visible only when a user chooses the Show Systems Table option.

Issues with the Compact on Close option will not only cause security problems but will also confuse users who come across the discarded databases that failed the compacting process. Do *not* use this option for important databases unless you monitor for failed compactions.

Overview for the IT Manager

Even if you don't add any other security to your database, you should review your databases with your DBA or developer and determine whether there are objects that you should hide from your users. This method isn't foolproof, but, coupled with setting the startup options, it will foil users who occasionally like to snoop around your database. No actions that a developer can take here cannot be undone by another developer or DBA, however. In other words, these changes are not at all foolproof but simply act as a deterrent to those small-time mischief-makers.

The Protection-Related Database Options

Access is a flexible software product, as is illustrated by the Options dialog box, with its comprehensive list of more than 50 different settings. Because this book focuses on issues of security, I have identified and will discuss only those options that either relate to security or will protect your database from inappropriate use.

Choose Tools ➤ Options to open the Options dialog box. This dialog box contains many options spread out over 10 different tabs. I will discuss the different options that we are interested in by grouping them into their respective tabs. Table 3-1, which gives you an overview of these protection-related options, lists the option, the tab that it can be found on, the version of Access when it was first introduced, whether the option is localized to the Windows user (WinUser) or to the current access database (CurrentDB), and the recommended protection value (if any).

Table 3-1. Database options and value recommended for protection

Tab	Option	Version	Applies To	Recommended Value
General	Recently Used File List	2000 or later	WinUser	Cleared *
	Compact on Close	2000 or later	CurrentDB	Cleared
	Remove Personal Information	2002 or later	CurrentDB	N/A **

Table 3-1. Database options and value recommended for protection (Continued)

Tab	Option	Version	Applies To	Recommended Value
Edit/Find	Confirm Record Changes	97 or later	WinUser	Selected
	Confirm Document Deletions	97 or later	WinUser	Selected
	Confirm Action Queries	97 or later	WinUser	Selected
Advanced	Default Open Mode	97 or later	WinUser	Shared
View	Show Hidden Objects	97 or later	WinUser	Cleared
	Show System Objects	97 or later	WinUser	Cleared

Table 3-1 notes:

* Unless your Windows account is secured (Window XP or Windows 2000)

** This value is only a temporary measure.

In the sections that follow, I describe each of these tabs in more detail. Those discussions will involve the specific options available, what value you need to specify to protect your database, and how the developer can interrogate and manipulate the option by using VBA code.

The General Tab

`Access 2000 or later`

The General tab applies to Access 2000. Changes to the General tab options take effect immediately (without your having to close and reopen the database) and apply to all databases that your computer opens. To view the options grouped under the General tab, choose Tools ➤ Options ➤ General, as shown in Figure 3-2. On that form, I have deliberately cleared the following protection-related options for better security:

- Recently Used File List

- Compact on Close

- Remove Personal Information from this File

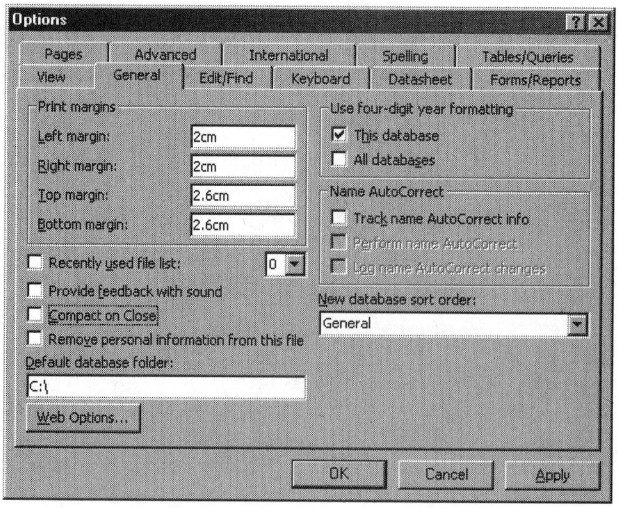

Figure 3-2. The Access 2002 General tab with the most secure settings selected.

Now I will discuss those particular General tab options in the sections that follow.

Recently Used File List

Access 2000 or later

The Recently Used File List option allows you to hide directory path links to the Access databases that you have used most recently (shown in Figure 3-3). As I explain in Chapter 12, hiding the location of your Access database is an important part of your security.

NOTE   This option is sometimes referred to as MRU, which means "most recently used."

Files used most recently are a security issue because people can observe this path while you are demonstrating your database or if Access is open when you are away from your desk.

Hiding Objects and Manipulating Options

| File | Edit | View | Insert | Tools | Window |

- New...   Ctrl+N
- Open...   Ctrl+O
- Get External Data   ▶
- Close
- Save   Ctrl+S
- Save As...
- Export...
- Search...
- Page Setup...
- Print...   Ctrl+P
- Print Preview
- Send To   ▶
- Database Properties
- 1 Gr-FX\gr\Books\hid2000.mdb
- 2 Gr-FX\gr\articles\...\dbNoPwd.mdb
- 3 temp\dbPwdIshello.mdb
- 4 Gr-FX\gr\Books\sta2000.mdb
- Exit

Figure 3-3. The MRU list reveals the location of databases that you have visited.

I read an article once that described a person who, while demonstrating an Excel spreadsheet to a supplier, inadvertently showed the names of other suppliers on the spreadsheet names. The lesson here is to consider turning off the most recently used option if you work at the same location as your users or if you are visiting a client who may have more than a passing interest in file names or directory locations.

TIP   In Access 97, you can manipulate this list only by changing the Windows registry by using VBA code. I am not sure that this risk is worth that level of sophistication. If you do have this problem, open a few sample databases just before you head to that important meeting, and the list will not reveal anything.

Most recently used lists appear in the Task pane in Access 2002. These lists do not appear if you turn this option off.

If you are using Windows XP and Access XP, you will find that you can keep your most recently used lists protected by setting up a new Windows account on your computer. This operating system protection works especially well with Access 2002 because each user has his or her own MRU lists when he or she starts Access. You can also protect yourself by introducing a password window. Both these protection methods are covered in more detail in Chapter 12. Also in Chapter 12, you will find out how to remove the Windows XP recent document list, which can also reveal the location and names of databases.

Now we will look at the personal information that is stored in the database options, then find out how the database options allow you to remove it.

Removing Personal Information

Access 97 or later

Microsoft Access allows you to store basic information to describe your database: who built it, where it originated, who developed it, and various other things. This information is readily accessible on the Summary tab (File ➤ Database Properties ➤ Summary), as shown in Figure 3-4. This descriptive information is stored in the Summary and Custom tabs, and you should be aware of this information before you distribute your database.

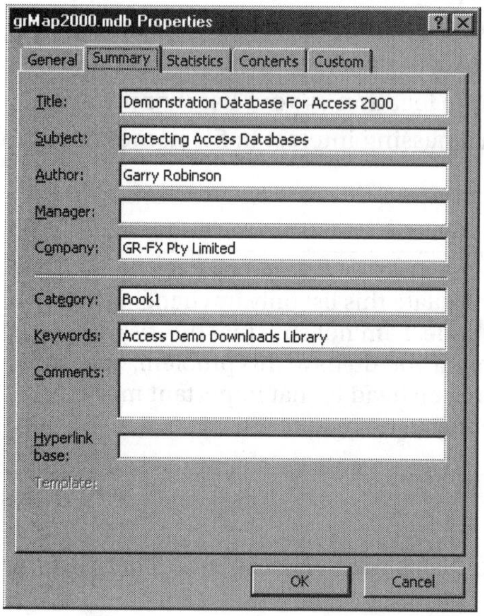

Figure 3-4. The Summary tab of database properties.

In Access 2002 or later, if you select the Remove Personal Information from this File option, Access erases the author, manager, and company descriptions from your database. The remainder of the Summary or General tab properties stay the same. If you use Microsoft Word regularly, you will find that these properties are very similar to the document properties.

You can also read this summary information directly from Windows Explorer. In Windows XP, you can hover your pointer above the file to see the summary properties (shown in Figure 3-5). To change the properties, right-click a database and choose the Summary tab. Keep in mind that on different computers and different operating systems, the properties that you can view and change will vary. I guess it's one of life's little mysteries.

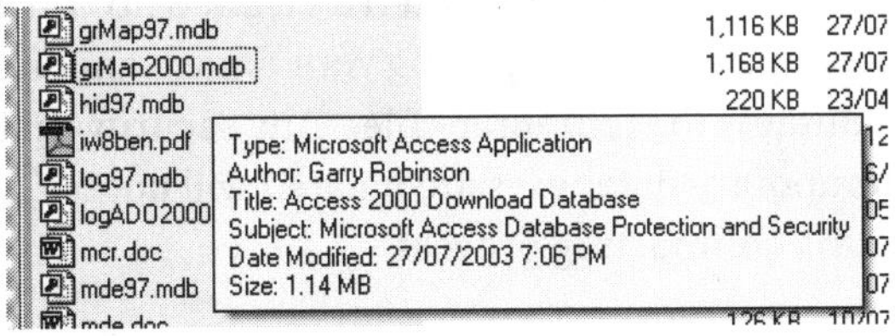

grMap97.mdb	1,116 KB	27/07
grMap2000.mdb	1,168 KB	27/07
hid97.mdb	220 KB	23/04
iw8ben.pdf	Type: Microsoft Access Application	12
log97.mdb	Author: Garry Robinson	6/
logADO2000	Title: Access 2000 Download Database	DE
mcr.doc	Subject: Microsoft Access Database Protection and Security	07
mde97.mdb	Date Modified: 27/07/2003 7:06 PM	07
mde.doc	Size: 1.14 MB	125 KB	10/07

Figure 3-5. The summary information is visible if you hover over the file in Windows XP.

Generally, database properties don't represent a huge security risk, and you may find that adding your company and personal information will assist in establishing ownership if the database ends up in the wrong place. For example, a former employee sends a database to a database recovery company to recover the data. In this case, a company address in the database properties would allow that recovery company to verify that the person asking for the recovery was bona fide. Though the database properties don't necessarily represent a security risk, they may represent a privacy issue or an embarrassing reference to a former employee.

Compact on Close

Access 2000 or later

In Access 2000, Microsoft introduced the Compact on Close option to ensure that your database is always in good condition. Compact on Close applies only to the current database, and the last person to leave the database will compact it. If you select the Compact on Close check box, the database will—theoretically—compact when the last person closes it.

Compacting Regularly Is Very Important

Compacting an Access database makes a copy of the file and rearranges how the file is stored on your disk. As part of this process, data and objects are stored in optimal order and all temporary information is removed from the database. Remember to compact both the front-end and the back-end databases.

Unfortunately, this option doesn't always work properly due to issues like data corruption or problems with ownership of files. As a result, temporary files with names such as db1.mdb and db2.mdb are left in the same directory as the database. In addition, if you move your database, you might inadvertently leave these temporary databases in the old folder. If these temporary files aren't "cleaned up" on a regular basis, they pose a reasonable security risk by exposing your data to anyone who has access to the location that contains the temporary files. Any security that you add to your database after the temporary databases are created will not be reflected in the databases that failed the compacting process.

TIP Do not use the Compact on Close option. Instead, find another way to compact your database.

A system table called MSysCompactError generally documents any compacting errors (shown in Figure 3-6). You will need to be able to view system tables by choosing Tools ➤ Options ➤ View, as explained later in this chapter.

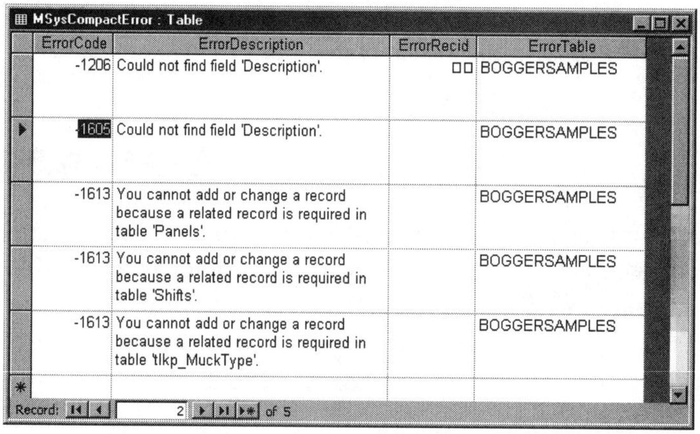

ErrorCode	ErrorDescription	ErrorRecid	ErrorTable
-1206	Could not find field 'Description'.	□□	BOGGERSAMPLES
-1605	Could not find field 'Description'.		BOGGERSAMPLES
-1613	You cannot add or change a record because a related record is required in table 'Panels'.		BOGGERSAMPLES
-1613	You cannot add or change a record because a related record is required in table 'Shifts'.		BOGGERSAMPLES
-1613	You cannot add or change a record because a related record is required in table 'tlkp_MuckType'.		BOGGERSAMPLES

Record: |◄| ◄| 2 |►| ►| ►*| of 5

Figure 3-6. The MSysCompactError table shows problems with compacting.

Dealing with an Auto Compacting Error

One of the sites where I work is a remote Australian copper mine. When I took over the geological database, a number of the tables were poorly set up and suffered from a lack of rules and database integrity. The database itself suffered from a lack of basic maintenance, such as compacting and repairing, and, even worse, ran Access 2 on two old PCs. After cleaning up the database and upgrading it to Access 2000, I decided to implement the Compact on Close option on the database. When I returned to the site a few months later, I found nine stray versions of the database, from db1.mdb to db9.mdb, in the same directory as the database itself. These temporary databases were all roughly the same size as the primary database and consumed more than 200 MB of disk space.

On investigating the problem, I found a new system table called MSysCompactError in the database (shown in Figure 3-6). The error descriptions in this table led me to the biggest table (50,000 records) in the database (called BoggerSamples). In that table, I found a number of dubious records (shown in Figure 3-7), which I removed. I imagine that these rubbish entries stopped the automatic compacting. This example illustrates the problematic nature of allowing Compact on Close to run on any user's PC because no user ever reports the problem. I resolved to turn off the Compact on Close option and instead built a simple menu option into the database to compact it. To complete the exercise, I showed the newly appointed DBA how to compact the database before I left the site.

sampid	date	shift	level	panel	drawPoint	Rin
##########	##########	#		###		
##########	##########	#		###		
##########	##########	#		###		
JR1	`	D	1590	C	11	
SS02368	`0020605	N	1615	D	10	
WG2	1	D	1590	C	11	
H7501	19951128	D	1700	A	1	
H7502	19951130	N	1700	A	99	

Record: 15 of 53431

Figure 3-7. The erroneous lines with "###" entries caused the Compact process to fail.

 CAUTION In Access 2000, a new database property called Auto Compact Percentage was also added to the database to allow for a more controlled and less frequent compacting of the database. This property never worked and was abandoned in Access 2002.

Changing the General Tab Options by Using VBA Code

To change the General tab options by using VBA code, you will need to use the Microsoft Access application object's `GetOption` and `SetOptions` methods. To find examples of the code, choose Chapter 3 in the download database and select the form called `frmGeneralOptions` (shown in Figure 3-8).

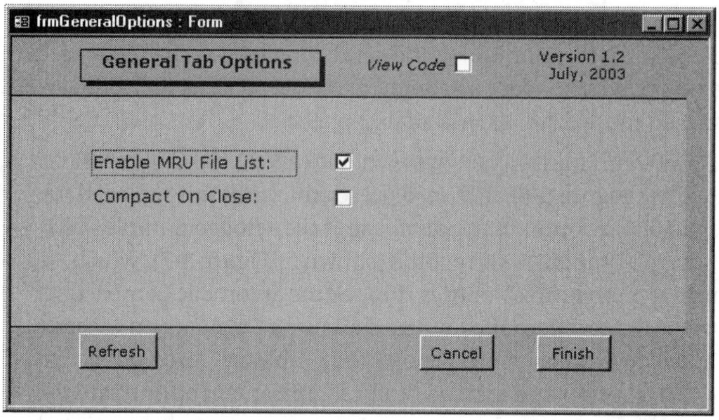

Figure 3-8. This form demonstrates the VBA code to change the General tab options.

Now if you want to find out the current values of the General tab options discussed, have a look at the code snippet from the Refresh button's onClick event. In this case, the values of the options returned are True or False, which is particularly suited to display in a check box.

```
Me!chkEnableMRU = Application.GetOption("Enable MRU File List")
Me!chkAutoCompact = Application.GetOption("Auto Compact")
```

As you are probably going to want to update the option values in code, you will need to look at the Finish button's onClick event. In this case, I will demonstrate the full subroutine so that you can also see how to open the Database Options dialog box with VBA code.

```
Private Sub updGeneralProps_Click()
' Update the General options and close the form.

Application.SetOption "Enable MRU File List", Me!chkEnableMRU
Application.SetOption "Auto Compact", Me!chkAutoCompact

If chkViewCode Then
' The next line displays the current subroutine.
  DoCmd.OpenModule "Form_" & Me.Name, Me.ActiveControl.Name & "_Click"
Else
  ' Close this form and display the database options dialog box.
  On Error Resume Next
  DoCmd.Close acForm, Me.Name
  RunCommand acCmdOptions

End If

End Sub
```

As you can see from these code samples, viewing and changing a database option really only takes one line of code. Sometimes I find it just as easy to enter a simple one-line expression like the following directly into the immediate window. If you want to do this, open the immediate window (press CTRL+G) and enter the line of code in that window. For example, you could turn off the MRU list by typing the following into the Immediate window on a new line:

```
Application.SetOption "Enable MRU File List", false
```

Now I will discuss the database options that allow you to specify whether the users are allowed a second chance when they delete some data or remove an object.

The Edit/Find Tab

Access 97 or later

Three Confirm options are on the Edit/Find tab (shown in Figure 3-9). Selecting these options will ensure that the users are prompted before these actions occur. These prompts notify users before they accidentally run queries on multiple records, accidentally delete objects, or change records without confirming the action. These Confirm options apply only to the current computer but will apply to every database that you open. To make a safer database, select all three options.

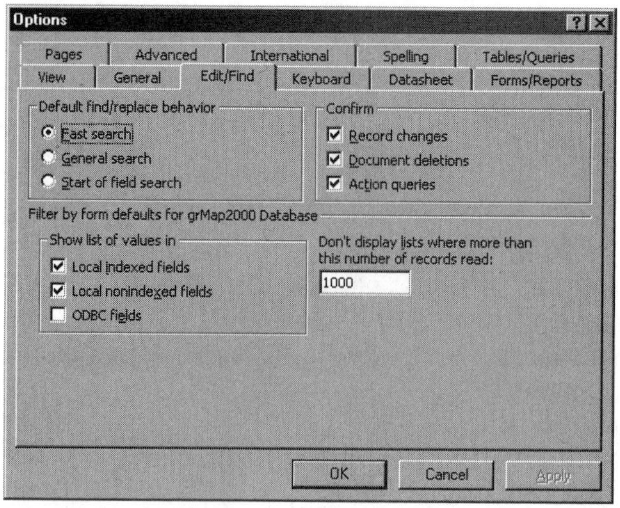

Figure 3-9. The Access 2002 Edit/Find tab options, shown with the most secure settings selected.

Now I will discuss how to change the Edit/Find settings by using VBA code, and then show you how I occasionally use VBA code to control when the user has to confirm an action query.

Changing the Edit/Find Settings by Using VBA Code

To change the Edit/Find tab options by using VBA code, you will need to use the Access application object's GetOption and SetOptions methods. To find examples of the code, choose Chapter 3 in the download database and select the form called frmEditFindOptions (shown in Figure 3-10).

Now if you want to find out the current values of the Edit/Find tab options discussed, have a look at the following code snippet from the Refresh button's onClick event. In this case, the values of the options returned are True or False, which are particularly suited to appear in a check box.

```
Me!chkRecordChanges = Application.GetOption("Confirm Record Changes")
Me!chKDocDelete = Application.GetOption("Confirm Document Deletions")
Me!chkActionQueries = Application.GetOption("Confirm Action Queries")
```

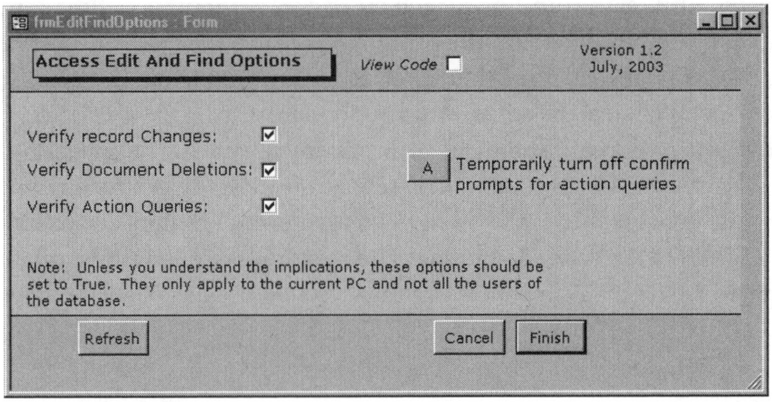

Figure 3-10. This form demonstrates the VBA code required to change the Edit/Find tab options.

As you are probably going to want to update the option values in code, you will need to look at the Finish button's onClick event. In this case, the following code snippet shows you how to update the option by using the value from the check box:

```
Application.SetOption "Confirm Record Changes", Me!chkRecordChanges
Application.SetOption "Confirm Document Deletions", Me!chKDocDelete
Application.SetOption "Confirm Action Queries", Me!chkActionQueries
```

Temporarily Turning Off the Confirm Prompts for Action Queries

If your users have selected the Confirm Action Queries option, which they should, the prompt that appears (shown in Figure 3-11) when they run action queries from your application may annoy them.

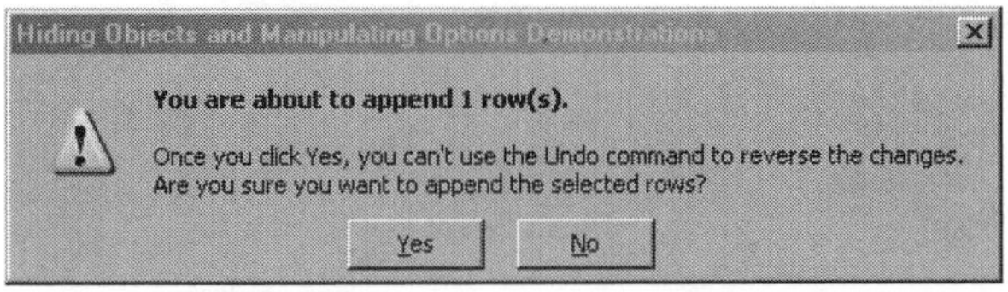

Figure 3-11. When you run an Insert query, you must confirm the action by responding to a prompt.

I find it best to turn off the prompt in each individual subroutine or function and, at the end of the subroutine, turn the prompt on again so that action query prompts always appear (as in Figure 3-11). To clear confirm action queries in your VBA code, you need to change the SetWarnings method from True to False. The following code example shows you how to stop an append message from appearing. You will notice that the SetWarnings method is set back to True just before the subroutine exits. In other words, it should happen after error handling and after the normal execution of the code. To demonstrate this process, open the form frmEditFindOptions. In the onClick event of button A, you will see the following code:

```
Private Sub actionQuery_Click()
Dim sqlStr As String
' Demonstration of how to turn action query messages on and off.

On Error GoTo actionQuery_Click_Error:

sqlStr = "INSERT INTO MyTable ( Field1, Field2 ) " & _
         "values ( 'Test 1' , 'Test 2');"
DoCmd.SetWarnings False
DoCmd.RunSQL sqlStr

actionQuery_Click_Exit:
DoCmd.SetWarnings True
Exit Sub

actionQuery_Click_Error:

   MsgBox Err.Description
   GoTo actionQuery_Click_Exit
End sub
```

NOTE   It is best to test your action queries thoroughly before disabling confirm prompts.

Now I will show you how you can change the default mode in which users open their databases.

The Advanced Tab

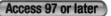

The only option on the Advanced tab (shown in Figure 3-12) that relates to your database's security is Default Open Mode.

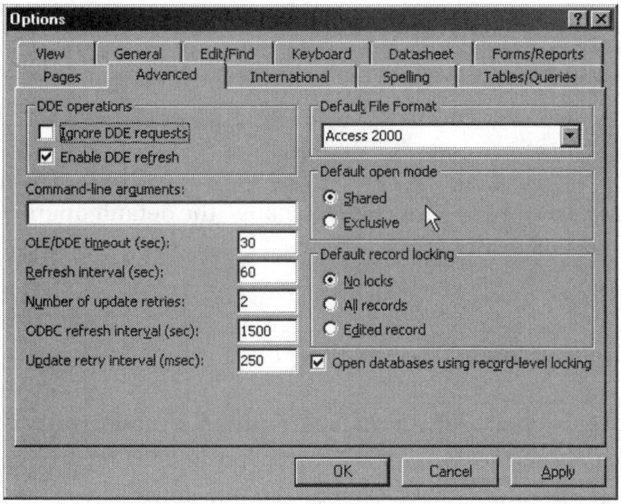

Figure 3-12. Access 2002 Advanced tab with the most secure settings selected.

If the Default Open Mode option is set to Exclusive, that computer will be able to open databases in exclusive mode whenever possible. This situation is generally one that you want to avoid, unless you are the administrator or the developer. This option only affects the way a database is opened on a single workstation; it does not affect the default setting for users on other computers. Another consequence of opening a database in exclusive mode is that an .LDB file will not be generated, which can be a useful pointer to a database that's being locked in exclusive mode. In Chapter 6, I discuss more about surveillance with some references to the .LDB files.

NOTE In Access 2000 and 2002, only if you are the only user of the database, it is possible to switch from shared ownership to exclusive ownership if you open a form, report, or module in design view.

If you set up Access workgroup security in your multi-user environment, you can ensure that users don't open a database exclusively by denying them Open Exclusive permission for that database. For more information on removing permissions, see Chapters 8 and 10 on workgroup security.

TIP   In Chapter 10, you will find out how you can set up your own desktop shortcuts so that you can open your database in exclusive or read-only mode, even if you specify shared mode as your default.

Now I will show you how you can use VBA code to change the default open mode for all databases that users open.

Changing the Default Open Mode by Using VBA Code

To change the default open mode on the Advanced tab by using VBA code, you will need to use the Microsoft Access application object's GetOption and SetOptions methods. To find examples of the code, choose Chapter 3 in the download database and select the form called frmAdvancedOptions (shown in Figure 3-13).

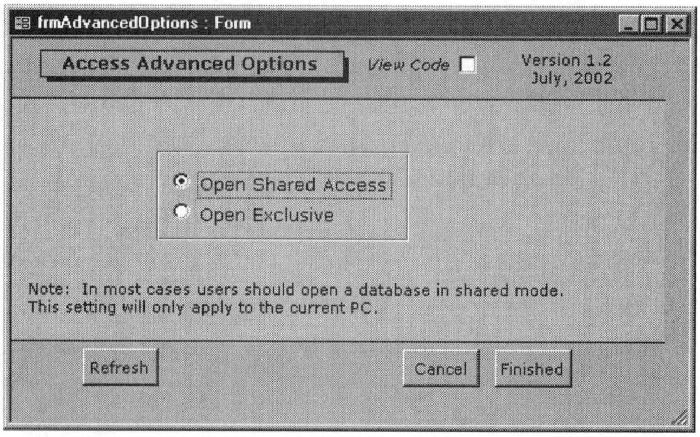

Figure 3-13. This form demonstrates the VBA code required to change the Advanced tab options.

Now if you want to find the current values of the Advanced tab options discussed, have a look at the following code snippet from the Refresh button's onClick event. In this case, the values of the options returned are integer constants. To show the correct integer constant, I have set up two options in a frame, and one option is selected according to the value returned from the GetOption method.

```
Const OPENEXCLUSIVE = 1
Const OPENSHARED = 0
Private Sub refrAdvancedProps_Click()
'Update the Option box frame to reflect the current system settings

If Application.GetOption("Default Open Mode for Databases") = OPENSHARED Then
  fraPrefOpen = OPENSHARED

ElseIf Application.GetOption("Default Open Mode for Databases") = _
OPENEXCLUSIVE Then
  fraPrefOpen = OPENEXCLUSIVE
End If

End Sub
```

As you are probably going to want to update the option values in code, you will need to look at the Finish button's onClick event. In this case, the following code snippet shows you how to update the option by using the value from the option frame.

```
If fraPrefOpen = OPENEXCLUSIVE Then
  Application.SetOption "Default Open Mode for Databases", OPENEXCLUSIVE
ElseIf fraPrefOpen = OPENSHARED Then
  Application.SetOption "Default Open Mode for Databases", OPENSHARED
End If
```

Time to Find the Magic Wand

We've come to the end of the discussion about options that protect or expose your database. Now we will look at one of the oldest tricks that Access magicians have up their sleeves—the ability to hide important objects in the Database window so that the casual explorer won't be tempted to modify an object or view the contents of a table.

Hiding Objects in the Database Window   Access 97 or later

Hiding your tables, queries, forms, macros, and modules from casual users who can open the Database window is one of the easiest ways to protect your database objects. I have to qualify this statement upfront, though, because the menus that you use to make an object visible take no more time than it does to hide the objects. The key difference is that once you have hidden an object, the casual user should be blissfully unaware of its existence. Now I will walk you through the manual steps required to hide an object:

1. Open the Database window.

2. Find the object that you want to hide.

3. Right-click the object (shown in Figure 3-14) and choose Properties.

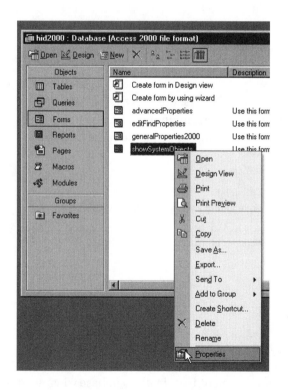

Figure 3-14. Right-click a table, query, form, report, macro, or module and choose Properties.

4. Select the Attributes: Hidden check box (shown in Figure 3-15).

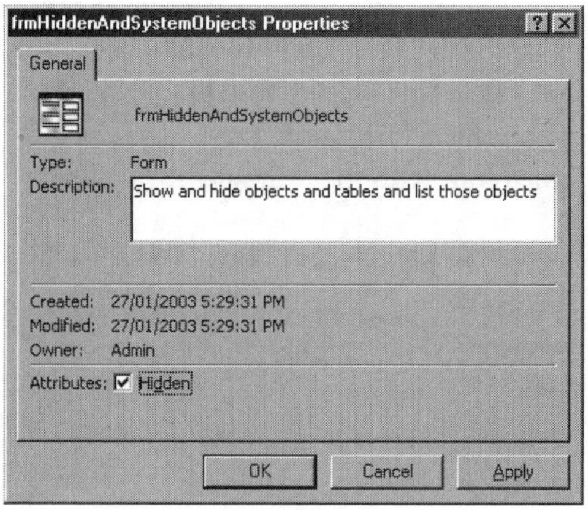

Figure 3-15. Select the Attributes: Hidden check box to hide the object.

This procedure will work the same for all objects in the database, but modules that you hide in the Database window will be visible in the Project Explorer in Access 2000 and later. In other words, this technique is designed only for "tricking" users who are having a "casual explore" of the Database window, rather than a database-savvy person. (For more on this issue, see the next section.)

You can view all hidden objects in the Database window by choosing Tools ➤ Options and selecting the View tab. Select the Hidden Objects check box (as shown in Figure 3-16), and the hidden objects appear in the Database window in gray rather than in the solid color used for visible objects.

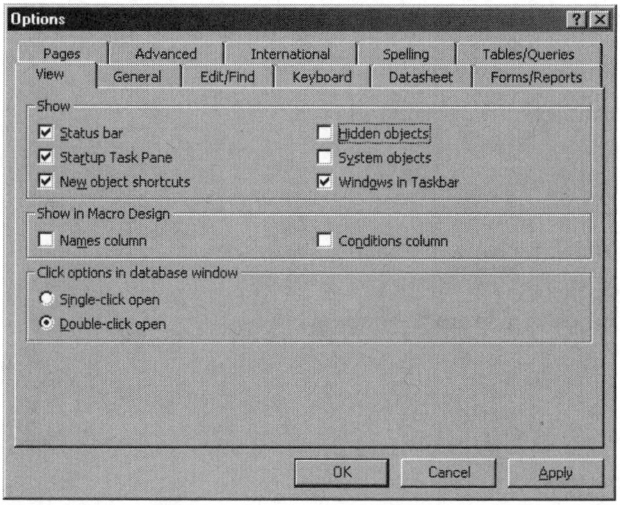

Figure 3-16. The Access 2002 View tab with the most secure settings selected.

You can also view all system objects by selecting the System Objects check box. All the system tables that will be visible through this process will be read-only and generally will not be useful to normal users. You should note that system tables should be left alone because they contain information that is vital for the database to operate correctly. System tables start with the MSys or USys prefix.

 TIP An easy way to hide your table like a system table is to give it the prefix of USys. I recommend this prefix only for tables that relate to program settings in your database.

Just so that you know the difference, hidden objects (tables, queries, forms, reports, macros, modules) are objects that the developer or the user has created. System objects generally are objects that Microsoft Access has created and that the developer or users cannot modify.

The VBA Editor Exposes a Hidden Module

Hiding objects in the database window is a neat way to protect objects from your database's users, but you need to be aware that VBA modules (and code behind forms) are more exposed because they are not hidden in Visual Basic Editor, or specifically, the Visual Basic Explorer. For example, I'll first show you how to hide a module, and then I'll show you how a casual user might find the module in a different way.

1. Open the demonstration database.

2. Open the Database window by pressing F11.

3. Select the Modules tab.

4. Create a module by clicking New.

5. Type the following subroutine into the code window:

```
Sub AussieWarning
  Msgbox "Watch out for the Crocodile!"
End sub
```

6. Save the module as MyHiddenModule and close it.

7. On the Module tab, right-click MyHiddenModule and choose Properties.

8. Select the Attribute: Hidden check box and click Apply.

9. If you can still see the module, choose Tools ➤ Options and select the View tab, and make sure that the Hidden check boxes are not selected.

10. Now create another new module and press F2 to open the Object Browser, as shown in Figure 3-17.

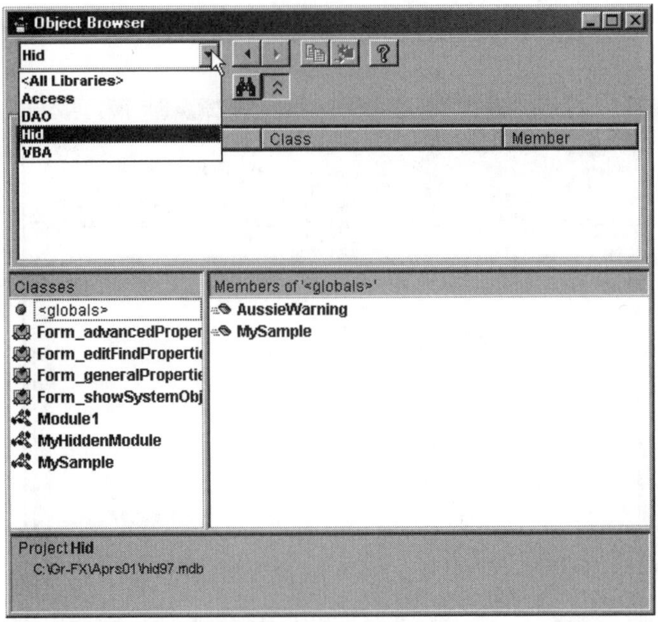

Figure 3-17. The Object Browser makes hidden modules visible. Example is from Access 97.

11. Select Hid from the drop-down list at the top of the form. Hid is the name of the current project name for this database, and this list provides all the modules and VBA code in the database.

12. You can now double-click MyHiddenModule, and you will be in the "hidden module."

In Access 2000 or later, it is even easier to find a hidden module, as I will demonstrate in the following instructions:

1. Create a new module as described in steps 1 through 9 of the previous procedure.

2. Open Visual Basic Editor by pressing ALT+F11 or by opening any module in design view.

3. On the left side of Figure 3-18, you will see a pane with a tree view of all the VBA code in the project. If you cannot see this window, choose View ➤ Project Explorer.

4. Now you or your users can explore down and double-click MyHiddenModule to get into the supposedly hidden module.

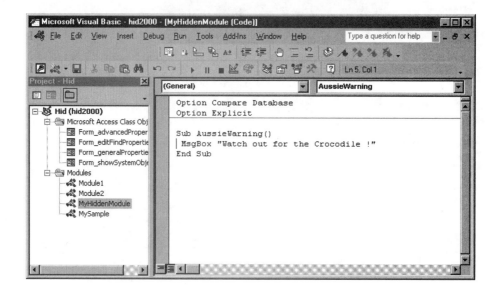

Figure 3-18. The Project Explorer window enables you to navigate to all modules and code in your project.

If you are starting to worry about the secrecy of your code, don't fret too much at this stage—I discuss solutions later on in this book. These solutions include creating security for your code by using the MDE format (Chapter 11), special code to protect your modules by using workgroup security (Chapter 8), and using the VBA project password (Chapter 11). Now we will review how you can hide objects in your database by using VBA code.

Hiding Objects in the Database Window by Using VBA Code

In the demonstration form called frmHiddenAndSystemObjects (shown in Figure 3-19), VBA code is illustrated to show you to change attributes to hide objects from users.

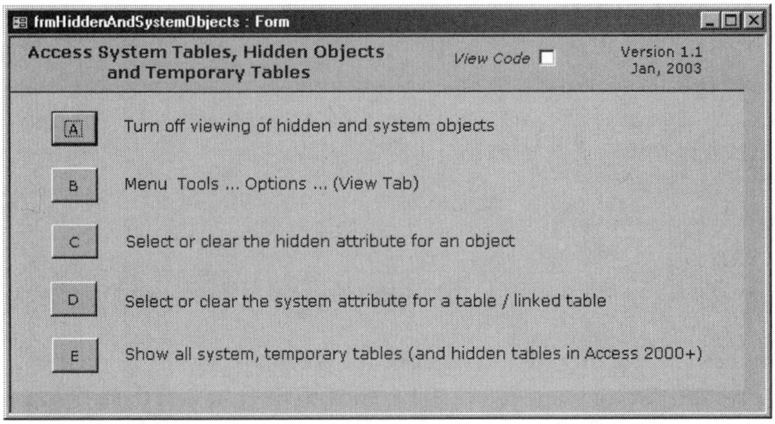

Figure 3-19. This form demonstrates VBA code options for system tables, hidden objects, and temporary tables.

The first step that we will need to do in the application is to make sure that users cannot see the hidden and system objects in the Database window. This step is accomplished in VBA code by the A button (shown in Figure 3-19), as follows:

```
Application.SetOption "Show Hidden Objects ", False
Application.SetOption " Show System Objects ", False
```

Now that you have cleared these two options, you should test that they work by choosing Tools ➤ Options and selecting the View tab. Button B on the demonstration form will also open the Options Tab form for you. Or, you can view options by using the VBA code example under Button B (Figure 3-19), as follows:

```
RunCommand acCmdOptions
```

Selecting or Clearing the Hidden Attribute for All Objects

Access 2000 or later

In Access 97, it was not possible to hide an object in the Database window by using VBA code. In Access 2000, the GetHiddenAttribute and SetHiddenAttribute methods were added to allow you to retrieve and change the attributes of all the objects in an Access database. The syntax for these two methods follows:

```
GetHiddenAttribute(objecttype, objectname)
SetHiddenAttribute(ObjectType, ObjectName, fHidden)
```

Note the following for the preceding code:

- ObjectType requires one of the following constants for Access objects: acDataAccessPage, acDiagram, acForm, acFunction, acMacro, acModule, acQuery, acReport, acServerView, acStoredProcedure, acTable.

- ObjectName is the name of object.

- fHidden is True if you want to hide the object and False if you want to view it.

In the demonstration form called frmHiddenAndSystemObjects, the VBA code example under button C (shown in Figure 3-19) shows you how first to find and then to swap the current value of the hidden attribute for both a table and a form.

```
Dim tableIsHidden As Boolean
Dim formIsHidden As Boolean
  tableIsHidden = Application.GetHiddenAttribute(acTable, "myTable")
  If tableIsHidden Then
    Application.SetHiddenAttribute acTable, "myTable", False
  Else
    Application.SetHiddenAttribute acTable, "myTable", True
  End If

  formIsHidden = Application.GetHiddenAttribute(acForm, "frmGotovb123")
  If formIsHidden Then
    Application.SetHiddenAttribute acForm, "frmGotovb123", False
  Else
    Application.SetHiddenAttribute acForm, "frmGotovb123", True
  End If

statusMsg = "The hidden attribute for the table myTable is currently set to " & _
tableIsHidden & vbCrLf & _
"The hidden attribute for the form frmGotovb123 is currently set to " & _
 formIsHidden
MsgBox statusMsg
```

Making a Table a Read-Only System Table

By using VBA code, you can change the attributes of a table so that it becomes a system table. Once you change this property with VBA code, the table will only be visible if you choose Tools ➤ Options, select the View tab, and select the System Objects check box (shown in Figure 3-16). More important, though, is the fact that the table is read-only in the database window, just like a system table.

You can use VBA code to change Access table attributes by manipulating the TableDef object. TableDef objects have an Attributes property that specifies the characteristics of the table. This property is confusing (to me anyway) because the clever developers at Microsoft have managed to store a variety of different options in the one number, which is then stored as the attribute property value. Included in this property value are numbers to signify that the table is a system table, a linked table, or just a table.

I've found that the following VBA code gives both tables and linked tables a system table attribute. The example under the D button (shown in Figure 3-19) on the frmHiddenAndSystemObjects form reverts the setting back to its original attribute if the table is already a system table. Here's the full procedure:

```
Private Sub swapSys_Click()
' To hide a table, make it a system object. If it already is a system object,
' then make it visible again by resetting its attributes to 0.

Dim dbs As DAO.Database

Set dbs = CurrentDb
With dbs.TableDefs("World_Demo")
' System/no system attribute for normal tables.
  If .Attributes = 0 Then
    .Attributes = dbSystemObject
  ElseIf .Attributes = dbSystemObject Then
    .Attributes = 0

' System/no system attribute for linked tables.
  ElseIf (.Attributes And dbAttachedTable) Then
    If (.Attributes And dbSystemObject) Then
      .Attributes = 0
    Else
      .Attributes = dbSystemObject
    End If
  End If
End With
End sub
```

Now that you have made a table a system table, if you open this table from the Database window, it will always open in read-only mode. This is a good safeguard for the database-exploring user.

NOTE The dbSystemObject table attribute makes a table hidden and read-only if you open it from the Database window. If you open the table through a form or a query, you can make changes and add records. The read-only attribute does not apply to linked tables (discussed in Chapter 4).

Temporary Tables and Hidden Tables

While searching the help files and the Internet for information on hidden tables and objects, I was misled by a table attribute called dbHiddenObject. After some research and a lot of reading, I found that Access seems to use a table's dbHidden attribute to define a temporary table. After looking through the relevant Access newsgroups, I found that many developers were making the mistake of using this attribute to hide a file, which in fact deletes the table when the database was compacted. Thankfully, there were a number of warnings on most of these postings about the problems associated with this attribute.

CAUTION To hide a table, do not use the hidden attribute in VBA code because Access uses this attribute to flag a temporary table. When you compact the database, Access uses the hidden attribute as a signal to delete all records from the table. You can use the hidden attribute when you want to save information, however, as for a temporary table. The following code is an example:

```
' Please do not use this code to hide a table. Use it make a temporary table.
CurrentDb.TableDefs("Table1").Attributes = dbHiddenObject
```

A note on Access 97: After much investigation, I have concluded that there is no supported way in Access 97 to hide an object in the database window by using VBA code. Access handles the hidden objects by making changes to the flag field in the MSysObjects system table, which is not a table that you can manipulate by using VBA code. If you want to give an object a hidden property, you must do it manually as I described previously in this chapter.

Now we will take a look at how we can document the system and temporary tables in your database.

Listing the System and Temporary Tables in Your Database

The final example on the frmHiddenAndSystemObjects demonstration form shows how you can loop through all the tables in your database and display only those that are system tables or temporary (dbhiddenobject) tables. If you look carefully at the code, you will see that system tables that have the "MSys" prefix are excluded from the list. To view the code, have a look at button E's onClick event, as follows:

```
Private Sub viewSystemTables_Click()
' Showing system and temporary tables requires a reference to the DAO library.

Dim dbs As DAO.Database, i As Integer, tablesStatus As String
Dim bolTempTbl As Boolean, bolSystemTbl As Boolean, bolHiddenTbl As Boolean
Dim prop As DAO.Property, tabDef As DAO.TableDef

tablesStatus = ""

Set dbs = CurrentDb
For i = 0 To dbs.TableDefs.Count - 1
  If Left(dbs.TableDefs(i).[Name], 4) <> "msys" Then

'   Test for temporary and system tables using table attributes.
    bolTempTbl = dbs.TableDefs(i).Properties!Attributes And dbHiddenObject
    bolSystemTbl = dbs.TableDefs(i).Properties!Attributes And dbSystemObject

'   Test if table is hidden.
  bolHiddenTbl = GetHiddenAttribute(acTable, dbs.TableDefs(i).Name)

    If (bolTempTbl = True) Or (bolSystemTbl = True) Or (bolHiddenTbl = True) Then
      tablesStatus = tablesStatus & (dbs.TableDefs(i).[Name]) & _
      IIf(bolTempTbl, " - Temporary table ", "") & _
      IIf(bolSystemTbl, " - System table ", "") & _
      IIf(bolHiddenTbl, " - Hidden table ", "") & vbCrLf
    Else
    End If
  End If
Next
```

```
If Len(tablesStatus) = 0 Then
  MsgBox "No hidden, temporary or system tables were found"
Else
  MsgBox tablesStatus, vbInformation, "Hidden, System and Temporary tables"
End If
End Sub
```

The manually hidden tables do not appear in Access 97 because this information is stored separately in the MSysObjects table. Now I will show you how you can be a little more specific in what you hide.

Hiding Columns from Users

For another way to hide information, you can choose the Hide Columns command in a table or a query. To hide a column in a table, you can right-click the top of a column and choose Hide Columns (shown in Figure 3-20).

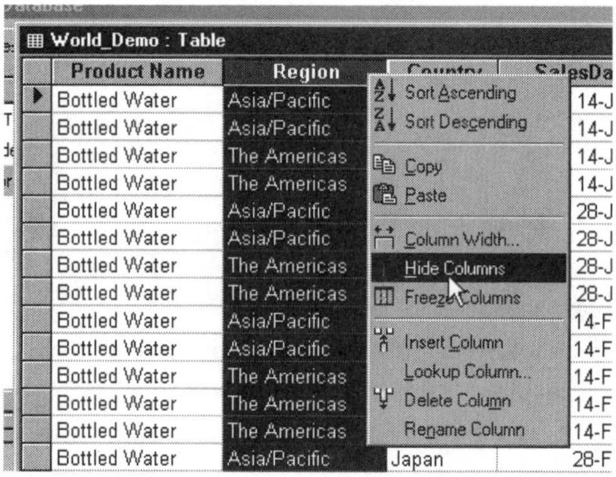

Figure 3-20. Hiding a column in a table or a query can help protect your information.

To make the column reappear, choose Format ➤ Unhide Columns. To program this procedure by using VBA code, search help for the ColumnHidden property.

That concludes the detail on using options and attributes to protect your database. Now I will describe where you can find additional resources on topics related to the discussions in this chapter.

Further Reading

As you might expect, there is never enough information when it comes to powerful products like Microsoft Access. To assist you with further investigations, I have put together a Web page with links to Web sites and articles on the issues that relate to material in this chapter, including:

- How to remove the registry entries for the most recently used files.

- Discussions on shared and exclusive ownership, plus saving design changes to a shared Access database.

- "How to Use the Attributes Property for TableDef Objects" (Microsoft Knowledge Base Article 117536).

- How you can document all the tables and other objects in your database.

- Discussion on the dangers of hiding a table by using the dbHiddenObject attribute.

You can find the further reading Web page for this chapter in the Downloads section of the Apress Web site (http://www.apress.com) or at the following address: http://www.vb123.com/map/hid.htm.

Reflecting on This Chapter

In this chapter, I concentrated on the options and attributes that will improve the protection of objects in the database. Though the default settings for these objects are generally safe, any user who can find Options on the Tools menu can easily change them. We learned that:

- The recently used file list and personal information can provide another person with information that we would like to hide.

- Compact on Close can produce copies of a database that are unknown to us. This option should be turned off.

- The confirmation settings on the Edit/Find tab should always be turned on.

- Manual methods can hide any objects in the Database window.

- VBA code can hide any objects in the Database window in Access 2000 and later.

- You can change table attributes to make them function like system tables. This capability provides them with more protection because they will be marginally harder to find than hidden tables and in read-only mode when they are viewed directly.

Understanding Access options is important, and you should consider putting VBA code in your database to make sure all that the options always reflect the manual settings. Also, hiding certain important objects in your Database window is a simple way to protect your database from most users. Finally, if you want a recommendation, I suggest that you start experimenting with each of these options one at a time and, as you become comfortable with them, start using these options in all your databases.

What's Next?

In the next chapter, I will explain some of the basics about setting up your database so that it's easier to protect. These basics include splitting your database into software and data components, starting up your database, and exploring some database design issues that will safeguard your data. Though these issues may seem a little introductory to some developers, they are fundamental and form an integral part of every database, protected or not.

Providing a Solid Foundation with Good Programming Practices

WHEN I THOUGHT about the demonstration material that I was providing with this book, three mechanisms stood out as being both relevant to your protection strategy and good database design in general:

- Using the AutoExec macro as a springboard for your application.

- Separating your tables and the relationships model into one database and placing all the remaining programming objects into a second database (called database splitting).

- Savvy and proactively using VBA code for Applications (VBA) error handling.

While reviewing the Access help files, other Access books, and even the Internet, I was surprised at the lack of prominence given to the first two of these programming topics. I feel they are fundamental because probably 90 percent of the databases that I've dealt with have used the database splitting technique, and most databases have an AutoExec macro. Therefore, in this chapter, I propose to redress that anomaly by featuring these two important topics.

VBA code error handling has been well covered in many publications. However, I shall underscore some of the common wisdom—adding my own perspective—and discuss error handling and its relevance to database protection. I'll even provide some useful tricks to improve your debugging efforts.

The demonstration material for this chapter includes a sample AutoExec macro and a module that will allow you to add your own relinking code to your split database. For Access 2002 users, I've included a demonstration of how to use the new FileDialog object to locate files. For errors and error handling, there are samples of standard, good, and nonexistent error handling. There are also samples of ignoring errors and trapping errors in lower-level procedures.

NOTE To find the demonstration material, open the download database for your version of Access (for example, grMAP2002.mdb) and select Chapter 4.

Is This Chapter Worth Reading Now?

Once again, I will provide three separate overviews—one for the developer, one for the DBA, and one for the IT manager. I do this because people in each of these categories will approach the chapter in a different way. The developer and the DBA will want to make sure that all but the smallest databases incorporate lessons detailed in this chapter. The IT manager will just want to recognize these practices and raise questions when they are not incorporated.

Overview for the Developer

The AutoExec macro is important because you can open your startup form and additional processes from the one location. If you follow the rules for writing a good AutoExec macro that are detailed in this chapter, you'll find that the macro will be easy to support and enhance.

Splitting a database into front- and back-end databases makes the task of improving an Access database match that of the traditional software development lifecycle. It is also the first step in making your Access front end independent of whether you store your data in an Access database (back end), SQL Server, Oracle, or other. Once you have made the split, you can program the front-end database without impacting the live databases. When the new front end is tested and complete, you can install it by replacing the existing live front end. If you are planning a career in providing contract development by using Access, splitting and relinking databases will be fundamental to your success.

When it comes to error handling, the discussions in this chapter focus on why error handling is an important element of database protection. This element especially applies when you clear the Allow Special Keys option in the Startup dialog. Also discussed are techniques that you can use to locate the source of your errors when you are using the debugger.

Overview for the DBA

The DBA needs to be fully aware of all the macros and VBA code procedures that are run when your database is started. These procedures are important because all the users' activities can be traced back to this point. In this chapter, I discuss a special macro called AutoExec that Access runs whenever anyone opens a database that has that macro in it. From this macro, you can open the main or home form, start any special administration procedures, and maybe even start a background surveillance process to help you administer the database.

After a database is split into a software front end and a data-only back end, the DBA will need to become fully conversant with the issues of table linking. Another consequence of splitting databases is that the DBA will need to know how to replace the front-end software database when the developer makes a new version available.

Overview for the IT Manager

When reading this chapter, an IT manager should be on the lookout for the following:

- A database used regularly by three or more people that has not been split into a software front end and back end. The problem with this scenario is that a developer requires exclusive ownership of the database to make changes to forms and reports, and when this happens, users may not be able to get on with their work.

- A database that has not been split that is being managed by a person in another company or another location. In this scenario, the database may have to be frozen while problems are fixed or objects in the database are modified. Even more worrying in this situation is that all your data may be transferred off-site while the changes are being made.

- Errors that occur on a regular basis. If this starts happening to your database(s), you need to make sure that your users respond in an appropriate manner. If they don't, then you will need to improve the error handling in your database and maybe even reconfigure your user interface to avoid the problems.

The AutoExec Macro Provides a Flexible Springboard

Access 97 or later

For those of you who started your programming life by using DOS as an operating system, you will probably be quite familiar with the autoexec.bat file, a file used to configure your PC. Though this batch file is almost a history lesson now, Access has a similar starting mechanism called the AutoExec macro. This macro has been around since Access 2 and is still an important foundation for protecting your database. When your database opens, Access first processes the startup options and then looks for and runs the AutoExec macro.

I consider the AutoExec macro to be an important protection mechanism because it acts as the springboard for your application. For example, you can simultaneously launch your startup form and any other procedures that you need to maintain your security and software integrity (see the working example that follows).

Of course, like most other things that you do in Access, there is an alternative way to add startup procedures to your application. Generally, this other method involves using VBA code that is processed in your startup form's onOpen event. If you want to see an example of this technique, see the onOpen event in the Northwind database's startup form.

Creating Your First AutoExec Macro

If your database doesn't have an AutoExec macro, create a sample to see how it works:

1. Open the Database window and select Macros.

2. Create a new macro by clicking New.

3. Select a check box in the Action column and type (or choose) "MsgBox."

4. In the bottom pane, you will find the custom action arguments suited to the action that you selected.

5. In the message box in the bottom pane, type "AutoExec is running."

6. Now close the macro and save it as AutoExec.

7. Close your database and then open it again.

8. You should now see the message "AutoExec is running."

Creating a Good AutoExec Macro

A good AutoExec macro can launch one or many different procedures or objects. In my view, the actions in the macro should either open a form or run a VBA function. Though a macro can do many things, I recommend that you restrict this macro to simple tasks and leave complex tasks to VBA.

If you open the demonstration database, you will find an AutoExec macro that opens two forms and runs a function called HideDBObjects. Figure 4-1 shows the AutoExec macro with the Expression Builder. It is important to note that Access macros will allow you to call only a function, rather than a subroutine or class module.

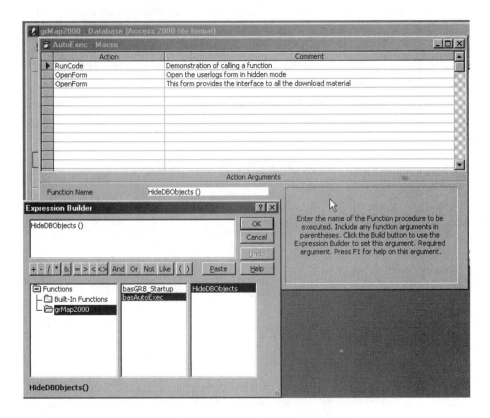

Figure 4-1. The AutoExec macro in the demonstration database includes a call to a function.

NOTE   If you don't want to run the AutoExec macro when you open the database, press SHIFT when the database opens. You can set the Allow ByPass option to False to avoid this security breach (described in Chapter 2).

How I've Used AutoExec Macros

When I started researching the AutoExec macro for this book, I thought I'd better review the databases that we have developed over the years. Not surprisingly, most of those databases used an AutoExec macro to control the startup actions. During the eight years that I've been programming Access databases professionally, I can't recall ever having had any problems with the AutoExec macro itself. As for the procedures and forms that the AutoExec macro runs, now *that's* been a different story. So what have I used the AutoExec macro for?

- Opening the database's main form.

- Minimizing the Database window.

- Modifying the startup options and other protection settings (just in case of user tweaking).

- Checking for VBA project reference failures.

- Opening the user logging form (see Chapter 6).

- Checking for regional date settings.

NOTE   An Autoexec macro runs only when you open the database or if you specifically run it from the Database window, from code, or from another macro. It will not run at any other time.

Using the AutoExec Macro to Launch Your Startup Form

In my view, the startup options are more accessible to the user than the AutoExec macro. Because of that, I recommend that you launch your startup form from the AutoExec macro. If you launch a form from both the Startup dialog and the AutoExec macro, the startup form will load first. Although it's possible to launch other code from your startup form, I don't recommend it because the form can be rewritten or lost.

 TIP   The macro environment is a good place to learn about the wide variety of functions that you can write in VBA code. I recommend that you work through the different macro actions (try the drop-down list in the Action column), and if an action attracts your interest, press F1 for help.

In the next section, I will show you how to make your database development more manageable by splitting the database into software and data databases.

Splitting Your Database to Make It Easier to Protect

Splitting the database into a back end with tables and relationships and front end with objects like forms and reports is an important step in protecting and securing the database. This additional protection comes about because you need to use different methods of protection for objects (in the front end) and data (in the back end).

After splitting a database, the front-end database communicates with the back-end database through linked tables. A linked table establishes a connection to data in another Access database or in a different format such as SQL Server, FoxPro, or MySQL. Linked tables follow all the rules of the remote Access database and allow you to use that information without opening the back-end database. Splitting the database into two Access databases is a very good way to become accustomed to working with a data-only database. By adopting this model, you are well on the way to making your database talk to other databases that offer enterprise-level database security, something that Access will never match.

The Database Splitting Wizard

To practice splitting a database, I suggest that you follow these steps. If you do not have a copy of the Northwind database or you would like to bring back the original, read the instructions in Chapter 1.

1. Open Windows Explorer, copy the Northwind database from the sample directory, and place it in a temporary directory on your computer, such as in C:\Temp.

2. Open the Northwind database in C:\Temp.

3. Start the Database Splitter wizard (shown in Figure 4-2), which you can open from Tools ➤ Add-ins in Access 97 and from Tools ➤ Database Utilities in Access 2000 and later. With Access 97, you may need to install the advanced wizards.

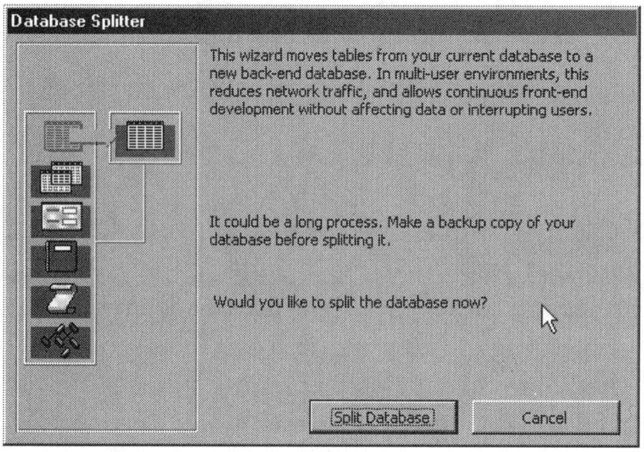

Figure 4-2. The Database Splitter wizard in action. Heed the warnings!

4. Enter a name for the back-end database (shown in Figure 4-3). This new back-end database will now hold all the tables and relationships from the current database (Northwind.mdb). The front-end database will now have links to these tables, which will be visible under Tables in the Database window (shown in Figure 4-4). I recommend that you place the back-end database in the same directory as the current database while you get used to working with linked tables.

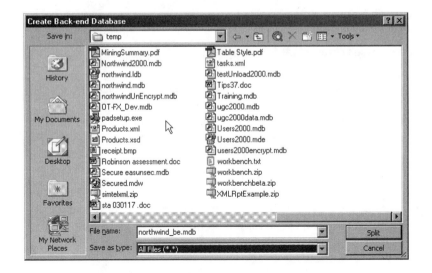

Figure 4-3. Enter the destination of the back-end database.

 TIP Access 2002 provides quick access to sample data. Simply choose Help ➤ Sample Databases, and you can select one of the sample files installed on your computer.

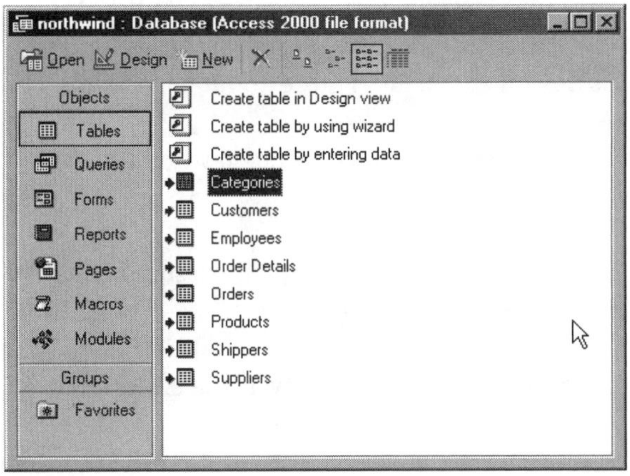

Figure 4-4. Arrows next to table names denote linked tables.

Why You Should Split Your Database

Splitting your database is important for many reasons:

- Development can proceed while people are using the database.

- Current wisdom says that one should split the user interface (UI) from the data (sometimes referred to as n-tier).

- Testing UI changes won't affect the "live" system's data.

- The quicker the users adopt a development database, the more likely the development will proceed in the right direction. I've yet to run into a user who really tests an application before it goes live.

- If you are an external developer, your client is far more likely to reuse your skills if you are maintaining the front-end database. I know this from personal experience.

- Splitting a database makes it much easier to plan for and convert to a server database such SQL Server or Oracle. Upsizing to SQL Server is made easier because you can modify the access table links to point to server-based tables with the same names. Once you have split the database, testing changed links can carry on independently of normal database operations.

- Front-end databases are very suited to conversions to the compiled Access database format (called MDE format). This format totally secures forms, reports, and modules (stops design view). Read more about it in Chapter 11.

- Protecting data in a back-end database is easy to focus on when the database isn't crowded with other objects.

- Users in a front-end database won't be able to change the design of a table unless they physically open the back-end database.

- Linked tables will adopt the same workgroup security as the tables in the back-end database.

Now I will explain how to deliver and install a front-end database.

Delivering a New Front-End Database with Linked Tables

Now that you've split your database, the next issue you will encounter is that the physical location of your development back-end database won't be the same as that of the live back-end database. The exception to this issue occurs in the early phase of development, when the person(s) who are testing your database are using local drives such as C: or D:. If that is the case, make the location of your development back-end database match the location of your live back-end database, and save yourself some of the steps here. Of course, if you are using local drives for development and even to store important data, make sure that you have a backup system in place and, even more importantly, make sure that you can retrieve it.

Now let's see what you have to do to install a new front-end database as the live database.

1. Before shipping a database to the DBA, always put a version number on the startup form in the database. This way, you can actually verify whether the version someone is testing is the latest update.

2. Before shipping a database, it is always a good idea to make a backup copy of the database. I make a compressed .ZIP file and give the .ZIP file a name that includes the version number. Then I ship the compressed .ZIP file to the DBA.

3. Once the DBA has the database, he or she should replace the existing front-end database with the latest version. Generally, the DBA should have a recent backup of the current live front-end database, but if he or she doesn't, he or she should make one. Having a recent backup is necessary in case someone has changed something in the database and the DBA needs to recover those changes.

4. The DBA should now open the front-end database that contains links to the tables. In Access 97, choose Tools ➤ Add-ins ➤ Linked Table Manager. In Access 2000 and later, choose Tools ➤ Database Utilities ➤ Linked Table Manager.

5. In the Linked Table Manager dialog box, click Select All (shown in Figure 4-5). This action selects all the linked tables in the database. Now click OK.

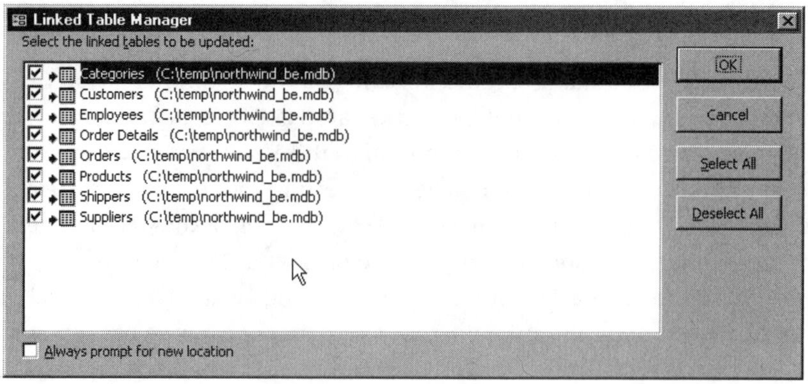

Figure 4-5. Update the links by clicking the Select All button.

6. Choose the location of the back-end database by using the Find File dialog box and click OK. This action refreshes the links to the tables in your back-end database.

7. Check that a couple of the tables are working correctly before releasing the database to your users.

NOTE If you rename or delete a table in the back-end database, you will need to delete the current linked table in the front-end database. If you rename a table, add a single link to the new table by right-clicking in Tables in the Database window and choosing Link Tables.

If you are still not sure about the benefits of linked tables, then why not ponder this little story from the days when Digital VMS and UNIX were a big part of my programming life.

User Story *My first Access problem was linking. I remember back in about 1994 when I was an Informix DBA and programmer. Our company purchased some data-mining software to monitor our production data. As part of this project, the software company had to produce an Access 2 database to manage the production data. The first version of the database came out, and our company tested it and made comments. The second version of the software was delivered, and we hired a data entry temp to punch thousands of lines of data into it. Naturally, the instant real data had to be added to*

the database and issues arose, so we contacted the developer. He came back with these comments: "You will have to stop the data entry, put the database on a floppy disk, send it to me by courier, and I will send it back when I've made the changes (in two days)." This process was not ideal from our company's point of view, so I started to read the help manual (yes, there was one in those days), and there on page 13 was a section that detailed the importance of splitting the database. We informed the developer (who, we found out, was new to Access), and he promptly split the database and our data entry temp got back to work. So too did the developer!

Your Very Own Link Manager

Sometimes the Tools menu is no longer visible because the Allow Full Menus startup option is cleared. Other times finding and using the Link Manager wizard can become a little too onerous for a busy client. If this is the case, you should consider installing a customized link manager of your own. To show you how to do this, I have included the following objects in the demonstration databases.

For Access 97 and Access 2000:

- frmRelinkDatabase. This form shows you how to call the link manager function.

- basGR8_RefreshTableLinks. This module refreshes the table links. If the back-end database does not refresh properly, the user can locate it with the Windows File dialog box.

- basGR8_Startup. This module has a number of shared routines.

For Access 2002 and Access 2003:

- frmRelinkDatabase. This form shows you how to call the Link Manager function and also how to use the FileDialog object in Office 2002.

- basGR10_Files. This module refreshes the table links. If the back-end database does not refresh properly, the user can locate it with the Office 2002 File dialog box.

Instructions for installing this link manager software onto the front end of your split database system follow:

1. Import the objects appropriate to your version of Access into your database.

2. Modify the VBA code under the relink button (button 1) in the frmRelinkDatabase form so that it refers to a table in your back-end database. Figure 4-6 shows the demonstration form in the Access 2002/2003 demonstration database.

3. Move the VBA code to a suitable utilities form in your database that is accessible only to the administrators.

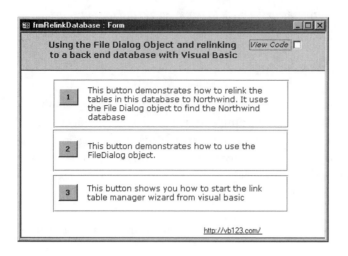

Figure 4-6 – The frmRelinkDatabase *demonstration form.*

The VBA code that initiates the relinking software is very easy, as follows (see the code under button 1 of the frmRelinkDatabase form):

```
If RelinkTables_FX("northwind.mdb", "orders", True, _
  "C:\", True) Then
  MsgBox "This database was relinked successfully."
Else
  MsgBox "Relinking was not successful."
End If
```

The code demonstrated for relinking had its origins in a database on the Access 97 CD-ROM called Solutions.mdb. The Access 2000 version of Solutions.mdb is available to download; see the Further Reading section at the end of this chapter for more information. I recommend this database as a useful resource. For the Access 2002/2003 database, I have rewritten the file selection code from the solutions database to use the FileDialog object that was bundled as a shared Office 2002 component.

Implementing the Relinking Software in Your Database

If you have cleared the Allow Full Menus check box in the startup options (as discussed in Chapter 2), the DBA won't have access to the conventional link manager to relink the tables. Therefore, you're going to have to start your own relinking software from your front-end database.

From my experience, I know that you will want to keep this relinking facility away from your users. The most common problem that I have experienced is when users try to relink from a drive mapped as F: when the linked path for the database was previously stored as the G: drive. In this instance, the links and the software the front end will stop functioning for all the users who have the G: drive mapping. For this reason, I add relinking software to the front-end databases in an Access form that is known only to the DBA. That way, this unwanted new link definition becomes much harder for the F: drive user to create.

Two other examples are on the frmRelinkDatabase form. Button 2 demonstrates how to use the FileDialog object to find a single database. Button 3 is a very simple demonstration on how to open the Link Manager wizard by using VBA code, as follows (only available in Access 2002–2003).

```
RunCommand acCmdLinkedTableManager
```

Now I will explain how you can avoid the incorrectly mapped drive issue by using the universal naming convention (UNC) for the network location of the back-end database.

Linking by Using UNCs Rather than Mapped Drives

Access 2002 help offers this advice: *"Important: If you link to a file on a local area network, make sure to use a universal naming convention (UNC) path, instead of relying on the drive letter of a mapped network drive in Microsoft Windows Explorer. A drive letter can vary on a computer or may not always be defined, whereas a UNC path is a reliable and consistent way for Microsoft Access to locate the data source that contains the linked table."*

An example of a UNC for a folder called "data" on a computer called "shared-Computer" is

```
\\sharedComputer\data
```

My experience with UNCs is that they are not very popular with people who are not network administrators. Therefore, it is difficult to get people at remote sites to use them. Most people just seem to get the G: drive (mapped letter) thing. In addition, I have found that if you are developing for a remote site, it is best not to use UNCs on your own network because it can take the Link Manager wizard a long time to resolve the links when the software is installed at that remote site. Users have reported that it can take up to 15 minutes to relink the databases that started with unknown UNCs, like our network paths. This amount of time, obviously, is not acceptable.

Databases that Should Not Be Split

Sometimes it's best *not* to split a database, such as when a database has a very small number of users and a simple user interface. In cases like this, it will almost invariably be possible to take the database out of production for a few hours while you make changes. Alternatively, if you keep track of which objects (forms, code, reports) that you change, you can import them into the live database. If you adopt this approach, do so because you understand the situation, not because it is too hard to split the database.

Another tricky situation is distributing your database and interface on CD-ROM. In this case, the database will be in read-only mode, so you may want to combine the data and the interface so that you do not need to relink. In this case, relinking is impossible because you cannot write the new linking information to the CD-ROM and, the way PCs are configured these days, the address of the CD drive will change from PC to PC.

Installing the Front-End Databases on the Client PC

One more touted benefit of splitting a database (in the Access manual and in a number of Access books that I have read) is that you can install the resultant front-end database on each user's PC to increase performance. Though this is true, this type of installation should only happen near the end of the development process, when you are happy that the front-end database is working well and that network traffic isn't an issue. In addition, if you are contemplating workgroup security or protection measures in the front-end database, test a shared network version of the database before installing that version on all the client PCs. Remember that the more versions you have out there in userland, the more databases you need to keep synchronized with the latest protection initiatives.

 CAUTION If you intend to use operating system security on your database, you should be careful installing the front ends on the client PCs because doing so allows the user to find the location of the back-end database. In fact, you really don't even want the user to copy the front-end database, if you can help it. Read Chapter 12 for more on this topic.

So now that you have learned why and how to split a database, let's move on and find out why the VBA code in the front-end database requires an error handler.

Error Handling Shields Your Code

VBA code, as the glue that binds your Access application together, must manage not only what the developer expects to happen but also the unexpected. When your code is set up properly, Access will trap errors when they happen and transfer them to a special section of code called an error handler. Error handling helps protect your database because it allows you to keep the logic of your application hidden from your less-technical users. It also is important to include error handling in all your code but especially for Access 2000 and later. If you don't include it and you have cleared the Allow Special Keys check box in the startup options, the following problems will occur:

- Your Access program will stop running where the error occurs.

- Your users will be oblivious to the nature of the error.

- Your users will be confused because they will not receive any response from the program.

Now that we have established that error handling is important, let's look at the standard error handling that is added to your VBA project by Access wizards that generate code.

Standard Error Handling Added by the Access Wizards

Whenever you run one of the Access code generation wizards, such as the Command Button wizard, the wizard adds a basic error handler section to the code it creates. For example, look at a sample procedure created by using the Command Button wizard. The code that this wizard creates opens a form in VBA code and comes complete with error handling code. All the code samples for error handling come from the demonstration form called frmErrorHandling (shown in Figure 4-7).

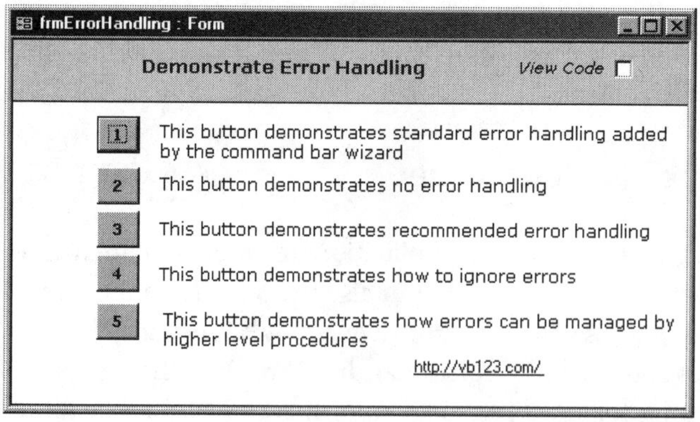

Figure 4-7. The frmErrorHandling *form demonstrates the error handling for VBA code.*

The first sample comes from the onClick event behind the cmdError1 button. This event intentionally tries to open a form that doesn't exist in the database.

```
Private Sub cmdError1_Click()
On Error GoTo Err_cmdError1_Click

    Dim stDocName As String
    Dim stLinkCriteria As String

    ' Try to open a form that doesn't exist.
    stDocName = "frmTasmanianTiger"
    DoCmd.OpenForm stDocName, , , stLinkCriteria

Exit_cmdError1_Click:
    Exit Sub

Err_cmdError1_Click:
    MsgBox Err.Description
    Resume Exit_cmdError1_Click

End Sub
```

This code has the following clearly identifiable sections:

- An onError statement is positioned at the top of the subroutine. When an error occurs, the code will be processed according to the onError statement's instructions. Generally, these instructions will involve jumping to the Error Handler section near the bottom of the procedure.

- The Main Body of the procedure is where all the working code is placed.

- The Exit section is where code requirements common to processing both the Main Body and the Error Handling section are tidied up, including closing open objects, variables, and files.

- The Error Handler section reports problems in processing to the users. This section is located at the bottom of the procedure. When this section is completed, the code generally jumps back to the Exit Section, and the procedure is closed.

So what happens when an error occurs in the code in the onClick event of button 1? On the line of code where the form is opened, an error occurs because the form does not exist in the database. The code then jumps to the Error Handler section at the bottom of the code, and a message box displays a descriptive error to the user (see Figure 4-8). The code then jumps back to the Exit Section and a graceful (if not successful) exit from the subroutine occurs. All unremarkable stuff for a seasoned developer but the important thing is that life carries on for the user and your code is safe from the prying eyes of casual users.

Figure 4-8. When an error occurs, the error handler displays a message box.

What Happens When You Do Not Have Error Handling

If you do not have error handling in your code and the user runs into a problem, you're going to expose your code to the user (illustrated in Figure 4-9). As you can see, the user can choose the a Debug or End button. If the user clicks the End button, your code is not exposed. If the user clicks the Debug button, however, the code is exposed on the line of VBA code that failed. Seeing the code will probably traumatize your beginner users and will tempt those users who like to explore.

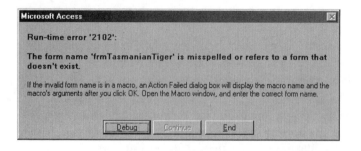

Figure 4-9. This message box is a result of no error handling.

NOTE   Not including error handling in the early stages of development and testing is acceptable because the debug option, as shown in Figure 4-9, allows you to see the problem code immediately. Forgetting to add your error checking when the system goes live is certainly not recommended if you are trying to protect your code.

To demonstrate what happens when there is no error checking, button 2 on the `frmErrorHandling` form shows what happens when you try to open a form that doesn't exist in the database (see Figure 4-9). In this code, the penultimate line is a `msgbox` statement that will never execute because the database will break on the problem line.

```
Private Sub cmdError2_Click()
' This button demonstrates what happens when you do not add error handling code.
' In particular, try this button with the Allow Special Keys option
' selected and then cleared in the Access startup properties.

' Open a form that does not exist to cause an error intentionally.
DoCmd.OpenForm "frmTasmanianTiger"

' The procedure should never get to the following line:
MsgBox "This demonstrates that the software has continued executing", vbInformation
End Sub
```

Clearly, we would like code to respond in a more consistent manner. If you can avoid these messy-looking debug prompts from appearing in your system, that would be a good outcome. So let's have a look at how you can ensure that the Debug button does not feature in your user interface.

Removing the Debug Button

In Access 97, you can stop the user from going into debug mode (also called break mode) by going to the Startup dialog and clearing the Allow Viewing Code After Error check box (shown in Figure 4-10). This action makes the Debug button unavailable.

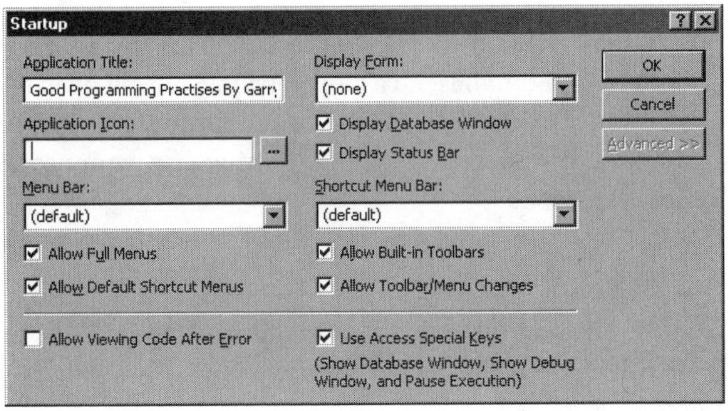

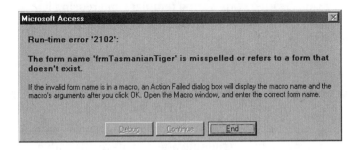

Figure 4-10. The Allow Viewing Code After Error check box in Access 97.

To try this procedure, change the startup options in the demonstration database, close the database, and open it again. Choose the frmErrorHandling form again and click button 2. Only the End button is available, as shown in Figure 4-11.

Figure 4-11. The disabled Debug button in Access 97.

Unfortunately, in Access 2000 or later, the Allow Viewing Code After Error check box is no longer included in the startup options. To stop the Debug button from appearing when errors occur, you must clear the Use Access Special Keys check box in the Startup dialog. This action leads to some unfortunate circumstances if you have not included an Error Handling section in your procedure.

To demonstrate these unfortunate circumstances, choose Tools ➤ Startup and clear the Allow Access Special Keys check box. Now restart the demonstration database, choose frmErrorHandling, and click button 2. The result: nothing happens. No prompt, no messages. Remarkably, Access doesn't display an error message and the code stops processing on the line that fails. The code under button 2 illustrates pause because a message box that should execute after the erroneous line never appears.

Therefore, the conclusion here is that if you have Access 2000 or later or are considering upgrading your Access 97 database to a later version, you will need to add error handling to all your applications, especially to any application for which you intend to remove the Allow Access Special Keys option. Otherwise, your users will be even more in the dark than usual!

NOTE   In Chapter 11, I discuss VBA project passwords and the MDE database format as good and great ways to hide your code.

Now that we have seen that error handling is pretty essential, what is the best way to organize your VBA code error handling? We'll address this next.

Writing Good Error Handling Code

Good error handling code results from having a good template and reusing it whenever you write a new procedure. Follow these basic principles:

- Always place an On Error GoTo statement before the first line of code.

- Place your error handling code at the bottom of the procedure.

- Test for and provide specific code for errors that you can easily anticipate or that occur frequently after you deploy the software. I manage this with a Case statement.

- Display all other errors with a generic error message by using the Err.Number and Err.Description methods. This way, users can report the error with both a number and a full description. You may even want to log this error in a table.

- Once you have completed the error messages, return the code to a common exit point so that the code can close all instantiated objects.

If you are like me, an example of code is always the best way to understand a software topic. To demonstrate the basic principles, look at the code for button 3's onClick event on the frmErrorHandling form that follows. As you can see, a GoTo statement is placed at the top of the procedure to ensure that all errors are trapped. At the bottom of the procedure, I have set up a Case statement to handle specific errors first. In this example, the divide-by-zero error number is 11. I like to define any specific error numbers by using a constant declared at the top of the procedure, which makes the code easier to read. The Case Else statement covers all other errors by displaying a message box that combines the number and its description. On completing the Error Handling section of the procedure, the code returns to the Exit section of the procedure.

```
Private Sub cmdError3_Click()

' This subroutine demonstrates error handling.
' The first error is opening a form that doesn't exist
' and the second is a number divided by zero.

Dim MyTotal As Double
Const DIVIDEBYZERO = 11

On Error GoTo err_cmdError3

MyTotal = 10
MyTotal = 5 * 10
MyTotal = 10 / 0                    ' This line will cause an error.
MyTotal = 10 / 5

MsgBox "MyTotal = " & MyTotal, vbInformation, "Mathematics Complete"

exit_cmdError3:

   Exit Sub
```

```
err_cmdError3:
  Select Case Err.Number
    Case DIVIDEBYZERO
      MsgBox "Problems with divide by zero  -> " & Err.Description, vbInformation
    Case vbObjectError + 1
      ' To see a line immediately after the error line, press CTRL+BREAK,
      ' then drag yellow arrow to Resume Next (below), then press F8.
      Resume Next
    Case Else
      MsgBox "Error No. " & Err.Number & " -> " & Err.Description, vbCritical
  End Select
  Resume exit_cmdError3
End Sub
```

That is the basic layout for handling errors in your software. You will have noticed that this layout differed from the error handler code generated by the Access code generation wizards that I explained earlier. If you are writing code for an unimportant part of your database, either layout will suffice. What is important is that you have some error handling in all your VBA code so that Access traps the errors.

Returning Your Code to the Location of the Error

One of the biggest problems with the error handler approach is that it forces the focus of the errors in the debugger to the bottom of the procedure. Then, you generally have to guess where in your code the error occurred. To compensate for this problem, I use a special technique. When the error message appears, I press CTRL+BREAK, which makes the code appear in break mode, as shown in Figure 4-12. In Access 2000 or later, you will need to click the Debug button that appears in a dialog box before you can see the code in debug mode. You will need to have selected the Allow Special Keys startup option for this trick to work.

In debug mode, you will see a yellow arrow on the left side of the code window. This arrow highlights the line of code that is about to be processed. You can click and drag the yellow arrow to the line of code that says Resume Next (as illustrated in Figure 4-12). Now press the Step Through Code key (F8), and the program will return to the line of code directly below the line where the error occurred. Now you can debug the error or allow the code to continue processing by using the debug hot keys.

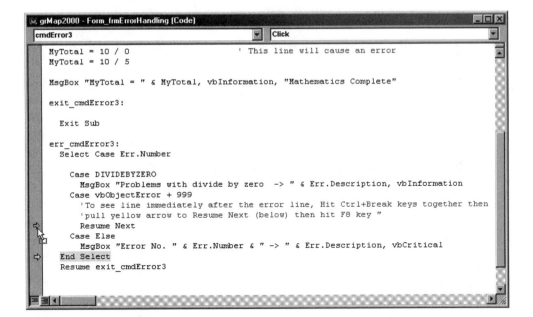

```
grMap2000 - Form_frmErrorHandling (Code)                         _ □ ×

cmdError3                        ▼   Click                          ▼

    MyTotal = 10 / 0                    ' This line will cause an error
    MyTotal = 10 / 5

    MsgBox "MyTotal = " & MyTotal, vbInformation, "Mathematics Complete"

    exit_cmdError3:

      Exit Sub

    err_cmdError3:
      Select Case Err.Number

        Case DIVIDEBYZERO
          MsgBox "Problems with divide by zero  -> " & Err.Description, vbInformation
        Case vbObjectError + 999
          'To see line immediately after the error line, Hit Ctrl+Break keys together then
          'pull yellow arrow to Resume Next (below) then hit F8 key "
          Resume Next
        Case Else
          MsgBox "Error No. " & Err.Number & " -> " & Err.Description, vbCritical
      End Select
      Resume exit_cmdError3
```

Figure 4-12. Viewing the code in break mode.

This discussion on error handling and debugging is a big topic, but it is one you don't need to learn all at once. I generally wait until I feel that something is getting repetitive before I look for the next little shortcut or technique. If you use the templates that I have provided and adopt the little debug trick to help you to locate your errors quickly, however, you will be well on the way to writing proficient error handling. The frmErrorHandling form has some other useful error-handling techniques: button 4 shows how to ignore errors in your code by using the Resume Next statement and button 5 demonstrates how a higher-level procedure can trap errors in lower-level subroutines and functions that have no Error Handler section.

That completes the discussion on good programming practices. To facilitate further research on these topics, I encourage you to follow up some of the Internet and Access help topics discussed in the next section.

Further Reading

As you can expect, there is never enough information when it comes to powerful products like Access. To assist you with further investigations, I have put together a Web page with links to Microsoft's and other Web sites plus key words to use when searching Access help on the issues relating to material in this chapter, including the following:

- Conditionally running the AutoExec macro when using automation.

- Hiding the Database window by modifying the AutoExec macro.

- Key words to use in the Access help guides to find out about linking tables. For example, Access 2002 help has a lot of material on linked tables, as shown in Figure 4-13.

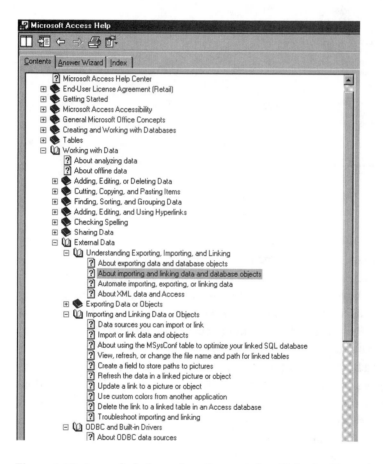

Figure 4-13. Access help has a lot of material on linked tables.

- An article I wrote on the FileDialog object for Smart Access.

- The File dialog and the FileSearch objects in Access 2002.

- Where to download the Access 2000 solutions database. This database includes source code for relinking tables and many other useful coding samples.

- Error handling in VBA, errors with DAO, ADO, DLL, and in class modules.

- How to turn off the Break on All Errors option in code.

You can find the further reading Web page for this chapter in the Downloads section of the Apress Web site (http://www.apress.com) or at this address: http://www.vb123.com/map/goo.htm.

Reflecting on This Chapter

In this chapter, you learned that AutoExec macros and database splitting are two fundamental parts of the Access application that you are building. You saw how the Database Splitter wizard divides your database into data and objects. Once this fundamental step is complete, you can proceed to improving your software without interfering with your users. There are many other reasons for splitting a database, but when you're concerned with protecting your database investment, separating software and data makes it easier to conceptualize the tasks of protecting your database. And developers will now be aware that it's better to use error handling in the recent version of Access so that users will receive an error message when a problem occurs in your code.

What's Next?

In the next chapter, we will be taking a good look at some different ways that you can back up the different objects in your database. Included in the next chapter are samples that will show you how to check if anyone is using the database, how to back up your database properly by compacting it, and how to convert all tables and objects to text. More importantly, the next chapter shows you how to recover the database if something goes wrong. The next chapter is important because it will help you protect the investment that you've already made in your database before one of life's little catastrophes heads your way.

Backing Up and Recovering Your Databases

IF YOU ARE INVOLVED with a multi-user Access database, you *must* learn how to back up the database properly. This chapter shows you how to check whether everyone has logged off, how to log off all users, how to back up a database properly, how to back up information while people are using the database, and then, when that fateful day comes, how to recover your information. As you progress through these topics, you will learn a good use for XML and even find out which objects in your database take up the most space.

The download material for this chapter includes forms and Visual Basic for Application (VBA) examples, as follows:

- Functions to find out whether anyone is using the database.

- A form to shut down the database at a set time.

- A form that will safely back up a database by using the compact process.

- A form that makes it easy for your users to compact their databases.

- A form to unload all tables to comma-delimited format.

- Two different ways to unload all tables to XML.

- A form to back up all objects to text.

- Special VBA recovery files that the text export procedures write automatically so that you can easily recover tables and objects.

NOTE To find the demonstration material, open the download database for your version of Access—for example, grMAP2002.mdb—and select Chapter 5. Before running any samples that involve data, you may need to relink the tables to the Northwind database on your computer.

What You Must Know About Database Backups and Recoveries

Once again, I will provide two overviews about the important issues covered in this chapter. The first provides an overview that's applicable to all IT professionals, because everyone should be concerned with backups. The second summary covers extra topics that are relevant to the developer.

Overview for the DBA, IT Manager, and the Developer

Backing up and recovering an Access database would be easy if you could instantly get everyone to log off the database just before the system backup was due to commence. This process used to be called tape backup, but these days, databases can be backed up to all sorts of media, such as portable hard drives and DVD burners. If people are using the database when your system backup runs, you risk copying a database that is in an unstable state, which could cause you problems when you need to recover the database. This chapter provides solutions to that issue by showing you how to:

- Make sure that your database is ready for a system backup.

- Show you how to back up your database to another location, including the new Access 2003 backup menu command.

- Provide insight into good backup procedures.

- Back up and recover individual tables while the database is in use by using both text and XML formats and objects that use the text format.

- Recover relationships, menus, and import/export specifications.

Of course, there are other reasons why you need to back up your databases, from computer equipment theft to the proverbial bus running over the laptop.

One extremely good reason to use some of the object- and table-exporting software is that someone may unknowingly delete something or lock something while implementing database protection. Because problems like these always lurk around the corner, the more alternatives that you have, the more chances that you have to save lost information.

 CAUTION   All the backup techniques described in this chapter can leave your security open to exploitation because you are creating yet more copies of the database and its objects for people to view. If you are serious about protecting and securing your backups, read Chapter 12 to find out how the operating system can protect the backup files. As part of this protection, you need to make sure that the Windows account that does the backups has write permissions for the backup directory.

Overview for the Developer

The gist of this chapter is to make it easy for you to incorporate backup routines into your own applications, and most of the material covered in this chapter will require that you integrate the demonstration material into a database. Apart from the benefits of the different backup processes discussed, you'll learn other important things:

- Different ways to identify all the tables and objects in your database.

- Another good use for XML.

- The undocumented and powerful `SaveAsText` and `LoadFromText` methods.

- Find out the very elusive facts about which are the biggest objects in your database, which is a very useful by-product of the object backup software in this chapter.

If that sounds like a lot of work, rest assured that most of the forms and functions from the demonstration database should not require too much customization when you add them to your database.

Now we will have a look in more detail about what you need to do to back up a database that has multiple users.

Backing Up Multi-User Databases

To back up an Access database correctly, every user must log off the database. If you back up a database when someone is using it, you risk saving the database in an unstable state. A user may have made changes to data and objects and not saved them, so that when you open the archived database, you may receive a message that states that the database is corrupt. You then will need to use the repair utility and, at best, only a small amount of information will be lost. Unfortunately, you will never be able to determine exactly what that was as any corrupted data is usually unrecoverable.

TIP   See the "Further Reading" section at the end of this chapter for a Web reference on database corruption.

To ensure that the database is ready to be backed up, you must have exclusive access to the database. This condition does not apply to some of the exporting backup options discussed in this chapter, but it is a good idea nonetheless. One way to tell whether someone else is in the database is to check for the existence of a file with the same name as the database and an .LDB extension, which indicates an Access locking file. As long as you don't see this file, you should be able to open the database in exclusive mode. There are exceptions, however, which I will explain.

NOTE   Chapter 6 discusses, at great length, different ways to find a list of users who are logged onto the database and even how to stop them from logging on to the database. Understanding these processes is important if you want to be the only person to have access to a database at a particular time. The .LDB locking file is discussed further in that chapter.

After you have exclusive access to the database, you can copy the file or export the information from the database. Before I describe some different ways to back up your database and data, I will show you how you can find out whether your database is being used.

Checking Whether Anyone Has the Database Open

The first and simplest way to determine whether someone's in the database is to check for an .LDB file with the same name as the database that you are using. You can check in Windows Explorer as follows:

1. Open Windows Explorer and navigate to the folder that your database is in.

2. Make sure that the display format of the folder is View Details or View List.

3. Sort the files in the display by file name.

4. Find the database and look for a file with the same name and the .LDB file extension.

The .LDB file is a good indicator of other people using the database, but sometimes a user turns off a computer or Windows crashes, and the .LDB file remains open. To cover for these contingencies, you can manually check whether you have exclusive access to a database by doing the following:

1. Open Access.

2. Choose File ➤ Open and navigate to the folder where your database is.

3. Select the file, click the Open button's drop-down arrow, and choose Open Exclusive (shown in Figure 5-1).

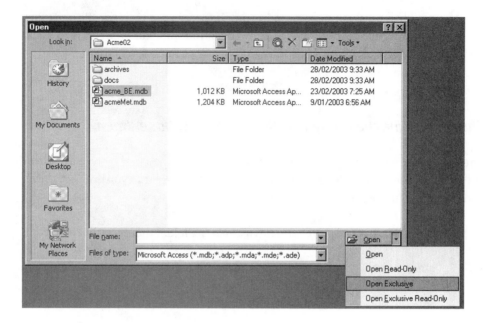

Figure 5-1. Testing whether you have exclusive access to a database.

If your database opens without any problem, then you can copy it to your backup media or compact it. If you are copying the file, you will need to close Access before doing the backup.

Unfortunately, these manual processes are a little tedious, and you may want to automate the process a bit more. To help with that, I have developed two equivalent functions that will tell you whether a database is being used.

Using VBA to Check Whether Anyone Is Using the Database

To find out whether someone is using a database, you will need to test whether you can open that database in exclusive mode. To try the demonstration form, open the sample database for the version of Access that you are interested in and choose Chapter 5 in the Demonstration Database Interface form. The first sample that I want to demonstrate is a form called frmIsDBopenDAO. Open this form in design mode because you may need to change the location of the Northwind database. The following code snippet demonstrates how you might use the IsDatabaseOpen function. If the (Northwind) database opens in exclusive mode, the function will return a True result.

```
' This form will test if it's possible to open a database exclusively.
Const MYDBPATH = "C:\Program Files\Microsoft Office\Office\Samples\northwind.mdb"
Dim myDbIsOpen As Boolean

myDbIsOpen = IsDatabaseOpen(MYDBPATH)
If myDbIsOpen Then
  MsgBox "Database is already open or an error occurred."
Else
  MsgBox "Database is not being used by anyone."
End If
```

The logic used in the IsDatabaseOpen function commences by opening a DAO workspace object. By using that workspace object, we then attempt to open a database reference in exclusive mode. If the exclusive reference fails, it returns an error. We can then check the error number to see why we couldn't open the database exclusively.

```
Function IsDatabaseOpen(strDbPath As String) As Boolean
' This function tests whether a database is open.

Const FILENOTFOUND = 3024
Const ALREADYOPEN = 3356
Const ALREADYOPENEXCL = 3045
Const DISKDOESNOTEXIST = 3043

Dim wsp As DAO.Workspace
Dim myDbs As DAO.Database

On Error GoTo IsDatabaseOpen_error
    ' Returns reference to default workspace.
    Set wsp = DBEngine.Workspaces(0)
    ' Attempts to open an exclusive reference to another database.
    Set myDbs = wsp.OpenDatabase(strDbPath, True)
    ' No one is using the database.
    IsDatabaseOpen = False
    Set myDbs = Nothing
    Set wsp = Nothing

IsDatabaseOpen_Exit:

  Exit Function

IsDatabaseOpen_error:
```

```
' Test for errors, which are probably caused by trying to open the
' database in exclusive mode.
IsDatabaseOpen = True
Select Case Err.Number

  Case FILENOTFOUND
    MsgBox Err.Description, vbInformation, "File Not Found"
  Case DISKDOESNOTEXIST
    MsgBox Err.Description & vbCrLf & vbCrLf & strDbPath, _
      vbInformation, "Disk does not exist"
  Case ALREADYOPEN
    ' Opened by one or more people. One name appears in message.
    MsgBox Err.Description, vbInformation, "File Already Open"
  Case ALREADYOPENEXCL  ' Already opened exclusively by someone.
    MsgBox Err.Description, vbInformation, "File Already Opened Exclusively"
  Case Else
    MsgBox "Error number " & Err.Number & " -> " & Err.Description
End Select
GoTo IsDatabaseOpen_Exit


End Function
```

When you try to use the IsDatabaseOpen function to open a database that someone is already using in shared mode, error number 3356 (signified by the constant ALREADYOPEN) returns an interesting error description. Unfortunately, because someone is using the database in shared mode, this description incorrectly says, "You attempted to open a database that is already opened exclusively by user 'Admin' on machine 'MY COMPUTER.' Try again when the database is available." Alternatively, if you have opened the database in exclusive mode and then use the IsDatabaseOpen function, it will return a message that says, "The file is already in use" (and doesn't mention it being exclusive at all).

I find this interesting because if you use the IsDatabaseOpenADO function, you will find in the frmIsDBopenDAO demonstration form that the equivalent code to check for exclusive access using the ActiveX Data Objects (ADO) library, the error descriptions returned are the same. Remember before running the code in the form that you will need to open this form in design mode because you may need to change the location of the Northwind database. That means that ADO is using exactly the same DAO calls to open the database. In addition, you can see that ADO returns only one error number for all the three errors provided in the DAO example. You then have to parse the error descriptions that accompany the numbers to establish what has gone wrong with the ADO exclusive open.

```
Function IsDBaseOpenADO(MyDBpath As String)
' This function tests whether a database is open
' by using the ADO Library.

Const ALREADYOPEN = -2147467259
Dim cnnDB As ADODB.Connection

On Error GoTo IsDBaseOpenADO_error

   Set cnnDB = New ADODB.Connection

   ' Open database for shared (by default), read/write access, and
   ' specify database password.
   With cnnDB
     .Provider = "Microsoft.Jet.OLEDB.4.0"
     .Mode = adModeShareExclusive
     .Open MyDBpath
   End With

   IsDBaseOpenADO = False
   cnnDB.Close
   Set cnnDB = Nothing

IsDBaseOpenADO_Exit:

   Exit Function

IsDBaseOpenADO_error:
   IsDBaseOpenADO = True
   Select Case Err.Number
     Case ALREADYOPEN
       ' Opened by one or more people. One name appears in message.
       If InStr(Err.Description, "not a valid path") Then
         MsgBox Err.Description, vbInformation, "File Not Found"
       ElseIf InStr(Err.Description, "file already in use") Then
         ' This database is opened exclusively.
         MsgBox Err.Description, vbInformation, "File Open Exclusively"
       Else
         ' This database is opened by other users.
         MsgBox Err.Description, vbInformation, "File Already Open"
       End If
```

```
      Case Else
        MsgBox "Error number " & Err.Number & " -> " & Err.Description
    End Select
    GoTo IsDBaseOpenADO_Exit
End Function
```

After working through both of these samples in detail, I prefer the DAO function to the ADO function because the DAO function returns better error numbers.

So now that we have examined how to find the "in-use" status of a database, let's see how to ensure that everyone logs off the database in time for the backup.

Setting Automatic Shutdowns Before Scheduled Backups

Unless you run a business that uses an Access database around the clock, there comes a time in the day when it should be safe to close the database. To make this easy, I have created a form called frmAutoShutdown that will shut down your Access database at a set time. To add this form to your database, import it and add a line to your AutoExec macro to open the form in hidden mode. From then on, the form will sit quietly in the background and check every few minutes to see if it is time to shut down the database. Just prior to the shutdown time, the form will issue a warning message to users. When the shutdown time arrives, the form will save any open objects or forms and then close the database. Because this process logs everyone off during the night, it is very useful for administering the database in the early morning.

To understand how the frmAutoShutdown form works—and possibly to change the setup—let's review the full form module that follows. The most important thing to be concerned with is the values of the module constants. Generally, you will be setting the SHUTDOWNHOUR constant to a time when everyone is tucked into bed and just before you run your scheduled backups. You will need to remember to modify that constant to an appropriate time when you are experimenting with the form. After that, you will see the warning messages and the actual shutdown constants. If you look at the form timer event, you will find that the MSGMINS constant decides the interval between triggers. When the shutdown hour arrives, the Quit method will shut down the database.

```
Option Explicit

' User administration constants
' Purpose: Shut down and user messages.
Const MSGMINS = 3               ' Minutes between checking for system shutdowns.
Const SHUTDOWNFLAG = True       ' If True, then the system shuts down once a day.
Const SHUTDOWNHOUR = 0          ' Automatic shutdown hour (24-hour time).
```

```
Const WARNSTARTMINS = O         ' Time in minutes that warnings start being issued.
Const WARNENDMINS = 10          ' Time in minutes that warnings stop being issued.
Const SHUTDOWNSTARTMINS = 10    ' Starting time in minutes for the shutdown.
Const SHUTDOWNENDMINS = 20      ' Final time in minutes for the shutdown.


Private Sub cmdOk_Click()
  Me.visible = False
End Sub


Private Sub Form_Load()


' Always hide this form; the user shouldn't know that it is there.
Me.visible = False
Me.TimerInterval = MSGMINS * 1000 * 60#


End Sub


Private Sub Form_Timer()


' Shuts down the database (in case anyone has left the database open).
Dim myDate, myDownTime, myUpTime, myMessage, minsDiff As Integer


On Error GoTo Quick_Exit


If SHUTDOWNFLAG Then
  If Hour(Time()) = SHUTDOWNHOUR Then
' The time to shut down is nigh.
    If Minute(Time()) > SHUTDOWNSTARTMINS And Minute(Time()) < SHUTDOWNENDMINS Then


' Safely huts down the database , saving all open objects.
      Application.Quit acQuitSaveAll


    ElseIf Minute(Time()) > WARNSTARTMINS And Minute(Time()) < WARNENDMINS Then
      Me.visible = True
      lblMessage.Caption = "This database will close soon for administration."
      Me.Caption = "Please Stop What You Are Doing."
    End If
  End If
End If


Quick_Exit:


End Sub
```

Now, if you use this form or something similar to shut down the open databases, you will be sure to produce a cleaner backup. Next, let me put my own ideas about conventional backups into the melting pot.

Normal Backups

Access 97 or later

Any database that you are involved with should be backed up to an alternative storage system such as a tape drive or CD-ROM. This backup should be *systematic* (routine—not something you only think about when a crisis strikes—and, ideally, scheduled) and have the following characteristics:

- Performed on a regular basis.

- Kept off-site.

- Stored on a good-quality storage medium, such as a backup tape, memory card, CD, DVD, or portable hard drive.

- Kept in a secure and fireproof location.

- Multiple copies on multiple mediums.

Naturally, your databases need not be the only files kept as part of the backup system. Under no circumstances should the backup be kept only on-site on a substandard medium like a floppy disk or saved by using backup system software and hardware that your supplier no longer supports.

Recovering the Backups

More important than the backup itself is regularly testing the recovery process. Make a note in your diary to test recovering your database at least once a month if personnel, software, or hardware changes and once a quarter when the process is stable. If a database becomes corrupt early in the working day, don't try to repair the database. Instead, move that corrupted database to a safe area and restore the backup version from the night before. That way, you are really testing your backup processes.

TIP When it comes to testing backups, it's useful to remember the Boy Scout motto: Be prepared. I also recommend that you plan quarterly "fire drills," where you try to restore your latest backup.

Boutique Hardware Issues

When you set up your backup hardware, you need to be aware of the long-term support for your hardware device in these days when backup mediums come in many configurations. One good example of the sort of backup issue that can arise is the use of these new portable and large hard drives. If you were to keep the hard drive off-site and the power unit on-site, a fire on-site could cause you to lose both your computer and the power for the backup. You would then be forced to purchase an additional power unit from your original supplier. Having tried to do that on a one-year-old model last year, I can tell you that there is no guarantee that they will be in stock.

On-Site Backups

It is a good idea to produce a backup at least once a day of any database that you are working on or using. An Access database can become corrupt occasionally, especially if a large number of users are on it. In this case, a backup from computer hard drive to computer hard drive will suffice. The farther these computers are apart, the better. For both off-site and on-site backups, I use a product called Second Copy (see Figure 5-2), but many backup software packages around will work. I personally prefer to use a backup system that stores data in either its original file formats or in a popular compressed format, such as .ZIP.

Another additional safeguard that developers can use is sending a copy of the development work to your client on a regular basis. This way, your client gets to see your work, and it may cover you if your office or computer sufferers a catastrophic event.

Now I will explain why compressed files and file versions are an important part of the developer's backup strategy.

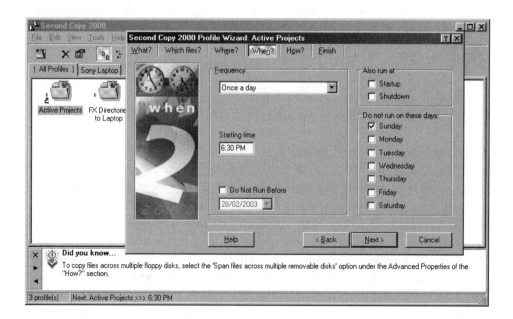

Figure 5-2. Backing up files on a regular basis is essential.

Creating Compressed (.ZIP) Archives

Probably the most vulnerable part of developing Access solutions is the developer. I personally am a little obsessed with cleaning up those objects in my database that just didn't work out. This routine occasionally leads to yours truly deleting the wrong object. Also, sometimes I will misunderstand a client's suggestions and make irretrievable alterations to a form or a module. So how do I get back to a previous point in the development cycle?

The answer is easy, and developers have used it since the beginning of computer time. It's called versions, and it's very simple to do. After you've made a number of alterations and you're happy with those changes, you give the database a version number. This number generally will be sequential and may involve major and minor version numbers or letters. For our business, we use the following procedure for front-end databases:

1. Update the version number on the startup form.

2. Save the database to a .ZIP or other type of compressed file with the same name as the database and a .ZIP file extension.

3. Rename the .ZIP file to include the version number.

TIP Always remember to make a brand new .ZIP file and then rename it. This action will ensure that you won't send the wrong version to a client. I once made the mistake of meaning to add a database to an existing .ZIP file but goofed up. The previous version of a database then went to the client for them to add data. When it came back, I replaced the development version with the client's older version.

To make a version archive, first make a new .ZIP file of your database, then rename the file to the version number shown by the files already in the folder (see Figure 5-3).

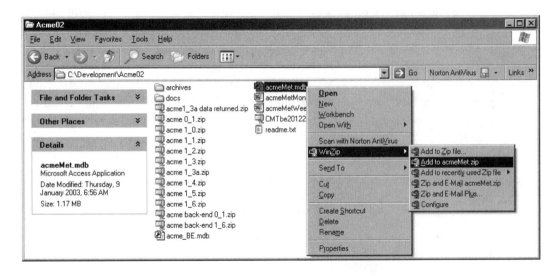

Figure 5-3. Adding the database to a .ZIP file.

With back-end databases, you have to be a lot more careful with managing both the changes and the archives because the client will have the latest data. What you really want to avoid is sending a copy of the back-end database back to the client and inadvertently having that file overwrite the live database. Always keep a copy of back-end databases that the client sends to you because the client could also have problems and might require a backup. Keeping multiple compressed versions of back-end databases whenever you change the data structure is a good idea. One exception to this rule is confidential information. You need to make sure that back-end databases that hold confidential information, such as credit card details, are not being stored on any computer other than those specially configured to protect that information.

TIP   Compression systems generally will have the option of a password. You may want to use a password when transferring files by email or when saving confidential or important databases in an archive.

Now I will review how you can use database compacting to back up your databases.

Compacting Databases

Compacting is good to use as a backup mechanism because it ensures that you have full ownership of the file when you do the transfer. Before I explain this backup technique, I will first describe how to compact a database, as using the compact option regularly on your Access database is an important administrative task. To compact a database, first open the database that you want to use and then choose Tools ➤ Database Utilities ➤ Compact and Repair. For Access 97, where the compact and repair functions are separated, you should regularly run the Repair option as well because doing so may resolve an as-yet unreported problem in the database.

NOTE   If you delete or modify tables or objects, your database will fragment. Fragmenting leads to a drop in performance and can be associated with database issues. Compacting from within a database makes a copy of the database, rearranging how the database file is stored on disk. Once that file is compacted, the new file replaces the existing database.

In installations where the DBA is actually an end user, I find that no matter how many times I ask the reluctant DBA, he or she forgets about the compacting option. To help resolve this issue, I will usually add a form to the database that will make compacting easier. I have called this form frmCompactEasy in the demonstration databases. It works by using the SendKeys method to send the keystrokes that drive the Compact Database menu option.

```
' Use the SendKeys command to compact the database safely.
  SendKeys "%TDC"
```

Compacting makes your database faster and more stable, and the following section explains how to use compacting to back up your database.

Using Compacting to Back Up Your Database

If you have used Access 2 or Access 95, you will remember that compacting databases was actually a three-step process. First, you had to use the compact option to make a new compacted database. Then you had to move the existing file to another folder, and finally you had to rename the compacted database back to the same name as the existing database. Naturally, compacting was not so popular in those days.

Even though the old method isn't used for compacting much these days, it can come in handy for doing backups. To use it, we will back up the database by compacting from the current database to a new one in a different location. To find this option, you will need to start Access without selecting any database and then choosing Tools ➤ Database Utilities ➤ Compact and Repair Database, as shown in Figure 5-4.

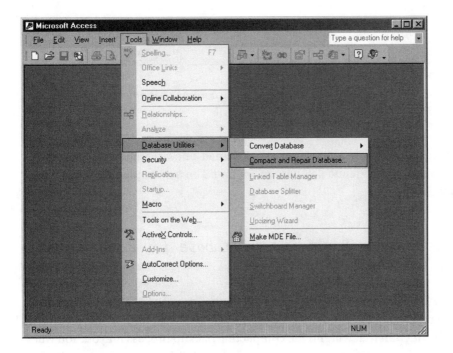

Figure 5-4. Choosing to compact a database for backup purposes.

You will then need to select the database (by using the File dialog) that you want to compact. After that, enter the name and location of the database that you want to backup and compact into (as shown in Figure 5-5). I suggest that you always give your backups a name that denotes it as a backup, and you should store it in a different folder so that the databases are not mixed up. I also advise that you save your backups in a folder that is difficult to find or protected from users by operating system permissions.

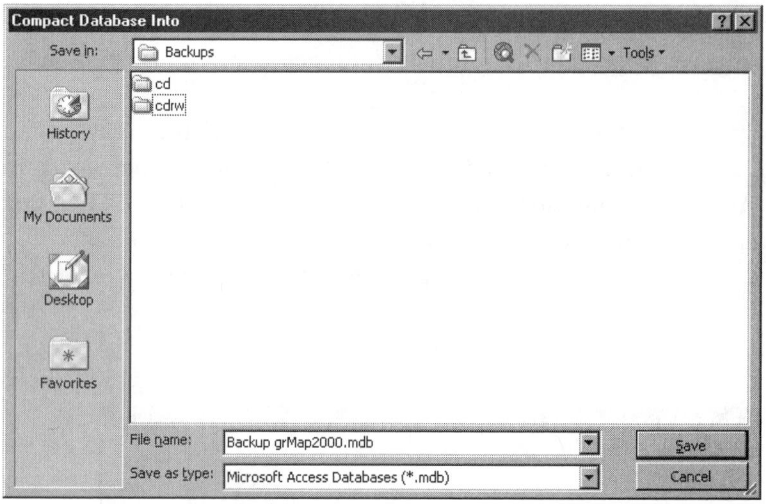

Figure 5-5. Selecting a new folder and entering a name that reflects that the database is a backup.

In Access 2002, the Application object gained a new method that made it easier to back up from one database to another. The next section demonstrates this method.

Compacting and Repairing a Database for Backups by Using VBA Code

Access 2002 or later

Access 2002 introduced a new VBA method—the CompactRepair method—that allows you to compact from one database to another. I've adopted this method as part of a function that will run the compacting backup process for you. You will find this code in the sample database in a form called frmCompactDatabase. When using this code, you will need to change the values of the constants to suit your own database and backup naming preferences.

```
Private Sub cmdCompactAnother_Click()
Dim compactOK As Boolean, backupName As String
Const COMPACTFROM = _
 "C:\program files\Microsoft Office\Office 10\Samples\northwind.mdb"
Const COMPACTTO = "C:\temp\northwind.mdb"

compactOK = CompactToNewMDB(COMPACTFROM, COMPACTTO, True)
If compactOK Then
  MsgBox "A newly compacted database called " & COMPACTTO & " has been created."
Else
  MsgBox "Compact was unsuccessful."
End If

End Sub
```

CAUTION The CompactToNewMDB function, described following, deletes an existing file if you set the deleteMdbToFirst argument to True. You should experiment with this function on an unimportant database before implementing it for your backup procedures.

The CompactToNewMDB function deletes the database before compacting is undertaken. If the database already exists in the location to which you want to compact, the Access CompaqRepair method will fail. For this reason, I have incorporated an optional deleteMdbToFirst argument to allow you to delete the destination database first. To run this process to generate multiple backups of your database, I suggest that you incorporate the date and time into the new database file name to make it unique.

```
Function CompactToNewMDB(mdbFrom As String, mdbTo As String, _
 Optional deleteMdbToFirst As Boolean) As Boolean
 ' Input values: the paths and file names of the source and destination files
 ' plus a Boolean flag that will delete your database if set to True.

On Error GoTo CompactToNewMDB_Error

  If IsMissing(deleteMdbToFirst) Then
    deleteMdbToFirst = False
  End If
```

```
    If deleteMdbToFirst Then

      If Len(Dir(mdbTo)) > 0 Then

        ' Delete the database that you are compacting to.
        Kill mdbTo
      End If
    End If

      ' Compact and repair the database. Use the return value of
      ' the CompactRepair method to determine if the file was
      ' successfully compacted.
    CompactToNewMDB = Application.CompactRepair(mdbFrom, mdbTo)

CompactToNewMDB_Exit:
  Exit Function

CompactToNewMDB_Error:
  ' You can add your own error handling code here.
  Select Case Err.Number
  Case Else
    MsgBox "Error number " & Err.Number & " -> " & Err.Description
  End Select

  Resume CompactToNewMDB_Exit

End Function
```

If you are using Access 97 or 2000, you will find examples of how to compact from one database to another in the VBA help. Search for the term "CompactDatabase" in the Visual Basic Editor.

In the remainder of the chapter, we will concern ourselves with backing up tables and objects from the database into text format.

Saving Tables to Text Files

This section explains the benefits of exporting data into text files and the methods of recovering that data into a (new) database. At anytime of the day, you can perform "live" extracts of all the information from a table to a text file. Exporting to text files is a good idea for the following reasons:

- You can generally do it at any time of the day, whether or not users are in the database. Only the currently saved records will be transferred. Keep in mind, though, that it would be better to rely on information that this software extracts when everyone has logged off, because getting information only from saved records may cause concurrency and contention issues.

- Long-term storage of data in text files will allow a DBA to read the information into multiple products. These text files probably will require accompanying documentation in a simple format so that the person who recovers the data does not have to guess the design of the tables that have been exported.

- Data exports are also a good idea to do prior to adding protection, such as passwords, to your databases.

Right from my early days as an Informix DBA, I learned that it was a good idea to export the tables in databases to text files. I like to do this so that I always know that a DBA looking at the text backups sometime in the future will be able to read the text files by using a text editor and import them into another system. What is more problematic is that you may not have a program that can read the database. As an example, contemplate how you would read information from an Access 97 database that you stopped using in 2002. When you pull the database from the archives and try to open it in 2008 by using the latest version of Access, you may unfortunately find that it doesn't support the Access 97 format. If you think that is unlikely, Microsoft has scheduled to remove Access 97 from its Web site sometime after the start of 2005. Though I don't imagine that Microsoft will drop support for Access 97 files for a long time, you never know. For more details on the support timetable for Microsoft products, see the links in the "Further Reading" section at the end of this chapter.

Saving Tables as Comma-Delimited Text Files

Access 97 or later

To demonstrate how you can export tables to text, use the following example to export all the tables in a database to a comma-delimited text format like that shown in Figure 5-6. You will find this sample under the only button in the details section of the download form called frmGR8_unloadAll. The sample works by first establishing the export folder. In this case, it will create a subfolder called Unload directly under the folder where the database is located. Then a DAO `TableDef` collection is established, and a loop is used to cycle through all the data tables in the collection. The `TransferToText` method then exports the table to comma-delimited format.

If you open one of the comma-delimited files, it may display in either a text editor or Excel, depending on your file type associations in Windows Explorer.

```
C:\Gr-FX\Aprs01\unload\Categories.csv                                    _ □ ×
"CategoryID","CategoryName","Description","Picture"
1,"Beverages","Soft drinks, coffees, teas, beers, and ales",
2,"Condiments","Sweet and savory sauces, relishes, spreads, and seasonings",
3,"Confections","Desserts, candies, and sweet breads",
4,"Dairy Products","Cheeses",
5,"Grains/Cereals","Breads, crackers, pasta, and cereal",
6,"Meat/Poultry","Prepared meats",
7,"Produce","Dried fruit and bean curd",
8,"Seafood","Seaweed and fish",
```

Figure 5-6. The exported comma-delimited file viewed in a text editor.

User Story *Exporting to text files means that, in all likelihood, you still will be able to read the files in 20 years—that's as long as CD-ROMs, tapes, or other such media will still be readable. Moreover, if you think that long-term recovery is unlikely, listen to this story. One project that I was involved with had a database of geological data that cost $50 million to put together. Another company bought the project, did nothing with the data for five years, and in the end couldn't read the backup tapes. When we were asked to help, we managed to recover the text data backups from our tapes, and these were used to build a reasonable copy of the database. We also recovered the database from tapes, but the format was proprietary, and the software that could read the proprietary format was long gone.*

The following example exports all the tables in a database to a comma-delimited text format.

```
Private Sub unload_all_Click()

' This form requires a reference to
' Microsoft DAO 3.6 or 3.51 library.

Dim i As Integer, unloadOK As Integer
Dim MyTable As DAO.TableDef
Dim MyDB As DAO.Database, MyRecords As DAO.RecordSet
Dim filen As String, unloadDir As String
```

```
' See Microsoft Knowledge Base Article 306144 if you want to
' change the following file type.

Const UNLFILETYPE = ".csv"
Const UNLSUBFOLDER = "unload\"

On Error GoTo unload_all_Failed

  unloadDir = GetDBPath_FX & UNLSUBFOLDER

  Set MyDB = CurrentDb
  If Len(Dir(unloadDir, vbDirectory)) = 0 Then

    unloadOK = MsgBox("All tables will be unloaded to a new directory called " & _
                unloadDir, vbOKCancel, "Confirm The Unload Directory")
    If unloadOK = vbOK Then
      MkDir unloadDir
    Else
      GoTo unload_all_Final
    End If
  End If

' Loop through all tables, extracting the names.

For i = 0 To MyDB.TableDefs.Count - 1
  Set MyTable = MyDB.TableDefs(i)

  ' Create the file name as a combination of the table name and the file type.

  filen = unloadDir & MyTable.Name & UNLFILETYPE
  If left(MyTable.Name, 4) <> "Msys" And left(MyTable.Name, 1) <> "~" Then

    ' Not an Access system table.
    'Export data in comma-delimited format with column headers.

    DoCmd.Echo True, "Exporting table " & MyTable.Name & " to " & filen
    DoCmd.TransferText A_EXPORTDELIM, , MyTable.Name, filen, True

  End If

Next i
```

```
        MsgBox "Unloaded all tables to ... " & unloadDir, 64, "Unloaded Tables"

unload_all_Final:
   Exit Sub

unload_all_Failed:
   ' Problems with unloading.
   Select Case Err.Number
     Case Else
       MsgBox "Error number " & Err.Number & " -> " & Err.Description, _
         vbCritical, "Problem unloading tables"

   End Select
   Resume unload_all_Final:

End Sub
```

 CAUTION   Not all exported tables will import into Access successfully from the comma-delimited format. This does not mean that there is any problem with the file. Generally, it means that there is a problem with the system that Access uses to predict what the field type of a column is in these external files. For example, when a decimal field is blank for the first 20 lines of the unload file, decimal number columns can be incorrectly classified as integer numbers. Once that incorrect classification has been made, for the rest of the import process, the decimal numbers are rounded to integer values. Also, some text fields can contain unusual characters (like ' or " or foreign languages enunciations), which will unload from the tables with unusual results. Generally, though, this type of data exporting is worth trying first because it is simple and because most systems will read comma-delimited files.

In the preceding code, a function called GetDBPath_FX helps to establish a sub-directory below where the current database exists.

I have made previous references to backups only being as good as the recovery process, so I now will show you how to recover a comma-delimited text (.CSV) file.

Recovering Data from a Comma-Delimited Text File

In the following example, I will show you how you can recover data from a comma-delimited text file. The steps to recover the data from the categories.csv file (shown previously in Figure 5-6) follow.

1. Create a new blank Access database by choosing File ➤ New Database.

2. Choose File ➤ Get External Data ➤ Import.

3. Choose files of type Text Files (*.TXT, *.CSV, *.TAB, or *.ASC) and click Import.

4. Navigate to the correct folder by using the Look In box and select the file.

5. On the first window of the Import Text wizard, choose Delimited and then click Next.

6. On the second window of the wizard, make sure Comma is selected as the type of delimiter, select the First Row Contains Field Names check box (as shown in Figure 5-7), and then click Next.

7. On the third window of the wizard, choose to load the file into a new table.

8. Accept the Access defaults by using the Next buttons, and on the last window, click Finish.

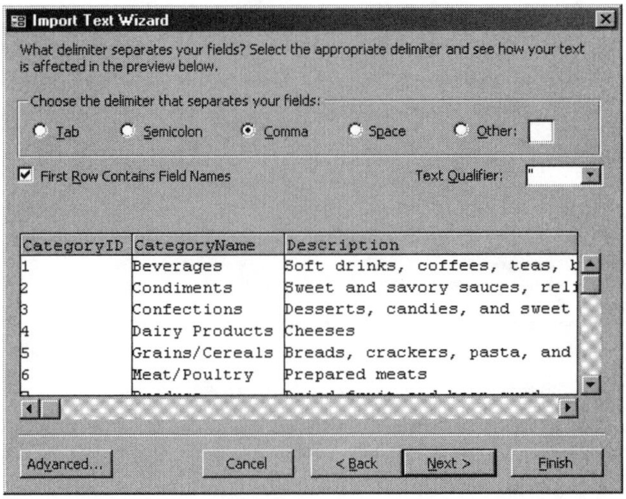

Figure 5-7. The second window of the Import Text wizard.

Now that you have the data loaded into a database, you can append, merge, or replace existing data tables as you see fit. Choosing whether to append, merge, or replace data would be specific to your own data structures and is not within the scope of this book.

Comma-delimited files can prove troublesome if you use them to recover from long-term storage if they are stored without documentation. To alleviate this risk, I recommend that you also store information about the structure of the data in the same location as the text files. Thankfully, there is now a popular new text standard called XML that will provide a more documented format for long-term storage of text files. I will now explain how you can instruct Access to use that format.

Using Access 2002 XML Methods to Export Tables

> **Access 2002 or later**

As I explained in the section on backing up to comma-delimited text files, there are some issues with recovering data from that format. A better way to back up tables to text files is by using the eXtended Markup Language (XML). Access 2002 provides a good platform to get involved in XML because you can easily save or retrieve tables and queries from the XML format by using the `ExportXML` and `ImportXML` methods of the application object. In every XML file that Access generates, you will find not only the data but descriptions of the structure of the data as well. This addition is an improvement on such text files as the comma-delimited format because there is no more guessing whether a field is text or integer or decimal. Figure 5-8 shows an XML file created from the Northwind Categories table.

```
<?xml version="1.0" encoding="UTF-8" ?>
- <root xmlns:xsd="http://www.w3.org/2000/10/XMLSchema" xmlns:od="urn:schemas-microsoft-
    com:officedata">
  - <xsd:schema>
    + <xsd:element name="dataroot">
    - <xsd:element name="Shippers">
      + <xsd:annotation>
      - <xsd:complexType>
        - <xsd:sequence>
          <xsd:element name="ShipperID" od:jetType="autonumber" od:sqlSType="int"
              od:autoUnique="yes" od:nonNullable="yes">
          + <xsd:element name="CompanyName" minOccurs="0" od:jetType="text"
              od:sqlSType="nvarchar">
          + <xsd:element name="Phone" minOccurs="0" od:jetType="text" od:sqlSType="nvarchar">
          </xsd:sequence>
        </xsd:complexType>
      </xsd:element>
    </xsd:schema>
  - <dataroot xmlns:xsi="http://www.w3.org/2000/10/XMLSchema-instance">
    - <Shippers>
        <ShipperID>1</ShipperID>
        <CompanyName>Speedy Express</CompanyName>
        <Phone>(503) 555-9831</Phone>
      </Shippers>
    - <Shippers>
        <ShipperID>2</ShipperID>
        <CompanyName>United Package</CompanyName>
        <Phone>(503) 555-3199</Phone>
      </Shippers>
    - <Shippers>
        <ShipperID>3</ShipperID>
        <CompanyName>Federal Shipping</CompanyName>
        <Phone>(503) 555-9931</Phone>
      </Shippers>
    </dataroot>
  </root>
```

Figure 5-8. The Shippers table from the Northwind database in XML format.

In the VBA example provided in the sample database, the procedure shown in the following code will export all the tables in the database to XML files. In this instance, I use the ADO Extensions for DDL and Security library (ADOX) to provide a list of all the tables in the database.

I use ADOX in this example because the database object types have properties that allow you to establish easily whether a table is linked or is normal (nonsystem). As the loop progresses to each table in the tables catalog, the ExportXML method is used. The code under the only button on the form called frmUnload2002xml demonstrates this.

```vba
Private Sub cmdUnlXML_Click()

' Set a reference for
' Microsoft Active X Data Object 2.5 library.
' Microsoft ADO Extensions 2.5 for DDL and security.

Dim tblsExported As String, cancel As Integer
Dim objT As ADOX.Table, objV As ADOX.View
Dim io As Integer, unloadOK As Integer
Dim adoxCat As ADOX.Catalog
Dim filepath As String
Dim xmlFolder As String, tableName As String
Const REBUILDFILE = "_RebuildMdbTables.txt"
Const INCLUDESCHEMA = 1

xmlFolder = GetDBasePath_FX & "backupXml\"
If Len(Dir(xmlFolder, vbDirectory)) = 0 Then

  unloadOK = MsgBox("All tables will be unloaded to a new directory called " & _
    xmlFolder, vbOKCancel, "Confirm the Unload Directory")
  If unloadOK = vbOK Then
    MkDir xmlFolder
  Else
    GoTo cmdUnlXML_Exit
  End If
End If

io = FreeFile
Open xmlFolder & REBUILDFILE For Output As io

Print #io, "public sub RebuildTables"
Print #io, ""
Print #io, "' Generated by software written by Garry Robinson"
Print #io, "' Import this into a blank database and type"
```

```
Print #io, "' call RebuildTables "
Print #io, "' into the Immediate Window"
Print #io, ""
Print #io, "msgbox ""This will a load a number of XML files into new tables. "", _"
Print #io, ", vbInformation"

Print #io, ""

On Error Resume Next
Set adoxCat = New ADOX.Catalog

adoxCat.ActiveConnection = CurrentProject.Connection

tblsExported = "Tables that were exported to " & xmlFolder & vbCrLf & vbCrLf
txtXMLFile.Visible = True
For Each objT In adoxCat.Tables

  If objT.Type = "Table" Or objT.Type = "Link" Then
    ' Queries are ignored in the exporting process.
    tblsExported = tblsExported & objT.Name & vbCrLf
    tableName = objT.Name
    DoCmd.Echo True, xmlFolder & tableName & ".xml"
    filepath = xmlFolder & tableName & ".xml"
    ' Export the table to an XML file.
    txtXMLFile = tableName
    ' Save the table as an XML file.
    ExportXML acExportTable, tableName, xmlFolder & tableName & ".xml", _
      , , , , INCLUDESCHEMA

    Print #io, "importXML """ & filepath & """, acStructureAndData"
  End If
Next objT

On Error Resume Next

Print #io, "msgbox ""End of table import from XML"""
Print #io, ""
Print #io, "end sub"
```

```
Close io
MsgBox tblsExported, vbInformation, "End Of Exports"
Set adoxCat = Nothing

cmdUnlXML_Exit:
End Sub
```

One good thing about the implementation of XML in Access 2002 is that you can export and import by using XML without truly understanding the format itself. The XML exports and imports work well because they correctly handle issues like unusual characters and bitmaps. In the next section, I show you how you can recover your XML files.

Recovering Data from an Access 2002 XML File

Access 2002 or later

You can use the Import command on the File menu to recover a table that has been exported to XML. Notice that when you import an XML file into a database that already has a table with the same name, you will create a table with the same name plus a numerical suffix, such as TableName1. The process for importing a single XML file in Access 2002 or later follows:

1. Choose File ➤ Get External Data ➤ Import.

2. Choose XML documents (*.XML, *.XSD) from the Files of Type drop-down list.

3. Choose the XML file, then click Import, and then click OK.

4. Be wary of choosing the Append to Existing Data option because you will need to check that all the records are new before you load them.

This process will work for a few files, but if you want to recover a number of tables, you may want to automate this process by using the VBA code recovery file generated by the preceding piece of code (found in form frmUnload2002xml). As part of the export process, this form generates a table recovery file (show in Figure 5-9) that you can use to load all the XML files into a blank database.

```
_RebuildMdbTables.txt - Notepad
File  Edit  Format  View  Help
public sub RebuildTables

' Generated by software written by Garry Robinson
' Import this into a blank database and type
' call RebuildTables
' into the Immediate Window

msgbox "This will create a new version of any tables with the same name in your database. " & _
       "Hit the Ctrl+Break keys NOW if you already have these tables in your database " & _
       "You will have to rename them from tableName1 to tablename if they are in the database" & _
       "and you will need to be careful with the database relationship model if you do so." _
, vbInformation

importXML "C:\Gr-FX\Aprs01\backupXml\Categories.xml", acStructureAndData
importXML "C:\Gr-FX\Aprs01\backupXml\Customers.xml", acStructureAndData
importXML "C:\Gr-FX\Aprs01\backupXml\Employees.xml", acStructureAndData
importXML "C:\Gr-FX\Aprs01\backupXml\Order Details.xml", acStructureAndData
importXML "C:\Gr-FX\Aprs01\backupXml\Orders.xml", acStructureAndData
importXML "C:\Gr-FX\Aprs01\backupXml\Products.xml", acStructureAndData
importXML "C:\Gr-FX\Aprs01\backupXml\Shippers.xml", acStructureAndData
importXML "C:\Gr-FX\Aprs01\backupXml\Suppliers.xml", acStructureAndData
msgbox "End of table import from XML"

end sub
```

Figure 5-9. The text file that can reload the tables into a blank database.

Here are the steps that will rebuild all the tables from the Access 2002 XML backup process:

1. Create a new blank Access database by choosing File ➤ Create Database.

2. Open the Visual Basic Editor by pressing ALT+F11.

3. Choose File ➤ Import File.

4. Choose all file types (*.*).

5. Find the table recovery file called _RebuildMdbTables.txt and click the Open button.

You've now created a module in your blank database called Module1. Review the code in this module. Now you can open the Immediate window by pressing CTRL+G or by choosing View ➤ Immediate Window. Type the following into the Immediate window to reload the tables:

```
call RebuildTables
```

If you are using Access 2000 or even Access 97, you can take advantage of XML by using the ADO 2.5 library to generate the XML. The next section describes a form that will show you how to do this.

Using ADO to Generate XML Files in Access 2000

Access 2000 or later

Long before I developed the automated XML export code discussed in the section "Using Access 2002 XML Methods to Export Tables," I used ADO 2.5 to export tables to text files. Using XML in this way isn't anywhere near as integrated into Access as the ExportXML method in Access 2002, but it does provide a way to generate XML files for backup. If you want to try this particular approach, open the demonstration database for Access 2000 (grMap2000.mdb) and choose the form called frmUnloadADOxml. This form has all the necessary code under the one button and is very similar in structure to that code discussed earlier in the chapter and demonstrated in the section on using Access 2002 XML methods to export tables.

The following code snippet illustrates how the ADO Recordset object's Save method saves a table to an XML file. Before exporting a database, you must delete the existing XML file by using the Kill function. The code snippet provided requires that you upgrade to at least version 2.5 of the ADO library (Microsoft ActiveX Data Object 2.5 library) and include this reference in your Access application.

If this method of exporting appeals to you, you can also use a proprietary and more compact Microsoft format to store the exported information. Select this format by changing the adPersistXML constant in the second argument of the Recordset object's Save method to use the adPersistADTG constant. This adPersistXML format may even appeal to you as a security precaution because the file format is binary and cannot be read in a text editor. Another advantage of the adPersistXML constant is that it will allow you to use the ADO 2.1 library that comes with Access 2000.

```
Set rst = New ADODB.RecordSet
rst.ActiveConnection = CurrentProject.Connection
datasource = objT.Name
rst.Open datasource

On Error Resume Next
  Kill cachedir & datasource
  rst.Save cachedir & datasource & ".xml", adPersistXML
  Set rst = Nothing
```

Now that you have seen a number of ways to save a table to a text file, the next section will show you how to save code and objects to text files and then recover the objects at a later date if necessary.

Exporting and Recovering Programming Objects

Access 97 or later

In this section, I will show you how to save queries, forms, reports, macros, and modules (which I'll call programming objects from now on) to text files. I encourage this particular backup approach because it offers additional recovery opportunities and helps you in these specific situations:

- If more than one person is developing software for the database, your systems for cooperating will not always be perfect, and someone's good hard work will be lost.

- If an object in a database becomes irretrievably damaged.

- If you're adding protection to the database, such as passwords and user-level security.

In all these scenarios, backing up the programming objects at regular intervals may help recover the object. Now I will describe how to save VBA code by using a menu.

Exporting a VBA Module to a Text File

Access 97 or later

Your VBA modules and class modules are the only objects in the database for which you can use a menu to save as text and recover from text.

1. Open the Database window (of any database with code).

2. Select Modules.

3. Select an individual module.

4. Choose File ➤ Export.

5. Save the file as a text (*.txt).

6. Select your folder and file name.

7. Select the Autostart check box and click Export.

Your VBA module will now be saved in a text file. In Access 2000 and later, you can also export modules from within the Visual Basic Editor. First, you need to select the object that you want to export in the Project Explorer, then you choose File ➤ Export, and the steps are similar to the preceding procedure. If you use the Visual Basic Editor to save the code, you can use more specific file types like *.BAS and *.CLS rather than *.TXT.

Importing the VBA Text File Back into the Database

In Access 97, the only way to import the VBA text file back into the database is to open the text file in a text editor like Notepad, select all, copy to the paste buffer, open a new module in Access, and paste the code into the new module. You can use this simple method in all versions of Access.

In Access 2000 and later, however, you can also import the VBA text file directly into the database by following these steps:

1. Open a new database.

2. Open the Visual Basic Editor (press ALT+F11).

3. Choose File ➤ Import File.

4. Find the file and click Open.

5. You will now find the module in the Project Explorer. If it is not visible, choose View ➤ Project Explorer.

The next section of this chapter will show you how to use the same formats that Microsoft Visual SourceSafe uses to save and recover all the programming objects in your database.

Saving and Retrieving Objects by Using Hidden Methods

Access 97 or later

Unless you suffer from the same compulsive Web-searching disorder that I am afflicted with, you will probably be blissfully unaware that it is possible to save all your queries, forms, reports, macros, and modules to text files. So what, you might ask? Saving objects as text files means that you have a copy of an object that is external to any database that you are developing. If an object is inadvertently changed, you can retrieve that object from the text file. Once you understand the concepts behind saving objects to text, you will find many possible uses for it, such as using the files to interchange objects between developers and recovering objects from corrupt databases.

To import and export programming objects, we can use two undocumented (hidden) methods of the Application object[1] called LoadFromText and SaveToText. These methods both require you to specify the object type by using the Access constants, the name of the Access object, and the destination or retrieval location of the file. To illustrate this process, open the Immediate window (press CTRL+G) in the Visual Basic Editor and type Application.SaveAsText. From then on, Intellisense will provide you with the list of constants and arguments to complete the statement. In Figure 5-10, I have put together an example to show how you can export and import a form.

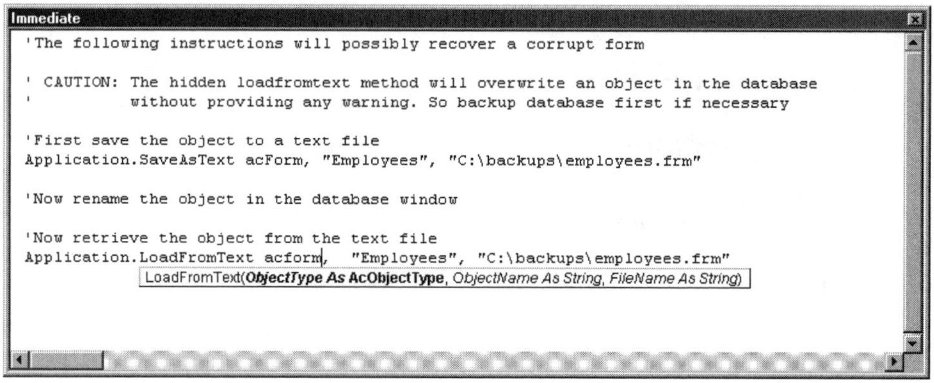

```
Immediate
'The following instructions will possibly recover a corrupt form

' CAUTION: The hidden loadfromtext method will overwrite an object in the database
'          without providing any warning. So backup database first if necessary

'First save the object to a text file
Application.SaveAsText acForm, "Employees", "C:\backups\employees.frm"

'Now rename the object in the database window

'Now retrieve the object from the text file
Application.LoadFromText acform,  "Employees", "C:\backups\employees.frm"
        LoadFromText(ObjectType As AcObjectType, ObjectName As String, FileName As String)
```

Figure 5-10. The SaveAsText *and* LoadFromText *methods viewed in the Immediate window.*

Exporting All Programmable Objects to Text Files

A good way to describe backing up objects to text is to work through an example from the demonstration database. This demonstration will create a file for each programmable object in the database. You will be able to run this utility even if other people are using the database. This example will coexist well with the exporting of all tables to text example described earlier in this chapter.

---

1. To show hidden members of objects such as the Application object, open the Object browser from the Visual Basic Editor. Right-click any object and choose Show Hidden Members from the menu.

To experiment with this download, do the following:

1. Make a copy of Northwind.mdb and then open the copy.

2. Import the following objects from the demonstration database: frmBackupAllObjects, basGR8_exportObjects, and basGR8_Startup.

3. Compile all the code by using the Debug menu in the Visual Basic Editor.

4. Open the form frmBackupAllObjects (shown in Figure 5-11) and click the Back Up All Objects to Text button to start the backups.

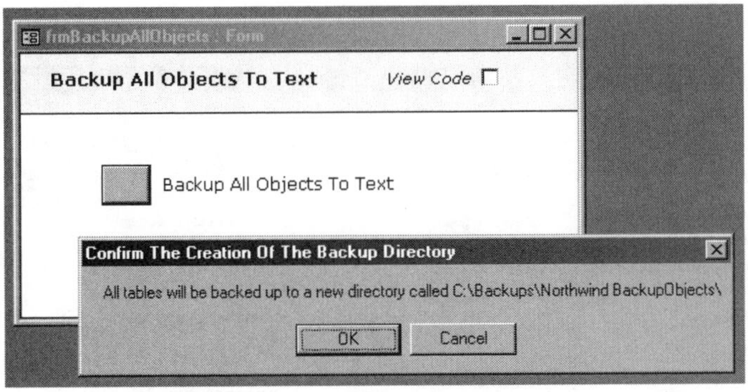

Figure 5-11. The Back Up All Objects to Text form.

5. When the exports are completed, a message box (as shown in Figure 5-12) will tell you where the text copies of the objects are. It will also tell you the name of a text file that you can use to recover all the objects into a blank database by using VBA.

Figure 5-12. The message that appears to tell you where the files went and how to recover them.

TIP   Before exporting a database or shipping it to clients, for that matter, it is wise to compile all modules in the database. To do this, open the Visual Basic Editor and choose Debug ➤ Compile Project for Access 2000 and later and Debug ➤ Compile All Objects for Access 97.

Now that the exports are complete, let's have a look at what has happened. All the objects are now stored in text files in a subfolder where the current database is located (shown in Figure 5-13). The file types used for saving the files are *.QRY for queries, *.FRM for forms, *.RPT for reports, *.MCR for macros, *.BAS for modules, and *.CLS for class modules.

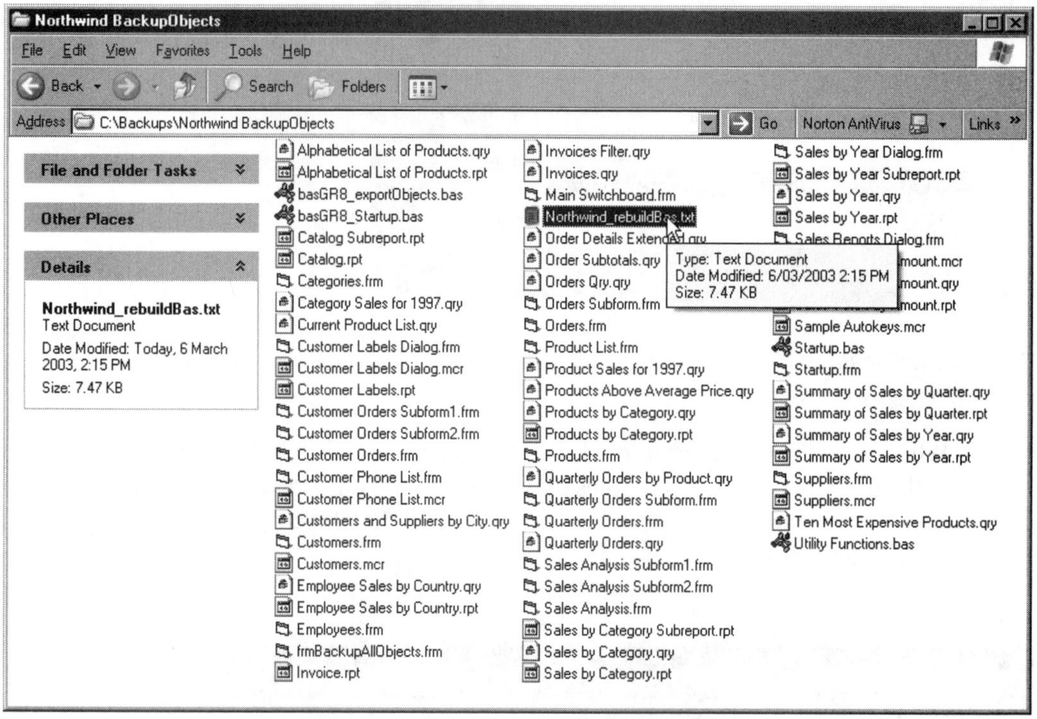

Figure 5-13. Folder showing all the objects exported to individual files.

To gain an understanding of the structure of the exported objects, let us look at the text version of a query that was created by the SaveAsText method (as shown Figure 5-14).

```
Product Sales for 1997.qry - Notepad
File  Edit  Format  View  Help
dbMemo "SQL" ="SELECT Categories.CategoryName, Products.ProductName, Sum(CCur([Order Details].U"
    "nitPrice*[Quantity]*(1-[Discount])/100)*100) AS ProductSales, \"Qtr \" & DatePar"
    "t(\"q\",[ShippedDate]) AS ShippedQuarter\015\012FROM (Categories INNER JOIN Prod"
    "ucts ON Categories.CategoryID=Products.CategoryID) INNER JOIN (Orders INNER JOIN"
    " [Order Details] ON Orders.OrderID=[Order Details].OrderID) ON Products.ProductI"
    "D=[Order Details].ProductID\015\012WHERE (((Orders.ShippedDate) Between #1/1/199"
    "7# And #12/31/1997#))\015\012GROUP BY Categories.CategoryName, Products.ProductN"
    "ame, \"Qtr \" & DatePart(\"q\",[ShippedDate]);\015\012"
dbMemo "Connect" =""
dbBoolean "ReturnsRecords" ="-1"
dbInteger "ODBCTimeout" ="60"
dbBoolean "FilterOn" ="0"
dbText "Description" ="Record source for Category Sales for 1995 query. Uses Sum and CCur functions."
dbBoolean "OrderOn" ="0"
dbByte "DatasheetGridlinesBehavior" ="3"
dbBoolean "OrderByOn" ="0"
dbByte "RecordsetType" ="0"
dbByte "Orientation" ="0"
dbByte "DefaultView" ="2"
Begin
    Begin
        dbText "Name" ="Categories.CategoryName"
        dbInteger "ColumnWidth" ="1620"
        dbBoolean "ColumnHidden" ="0"
    End
    Begin
        dbText "Name" ="Products.ProductName"
        dbInteger "ColumnWidth" ="3210"
        dbBoolean "ColumnHidden" ="0"
    End
    Begin
        dbText "Name" ="ProductSales"
        dbInteger "ColumnWidth" ="1410"
        dbBoolean "ColumnHidden" ="0"
        dbMemo "Caption" ="Product Sales"
        dbText "Format" ="$#,##0.00;($#,##0.00)"
    End
    Begin
        dbText "Name" ="ShippedQuarter"
        dbInteger "ColumnWidth" ="1665"
        dbBoolean "ColumnHidden" ="0"
    End
End
```

Figure 5-14. The Product Sales query after being exported to a backup text file.

As you can see, not only is the SQL stored, but the column properties, field types, and other details are also stored in the file. It is this complete detail that allows Access to import the objects that are exported, which allows us then to recover a damaged or deleted object.

Okay, so now we have created all the text copies of the database; what use are they if we cannot recover them? To assist in loading all these files back into a database, the export process generated an object recovery file. This file has all the necessary VBA code to import the objects back into an empty database, which I will now describe how to do.

Importing All Programmable Objects into a Blank Database

Retrieving all or some of these objects back from a folder requires you to create VBA code by using the Application object's LoadFromText method once for every object in the database. Writing this sort of code manually for even a small database such as Northwind would be very tedious. To automate this process, the Export All

Objects software automatically generates a text file called Northwind_rebuildBas.txt (shown in Figure 5-15). This file contains VBA code that will load all the objects into a blank database.

```
public sub RebuildDatabase

' Generated by software written by Garry Robinson
' Import this into a blank database and type
' RebuildDatabase into the debug window

msgbox "This will OVERWRITE any objects with the same name in your database. " & _
       "WARNING - Hit the Ctrl+Break keys NOW " & _
       "If you already have these objects in your database " & _
       "You will not be able to retrieve the current objects if you continue"

LoadFromText acQuery,"Alphabetical List of Products" , "C:\Backups\Northwind BackupObjects\Alpha
LoadFromText acQuery,"Category Sales for 1997" , "C:\Backups\Northwind BackupObjects\Category Sa
LoadFromText acQuery,"Current Product List" , "C:\Backups\Northwind BackupObjects\Current Produc
LoadFromText acQuery,"Customers and Suppliers by City" , "C:\Backups\Northwind BackupObjects\Cus
LoadFromText acQuery,"Employee Sales by Country" , "C:\Backups\Northwind BackupObjects\Employee
LoadFromText acQuery,"Invoices" , "C:\Backups\Northwind BackupObjects\Invoices.qry"
LoadFromText acQuery,"Invoices Filter" , "C:\Backups\Northwind BackupObjects\Invoices Filter.qry
LoadFromText acQuery,"Order Details Extended" , "C:\Backups\Northwind BackupObjects\Order Detail
LoadFromText acQuery,"Order Subtotals" , "C:\Backups\Northwind BackupObjects\Order Subtotals.qry
LoadFromText acQuery,"Orders Qry" , "C:\Backups\Northwind BackupObjects\Orders Qry.qry"
LoadFromText acQuery,"Product Sales for 1997" , "C:\Backups\Northwind BackupObjects\Product Sale
LoadFromText acQuery,"Products Above Average Price" , "C:\Backups\Northwind BackupObjects\Produc
LoadFromText acQuery,"Products by Category" , "C:\Backups\Northwind BackupObjects\Products by Ca
LoadFromText acQuery,"Quarterly Orders" , "C:\Backups\Northwind BackupObjects\Quarterly Orders.c
LoadFromText acQuery,"Quarterly Orders by Product" , "C:\Backups\Northwind BackupObjects\Quarter
LoadFromText acQuery,"Sales by Category" , "C:\Backups\Northwind BackupObjects\Sales by Category
LoadFromText acQuery,"Sales by Year" , "C:\Backups\Northwind BackupObjects\Sales by Year.qry"
```

Figure 5-15. The VBA recovery file that helps import all the objects into a blank database.

To load all the objects into a new database, follow these steps:

1. Open a new blank database.

2. Open the Visual Basic Editor (press ALT+F11).

3. Choose File ➤ Import File.

4. Find the file (its name should be Northwind_rebuildBas.txt) and click Open.

5. Find the module in the Project Explorer, which you can view by choosing View ➤ Project Explorer.

6. Open the Immediate window.

7. Type "call RebuildDatabase" into the Immediate window.

8. Because this database started as a blank project, you need to check your VBA project references by choosing Tools ➤ References. You will probably be missing references such as DAO and Microsoft Office 10.

As an alternative, you can actually use the LoadFromText method to load the individual VBA object recovery files into the database. To do this, open the Immediate window and type

```
LoadFromText acModule, "RebuildDatabase", _
  "c:\Backups\Northwind BackupObjects\Northwind_rebuildBas.txt"
```

CAUTION The LoadFromText method will copy over the existing objects without warning. If you are using this method, you probably should open a new blank database and then compare the object with your existing database before importing.

Now I will retrace my steps a little to discuss the VBA code that makes backing up and recovering objects possible.

How Exporting of Objects to Text Works

The following onClick procedure for the form frmBackupAllObjects shows you how to integrate the exporting software into your database. This procedure establishes both a folder for the backup plus a name for the VBA recovery file. It then calls the exportObjectsToText_FX subroutine, which you will find in the basGR8_exportObjects module.

```
Private Sub cmdBackupToText_Click()
' Back up all queries, forms, reports, macros, and modules to text files.

Const OBJFOLDER = "BackupObjects\"
Const REBUILDOBJ = "_rebuildBas.txt"

Dim exportAllOK As Boolean, backUpFolder As String
Dim dbNameStr As String, rebuildFile As String
```

```
backUpFolder = GetDBPath_FX(, dbNameStr)
backUpFolder = backUpFolder & dbNameStr & " " & OBJFOLDER

' Back up all objects to text.
rebuildFile = dbNameStr & REBUILDOBJ
exportAllOK = exportObjectsToText_FX(backUpFolder, rebuildFile)

If exportAllOK Then
  MsgBox "Database objects have been exported to text files in " & backUpFolder & _
  ". These files can be recovered into a blank database using VB in the file " _
  & rebuildFile
Else
  MsgBox "Database export to " & backUpFolder & " was not successful"
End If
End Sub
```

Now we will look at the exportObjectsToText_FX subroutine in detail. Initially, the function creates a folder plus the instructions section of the VBA recovery file. You will be able to recognize the VBA code that creates the VBA recovery file by looking for lines that include the output channel variable io and the text file creation commands Open, Print, Close, and FreeFile. The first half of the subroutine follows:

```
Public Function exportObjectsToText_FX(folderPath As String, _
                rebuildFile As String) As Boolean

' Export all queries, forms, macros, and modules to text.
' Build a file to assist in recovery of the saved objects
' in a clean database.

' This function requires a reference to
' Microsoft DAO 3.6 or 3.51 Llibrary.
'Requires the modules basGR8_exportObjects and basGR8_Startup.

On Error GoTo err_exportObjectsToText

Dim dbs As DAO.Database, Cnt As DAO.Container, doc As DAO.Document
Dim mdl As Module, objName As String
Dim io As Integer, i As Integer, unloadOK As Integer
Dim FilePath As String
Dim fileType As String

If Len(Dir(folderPath, vbDirectory)) = 0 Then
```

```
  unloadOK = MsgBox("All tables will be backed up to a new directory called " & _
          folderPath, vbOKCancel, "Confirm the Creation of the Backup Directory")
  If unloadOK = vbOK Then
    MkDir folderPath
  Else
    GoTo Exit_exportObjectsToText
  End If
End If


' The location of all the text files should be in a folder that is
' backed up and kept off-site.

io = FreeFile
Open folderPath & rebuildFile For Output As io

Print #io, "public sub RebuildDatabase"
Print #io, ""
Print #io, "' Import this into a blank database and type"
Print #io, "' RebuildDatabase into the debug window"
Print #io, ""
Print #io, _
"msgbox ""This will OVERWRITE any objects with the same name. "" & _"
Print #io, _
"          ""WARNING: Press CTRL+BREAK NOW "" & _"
Print #io, _
"          ""If you already have these objects in your database "" & _"
Print #io, _
"          ""You will not be able to retrieve the current objects if you continue"""
Print #io, ""
```

The function must now iterate through the different collections of objects in the database by using DAO. When the loop moves to the next object, the object is saved to text and another line is written to the VBA recovery file. When it comes to exporting modules, I like to differentiate between modules and class modules by saving them to a different file type, which requires that I open the modules in design mode first. If you like, you can remove this additional code and save all class modules as .BAS files. This change will not affect the recovery process at all. Before I start this part of the subroutine, I find it useful to test whether the database has been compiled and then compile it as a final test of the quality of the database. The second half of the exportObjectsToText_FX follows.

```
If Not Application.IsCompiled Then
  ' If the application is not compiled, compile it.
  RunCommand acCmdCompileAllModules
End If


' Now test again whether the database is compiled.
' First, test whether the database is compiled.
If Application.IsCompiled Then
  Set dbs = CurrentDb()

  For i = 0 To dbs.QueryDefs.Count - 1
    objName = dbs.QueryDefs(i).Name
    FilePath = folderPath & objName & ".qry"
    If left(objName, 1) <> "~" Then
      SaveAsText acQuery, objName, FilePath
      Print #io, "LoadFromText acQuery,""" & objName & _
        """" , """ & FilePath & """"
    End If
  Next i


  Print #io, ""


  Set Cnt = dbs.Containers("Forms")
  For Each doc In Cnt.Documents
    FilePath = folderPath & doc.Name & ".frm"
    SaveAsText acForm, doc.Name, FilePath
    Print #io, "LoadFromText acForm,""" & doc.Name & _
      """" , """ & FilePath & """"
  Next doc


  Print #io, ""


  Set Cnt = dbs.Containers("Reports")
  For Each doc In Cnt.Documents
    FilePath = folderPath & doc.Name & ".rpt"
    SaveAsText acReport, doc.Name, FilePath
    Print #io, "LoadFromText acReport,""" & doc.Name & _
      """" , """ & FilePath & """"
  Next doc


  Print #io, ""
```

```
' Scripts are actually macros.
  Set Cnt = dbs.Containers("Scripts")
  For Each doc In Cnt.Documents
    FilePath = folderPath & doc.Name & ".mcr"
    SaveAsText acMacro, doc.Name, folderPath & doc.Name & ".mcr"
    Print #io, "LoadFromText acMacro,""" & doc.Name & _
      """ , """ & FilePath & """"
  Next doc

  Print #io, ""

  Set Cnt = dbs.Containers("Modules")
  For Each doc In Cnt.Documents
' Modules need to be opened to find if they are class or function modules.
' You can turn off open module to save all files as .BAS types.
    DoCmd.OpenModule doc.Name
    If Modules(doc.Name).Type = acClassModule Then
      fileType = ".cls"
    Else
      fileType = ".bas"
    End If
    FilePath = folderPath & doc.Name & fileType
    DoCmd.CLOSE acModule, doc.Name
    SaveAsText acModule, doc.Name, FilePath

    Print #io, "LoadFromText acModule ,""" & doc.Name & _
      """ , """ & FilePath & """"

  Next doc

  exportObjectsToText_FX = True
  Print #io, "msgbox ""End of rebuild"""
  Print #io, ""
  Print #io, "end sub"

Else

  MsgBox "Compile the database first to ensure the code is OK .", _
    vbInformation, "Choose Debug, Compile All Modules from the VBA window."
  exportObjectsToText_FX = False
End If
```

```
Exit_exportObjectsToText:

On Error Resume Next
  Close io
  Set doc = Nothing
  Set Cnt = Nothing
  Set dbs = Nothing

  Exit Function

err_exportObjectsToText:
  Select Case Err.Number          ' Problems with unload process.

    Case Else
        MsgBox "Error No. " & Err.Number & " -> " & Err.Description
  End Select
  exportObjectsToText_FX = False

  Resume Exit_exportObjectsToText

End Function
```

Now that you have seen how to import all the objects, let's have a look at how the file size of the text files will tell you the relative size of the objects in the database.

Size Does Matter: How the Text Backup Files Will Help

This section shows that unloading to text backup systems provides a tool for working out the biggest objects and tables in our databases. If a database is getting large, you will start to wonder about what is taking up all the space. Sure, you can look at the tables, find the one with the most records, and then see if you can reduce its size. But this is a hit-or-miss approach, and you'll miss many good opportunities to decrease your database size. If you think that missing these opportunities is not all that important, ponder this disaster.

 User Story *One database I was called in to fix was 100MB large and was performing very poorly. Naturally, I assumed that no one had ever compacted it. Unfortunately, it was in such a mess, it wouldn't compact. After importing all the objects into another database, I managed to compact the database and save 20MB. I then hunted through the system and found a few table changes that saved another 5MB. Next, I tried for another favorite space*

saver of mine: embedded graphs that have too many rows of data stored directly in the graph object. This repair saved a couple more megabytes. Finally, I came across an innocuous small company logo in the corner of every one of the 100 reports. I took a copy of the database and removed this picture from 20 reports. Bingo—10MB saved. I then discovered that the logo was actually a large picture that had been shrunk to a small size. I asked for permission from the manager to remove the logo from the reports, and the database shrunk to only 20MB. I then split the database, and the front-end database reduced to only 4MB. If I had known the relative size of all the objects in the first place, however, this process would have been so much easier.

It's at this point where text backups are so useful because the size of the text files for both the tables and the objects provides a relative indicator of the size of the objects inside the database. If you look at the exports from the Northwind database, you will find that the Orders and OrderDetails XML table export files are the largest. The size reflects the database where these two tables clearly have the most records. Surprisingly, the Categories table is the third biggest text file. It only has five records, but each record includes a bitmap. If this table had many records, the bitmaps would really consume a lot of space unnecessarily and would probably be better stored outside the database. If you sort the programmable object exports folder by file size, the Catalog report and the Customers form are the largest at 150KB each. Though these are not large objects, both these objects have embedded pictures that may not be necessary. If you remove the picture from these objects, they shrink to 50KB when exported.

Though the Northwind object sizes may not be that exciting to you, this file size assessment technique will have a bigger impact on you when you try saving all objects from your databases.

Now we will have a look at backing up and recovering the information not covered by the table and object exports.

Backing Up Other Information

Database properties, relationship diagrams, menus, and import/export specifications can only be backed up to another Access database or documented by printing. To produce a report on the database properties and relationship diagrams as a form of backup:

1. Open a database.

2. Choose Tools ➤ Analyze ➤ Documentor.

3. Select the Current Database tab and select both Properties and Relationships. This action will produce a report that shows both database properties (see Figure 5-16) and descriptions of the relationships.

C:\Backups\Northwind.mdb		Friday, 14 March 2003
Database: C:\Backups\Northwind.mdb		Page: 1

Properties

AccessVersion:	08.50	AllowBreakIntoCode:	True
AllowBuiltInToolbars:	True	AllowFullMenus:	True
AllowShortcutMenus:	True	AllowSpecialKeys:	True
AllowToolbarChanges:	True	ANSI Query Mode:	0
Auto Compact:	0	Build:	702
CollatingOrder:	General	Four-Digit Year Formatting:	0
Log Name AutoCorrect Chan	0	PagesFixed:	true
Perform Name AutoCorrect:	1	ProjVer:	24
QueryTimeout:	60	RecordsAffected:	0
Remove Personal Informatio	0	RemovePersonalInformation	0
Row Limit:	10000	Show Values in Indexed:	1
Show Values in Non-Indexed	1	Show Values in Remote:	0
Show Values in Server:	0	Show Values in Snapshot:	1
Show Values Limit:	1000	StartUpForm:	Startup
StartUpShowDBWindow:	True	StartUpShowStatusBar:	True
Track Name AutoCorrect Inf	1	Transactions:	True
Updatable:	True	Use Default Connection File:	0
Use Default Page Folder:	0	Use Hijri Calendar:	0
UseAppIconForFrmRpt:	False	Version:	4.0

Figure 5-16. The database documentor output shows important database properties.

An additional way to back up the table relationships is to print out the relationship model diagram. To find this option:

1. Open the back-end database where the table relationships are stored.

2. Open the relationships window.

3. Choose File ➤ Print Relationships.

The output from this menu command is shown in Figure 5-17. This option became available in Access 2000, but a download wizard was available from Microsoft for the same purpose in Access 97.

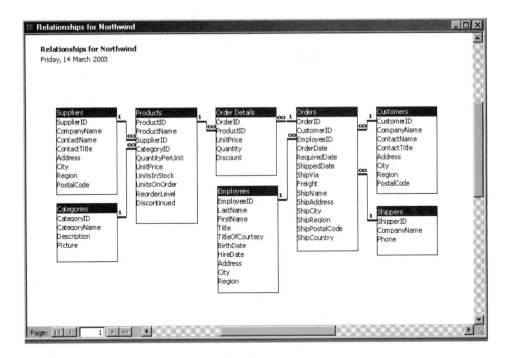

Figure 5-17. The relationship window, which you can print as part of your backup material.

Recovering Your Relationships, Menus, and Import/ Export Specifications

If you import or export data to text files regularly, you can save the definition of the responses that you used for that work into an import/export specification. These specifications can take a while to re-create if lost. If you have created menus and toolbars in your application (discussed in detail in Chapter 7) or relationships between tables, then you will wonder how to back up or move that information around. The only practical way to transfer these items is to use the Import Objects wizard.

To open the Import Objects wizard, choose File ➤ Get External Data ➤ Import. To import the relationships, menus, and import/export specifications, click the Options button and then select the three check boxes in the lower left of the wizard (as shown in Figure 5-18).

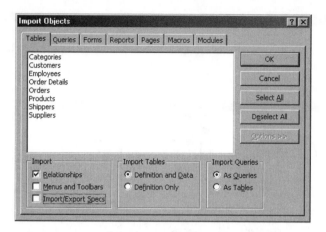

Figure 5-18. The Import Objects wizard after the Options button is clicked.

Select the Relationships check box to include the relationships defined between the tables and queries you import. It is important to note that the only relationships transferred will be those common to the tables that you are importing. Select the Menus and Toolbars check box to import all custom menus and toolbars in the database. If a custom toolbar or menu with the same name exists in the current database, that toolbar won't be imported. Select the Import/Export Specs check box to include all import and export specifications from the database you are importing.

NOTE It is quite acceptable to use the Import command from the Access main menu to import all objects into a blank database. This procedure will form quite an acceptable form of backup. Chapter 9 discusses in detail why the Import command is one of the bigger weaknesses in the Access protection mechanisms.

Backing Up Your Database by Using Access 2003

With the arrival of Access 2003, a new menu command will handle the naming conventions for backing up a database, and it's an option well worth considering for any DBA who is interested in a simple, well-organized backup process for their Access 2000, 2002 format database. The system works by asking you for the folder of your backup database (as shown in Figure 5-19).

Figure 5-19. The Backup menu command.

It then compacts the current database to that folder. The file name suggested for the backup results from concatenating the name of the current database with a date string. If you back up your database more than once a day, the name of the backup database will also receive a numerical suffix to differentiate between each of the backups for the day (as shown in Figure 5-20).

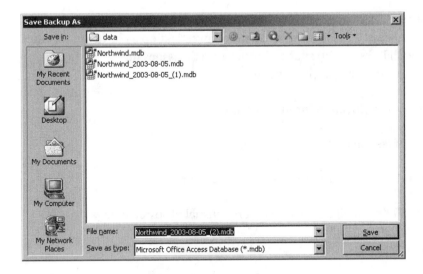

Figure 5-20. Access 2003 backup wizard in action.

Naturally, there are some complications with this process, such as:

- You need to store the backups in a safe place if you are trying to protect the information in the database.

- You will need to make sure that everyone has logged off the database before running the backup.

- You need to make sure that you back up both the front-end and back-end databases.

- You will need to clean up all the old backup databases by using Windows Explorer or some other system that lists files in the directory.

Now that we have reached the end of the descriptions of the backup techniques, I will provide you with some links so that you can continue reading on these topics.

Further Reading

As you might expect, there is never enough information when it comes to powerful products like Access. To assist you with further investigations, I have put together a Web page with links to Web sites and articles on the issues that relate to the material in this chapter. This page includes

- The download location for ADO libraries.

- A page of resources for Access corruption.

- Microsoft product support rules and regulations.

- Microsoft Knowledge Base articles on unusual file extensions.

- How to use XML exports to generate Web reports.

- Information on the `AddFromFile` method.

- How to program your own documentation of tables, indexes, and relationships.

- How to find the Access 97 Relationship Printer wizard.

You can find the further reading Web page for this chapter in the Downloads section of the Apress Web site (http://www.apress.com) or at the following address: http://www.vb123.com/map/bac.htm.

Reflecting on This Chapter

In this chapter, we have seen that there is a bit more to backing up a database than you would think. Sure, the DBA can put a new tape in the tape drive every night, and your database will be on the tape in the morning. If you ever need to recover that database, that process is probably okay. But if this is all that you do, you are missing an opportunity to introduce some additional safeguards and flexibility into your backup process.

My recommendations for you:

- Add the demonstration form (frmAutoShutdown) to your startup sequences in your front-end databases to help to ensure that everyone has logged off by backup time.

- If you need to back up during the day, make sure that everyone has logged off by using the frmIsDBopenDAO form demonstrated at the start of the chapter.

- Once a month or more, export all tables and objects to text files to create an additional safeguard.

- If you have a busy database, run the backup to XML or comma-delimited format procedures described in this chapter sometime during the day. This action will protect you from unfortunate incidents such as someone deleting a large number of records.

Finally, remember to test your recovery procedures on a regular basis.

What's Next?

In the next chapter, we will be looking at different ways that you can monitor who is in the database. Knowing who is in the database is very useful information if you have trouble with your backups or software updating because your database is open. You will also learn other useful administration techniques, such as logging when and by whom a database is opened and closed, logging when someone opens an object, and even how to keep people from logging onto the database. Also, I'll introduce an Access form that will show who is connecting to or sneaking into your databases without using the startup form or AutoExec macro.

CHAPTER 6

User and Object Surveillance

IN THIS CHAPTER, you will learn how to find out who and how many people are using your database. This important surveillance information can help you with administration issues such as asking users to log off the database or network for maintenance and upgrades and with targeting security for your database. To help you with these issues and other related topics, this chapter has a number of easy-to-install Access objects and discusses some free products that you can use. You should consider deploying some of these solutions in your database because they may help you balance speculation with facts, something that is always a good idea before embarking on software upgrades, such as adding security.

To get you up to speed quickly with the tools necessary for surveillance, I start by providing you with an Access form that will allow you to view computer and Access workgroup logon names. Though this tool is useful for individual databases, if you have a large number of databases, you may want to use a tool such as the LDBView or the Access Workbench to find who is using these databases without opening the database itself.

There are a number of occasions where it is useful to keep a detailed log of who is using the database. To assist you with that, you can include software from the download database to capture the Windows user account and time that someone opened and closed the database. What I find useful about this information is that it allows you to monitor usage over time and diagnose who was using a database when a problem occurred. I will also show you how to detect whether someone has connected to your database without using the startup form or the AutoExec macro.

To be more specific, the demonstration material included for this chapter includes a number of forms and Visual Basic for Applications (VBA) examples like the following:

- A form that lists computer names and allows you to stop new users from opening the database.

- A free license for Access Workbench 1.3 that I wrote. This license allows you to list all users of your database, even if it is protected by workgroup security or a database password.

- Access objects that log Windows user IDs, computer names, workgroup IDs, and the time that the user opens and closes the database.

- Access forms and modules that log the use of forms or reports in the database.

- A form that identifies database users who deliberately or unintentionally avoid your startup form or AutoExec macro.

 NOTE To find the demonstration material, open the download database for your version of Access—for example, grMAP97.mdb—and choose Chapter 6.

Will Surveillance Really Help?

Once again, I will provide three separate overviews: one for the developer, one for the database administrator (DBA), and one for the IT manager. I do this because people in each of these categories will approach the chapter in a different way. The developer will want to know how to add these surveillance techniques to a database, the DBA will want to find out about users unless they can see all the users of the database from their desk, and the IT manager should be aware of who, when, and how people are using databases when additional development is requested or performance and stability are proving troublesome.

Overview for the Developer

Any Access 2000 or later database can import a form called `frmJetUserRoster` from the demonstration database. The user logon form and software demonstrated here are easy to add to your database and can provide you with a list of all the users currently connected to your database.

The functions provided in the demonstration database to log usage of forms and the reports complement the `DoCmd` object's `OpenForm` and `OpenReport` methods. The information that these functions gather provides you with an easy and practical way to assess which parts of your application are being used the most. The computer name and Windows user IDs functions are also handy if you want to set up customized security of your own.

Overview for the Database Administrator

If you administer a reasonably active multi-user Access database, it's a good bet that you'll routinely need to compact it. Less frequently, you'll probably also change objects in your database. Both of these activities require you to ask all the users in your database to log off. To help you with this task, you'll learn a number of different ways to view a list of computers that are accessing your database. You'll also learn how to stop additional users from opening your database when you're trying to shut it down.

Many DBAs will want to log access and changes to certain databases, a feature that allows you to monitor Windows users' IDs and the times when users opened and closed your database or forms and reports in your database.

Overview for the IT Manager

The IT manager has a lot to gain from Access surveillance. Viewing user lists and logs can give you quantitative information on database use. This information is useful for deciding whether you need to upgrade to an industrial-strength database, such as a SQL Server, or invest additional money in improving your Access database software and database design.

The object logging functions can provide quantitative information on the use of forms and reports in your database. This sort of information allows you to focus the development effort on the most used elements of your Access database. It may also allow you to decide whether you can remove under-used parts of the application, saving you money on long-term development and maintenance costs.

NOTE   If the "S" word—"surveillance"—raises images of Big Brother, then I'm glad that I have your attention. You may want to refer this sort of data collection to a company ethics committee if you see any problem with the technology that is demonstrated in this chapter.

The Jet User Roster Form

`Access 2000 or later`

As I was putting this chapter together, I kept hunting for a surveillance tool that would be easy for readers to implement. Finally, I decided on developing an Access 2000 form called `frmJetUserRoster` (shown in Figure 6-1) that is included in the demonstration database. You can import this form into your database and it should work straight away. The descriptions about the technology behind the form are complex, and you can skip those discussions if you're happy with the way the form works.

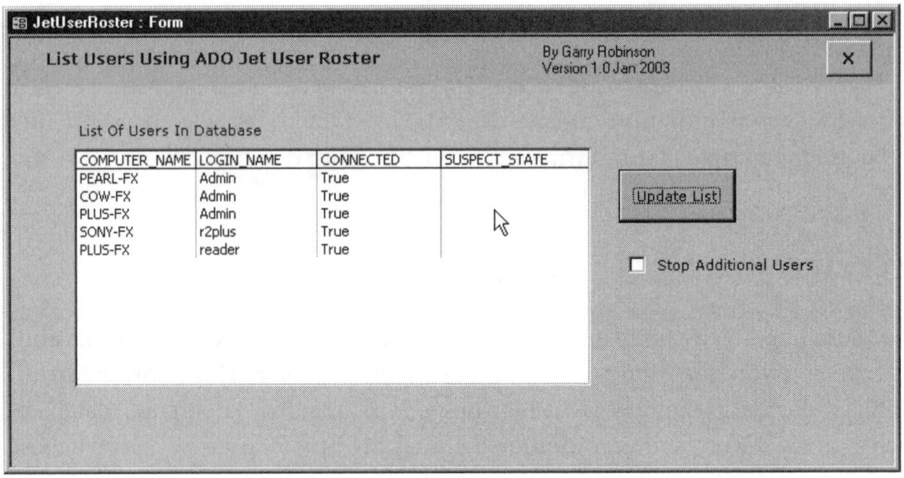

Figure 6-1. The Jet User Roster form, which shows users in a database.

So what does `frmJetUserRoster` do? When the form opens, the onLoad event triggers VBA code to generate a list of computer names, Access workgroup names, and two codes that show the state of the users' connection to the current database.

NOTE Workgroup security is also referred to as user-level security in Access help manuals and other Access books.

This list includes all the users who are currently connected to the database. The user list is obtained by using an ActiveX Data Objects (ADO) schema rowset (see the description following) that has been specially written for Access databases. Adding the `frmJetUserRoster` form to your database is relatively hassle free because the ADO library is fully set up on any computer that has a default installation of Access 2000 and 2002. This form will work in Access 97 and will work with a reference to the Microsoft ActiveX Data Objects 2.1 Library (or later).

NOTE ADO consists of three libraries: 1) the Microsoft ActiveX Data Objects 2.x library that I use in this chapter, 2) the Microsoft ADO Ext. 2.1 for DDL and Security, and 3) the Microsoft Jet and Replication Objects 2.1 library. You don't need a library reference to either of the latter two for anything demonstrated in this chapter. Find out more in the "Further Reading" section at the end of this chapter.

The list box on the `frmJetUserRoster` demonstration form displays the following information:

- Computer Name, which identifies the workstation as specified in the Control Panel under Network for NT/Windows 98 or System for Windows XP/2000.

- Login Name, which specifies the Access workgroup user name the user entered to log on to the database. If the user name and password prompt does not appear, this field returns Admin, the default Access user name. An exception to this rule is when a Windows shortcut file or an executable supplies the user name and password to open the database.

- Connected, which returns True (-1) if there's a corresponding user lock in the .LDB file. If the connection is False, this column indicates issues that may lead to corruption of the database.

- Suspect State, which returns True (-1) if the user has left the database in a suspect state. This state can happen if a computer loses power, Windows crashes, or other unnatural events occur. Otherwise, this value is Null.

NOTE Connection and suspect state problems indicate that you may need to review issues that cause corruption in the database. See Microsoft Knowledge Base Article No. 109953 for more information.

Preventing More Users from Logging On

One of the features of the `frmJetUserRoster` form is a check box that allows you to stop additional users from logging on to the database. Once you have selected the Stop Additional Users check box, you can be confident that no new users will connect or open the database. If a user opens the database, he or she will receive a warning (shown in Figure 6-2) and will be shut out of the database.

Figure 6-2. Warning received when users try to connect to a database that has been locked.

NOTE   Database Administrators: Introduced in Access 2000, formal control of the development process is available to you through shared and exclusive ownership of the database. This control is important because you will regularly be involved with issues that arise from exclusive ownership requirements when you are trying to upgrade the database. In all versions of Access, you will need exclusive rights to the database to undertake very necessary maintenance, such as compacting and repairing. That's why obtaining user lists and stopping more people from logging on to the database is very important.

Retrieving the User Roster by Using VBA Code

When you click the Update List button (shown in Figure 6-1), you start the following VBA subroutine. This subroutine includes establishing your ADO connection by using the CurrentProject object. Now a recordset is established because the OpenSchema method of the Connection object responds to a unique text string, called a global unique identifier (GUID); specifically, {947bb102-5d43-11d1-bdbf-00c04fb92675}.

```
Private Sub updateList_Click()

' Find a list of users in an Access database by using the JetUserRoster
' data provider that is provided with the ADO library.

Dim adoRS As New ADODB.Recordset
Dim i As Long, j As Long, strUserList As String
```

```
On Error GoTo updateList_Error

strUserList = ""
Set adoCn = CurrentProject.Connection

Set adoRS = adoCn.OpenSchema(adSchemaProviderSpecific, , _
"{947bb102-5d43-11d1-bdbf-00c04fb92675}")
```

Now that you have established the recordset, you will find that it has a row for every Access session that has opened the database plus four columns of information, as illustrated in Figure 6-1.

A four-column list box then shows the recordset by using the following steps:

1. The field names of the recordset produce the headers.

2. The four columns of the schema information are added to these headers, and all this information is stored in a semicolon-delimited text string.

3. To display the string, set the rowsource property of the list box to the text string with the schema headers and semicolon-delimited data.

NOTE   You may need look at the properties of the list box in the form to see exactly how this is displayed.

```
' Generate the list of all users in the current database.

strUserList = adoRS.Fields(0).Name & ";" & adoRS.Fields(1).Name & _
            ";" & adoRS.Fields(2).Name & ";" & adoRS.Fields(3).Name & ";"

While Not adoRS.EOF
  strUserList = strUserList & TrimToNull(adoRS.Fields(0)) & ";" & _
              TrimToNull(adoRS.Fields(1)) & ";" & _
              TrimToNull(adoRS.Fields(2)) & ";" & _
              TrimToNull(adoRS.Fields(3)) & ";"
  adoRS.MoveNext
Wend

DisplayJetRoster.RowSource = strUserList
```

Now the form procedure uses a special property of the ADO connection object, which allows us to stop any more users from logging on to the database. This property can be set to True or False, as shown here, and will work only if you select the Stop Additional Users check box.

```
Const NewConnectStop = 1
Const NewConnectOK = 2

If chkStopMoreUsers = True Then

' Stop additional users from logging on to the database.
  adoCn.Properties("Jet OLEDB:Connection Control") = NewConnectStop
  MsgBox "The database is now locked to new users" & _
    vbCrLf & vbCrLf & "Open a new instance of the database to see the warning " & _
    "that the user receives when the database is locked", _
    vbInformation, "Database Locked."

ElseIf chkStopMoreUsers = False Then
' You can now allow users to open the database again.
  adoCn.Properties("Jet OLEDB:Connection Control") = NewConnectOK

End If
```

The user roster recordset isn't quite as simple to decode as the Microsoft MSDN examples lead you to believe. If you try to display the user list in a combo box, a list box, or save the information in the table, you will find that the information in the recordset has a null character at the end of each field of text. This null can create some unwanted outcomes. To resolve this problem, I've written a function called TrimToNull that removes these unnecessary characters from the end of the string (as follows).

```
Private Function TrimToNull(valueReq As Variant) As String

' Make the value a text string.
' Remove all values after the null character.

Dim trimStr As String
Dim nullPos As Long

  On Error GoTo TrimToNull_Err

  trimStr = CStr(valueReq)
```

```
' Locate the terminating null (if any).
  nullPos = InStr(1, trimStr, Chr$(0))
  If nullPos > 0 Then
' Return the characters before it.
    trimStr = Left(trimStr, nullPos - 1)
  Else
    trimStr = trimStr
  End If

TrimToNull_Exit:
  TrimToNull = trimStr
  Exit Function

TrimToNull_Err:
  trimStr = ""
  Resume TrimToNull_Exit

End Function
```

If you find that you want to extend this software to use your own ADO Connection string rather than the CurrentProject Connection string, you may need to read more about connecting to password- and workgroup-secured databases. I provide a link to an article on this material at www.vb123.com in the "Further Reading" section of this chapter, or you might just want to use the Access Workbench, which handles this problem by securely storing your security information.

The LDBView Utility

Access 97 or later

If you have a number of Access databases on which you want to conduct surveillance, you may want to use a specific piece of software that's suited to the job. One tool that you should look at is LDBView, a program that Microsoft wrote for Access 97 that still works well on any database on any version of Access. This program comes as part of a download file from www.microsoft.com called JetUtils.exe. Download this file by using the link provided in the "Further Reading" section at the end of this chapter. On this download, you will find the following:

- The LDBView program, which helps you look at who is using your database.

- A comprehensive white paper on Jet database engine locking and .LDB (locking information) files.

- A program called DBLock that can help you understand record locking conflicts in your database.

From this package, the most important tool is the LDBView utility (shown in Figure 6-3). This program is easy to install and easy to use. Microsoft Knowledge Base Article No. 176670 says that the LDBView accomplishes the following tasks:

- Discover which users have been connected to the database and which users are currently connected to the database.

- Determine which user or users have left the database in a suspect state.

To use the utility, open LDBView.exe and then select a database by choosing File ➤ Open, as shown in Figure 6-3.

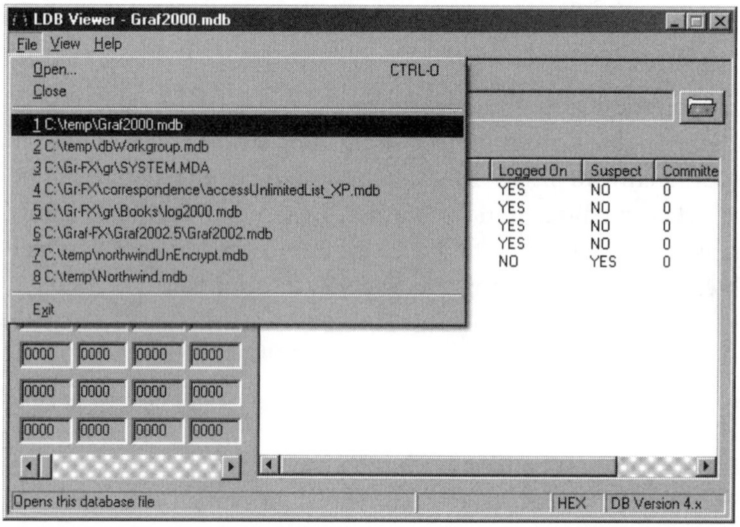

Figure 6-3. Finding a database from which you require a list of users.

The LDBView utility will work only if someone has the database open (in shared mode) and an .LDB file is generated. Once you have selected the database, you will see a form similar to that shown in Figure 6-4.

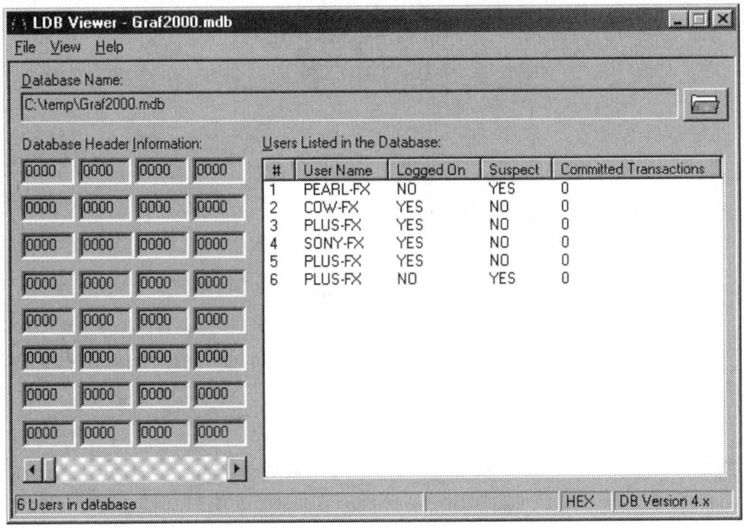

Figure 6-4. LDB Viewer, showing a list of users in a database.

The list on the right side of that form shows the following important information:

- User Name, which identifies the workstation as specified in the Control Panel under Network for NT/Windows 98 or System for Windows XP/2000.

- Logged On, which specifies the Access workgroup user name the user entered to log on to the database. If the user name and password prompt does not appear, this field returns Admin, the default Access user name.

- Suspect State, which returns True if the user has left the database in a suspect state. Otherwise, this value is Null.

- Committed Transactions, an integer value whose purpose this author was unable to determine. In addition, Access 97 databases were the only version where this column was populated.

CAUTION If you are using Access 2000, the suspect state will have a value of Yes once a user logs off. Also, the number of committed transactions will always remain 0. The database header information also always remains 0, but you really need to consider finding a *new life* if you find this interesting. When everyone closes down the database, the connection to the database ceases and the display is cleared.

The LDBView utility has the advantage that it looks directly at the .LDB file and skips Access security such as database passwords and workgroup security. Please note that the .LDB file holds no information that will compromise your database's security.

A Little More on the .LDB File

Whenever you open an Access database, Access will open a file with the same name as the database and an extension of .LDB. This file type is known as a locking information file. For example, if you open Northwind.mdb in the samples directory of your Access/Office installation, a file called Northwind.ldb will be generated. This new file keeps track of users and the locking status of every object that requires some form of locking in the database. When all users have exited the database by closing it in an orderly manner, Access will close the .LDB file and delete it.

The internals of the .LDB file are important for database sharing. The file stores the computer name and workgroup file security names of those users who are currently logged on to the database (with the occasional exception). It also stores the objects that that user has open or locked in a special and flexible part of the workgroup file.

NOTE   Access needs to delete the .LDB file when it closes so that replicated databases work properly and to allow for performance improvements when determining which other users have locks. Therefore, everyone who uses the folder in which the database is stored will need write and delete permissions for files in that folder. You will find out more about Windows folder permissions in Chapter 12.

To find out more about the .LDB format, read the white paper *Understanding Microsoft Jet Locking (LDB Files)* by Kevin Collins. This paper is included in the LDBView download files, or you can find a link to it in the "Further Reading" section with other .LDB pages at the end of this chapter.

The Who Logged On Form

I've included a form in the demonstration database called frmWhoLoggedOn. (Australian Mark McNally wrote the form in 1996, as far as I can tell.) This form shows you how to read an .LDB file directly and displays the results in a list box. This form continues to show users after they have logged off until Access deletes the .LDB file. This file may be of interest if you want to find all users who have attached to a database rather than just those who were in the database when you looked at the user roster through ADO or the LDBView utility.

The Access Workbench

`Access 97 or later`

I have written an Access Workbench program that uses newer technology to find out information similar to the LDBView. The Access Workbench program uses the ADO Jet User Roster form I described earlier. This program—version 1.3, which is quite a popular download—is available to be downloaded and comes with free registration that is described in Appendix B. This program has an advantage over the LDBView in that it also lists the name of the Access workgroup user name that the user has selected to log on to the database.

Using the Access Workbench

In the following instructions, I will show you how you can use the Access Workbench to find who is using an Access database. Before you start, please following the installation instructions in Appendix B.

1. Open the Access Workbench by choosing Start ➤ Programs ➤ vb123.com ➤ Access Workbench.

2. Click Select and browse to the folder where your database is kept (shown in Figure 6-5).

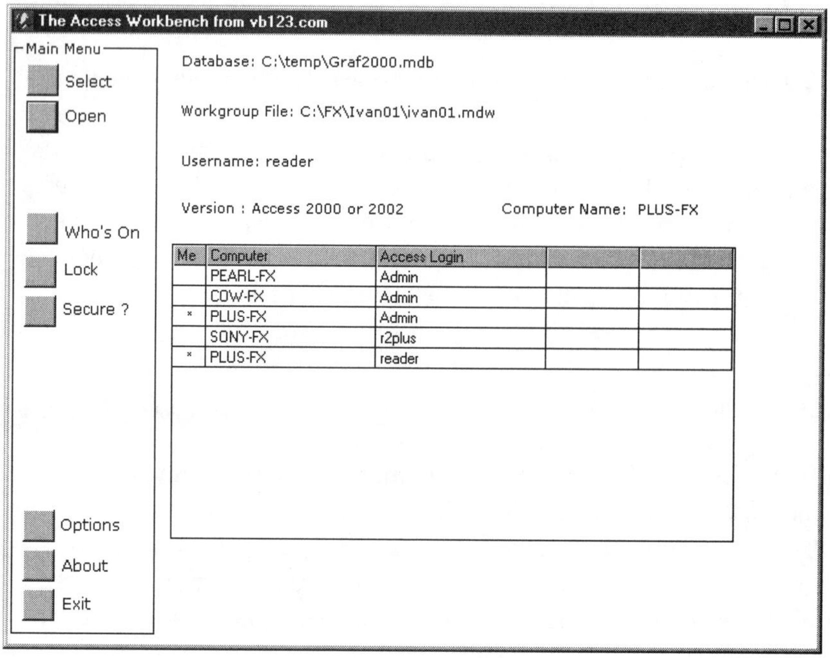

Figure 6-5. The Access Workbench, showing a list of computers in a database.

3. Choose from any of the Access databases that are in the current directory, including normal databases (.MDB), compiled databases (.MDE), and workgroup files (.MDW). You can also select from Access locking databases (.LDB).

4. Once you have selected the database, a list of users who are currently logged on to the database will appear on the form (shown in Figure 6-5).

5. Click the Who's On button (F5) to refresh the list of users who are currently logged on to the database.

Five columns appear on the Access Workbench, as follows.

- Me. An asterisk appears in this column if you're viewing the database.

- Computer. This column shows the actual computer name on which the Access session is taking place.

- Access Login. Specifies the Access workgroup user name that the user entered to log on to the database. If the user name and password prompt does not appear as you log on to Access, this field returns Admin, the default Access user name.

- Skipped LDB (hidden unless a database error has occurred). This column shows users who have avoided using the locking database. Values in this column are very rare.

- Suspect Exit (hidden unless a database error has occurred). This column shows users whose Access session ended abruptly. An abrupt close can happen if a computer loses power or other such rare events.

If you think that a workgroup has secured a database and you have Admin users in this list, then it is possible that your workgroup security has not been set up correctly.

Secure Workgroups and Password-Protected Databases

One complication of using the `frmJetUserRoster` form is that it requires you to adjust the ADO connection string if your database uses password protection or workgroup security. The workbench adjusts for this as follows:

- If an Access database password secures your database, the Access Workbench will ask you to enter it.

- Some Access databases may be protected through workgroup security. If that is the case, you will need to set up details about the workgroup, the workgroup administrator, and its password before you can retrieve a list of people who are using your database. Figure 6-6 shows the warning message that appears when the Access Workbench doesn't have this security information.

DB Pwd

Options

About

Exit

The software has been unable to refresh the list of computers/users due to protection issues. If the database is password protected, choose the { DB Pwd } button on the left. If your database is secured by a workgroup or you are using the wrong workgroup, choose the Options button to setup your workgroup and username/password.

Figure 6-6. The no security details warning from the Access Workbench.

Locking Out Users

The Access Workbench provides the same facility as the `frmJetUserRoster` form in that it uses ADO to stop additional users from logging into a database. This worthwhile management tool works best for databases that have more than a handful of users. To use it in this version of the Access Workbench, click the Lock button.

Other Commercial Software

FMS recently brought out a new product called Total Access Admin. This product uses a similar approach to many of the techniques discussed here for logging users and stopping new users from logging on. You can find a link for this product in the "Further Reading" section at the end of this chapter.

Logging Windows Users, Computers, and Access Accounts

Access 97 or later

Because it is not feasible on most networks to restrict the use of a computer to a single person, the computer name provided by the ADO `frmJetUserRoster`, LDBView, and the Access Workbench (already mentioned in this chapter), may not provide enough information to track down an individual. The computer name also makes it difficult to find a user when that user uses a database on a variety of computers. To reduce this confusion, it is good practice to log the Windows user ID each time the user opens the database. Other information that I find useful to log is the Access workgroup user name and the time the person opens and closes the database.

NOTE A Windows user ID is the name that is used to log on to a Windows 2000, Windows XP, Windows NT, or Windows 98 network or computer.

An Access workgroup user name is the name that you select when logging on to Access. Access workgroup user names are explained in more detail in the chapter on workgroup security (Chapter 8).

The demonstration database for this chapter includes a form called `frmUserObjectLogs` (shown in Figure 6-7), which demonstrates what objects you need to log user activity in your database. This form also demonstrates how to log usage of individual Access forms and reports.

frmUserObjectLogs : Form		_ □ ×

User and Object Logs Demonstration   View Code ☐ | × |

Description

[ ]	Open the userlogging form	The userlogging form writes a log of when a person enters and exits a database.
[ ]	View the userlogs table	The userlog table stores the user access to the database. This can be used to find out who is using the database at the current time.
[ ]	Open a form and log username and time	These buttons show how to open either a form or a report and log the username and time the object was opened to the UserObjectLogs table.
[ ]	Open a report and log username and time	The openForm and OpenReport functions have been setup so that they are like the doCmd.OpenForm and doCmd.OpenReport
[ ]	Open object logs table	The objectslog table stores information as to when a form or a report was opened and by whom. This can be used to find out what is being used in a database for software management.

Import the UserLogs, UserObjectLogs tables into your database. You will also need to import the FXL8_UserLogs form, FXL8_Startup module and FXL8_UsersLoggedInNow query into your database.

Review the code under the buttons and copy what you need.

Figure 6-7. The `frmUserObjectLogs` *form shows how to log users and object use.*

Here's a list of what you will need to import into your database to make the demonstration examples work.

- `UserLogs` table

- `UserObjectLogs` table

- `frmMakeUserLogs` form

- `basGR8_Startup` module

- `qryGR8_UsersLoggedInNow` query

- `rptGR8_UserLogs` report

 User Story *A database that I've been working on for the last three years has about 25 different users every day who either make changes or run reports and query information. When I have to sort out problems or upgrade the software, the first task is always to ask all the users to log off the database. After a bit of "polite shouting" across the desks, we generally reduce the list to about five remaining users. These people can usually be found at meetings or buying a coffee downstairs. To find out who these users are and where they are*

*located, I look at the log of Windows user IDs in the database and filter the
list to the names of those who've not logged off during the day. I then have
a few Windows 2000 user IDs that I can give to the manager to find out
where those people sit. Then we try to contact those people and, when all
else fails, we go to their computers and shut them down.*

Initiating a User Log

To generate details that log when the user opens and closes the database, I open
an Access form called frmMakeUserLogs (shown in Figure 6-8). I have designed this
form deliberately to look like a system message. A startup AutoExec macro opens
the frmMakeUserLogs as a hidden form, which the following VBA code snippet
illustrates:

```
DoCmd.OpenForm "frmMakeUserLogs", , , , , acHidden
```

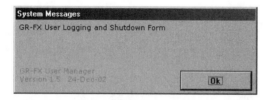

Figure 6-8. The hidden user logging form.

The form's load event in the form frmMakeUserLogs collects information for the
log by using the following VBA code:

```
Dim sqlStr As String
Const dateTimeFmt = "dd-mmm-yyyy hh:mm"

Private Sub Form_Load()

Dim UserNameStr As String, ComputerNameStr As String
dim LoginTime As Date, wkgUserStr As String

Me.visible = False
```

```
' Though this form is important, it should not interfere with the user
' interface. That is why there is a quick exit.

On Error GoTo Quick_Exit

UserNameStr = User_FX
ComputerNameStr = ComputerName_FX
LoginTime = Now
wkgUserStr = CurrentUser
```

The VBA code shown gathers information by using the following functions:

- `User_FX`, which finds the Windows user ID by using the system that the application programming interface (API) calls.
- `ComputerName _FX`, which finds the computer name by using the system that API calls.
- `CurrentUser`, which returns the current workgroup user name.

Now that we have that vital information, we need to save it to the UserLogs table (shown in Figure 6-9).

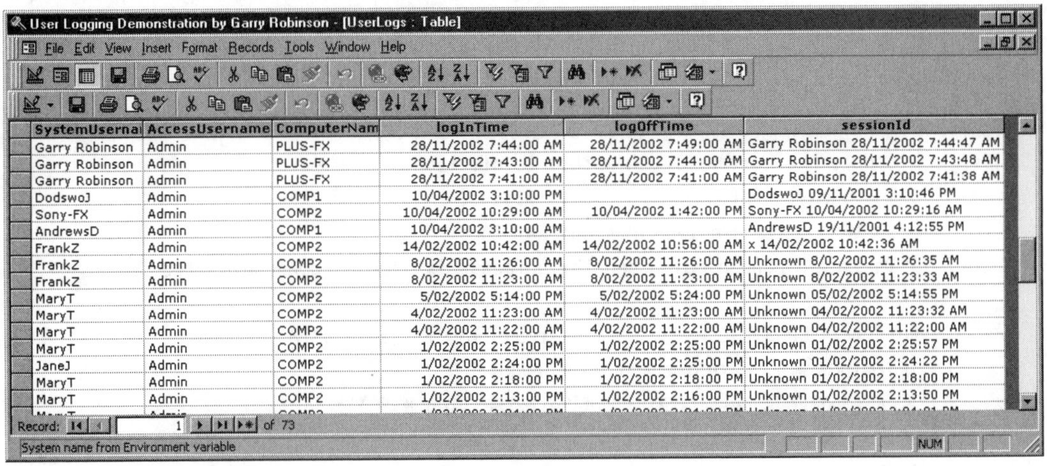

SystemUserna	AccessUsername	ComputerNam	logInTime	logOffTime	sessionId
Garry Robinson	Admin	PLUS-FX	28/11/2002 7:44:00 AM	28/11/2002 7:49:00 AM	Garry Robinson 28/11/2002 7:44:47 AM
Garry Robinson	Admin	PLUS-FX	28/11/2002 7:43:00 AM	28/11/2002 7:44:00 AM	Garry Robinson 28/11/2002 7:43:48 AM
Garry Robinson	Admin	PLUS-FX	28/11/2002 7:41:00 AM	28/11/2002 7:41:00 AM	Garry Robinson 28/11/2002 7:41:38 AM
DodswoJ	Admin	COMP1	10/04/2002 3:10:00 PM		DodswoJ 09/11/2001 3:10:46 PM
Sony-FX	Admin	COMP2	10/04/2002 10:29:00 AM	10/04/2002 1:42:00 PM	Sony-FX 10/04/2002 10:29:16 AM
AndrewsD	Admin	COMP1	10/04/2002 3:10:00 AM		AndrewsD 19/11/2001 4:12:55 PM
FrankZ	Admin	COMP2	14/02/2002 10:42:00 AM	14/02/2002 10:56:00 AM	x 14/02/2002 10:42:36 AM
FrankZ	Admin	COMP2	8/02/2002 11:26:00 AM	8/02/2002 11:26:00 AM	Unknown 8/02/2002 11:26:35 AM
FrankZ	Admin	COMP2	8/02/2002 11:23:00 AM	8/02/2002 11:23:00 AM	Unknown 8/02/2002 11:23:33 AM
MaryT	Admin	COMP2	5/02/2002 5:14:00 PM	5/02/2002 5:24:00 PM	Unknown 05/02/2002 5:14:55 PM
MaryT	Admin	COMP2	4/02/2002 11:23:00 AM	4/02/2002 11:23:00 AM	Unknown 04/02/2002 11:23:32 AM
MaryT	Admin	COMP2	4/02/2002 11:22:00 AM	4/02/2002 11:22:00 AM	Unknown 04/02/2002 11:22:00 AM
MaryT	Admin	COMP2	1/02/2002 2:25:00 PM	1/02/2002 2:25:00 PM	Unknown 01/02/2002 2:25:57 PM
JaneJ	Admin	COMP2	1/02/2002 2:24:00 PM	1/02/2002 2:25:00 PM	Unknown 01/02/2002 2:24:22 PM
MaryT	Admin	COMP2	1/02/2002 2:18:00 PM	1/02/2002 2:18:00 PM	Unknown 01/02/2002 2:18:00 PM
MaryT	Admin	COMP2	1/02/2002 2:13:00 PM	1/02/2002 2:16:00 PM	Unknown 01/02/2002 2:13:50 PM

Figure 6-9. The UserLogs table, which stores logging details at time of entry and exit.

A SQL insert statement generates the log when the user opens the database, as follows:

```
Me!txtSession = UserNameStr & " " & LoginTime
DoCmd.SetWarnings False

sqlStr = "insert into UserLogs " & _
  "( SystemUsername, AccessUsername, ComputerName, loginTime, sessionID ) " & _
  " values ('" & UserNameStr & "','" & wkgUserStr & "','" & ComputerNameStr & _
  "',#" & Format(LoginTime, dateTimeFmt) & "#,'" & Me!txtSession & "')"
DoCmd.RunSQL sqlStr

Quick_Exit:
DoCmd.SetWarnings True
End Sub
```

Completing the User Log

Of importance is the key field in the UserLogs table, which includes the Windows user ID and the time. The key field value is first stored in a hidden text field on the form and added to the UserLogs table (demonstrated by the previous insert SQL statement). You then reuse that key field value by using the form close event to update the time that the person logged off into the table by using an update SQL statement, as follows:

```
Private Sub Form_Close()

' Update the current logon with a logoff time.
' You always want this process to finish,
' so turn off error messages and warnings.
' It should happen only when the database is closing down normally.

sqlStr = "UPDATE UserLogs SET UserLogs.logOffTime = #" & _
  Format(Now(), dateTimeFmt) & "# WHERE " & _
  " (((UserLogs.sessionID)='" & Me!txtSession & "'));"

On Error Resume Next
DoCmd.SetWarnings False
DoCmd.RunSQL sqlStr
DoCmd.SetWarnings True
On Error GoTo 0

End Sub
```

You may be curious to know how the form closes when the user shuts down Access. Thankfully, Access closes all open forms when it shuts down, and the close form event will be fired. If the database is shut down by an unforeseen event, such as a power failure, the open forms are not closed properly and the UserLogs table will not have an entry in the LogOffTime column (shown in Figure 6-9).

To view this information, you can either go directly to the UserLogs table or view the information in a query or a report. The rptGR8_UserLogs report (shown in Figure 6-10) summarizes the number of times that users have opened a database (logged on), when they last opened it, and whether they still have the database open. This information is quite useful for administration purposes.

Microsoft Access User Logs

System Username	No. Times Logged In	Last Date Logged In	Total Hours Logged In	Logged In Now
Garry Robinson	52	03-Sep-03	19.0	Yes
AndrewsD	4	10-Apr-02	16.9	
DodswoJ	3	10-Apr-02	6.0	
FrankZ	4	14-Feb-02	0.2	
JaneJ	1	01-Feb-02	0.0	
MarsfieldG	7	20-Nov-01	25.7	
MaryT	8	05-Feb-02	0.2	
Owner	1	08-Jun-03	0.3	
PetersC	1	21-Nov-01	0.1	
SmithJ	1	21-Nov-01		
Sony-FX	1	10-Apr-02	3.2	
ThatcherD	4	21-Nov-01	19.7	

Figure 6-10. A report that shows Windows user ID information.

The final piece of administration that I like to handle with this frmMakeUserLogs form is closing down the database at midnight by using the form timer event, as follows:

```
Private Sub Form_Timer()

' Close the database at midnight (in case anyone has left it on).
' This step closes the database in a safe manner, saving all open
' database objects.

If Hour(Time()) = 0 And Minute(Time()) < 20 Then

  DoCmd.Quit acQuitSaveAll

End If

End Sub
```

NOTE   Surveillance works best if you manage your startup properties well, as described in the startup properties chapter (Chapter 2).

I like to use this method this because it leaves the database free for early morning maintenance. Now I will discuss how to conduct surveillance at the object level.

Recording When Objects Are Opened   `Access 97 or later`

Another important surveillance technique that I have used is to log the Windows user ID and time when a person opens an Access form or report. This information is useful as the precursor to implementing more stringent security measures because it can help you diagnose if you have a problem in the first place.

So how and why will you do this? To make the transition to object logging easy, I've created two functions that mimic the DoCmd.OpenForm and DoCmd.OpenReport methods. You use these functions to log the Windows user ID and the current time when users open the form or the report. The best way to illustrate this function is first to show the old VBA code, as follows:

```
Docmd.OpenForm  "AnotherForm", acNormal
Docmd.OpenReport "rptGR8_UserObjectLogs", acPreview
```

The converted code follows:

```
OpenForm_FX "AnotherForm", acNormal
OpenReport_FX " rptGR8_UserObjectLogs", acPreview
```

As you can see, there is very little difference between the two methods of opening the form and report. Once I have tested this function in a live database, I have found it relatively simple to do global find-and-replaces to change all the `DoCmd.Open` methods in the VBA project. We will examine these two functions in more detail later in this chapter.

 User Story *The same 25-user database that I described ear-lier had been earmarked for a total conversion to Visual Basic 6 and SQL Server. Converting this database was necessary because other software and databases required information from this database so its reliability was very important. The IT manager was keen to convert only the forms and reports from the database that were still in constant use. Because there were 100 reports, reducing that list to 50 would bring considerable savings in development time.*

To find the active reports, I integrated the object logging software into the database and let it run for a couple of months. Then, when the IT manager attended design meetings with users, he could provide quantitative information, such as "This report has been used only once in two months." This specific information was more useful than asking users who generally answer, "We use all those reports" when questioned about the list of reports. I generally display this table in a summarized format by using the rptGR8_UserObjectLogs *report (shown in Figure 6-11). This report shows the object and its frequency of use. It also shows the last Windows user IDs to open the form or report. This user can then assist in determining why that form or report is used.*

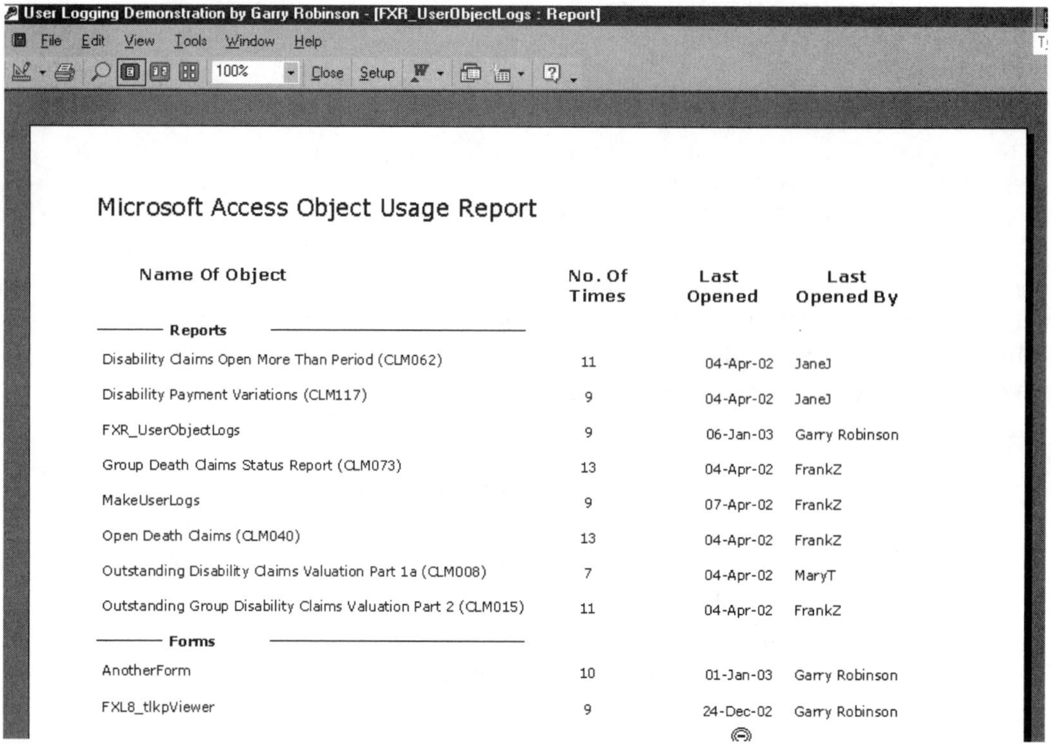

Microsoft Access Object Usage Report

Name Of Object	No. Of Times	Last Opened	Last Opened By
——— **Reports** ———			
Disability Claims Open More Than Period (CLM062)	11	04-Apr-02	JaneJ
Disability Payment Variations (CLM117)	9	04-Apr-02	JaneJ
FXR_UserObjectLogs	9	06-Jan-03	Garry Robinson
Group Death Claims Status Report (CLM073)	13	04-Apr-02	FrankZ
MakeUserLogs	9	07-Apr-02	FrankZ
Open Death Claims (CLM040)	13	04-Apr-02	FrankZ
Outstanding Disability Claims Valuation Part 1a (CLM008)	7	04-Apr-02	MaryT
Outstanding Group Disability Claims Valuation Part 2 (CLM015)	11	04-Apr-02	FrankZ
——— **Forms** ———			
AnotherForm	10	01-Jan-03	Garry Robinson
FXL8_tlkpViewer	9	24-Dec-02	Garry Robinson

Figure 6-11. The rptGR8_UserObjectLogs *report, showing activity for forms and reports.*

Using VBA Code to Log Use of Individual Access Forms and Reports

Now that you have seen how useful this object logging software can be in working out what parts of the database are being used and when, let's have a look under the hood to see what actual code was used. You can find the procedures to open and log a form and a report in the demonstration database in a module called basGR8_Startup. Now I will review each of these functions.

The OpenForm_FX Function

This function uses the same arguments as DoCmd.OpenForm to open the form and logs the Windows user ID and time when it was called. To use it, substitute OpenForm_FX for DoCmd.OpenForm and keep all the other arguments the same.

The following sample VBA code shows how you can open a form called `MyForm` in datasheet mode and only show records from the company Acme, for example:

```
OpenForm_FX "MyForm", acFormDS,,"Company='Acme'"
```

After opening, the `OpenForm_FX` function logs the user details to the `UserObjectsLogs` table, as follows:

```
Public Const dateTimeFmt = "dd-mmm-yyyy hh:mm"
Function OpenForm_FX(formName As String, Optional viewType As Variant, _
          Optional filterName As Variant, Optional WhereCondition As Variant, _
          Optional DataMode As Variant, Optional WindowMode As Variant, _
          Optional OpenArgs As Variant)
On Error GoTo OpenForm_FX_Error

If IsMissing(viewType) Then
  viewType = acNormal
End If
If IsMissing(WhereCondition) Then
  WhereCondition = Null
End If
If IsMissing(DataMode) Then
  DataMode = acFormPropertySettings
End If
If IsMissing(WindowMode) Then
  WindowMode = acWindowNormal
End If

' Open the form by using the arguments provided.
DoCmd.OpenForm formName, viewType, filterName, WhereCondition, DataMode, _
                WindowMode, OpenArgs
' Log the user information to a table.
Call UserObjectLogs_FX(formName, acForm)

OpenForm_FX_Exit:

  Exit Function

OpenForm_FX_Error:
  MsgBox "Error Number { " & Err.Number & " } " & vbCrLf & vbCrLf & _
    Err.Description, vbExclamation, "Problems with OpenForm_FX"
  GoTo OpenForm_FX_Exit
End Function
```

TIP I have found that it is better to first use the Access DoCmd.OpenForm procedure to first test the way that the form opens before converting to the OpenForm_FX function.

From a programming viewpoint, the OpenForm_FX function is interesting because it uses the optional parameter in the functions arguments, which allows you to leave out values while calling the function by using VBA code. To handle these optional arguments, the function uses the IsMissing function to find the unused arguments and thereafter adds the default value instead. Now I will show you how to use a function that works in the same way to open a report.

The OpenReport_FX Function

To log the use of a report and the person's computer and user name, you can substitute OpenReport_FX for DoCmd.OpenReport and keep all the other arguments the same:

```
OpenReport_FX "MyReport", acPreview,,"Company='Acme'"
```

This code opens MyReport in preview mode and shows information only for the company Acme. After opening, it logs the user name and computer to the UserObjectsLogs table.

The Time Logging Functions

Finally, both the OpenForm_FX and OpenReport_FX functions handle logging through a subroutine called UserObjectLogs_FX. This subroutine logs an object's Windows user ID and time.

```
Public Sub UserObjectLogs_FX(ObjectName As String, ObjectType As Integer)
On Error Resume Next
Dim UserNameStr As String, ObjectTime As Date, sqlStr As String
UserNameStr = User_FX
ObjectTime = Now
DoCmd.SetWarnings False
```

```
sqlStr = "insert into UserObjectLogs " & _
 "( SystemUsername, ObjectName, ObjectType, OpenTime ) " & _
 " values ('" & UserNameStr & "','" & ObjectName & "'," & _
 ObjectType & ", #" & Format(ObjectTime, dateTimeFmt) & "#)"

DoCmd.RunSQL sqlStr
DoCmd.SetWarnings True

End Sub
```

If you are wondering how good this function will be in identifying single record changes and deletions, you will probably guess that it is a quite a coarse logging system and may not suffice for that sort of surveillance. Nevertheless, for most systems that have only a few users, logging the open data event can be quite a revelation, especially if you find that certain people are using forms and reports that you never planned that they should use. At this stage, you really can plan the next stage of your security.

In the next section, I will explain the VBA code that you need to retrieve the different user information that I have been demonstrating for the different logging systems.

Retrieving the Computer Name, Windows User ID, and Access Workgroup ID by Using VBA Code   Access 97 or later

In Microsoft Windows NT or Windows 95 or later, you can use the Win32 application programming interface (API) to retrieve network information, such as the user name, workgroup, and computer name, about the currently running computer.

Access does not offer the built-in functionality to access the computer's current user name. You can, however, use the Declare statement in a VBA procedure to call a Microsoft Windows function that will return the current user name.

NOTE An application programming interface (API) is a set of routines that application programs use to request and perform lower-level services. The operating system performs these lower-level services.

When you need capabilities that go beyond the core language and controls provided with VBA, you can make direct calls to procedures contained in dynamic-link libraries (DLLs). By calling procedures in DLLs, you can access the thousands of procedures that form the backbone of the Microsoft Windows operating system, as well as routines written in other languages.

As their name suggests, DLLs are libraries of procedures that applications can link to and use at runtime rather than link to statically at compile time. The libraries can be updated independently of the application, and many applications can share a single DLL. Microsoft Windows itself uses many of these DLLs, and other applications call the procedures within these libraries to display Windows and graphics, manage memory, or perform other tasks.

You can find the procedures to retrieve the Windows user ID, computer name, and workgroup ID in a module called basGR8_Startup in the demonstration database.

Probably the most important item of information that you need to retrieve for logging is the Windows user ID. Figure 6-12 shows the Windows XP fast logon form. In this case, the Windows user ID could be either "Garry Robinson" or "Guest."

Figure 6-12. The Windows XP user ID as shown in fast user switching mode.

Retrieving the Windows User ID

To retrieve the Windows user ID, you have to leave the confines of Access VBA and venture into Windows API programming. Though this may seem a little risky and difficult, I can assure you that these examples are both well tested and will work on all Windows platforms from Access 98 and later. First, you need to make a declaration at the top of the module, as follows:

```
Public Declare Function GetUserName Lib "advapi32.dll" _
  Alias "GetUserNameA" (ByVal lpBuffer As String, nSize As Long) As Long
```

This declaration refers to a file called advapi32.dll. You can search for this file in your Windows software directory. Now the VBA code that retrieves the Windows user ID follows:

```
Public Function User_FX() As String
On Error Resume Next
Dim lSize As Long
Dim lpstrBuffer As String, trimStr As String
lSize = 255
lpstrBuffer = Space$(lSize)
If GetUserName(lpstrBuffer, lSize) Then
  User_FX = left$(lpstrBuffer, lSize - 1)
Else
  User_FX = "Unknown"
End If
End Function
```

The following code snippet shows how to use this function:

```
Msgbox "Your Windows User ID is : " & User_FX
```

Retrieving the Computer Name

The second useful piece of information that you will want to log is the name of the currently running computer. This name too is retrieved by using a Windows API and requires a declaration at the top of the module. After that declaration, you will find the code for the module ComputerName_FX:

```
' API declared to find the current computer name.
Public Declare Function GetComputerName Lib "kernel32" Alias _
  "GetComputerNameA" (ByVal lpBuffer As String, nSize As Long) As Long

Public Function ComputerName_FX() As String
' Function calls the API function and returns a string of the computer name.
On Error Resume Next
Dim lSize As Long
Dim lpstrBuffer As String
lSize = 255
lpstrBuffer = Space$(lSize)
If GetComputerName(lpstrBuffer, lSize) Then
  ComputerName_FX = left$(lpstrBuffer, lSize)
Else
  ComputerName_FX = ""
End If
End Function
```

In the next line of code, I show you how you might use this function in your application:

```
Msgbox "The Computer that I am using is called: "  & ComputerName_FX "
```

Retrieving the Workgroup User Name

The other useful piece of information that I like to add to the UserLogs table is the Access workgroup user name. The Access CurrentUser method returns the user name, as shown in the following example:

```
MsgBox("The current user is: " & CurrentUser)
```

If you are wondering what I am talking about when I say logged into a workgroup or workgroup user name, you probably are in the same boat as all database users who don't have workgroup file security. In this case, you most likely have used the workgroup file that does not have a password for the default Admin account. When that happens, you never actually have to enter a user name and password and the CurrentUser function returns "Admin." You may want to test for this Admin account in your software to find users who are using one of these types of workgroups. The following example shows you a test that you can use:

```
If CurrentUser = "Admin " Then
   msgBox "Please use the correct Access workgroup file."
   doCmd.Quit
end if
```

Workgroup file security is an integral part of Access security, so you can rest assured that a lot of black ink will be devoted to that topic in Chapters 8 through 11. But for the time being, let's now explore what we can do to log people who are using our database but have avoided our user surveillance and are opening the database without using our startup software sequences.

Checking for Users Who Skip the Startup Sequence

Access 2000 or later

Because Access offers a variety of ways to open or connect to a database, you cannot ensure that your users will open the database by using the startup form or AutoExec macro that you set up for them. To alleviate this problem, you can turn off accelerator key sequences such as the Allow Bypass key, as explained in Chapter 2 on startup properties.

Wouldn't it be great if you could find out whether people were sneaking into your database by using ways that you haven't protected against? There is a way, and it involves comparing the logged record of all computers whose users opened your database by using your startup sequence (see the section "Logging Windows Users, Computers, and Access Accounts" earlier in this chapter) against the computer names returned from the JetUserRoster schema.

Another way to consider this possible security breach is that if a computer has a connection to a database and it is not in your custom UserLogs table, then that person is not opening the database as planned.

In the Access 2000 demonstration database, you will find a form called frmFindNoStartups that you can use in your database with the other user logging samples for this special monitoring purpose. The VBA code to find these users involves opening a recordset by using a query that retrieves a unique list of all computers that have your database open. To define "currently," I assume that a person has opened the database today and has not closed it.

 NOTE You will need a UserLog table, as described earlier in the chapter.

```
strUserList = ""
Set adoCn = CurrentProject.Connection

sqlStr = "SELECT ComputerName" & _
        " FROM UserLogs" & _
        " WHERE (((Format([loginTime],'yyyy-mm-dd'))=" & _
        " Format(Date(),'yyyy-mm-dd'))" & _
        " AND ((UserLogs.logOffTime) Is Null))" & _
        " GROUP BY UserLogs.ComputerName;"
```

Now you will establish a second ADO recordset that retrieves the `JetUserRoster` form of all the computers that are connected to the current database, as follows:

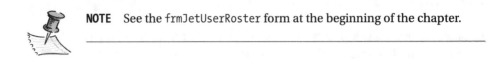

NOTE   See the `frmJetUserRoster` form at the beginning of the chapter.

```
Set usersRS = New ADODB.Recordset
usersRS.Open sqlStr, adoCn ' , adOpenStatic, adLockReadOnly

Set adoRS = adoCn.OpenSchema(adSchemaProviderSpecific, , _
"{947bb102-5d43-11d1-bdbf-00c04fb92675}")

  'Setup the column headers for the list box
strUserList = adoRS.Fields(0).Name & ";" & adoRS.Fields(1).Name & _
        ";" & adoRS.Fields(2).Name & ";" & adoRS.Fields(3).Name & ";"
```

Now you need to move through the `JetUserRoster` recordset one record at a time and compare the computer name against the unique list of computer names in your own UserLogs table. If your computer name is legitimate, you can jump to the next computer name in the roster.

```
While Not adoRS.EOF

' First test whether the computer name is in the the UserLogs table.

  usersRS.MoveFirst
  While Not usersRS.EOF
```

```
   If TrimToNull(adoRS.Fields(0)) = usersRS!ComputerName Then
' Computer has been legitimately logged.
     GoTo userLegitimate
   End If
   usersRS.MoveNext
 Wend
```

If a computer name is not found, then this connection has not opened the startup user logging sequence correctly and needs investigating. You may at this stage want to send an email or open a message box to warn the administrator of a possible security breach.

```
' Computer has not been logged. User has entered the database the wrong way.
  strUserList = strUserList & TrimToNull(adoRS.Fields(0)) & ";" & _
               TrimToNull(adoRS.Fields(1)) & ";" & _
               TrimToNull(adoRS.Fields(2)) & ";" & _
               TrimToNull(adoRS.Fields(3)) & ";"

userLegitimate:

  adoRS.MoveNext

Wend

DisplayJetRoster.RowSource = strUserList

updateList_Exit:
  Set adoRS = Nothing
  Set usersRS = Nothing
  Exit Sub
```

To enhance this form, you can add a timer event to check security breaches on a regular basis.

Further Reading

As you might expect, there is never enough information when it comes to powerful products like Access. To assist you with further investigations, I have put together a Web page with links to Web sites and articles on the issues relating to the material in this chapter. This page includes the following:

- The location of the Jetutils.exe download.

- The latest and the free versions of the Access Workbench, as discussed in Appendix B.

- White paper on *Understanding Microsoft Jet Locking (LDB Files)* by Kevin Collins.

- Where to find the Total Access Admin product from FMS.

- Article on how to use ADO to return a list of users connected to a database (JetUserRoster).

- Papers that discuss the .LDB file and how it works.

- Articles on record locking.

- More on the Jet roster and a technique to identify users.

- Use Connection Control to Prevent User Log On at Run Time in Access 2000 (Microsoft Knowledge Base Article No. 198756).

- How to troubleshoot corruption issues to reduce suspect state and connection problems.

- Access passwords, workgroups, and ADO and customized connection strings.

- How to Shut Down a Database Remotely (Microsoft Knowledge Base Article No. 304408).

- New features in ADO, ADOX, and JRO, including the Jet UserRoster.

- API to Retrieve the Windows User ID (Microsoft Knowledge Base Article No. 152970).

- API to Retrieve the Computer Name (Microsoft Knowledge Base Article No. 148835).

- How to detect idle time or inactivity.

- Learn about ADO and find the latest downloads.

You can find the further reading Web page for this chapter in the Downloads section of the Apress Web site (http://www.apress.com) or at the following address: http://www.vb123.com/map/log.htm.

Reflecting on This Chapter

If you look back on the chapter, you may conclude that you now have a number of ways to monitor your users—and that is certainly the case. The reality over time, however, is that these techniques end up being very useful management tools for assisting you with database management and for reviewing possible software changes, be they for security reasons or just normal improvements. So let's review how you can put in place some of the topics and software discussed in this chapter.

Sometime before you start getting more sophisticated with security and the ensuing issues, like training your users how to do things in a more secure application, it certainly may be worth undertaking surveying your database to find out whether you actually have a problem in the first place. In the first instance, I would recommend that you import the frmJetUserRoster demonstration form into your database to view computer and Access workgroup logon names. This form allows you both to assess the number of users in a database and to understand who is using the database. If you have a large number of databases, you may want to use a tool such as LDBView or the Access Workbench to view this information in any of your databases. Once you have these tools working, you will probably use them to help manage the database for administration issues, such as asking users to log off the database for database or network maintenance and upgrades.

In larger networked environments, the value of the computer names supplied by the Jet User Roster may not be all that useful. At this stage, I find it more informative to use a customized logging system in the database to capture and store the details. This system has the advantage that the UserLog table can store the Windows user IDs plus creates a good record of who has used the database. The Window user ID and the time that the user opened the database are very useful for managing the database users.

Finally, as I explained in the chapter on startup options (Chapter 2), it is possible for users to open your database and skip your startup form or AutoExec macro, and thus, no UserLog entry is generated. The frmFindNoStartups form in the Access 2000 demonstration database can identify this possible security breach.

What's Next?

In the next chapter, we will look at how you can add custom menus and toolbars to your Access database to replace the rather powerful menus that are bundled with Access. This important phase in the development of your database indicates that you can start to remove the complexity from your application. Though developers are usually very entertained by the prospect of hundreds of features, giving end users more than a few options will serve only to confuse them and increase your training costs. Menus also provide added protection to objects and data in your database. Naturally, as soon as you put a menu in place, the developer and the database administrator are going to want to do something more powerful than your own menus and toolbars can provide. The menu chapter shows you how to get around this as well.

Protecting Your Database with Menus and Toolbars

TOOLBARS AND MENUS allow Access users and developers flexible access to all the built-in menu items and, indirectly, to any objects in your database. Though this flexibility is good for a developer's productivity, it is not necessarily so good when it is available to the users of your database. In my experience, most users are interested in software that makes their job easier. Toolbars and menus bulging with developer options (such as the Design View and Database Window commands) probably do not assist in that aim. In addition, if users are technologically competent, they may be tempted to alter the programming objects of your database. Therefore, it is important that you learn how to use both toolbars and menus to set up a good user interface and to protect your database at the same time.

This chapter teaches you first how to build menus and toolbars. Included are plenty of pictures of all the tricky graphical steps that are required. Once you understand how to build toolbars, you will then learn how to apply those toolbars to your database using either form and report properties or the Access startup options. If you combine these skills, you will have a database that is both simple to use and hard for most users to crack. In addition, because users will not see the developer-specific toolbar and menu commands, there will be little visual incentive for your users to wander about your application. To conclude the discussions, the chapter shows you how you can permanently disable the developer-specific commands on end-users' computers.

The demonstration material for this chapter includes a number of forms and Visual Basic for Applications (VBA) examples:

- A form to change the default toolbar and shortcut menu for all forms.

- A form to change the default toolbar and shortcut menu for all reports.

- A form to disable developer-related commands in the built-in menus.

- Code to find all the custom menus and toolbars in a database.

- Code to find all the menu items on a menu.

 NOTE To find the demonstration material, open the download database for your version of Access—for example, grMAP97.mdb—and select Chapter 7.

Will Menus and Toolbars Help Protect My Database?

Menus, toolbars, and the way that they are applied are important cogs in the overall protection of your Access database. Because different audiences will read this chapter, I provide alternative overviews about the important issues covered in this chapter because people in each of these categories will approach the chapter in a different way.

Overview for the IT Manager

Access menus and toolbars are a good way both to protect your database and to make it simpler to use. Your developer or DBA can produce simple custom menus and toolbars at a low cost by using the top-level forms in your database and a subset of the commands that Microsoft installs as part of the Access setup. These custom menus can then be combined with the database startup options to form a reasonable level of protection. Near the end of the chapter, I explain how you can permanently disable some of the developer menu and toolbar commands on an end user's computer.

Overview for the DBA

Creating Access toolbars and menus is not a difficult skill to master, and you can use them to provide a consistent and easy interface for your database users. DBAs should first become familiar with the basics of toolbar design because you can use custom toolbars and menus across all your databases. Once these skills are mastered, DBAs should review in detail the effect of the five toolbar-specific Access startup options. Finally, DBAs should discuss with management whether disabling Access menu options permanently is appropriate for some of your Access users.

Overview for the Developer

Getting started with toolbars and menus in an Access database is all about understanding the little tricks. That mastered, the next skill is knowing how to plug the protection holes that the built-in menus and toolbars provide for users. Once you have those basics mastered, further toolbar development is a balancing act between good interface design and the power that toolbars can bring to your application. This chapter will show you how to set up toolbars, menus, and shortcut menus. The download software will ensure that your entire application is using your menus and toolbars, and the discussions on startup options will show you how and why these options are important for your database protection. In addition, you may want to discuss with your manager or clients whether it is appropriate to disable menu items permanently on your end users' computers. Finally, some additional samples in the download database show you how to program the CommandBar object to manipulate the toolbars.

Building Toolbars, Menus, and Shortcut Menus

Access 97 or later

What is a toolbar? A toolbar is primarily a collection of buttons or text and can occasionally include other controls such as combo boxes and text boxes. A toolbar can be organized horizontally, vertically, or in a floating rectangle. Its appearance in the Access window depends on whether it is defined as a menu, a toolbar, or a shortcut menu. Because menu bars and shortcut menus are just different types of toolbars, you can customize all three the same way. Though you probably will be very familiar with toolbars and menus, you may not be conversant with the terminology. Figure 7-1 illustrates the different types of toolbars. These are:

- A horizontal menu bar that runs across the window with commands such as File, Edit, and View.

- A vertical menu bar with commands such as New Database and Open Database. The vertical menu bar will normally be attached to a menu bar.

- A toolbar, which is a collection of buttons and sometimes text, that can be organized in rectangles anywhere within the Access window. Sometimes you can position toolbars next to each other in the same row. Sometimes multiple toolbars may not fit into the space across or down the screen but are flexible enough that users can generally place them where they want in the Access window.

- A special vertical menu called a shortcut menu (or pop-up menu). This menu appears when you right-click a form, report, other objects, and some form controls.

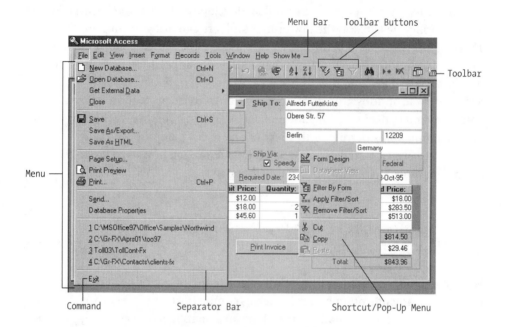

Figure 7-1. Menus, toolbars, and shortcut menus.

Menus and toolbars behave in different ways in your application, depending on whether or not Microsoft developed it. Menus placed on your computer at the same time as the Access installation are called built-in menus. You can customize built-in menus on your computer, and these changes will never appear on any other computer. Therefore, you have to be aware that manually modifying built-in menus will not provide much protection for your database.

A custom menu is a menu or toolbar that you create for your application. Custom menus allow you to create a user interface within your own Access database that has the look and feel of a Microsoft Windows application. If you create a custom menu for a database, that menu will be available only within that database. It is possible to share menus and toolbars between databases by referencing another database, but I advise sharing only if you are using the referenced database as a code library. Within the menu environment you can create, delete, and rename your own custom toolbars, menu bars (including submenus), and shortcut menus.

Building a Custom Toolbar Menu

The easiest custom menu that you can add to your database is a toolbar. The first custom toolbar that you should design for your database is one to replace the built-in Form View toolbar. This built-in toolbar has a number of developer-specific commands (such as Design View and Database Window). Therefore, if you create a version that is suited to users, this custom toolbar will protect your application and reduce clutter by removing a number of buttons from your user interface.

Now I will show you the steps to create a custom toolbar. The purpose of the toolbar will be to provide users with buttons that are suited to forms with records. For these instructions, I will use a copy of the Northwind database, and I suggest that you do likewise.

1. First, open the Customize dialog either by choosing View ➤ Toolbars ➤ Customize, as shown in Figure 7-2, or by right-clicking any toolbar or menu and choosing Customize, as shown in Figure 7-3.

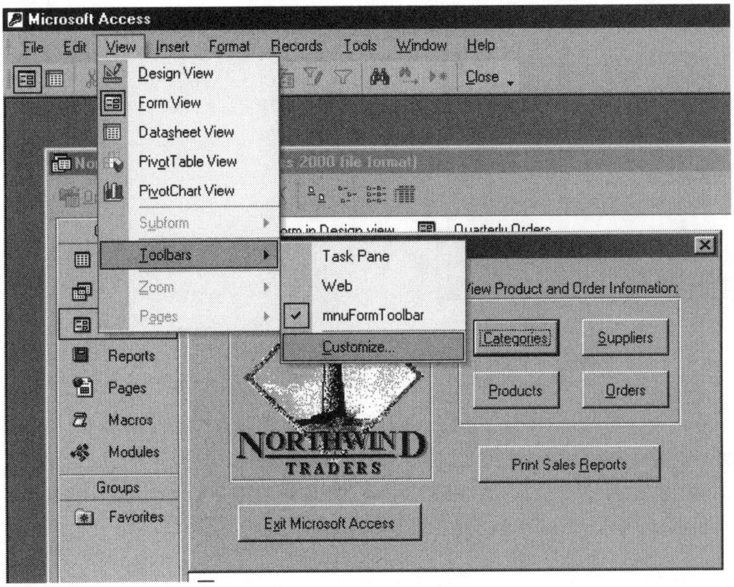

Figure 7-2. Customizing toolbars by using the View menu.

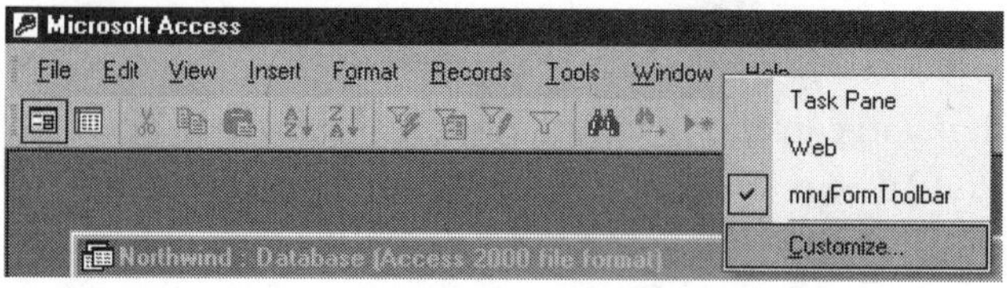

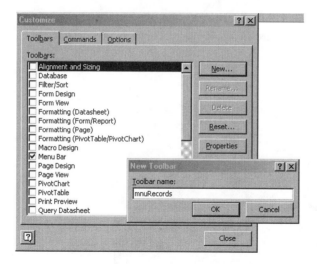

Figure 7-3. Customizing toolbars by right-clicking.

2. When the Customize dialog opens, select the Toolbars tab, click New, and give your toolbar a name, such as mnuRecords (as shown in Figure 7-4). Click OK.

Figure 7-4. Naming a new custom toolbar.

3. A small, blank toolbar will appear near the Customize dialog. Select the Commands tab so that you can add some of the built-in commands to your new toolbar (as shown in Figure 7-5).

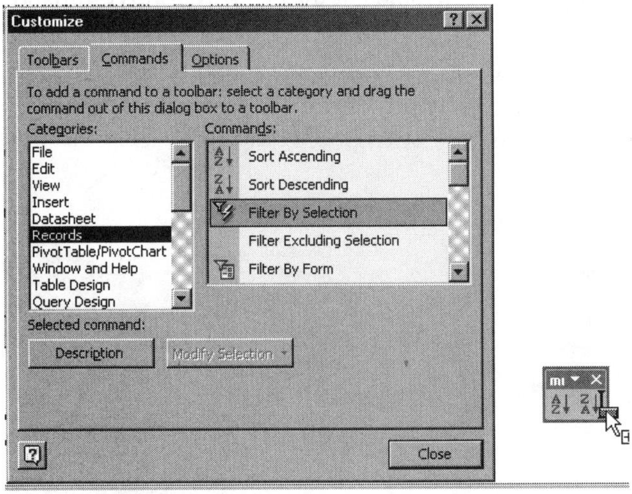

Figure 7-5. Selecting the commands that you need for your toolbar.

4. It is probably a good idea at this stage to open another Access database in another window and look at the Form View toolbar. From this second database, you can now decide which of the commands you need for your new custom toolbar.

5. Rummage through the different lists to find the commands that you want. Your focus here should be to choose those buttons that your users will need to work with the data in the database, but not those commands that allow users to modify the design of the objects in the database. You will find most of the Form and Report View-related commands in the list next to the Edit, View, and Records categories.

6. To add a command to the new toolbar, drag and drop it onto the toolbar.

7. If you add the wrong command or want to eliminate an existing command, drag and drop the button from the new toolbar to a blank part of the Access window. This action deletes the button.

Once you have dragged all the relevant built-in commands to your new toolbar, you can modify the look of the toolbar buttons by right-clicking the command (as shown in Figure 7-6). One useful addition to a toolbar is the Begin a Group command. This command adds a line that subdivides the toolbar. As you can see, there are plenty of options to modify your toolbar. My thoughts on toolbar visual changes are that these modifications should not stray too far from the conventions used in Microsoft Access or other popular Windows software.

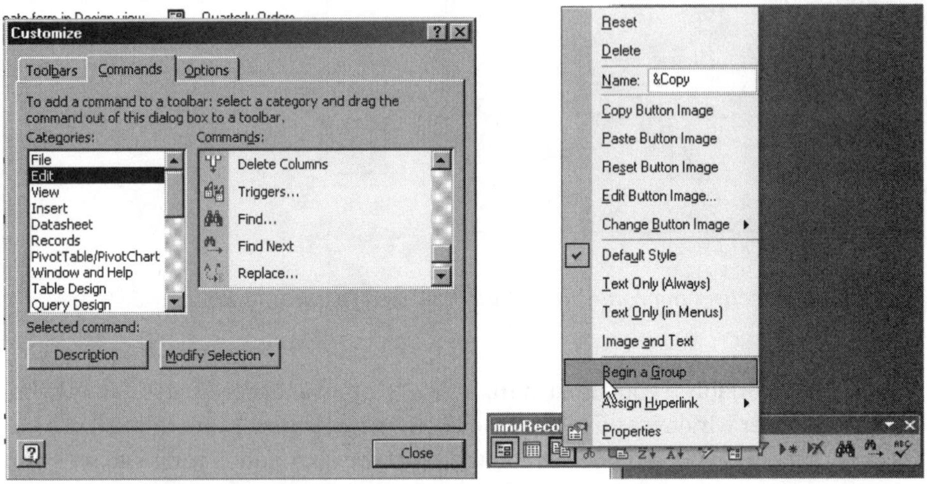

Figure 7-6. Adding a separator with the Begin a Group command.

Now, if you right-click any toolbar, you will see the name of the custom toolbar that you have created. Click it to display or hide the toolbar. In the next section, I will show you how to build a custom menu.

Building a Custom Menu

Building custom menus is a good way to protect your database and make it easier to use at the same time. A custom menu can be either a simple structure that provides access to the top hierarchy of objects in your database, a full user interface that replaces the more conventional buttons on forms, or the interface provided by the Switchboard Manager wizard in Access 2000 or later.

When it comes to building menus, the techniques are very similar to those used for building toolbars. Once again, I will combine descriptions with a pictorial representation because I find that this best illustrates the subtle tricks required to put the menu together.

1. In your copy of the Northwind database, open the Customize dialog, select the Toolbar tab, and create a new toolbar.

2. Click the Toolbar Properties button and change the Type to Menu Bar, as shown in Figure 7-7.

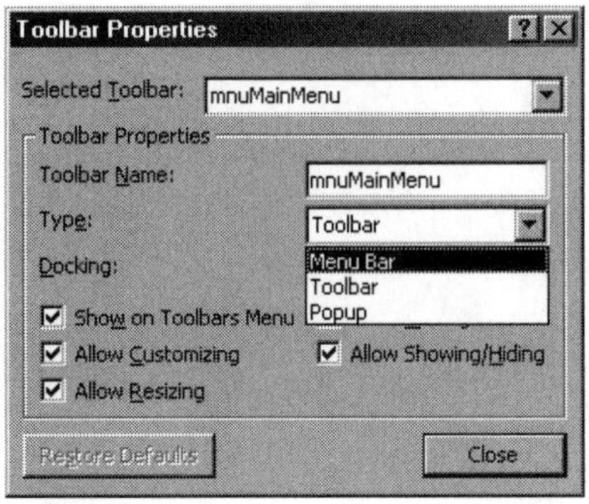

Figure 7-7. *Converting a toolbar to a menu bar.*

TIP   The Toolbar Properties dialog shows the selected toolbar options in a drop-down list. Make sure first that you are indeed using the correct toolbar. If you have selected the wrong toolbar, you can use the drop-down list to change your selection.

---

3. After you have changed the toolbar to a menu bar, the toolbar will look different, as shown in the Access 2002 sample in Figure 7-8.

4. Close the Toolbar Properties dialog and switch to the Commands tab. You have two options when building your new menu. If you drag the commands (like Open form) across to the menu bar, they will line up horizontally across the menu bar. The second and more likely choice is to make a vertical menu, which you can do by dragging the New Menu command to your menu bar (shown in Figure 7-8).

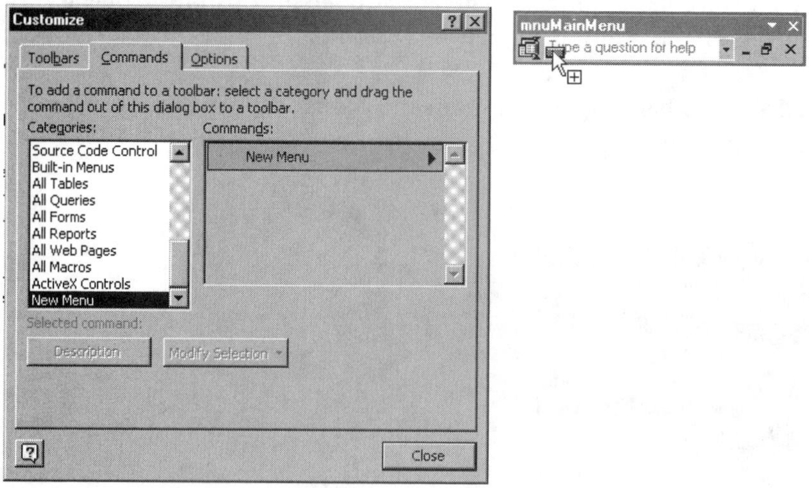

Figure 7-8. Dragging New Menu to the menu bar.

5. Right-click the new menu item and rename the menu to "&Northwind."

TIP   You can create an accelerator key for your menu item so that users can access it with the keyboard. To do so, type an ampersand (&) in front of the letter that you want to use. For example, to use "N" as the accelerator key for the Northwind menu, type "&Northwind." The "N" in your command name is underlined, and users can carry out the command by pressing ALT+N.

---

6. Now we are going to add a form to this menu and, believe me, it isn't all that obvious what you have to do. While the Customize dialog is still open, on the Commands tab, select the All Forms category (as shown in Figure 7-9).

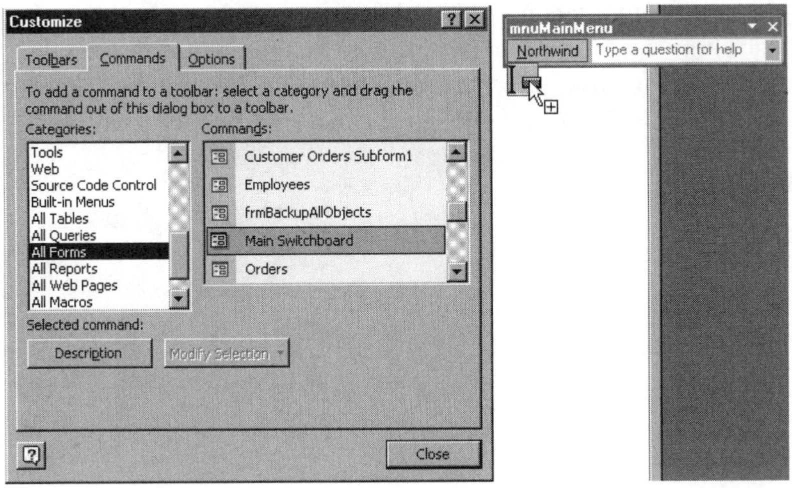

Figure 7-9. Adding a form to a custom menu.

7. Select the Main Switchboard form command, drag it to the Northwind menu, and hover over the menu until a blank toolbar appears directly under it. Then drop the Main Switchboard button onto the blank toolbar.

8. If you are using Access 2002, you might want to right-click the new menu bar and clear the Type a Question for Help check box.

9. Close the Customize dialog, and try out your new menu.

While you're in the Customize dialog, you might also want to add some other forms from the Commands form to your menu. Remember to hover above the menu (Northwind) when you drag the command from the Commands tab in the Customize dialog.

Before rushing off and spending lots of time enhancing menu bars, remember that you should avoid duplicating too many commands in both your forms and the menu system because it may prove difficult to synchronize both systems. I suggest that if you want to build a comprehensive system of menus, you should avoid having too many equivalent buttons in the forms themselves. In the applications in which I have used menus (as in Figure 7-10), I found that it is best to avoid anything more than top-level forms in your custom menu bars. Most Access users who I have dealt with like to see the options on a form rather than tucked away in menus at the top of the Access window.

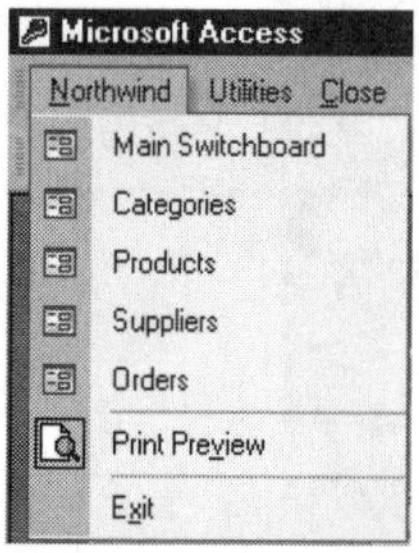

Figure 7-10. A custom menu for the Northwind database.

In the next section, we will look at another type of toolbar that the Microsoft Office toolbars environment supports.

Building a Shortcut Menu

A shortcut (pop-up) menu appears whenever you right-click a form or a report in preview mode. If you leave the built-in menus in place, the shortcut menu will include the Design View command. Naturally, you probably won't want this command to be available in a protected database, so let's find out how to build a custom shortcut menu that replaces the built-in Form View shortcut menu:

1. Open the Customize dialog, select the Toolbars tab, and create a new menu.

2. Click the Properties button and select Popup from the Type drop-down list. This action brings up a message box, shown in Figure 7-11, that tells you that the menu is about to disappear and that you will have to find it again. Weird, but true!

3. Click OK and then click Close.

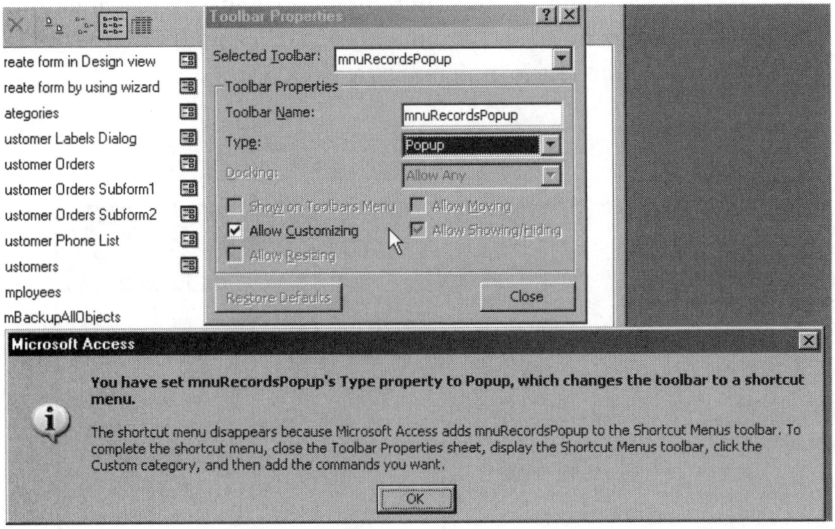

Figure 7-11. The message invoked when you make a toolbar into a shortcut (pop-up) menu.

4. To start adding commands to your new shortcut menu, choose the Toolbars tab.

5. Select the Shortcut Menus check box (as shown in Figure 7-12). Find the new shortcut menu under the Custom menu on the right side of the Shortcut Menus bar.

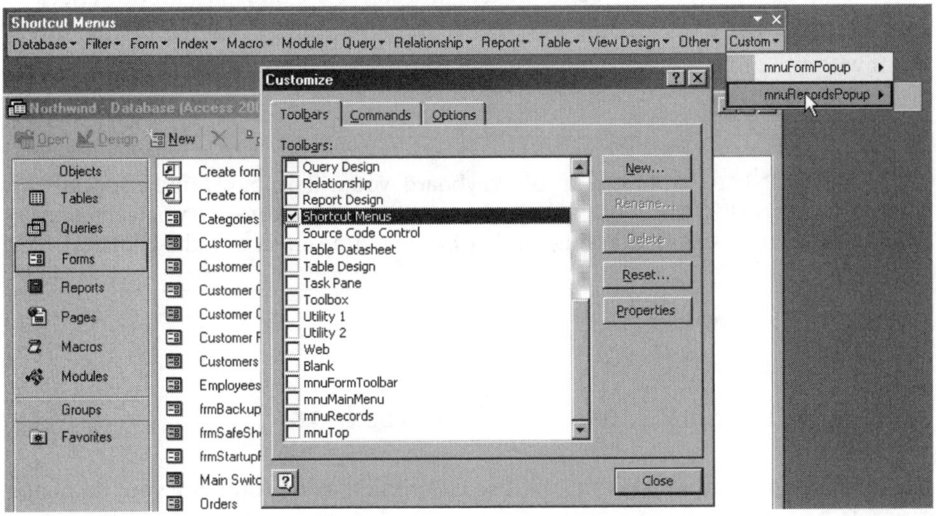

Figure 7-12. Displaying shortcut menus with other toolbars.

6. Now that you have found the new shortcut menu, you can drag and drop all the record and form-related commands onto the menu, such as the Form View menu that I have built in Figure 7-13.

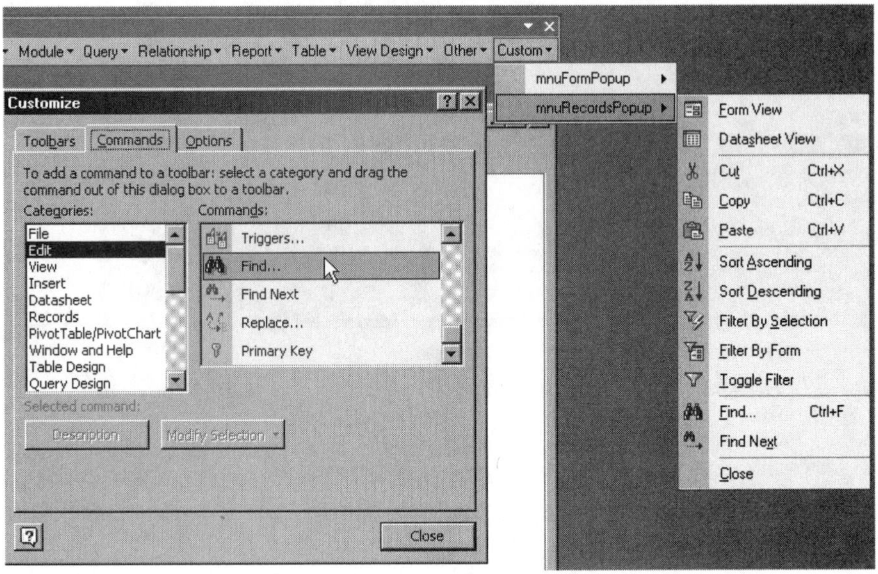

Figure 7-13. A demonstration of a Form View shortcut menu.

Whenever you want to edit the shortcut menu further, you need to open the Customize dialog, select the Toolbars tab, and select the Shortcut Menus check box. Alternatively, you can find your shortcut menu by selecting the menu you want with the drop-down list at the top of the Toolbars tab.

TIP At the bottom of your keyboard, you will probably find a special key called the Shortcut key, which has a small picture of a vertical menu with an arrow. Pressing this key has the same effect as right-clicking.

Adding Your Functions to Your Toolbars

Throughout this chapter, the toolbar discussions focus on protecting your database by replacing or disabling built-in Access commands. These discussions gloss over the fact that one of the strengths of the Access toolbars (and menus) is that you can add custom toolbar commands that run your own VBA functions or macros.

I will now illustrate how this works:

1. Create and save a new module with the very simple function that follows. This function will display the startup options from the Tools menu.

```
Function showStartupOptions()
    ' Show the startup option dialog.
    RunCommand acCmdStartupProperties
End Function
```

2. Select the Customize dialog box, select the Toolbars tab, and choose an existing toolbar.

3. Select the Commands tab and choose the File category.

4. Drag the Custom command across to your toolbar.

5. Right-click the Custom command and choose Properties.

6. In the On Action box, type an expression to run your VBA function. The expression must use the following syntax: =functionname(). For our startup options function, type =showStartupOptions(). You can also use the On Action drop-down list to select a macro, if you want to.

If you start to rely on toolbars a lot in your application, you may want to investigate other toolbar properties, such as:

- Adding help information to menu items.

- Protecting changes to toolbars, such as movement and resizing.

As previous demonstrations have shown, building the different types of toolbars is a graphical process with a few tricks here and there. Fortunately, the results are high quality and should improve your Access user interface. In the next section, I'll show you how to add custom toolbars to your application so that they appear when you want them.

Integrating Menus into Your Forms and Reports

Adding a toolbar or menu to your Access user interface requires no more than changing a few properties on your forms and reports. These properties are the Menu Bar, Toolbar, Shortcut Menu, and Shortcut Menu Bar, and they can be found in the Other tab of the Form properties dialog (shown in Figure 7-14). To add a custom menu or toolbar to a form, open the form in design view and show the form's Properties dialog. Now select the Other tab to add your custom menus to a form.

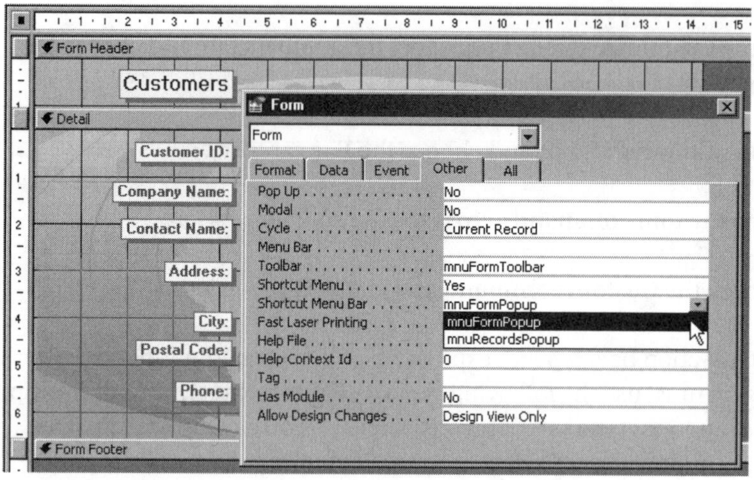

Figure 7-14. Adding custom menus and toolbars to your form.

To experiment with the examples in this section, you can use the toolbars and menus created earlier in the chapter, or you can import the menus from the demonstration database. I will use the toolbars called mnuFormToolbar and mnuFormPopup in the example, but you can easily change these by varying the constants at the top of the procedure. The steps to import those toolbars follow:

1. Open your copy of the Northwind database.

2. Choose File ➤ Get External Data ➤ Import.

3. Find the database (grMap97.mdb, grMap2000.mdb, etc.), and click OK.

4. Click the Options button.

5. Select the Menus and Toolbars check box, clear the Relations check box, and click OK.

This procedure imports any custom toolbar from the demonstration database that doesn't have an equivalent name in your current database. No toolbars will be replaced, even if they are newer than the one in your database. To check what was imported, open the Customize dialog and look on the Toolbars tab for toolbars with names starting with mnu. To see the shortcut menus that were imported, remember to select the Shortcut Menus check box on the Toolbars tab.

TIP   To select the properties of a form, you can click the little gray box in the top left corner of the form (see top left of Figure 7-14). This action adds a tiny black square to this box to signify that the properties displayed are for the form and not for one of the controls placed on it.

When you select the menu bar, toolbar, or shortcut menu bar properties of a form, a drop-down list appears, showing you all the appropriate custom toolbars in your database. To hide the shortcut menu, set the Shortcut Menu property to No.

You will generally not add menus to individual forms but will instead rely on a menu defined by the startup properties described later in this chapter. Once the top menu bar is defined in the startup options, it will stay in place until you change the menu with your application.

Though the menu bar at the top of the form requires a change only to the startup options, the toolbar property does not have an equivalent startup option. Therefore, it is necessary that you allocate a safe custom toolbar to all the forms in the database. If you don't, then the forms will revert to the built-in toolbar, leaving the forms and the database vulnerable. The best way to avoid this loophole is to use the VBA code described in the next section.

Adding Custom Toolbars and Shortcut Menus to All the Forms

Writing a good Access system with toolbars and menus will require you to make changes to the toolbar and menu properties of all the forms and reports in your database. Though you will need to tailor your own approach to your application, you generally will follow the principles used in the sample in the frmSafeFormMenus form. This sample shows you how to cycle through all the forms to change the toolbar and shortcut menu properties.

To work through this sample, you will need to import the frmSafeFormMenus form and the toolbars from the demonstration database into the copy of the Northwind database. To do this:

1. Choose File ➤ Get External Data ➤ Import.

2. Choose the form `frmSafeFormMenus`.

3. Click the Options button.

4. Select the Menu and Toolbars check box, and start the import by clicking the Import button. I recommend that you first try this option on a copy of the Northwind database (or something similar).

5. Once the import is finished, use the Customize menu's dialog to verify that the two menus, `mnuFormToolbar` and `mnuFormPopup`, are in the database.

 NOTE The demonstration database includes a form called `frmSafeReportsMenus`. This form will change the toolbars and shortcut menus for all the reports in your database. To support this form, I have included two other menus: `mnuPreviewPrint` and `mnuReportPopup`. These menus will also be imported into your database if you import menus from the demonstration databases.

When you open the form `frmSafeFormMenus`, you will see one button. If you click the button, the software will first check whether all the modules in the database have been compiled. If they have not, then the form will attempt to compile them for you. Then a message will appear (shown in Figure 7-15). Click Yes to add the toolbar and shortcut menus to all the forms in your database or No to reverse the changes made. If a form already has a menu in the toolbar or shortcut menu properties, these entries will remain as is. Before you run the program for the first time, you should view the VBA code to make sure that it is using toolbars that actually exist in your database. The toolbar names used for the forms are defined by constants at the top of the code that follows.

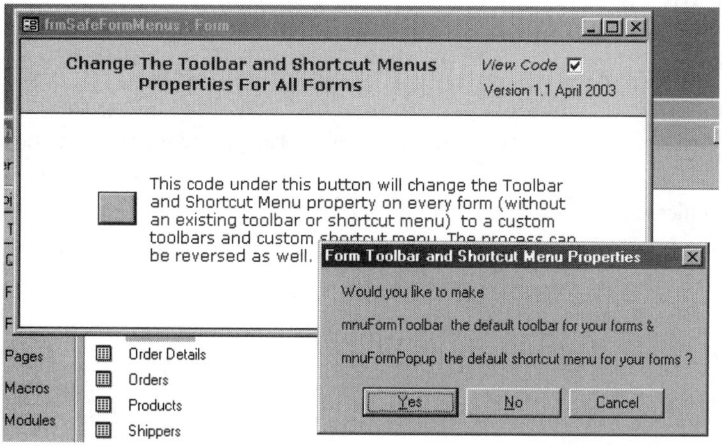

Figure 7-15. The frmSafeFormMenus *form, which changes all form shortcut and toolbar properties.*

The essence of this VBA code is that the DAO library obtains a collection of forms in the database. The code circulates through all the forms. If the form is open, the developer can choose to close the form and continue. The code then opens the form in design mode and the toolbar or shortcut menu bar properties are checked. If these are blank, then the code will modify the properties' values to equal the values as defined by the constants at the top of the procedure. The code can also undo the property changes that it makes.

```
Private Sub cmdSafeShortcuts_Click()

' Export all queries, forms, macros, and modules to text.
' Build a file to assist in recovering the saved objects
' into a clean database.

' This subroutine requires a reference to
' Microsoft DAO 3.6 or 3.51 library.

On Error GoTo err_cmdSafeShortcuts

Dim dbs As DAO.Database, Cnt As DAO.Container, doc As DAO.Document
Dim mdl As Module, objName As String, strDocName As String
Dim i As Integer, modifyMenus As Integer
Dim FilePath As String
Dim fileType As String
```

```
Const CONDOCSTATECLOSED = 0
Const FORMTOOLBAR = "mnuFormToolbar"
Const FORMPOPUP = "mnuFormPopup"
Const SHOWPOPUPMENU = True     ' Set to false to hide shortcut menus altogether.
Const FORMSAVEMODE = acSave    ' Use acSavePrompt if you want to confirm changes.


If Not Application.IsCompiled Then
  MsgBox "This module is about to compile all the VBA code in your database", _
    vbInformation
  RunCommand acCmdCompileAllModules
End If


If Application.IsCompiled Then
    modifyMenus = MsgBox("Would you like to make " & vbCrLf & vbCrLf & _
                FORMTOOLBAR & "  the default toolbar for your forms and " & _
                vbCrLf & vbCrLf & FORMPOPUP & _
                "  the default shortcut menu for your forms ? ", _
                vbYesNoCancel, "Form Toolbar and Shortcut Menu Properties")
    If modifyMenus = vbYes Or modifyMenus = vbNo Then
        Set dbs = CurrentDb()
        Set Cnt = dbs.Containers("Forms")
        For Each doc In Cnt.Documents
            strDocName = doc.Name
            If Me.Name <> strDocName Then  ' Do not open this form with this code.

                ' Test whether the form is already open and close it with a prompt.
                If SysCmd(acSysCmdGetObjectState, acForm, strDocName) <> _
                        CONDOCSTATECLOSED Then
                    DoCmd.Echo True, "Closing an open form"
                    DoCmd.CLOSE acForm, strDocName, acSavePrompt
                End If

                DoCmd.OpenForm strDocName, acDesign
                ' Change the settings for the toolbar menu.
                If Len(Forms(strDocName).Toolbar) = 0 Or _
                        Forms(strDocName).Toolbar = FORMTOOLBAR Then
                    ' Only change forms with no toolbar or our toolbar.

                    If modifyMenus = vbYes Then
                        ' Make this the default toolbar.
                        Forms(strDocName).Toolbar = FORMTOOLBAR
```

```
            Else
                ' Clear the toolbar menu from the form.
                Forms(strDocName).Toolbar = ""
            End If
        End If


        ' Change the settings for the shortcut menu.
        If Len(Forms(strDocName).ShortcutMenuBar) = 0 Or _
                Forms(strDocName).ShortcutMenuBar = FORMPOPUP Then
            ' Only change forms with no shortcut menu or
            ' our shortcut menu.

            If modifyMenus = vbYes Then
                ' Make this the default shortcut menu.
                Forms(strDocName).ShortcutMenu = SHOWPOPUPMENU
                Forms(strDocName).ShortcutMenuBar = FORMPOPUP
            Else
                ' Clear the new shortcut menu from the form.
                Forms(strDocName).ShortcutMenu = SHOWPOPUPMENU
                Forms(strDocName).ShortcutMenuBar = ""
            End If

            DoCmd.Echo True, "Closing the form that has had " & _
                            "its popup properties modified"
            DoCmd.CLOSE acForm, strDocName, FORMSAVEMODE
        Else
            ' No action to be taken on this form; close the form.
            DoCmd.CLOSE acForm, strDocName, acSaveNo
        End If
    End If
    Next doc
    End If
Else
    MsgBox "This database needs to be compiled first for safety reasons", _
            vbInformation, "Choose menu { Debug ... Compile All Modules} " & _
            "from the VBA window"

End If

Exit_cmdSafeShortcuts:
```

```
On Error Resume Next

    Set doc = Nothing
    Set Cnt = Nothing
    Set dbs = Nothing
    Exit Sub

err_cmdSafeShortcuts:
    Select Case Err.Number          ' Problems with unload process.

       Case vbObjectError + 999
          ' To see line immediately after the error line, press CTRL+BREAK,
          ' drag yellow arrow to Resume Next, then press F8.
          Resume Next
       Case Else
          MsgBox "Error No. " & Err.Number & " -> " & Err.Description
    End Select

    Resume Exit_cmdSafeShortcuts
  End Sub
```

You could make some easy extensions to this sample, such as adding report-specific toolbars, adding simpler toolbars when the form has no record source, or turning off the pesky Form Allows Design Changes property in Access 2000 and later. If you want to add toolbars and shortcut menus to your reports, use the frmSafeReportMenus form, which has very similar software, in the demonstration database. Now we will look at how to combine the startup options with menus to provide better database protection through menus.

The Menu and Toolbar Startup Options

In Chapter 2, I discussed in detail the ways in which you can manually and pro-grammatically change the Access startup options. During those discussions, I refrained from detailed analysis of the five toolbar-related options because I felt it would be better to introduce some background on toolbars first. Now that you have the knowledge to build custom toolbars, you can use those toolbars with the startup options to protect your database.

Before starting, I suggest that you build a protection toolbar that will provide shortcuts to some of the protection forms and techniques illustrated in this book. This toolbar will help you as we work through the startup options by making it easy to undo the changes that we make. You may also want to build on this toolbar while you are working through this book so that you have easy access to the samples that you think are suited to your applications. So, to build the protection toolbar:

1. Open your copy of Northwind.mdb.

2. Open the Customize dialog and select the Toolbars tab.

3. Create a new toolbar called mnuProtection.

4. Select All Forms on the Commands tab.

5. Drag New Menu to the mnuProtection toolbar and rename it Protection.

6. Drag the following forms to the mnuProtection toolbar (you may need to import these from the demonstration database): frmStartupProperties, frmSafeFormMenus, frmSafeReportMenus, frmDisableMenuItems.

7. Put the toolbar on the same level as the current toolbar and place it on the right side, as shown in Figure 7-16.

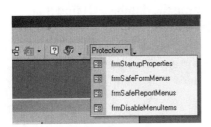

Figure 7-16. Adding the Protection menu, which includes forms from the demonstration database.

Now we are in a position to test the startup options without making our database difficult to open. So let's have a look at the ramifications of changing each of the five toolbar-related startup options (shown in Figure 7-17). When you decide which one of the options to adopt, remember to clear the Display Database Window check box, as these options provide little protection if you allow the Database window to appear.

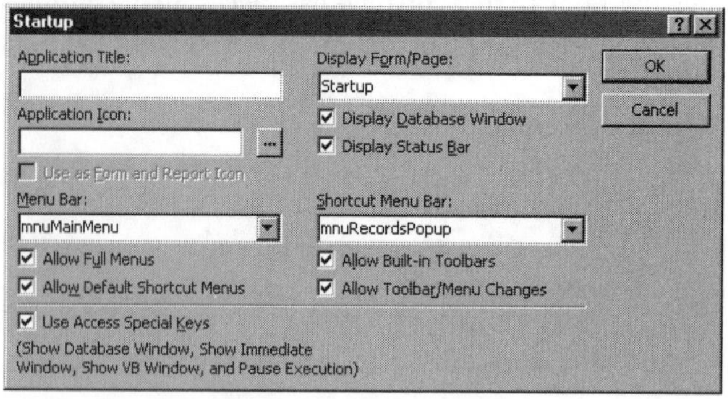

Figure 7-17. The startup properties, which include information on menus and toolbars.

TIP The easiest way to open and close a database to test the startup options is to choose Tools ➤ Database Utilities ➤ Compact Database.

Remember when you try out any of these options that you can fall back on the `AllowByPassKey` property (press SHIFT when opening the database). I find that when I am experimenting with these menu-related startup options, it is easier to turn off one option at a time so that I fully understand what does what. In addition, remember that these changes apply only to the current database and, for greater clarity, you should only experiment with one of these startup options at a time.

Setting the Startup Menu Bar

When you click the Menu Bar drop-down list, you will see a list of all the custom menus in your database (specifically a toolbar where the `Type` property equals Menu Bar). If you choose one like the `mnuMainMenu` menu bar and restart the database, the new menu will replace the built-in Access main menu bar (as shown in Figure 7-18). To return to the full menu, try pressing CTRL+F11. If that fails, click the `frmStartupProperties` command on the newly established Protection toolbar.

Figure 7-18. The menu bar at the top of the page, which now becomes your custom menu.

Now set the menu bar in the startup properties back to Default so that you can see the effect of the other menus.

Allowing Full Menus

Clearing the Allow Full Menus check box is a good way of protecting the database because it removes all the developer-related menus items from the built-in menus (as shown in Figure 7-19). This action removes the following:

- Complete Tools menu (startup, options, security)

- Complete View menu (design and toolbar customization)

- Hide and Unhide columns on the Format menu

- Get External Data command (import and link) on the File menu

- Database properties command on the File menu

- Hide and Unhide commands on the Windows menu

- About Microsoft Access and Help on the Web on the Help menu

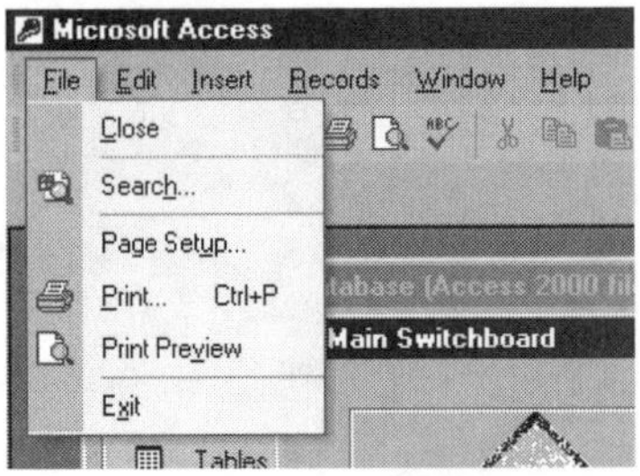

Figure 7-19. Fewer menu items available in the built-in menus.

Because this action will make your interface less cluttered for your users, it's a good option to select. Unfortunately, this option does not remove developer-related commands from your built-in toolbars or shortcut menus.

Allowing Built-In Toolbars

Selecting the Allow Built-In Toolbars check box hides the toolbars that Access applies when a form or report is open. Clearing this option is best when the toolbar property for the form or report has been set to a Custom toolbar (discussed earlier in the chapter). If you don't provide an alternative toolbar, you will probably need to ensure that your forms and menus adequately compensate for the missing toolbar menu. Clearing this option gives more window space to the Access interface because the space allocated to the toolbar will disappear.

Setting the Startup Shortcut Menu Bar

Selecting a menu from the Shortcut Menu Bar drop-down list allocates a custom shortcut menu as the startup shortcut menu that appears for all your forms, as well as for any reports shown in preview mode. You should tailor your custom menu to mimic most of the functionality of the built-in Form View shortcut menu, but without the Design View command.

Allowing Default Shortcut Menus

Selecting the Allow Default Shortcut Menus check box stops built-in shortcut menus from appearing when you open a form or a preview a report. If you clear this option, you should implement an alternative shortcut menu because users will expect something to happen when they right-click in your Access application.

Clearing this check box does not override any custom shortcut menu bar defined in the Shortcut Menu Bar property of a form. As an aside, when you clear this option, you will not be able to right-click a menu or toolbar to make changes.

Allowing Toolbar/Menu Changes

If you clear the Allow Toolbar/Menu Changes check box, you will not be able to close a toolbar or right-click to customize or select a toolbar. Also, the View ➤ Toolbars ➤ Customize command will be disabled. This option applies to all the toolbars, including the built-in ones.

Some Easy VBA to Help You Manage Your Menus

Even though the toolbars and menus are fully programmable, here are some little tricks to help you manage your menus. In the Immediate window or with VBA code, you can:

- Tell the built-in menu bar to go away:

```
Application.Commandbars("Menu Bar").Enabled = False
```

- Tell the Access application to use your menu bar instead:

```
Application.Menubar = MyMenuBarName
```

- Tell Access to stop using your menu bar and return to the default Access menu bar by using an empty text string:

```
Application.Menubar = ""
```

- Delete a shortcut menu (or any toolbar, for that matter):

```
Application.CommandBars("My Shorcut Menu").Delete
```

TIP   You can switch between the application menu bars and your custom menu bar by pressing CTRL+F11. This option does not apply if you have cleared the Allow Special Keys check box in the Startup options dialog.

Now we will take a stricter corporate approach to menu management by showing how you can disable certain built-in toolbar and menu items on a particular computer.

Modifying the Built-In Menus and Toolbars

If you work for a large company with some in-house programming staff, you may feel that the programming features built into Access are not something that all staff in your organization should have access to. This section shows how you can disable certain commands for all Access databases used by a single computer. You could run this VBA code after installing Access on a computer. If a user then requests the additional functionality, the same software with a slight modification will enable the commands that were disabled. This modification works out to be very effective in a database where Access to the VBA code is restricted to the developer or if the database is in MDE format. Of course, the same users could use VBA in another database to turn these menu bars on again, supposing that they actually could find out what was going on. If this possibility worries you, you will have to add the same code to the startup procedures of all your important databases. Though this may seem heavy-handed, remember that some organizations have corporate IT policies that assume that control of in-house development produces a better result than the empowerment of end users.

 NOTE The built-in menus remain disabled even if you use the AllowByPassKey property to open the database.

To disable the toolbar commands, I have written a subroutine that disables the critical menu and toolbar items in the Access environment. This software is located in the VBA code behind the frmDisableMenuItems form (as shown in Figure 7-20). The sample restricts itself to the commands that are available from the Form View and Report Preview mode. Disabling commands has the effect of making the commands unavailable but still visible on the menus (see Figure 7-21).

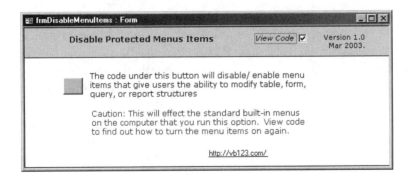

Figure 7-20. The frmDisableMenuItems *form, which disables/enables developer commands.*

Figure 7-21. The sample software, with disabled commands on the Access built-in menus.

NOTE When you change a built-in menu, you actually create a new Access menu called a global menu bar. This global menu bar now becomes the default menu for your computer, and the built-in menu isn't used any more. The same applies for toolbars and shortcut menu bars.

To disable the commands, I use a function that I have written (called EnableMenuItem) that enables or disables a menu item by using the CommandBar object. As you will see in the VBA code that follows, I identify the menu commands by using the text names that appear on the built-in menus themselves. I have used this approach because it is far more self-explanatory. For one of the commands, I have resorted to using the numerical identifier for a toolbar because the built-in toolbar and shortcut menu both have the same names (Form View). I have one big apology here for anyone reading this text that uses a foreign language version of Access: The text names for these commands could be different on your computer. Anyway, here is the code that you can use to disable built-in menu items.

```
Private Sub cmdDisableMenusItems_Click()

' Enable/disable all the command bars controls that a user could
' use to elude the protection in your database.

On Error GoTo err_cmdDisableMenusItems

' To disable the toolbar commands, set the following constant to False.
Const ENABLEITEM As Boolean = True

enableMenuItem "File", "Get External &Data", ENABLEITEM ' Access 97 caption.
enableMenuItem "File", "&Get External Data", ENABLEITEM ' Access 2000 caption.

enableMenuItem "View", "&Design View", ENABLEITEM
enableMenuItem "View", "&Toolbars", ENABLEITEM

enableMenuItem "Tools", "&Relationships...", ENABLEITEM
enableMenuItem "Tools", "Anal&yze", ENABLEITEM
enableMenuItem "Tools", "Securi&ty", ENABLEITEM
enableMenuItem "Tools", "Re&plication", ENABLEITEM
enableMenuItem "Tools", "Run &Macro...", ENABLEITEM      ' Access 97 caption.
enableMenuItem "Tools", "&Macro", ENABLEITEM             ' Access 2000 caption.
enableMenuItem "Tools", "Start&up...", ENABLEITEM
enableMenuItem "Tools", "ActiveX &Controls...", ENABLEITEM ' Access 97 caption.
enableMenuItem "Tools", "Active&X Controls...", ENABLEITEM ' Access 2000 caption.
enableMenuItem "Tools", "&Customize...", ENABLEITEM
enableMenuItem "Tools", "&Options...", ENABLEITEM

' Caution: If you disable the database utilities option, that will remove
' the compact options.
enableMenuItem "Tools", "&Database Utilities", ENABLEITEM
```

```
' To test that the menu item exists, use the following code:
If Not enableMenuItem("Window", "&Unhide...", ENABLEITEM) Then
    MsgBox "Problem with the Unhide Menu Item"
End If


' Now disable the protection related buttons on the form and report toolbars
enableMenuItem "Form View", "View", ENABLEITEM
enableMenuItem "Form View", "&Design View", ENABLEITEM
enableMenuItem "Form View", "&Database Window", ENABLEITEM
enableMenuItem "Form View", "&New Object", ENABLEITEM
enableMenuItem "Print Preview", "View", ENABLEITEM
enableMenuItem "Print Preview", "Design &View", ENABLEITEM
enableMenuItem "Print Preview", "&Database Window", ENABLEITEM
enableMenuItem "Print Preview", "&New Object", ENABLEITEM


' For the shortcut toolbar, use the index of the toolbar for the
' actual name of "Form View," which is the same name used for toolbars.
enableMenuItem 85, "Form &Design", ENABLEITEM


' For the shortcut toolbar, use the index of the toolbar for the actual
' name of  "Print Preview," which is the same name used for toolbars.
enableMenuItem 95, "Report Desig&n", ENABLEITEM


If ENABLEITEM Then
    MsgBox "All protection related menus items on this computer are Enabled", _
          vbInformation, "Built-In Menu Items Unprotected"
Else
    MsgBox "All protection-related menus items on this computer are Disabled", _
          vbInformation, "Built-In Menu Items protected"
End If


Exit_cmdDisableMenusItems:


On Error Resume Next
    Exit Sub


err_cmdDisableMenusItems:
    Select Case Err.Number          ' Problems with unload process.
        Case vbObjectError + 999
            ' To see line immediately after the error line, press CTRL+BREAK,
            ' drag yellow arrow to Resume Next, then presss F8.
            Resume Next
```

```
      Case Else
          MsgBox "Error No. " & Err.Number & " -> " & Err.Description
      End Select

      Resume Exit_cmdDisableMenusItems

End Sub
```

In the `enableMenuItem` function that follows, the `CommandBar` object from the Microsoft Office Object Library is used. This function iterates through all the controls (we call them commands) in a particular command bar (toolbar) until the command we want is found. The Boolean value passed as an argument to the function enables or disables the menu command.

```
Function enableMenuItem(varCBBarName As Variant, strCBarCtlCaption As String, _
                        booEnabled As Boolean) As Boolean

' Turn menu items on and off.
' There is no error trapping in this subroutine.
' You should handle this in higher-level procedures.

' Caution: This function will disable a menu item if booEnabled = True.

' This procedure requires a reference to the
' Microsoft Office X Object Library.

Dim cbrReq As CommandBar
Dim ctlName As CommandBarControl

Set cbrReq = CommandBars(varCBBarName)
For Each ctlName In cbrReq.Controls
   If ctlName.Caption = strCBarCtlCaption Then
      ctlName.Enabled = booEnabled
      enableMenuItem = True
      GoTo enableMenuItem_Exit
   End If
Next ctlName

enableMenuItem = False

enableMenuItem_Exit:
   Set cbrReq = Nothing
End Function
```

NOTE Because you may have trouble enabling a particular command, you can restore the toolbar to its installation settings. Open the Customize dialog, select the Toolbar tab, choose the toolbar, choose properties, and click the Restore Defaults button.

Now I will briefly review some samples that were not discussed in this chapter and discuss links to relevant Internet material. The samples include VBA code that I used to establish the numerical identity numbers of the Form View shortcut menu.

Further Reading

As you can expect, there is never enough information when it comes to powerful products like Access. To assist you with further investigations, I have put together a Web page with hyperlinks to Web sites and articles on the issues relating to material in this chapter, including

- Tuning Up Your Design Toolbars in Access 2000/97

- All About Command Bars: Menu Bars, Toolbars, and Shortcut Menus

- Command Bars in Access 97

You can find the further reading Web page for this chapter in the Downloads section of the Apress Web site (http://www.apress.com) or at the address http://www.vb123.com/map/too.htm.

Now I will introduce some additional VBA code samples that are included in the downloadable database.

Additional Toolbar Programming

The CommandBar object is a powerful tool that has many properties and methods that you can learn. In the download database, I have provided VBA code samples in the form called frmShowMenus (see Figure 7-22) that will:

1. Show you how to list all the commands in a shortcut/pop-up menu.

2. Find all the custom menus in your database and display them in a separate list box for each toolbar type. You can easily turn off the custom toolbar filter and use the same form to list the built-in toolbars and menus as well.

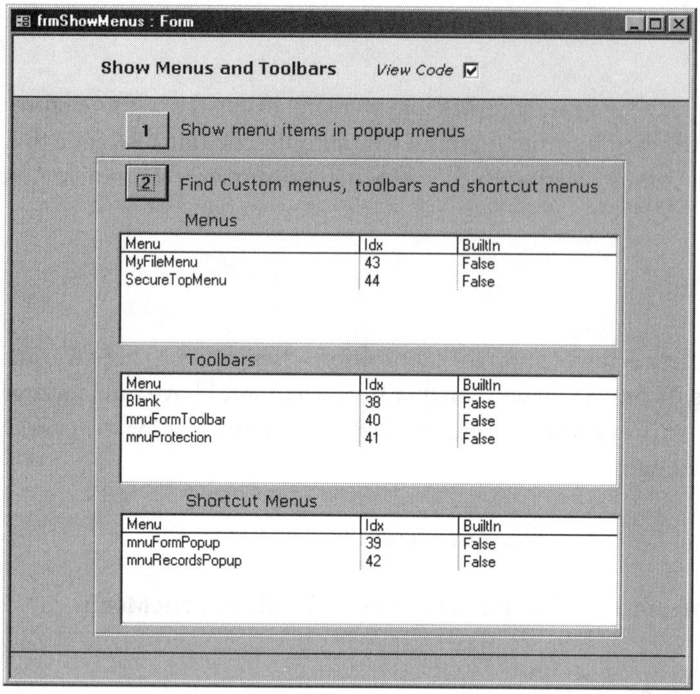

Figure 7-22 - Additional toolbar VBA code in the frmShowMenus *form.*

Runtime Menus

Another way to restrict the menu items in an Access database to those that are essential for forms and reports is to use the Access runtime options. You can bring up the runtime environment in two ways:

1. Include the /Runtime option in an Access shortcut file (explained in Chapter 10).

2. Install the runtime environment on a computer that doesn't have Access installed. This packaging system is available if you purchase the Office Developer edition of Access.

The menus displayed are the same as those if you clear the Allow Full Menus startup check box. It is necessary to have a startup form before starting Access in runtime mode. You can read more about runtime systems in Chapter 12.

Managing Menus Across Multiple Databases

To use the same menus across multiple databases, I recommend that you keep all your standard menus in one library database and give the menus a name (prefix/suffix) that identifies them as coming from that database. Then, if you need the menus, import them into your current database to install them. If you make any enhancements to the menus, do so in the library database. If you decide to customize the default characteristics of the custom menu, you will need to rename it so that you know that it is now specific to the current database.

Reflecting on This Chapter

Access is a multifaceted interface designed for both developers and users. Nowhere is that more apparent than in the toolbars and menus part of the user interface. Like other parts of the Access environment, this flexibility means that there are a lot of holes to plug to protect your database. This chapter should have provided you with the skill and knowledge to help you in that regard by discussing these relevant issues:

- How to build custom toolbars, menus, and shortcut menus.

- How to add VBA code to the custom toolbars.

- How to use VBA to change the relevant properties in your forms so that they use your custom toolbars and shortcut menus.

- What the toolbar related startup options are, how they work, and how custom menus are an important part of that mechanism.

- How to disable developer-specific toolbar commands on end-user computers.

Of course, this seems like a lot of material, but I can assure you that though toolbars and menus seem a little tricky at first, they really are quite easy to set up. As a first step, you should ensure that the developer-specific commands are not available to the end user, because this precaution will better protect your database and make it easier for your users.

What's Next?

In the next chapter, we will be looking at how you can secure your database by using workgroup (user-level) security. The particular emphasis in this chapter is on how to set up workgroup security so that the developers of the application have secure ownership of the objects. Other users who open the database will have the ability to use the database but not make any changes to the design of the database. This particular setup is as secure as you can get and does not require the users to enter any user names or passwords before opening the database. If you are serious about protecting your database, this next chapter will be vital reading.

CHAPTER 8

Developer Workgroup Security

THIS CHAPTER WILL show you how to use the Access workgroup (user-level) security system to secure your user interface and most of the objects in your database. To achieve these worthwhile goals, you need to follow some fundamental steps, such as creating a secure workgroup file, changing object ownership in the your database, and setting permissions on all or some of these objects. Just undertaking these tasks can all get a little complex, especially if you are unsure of what you are doing or what you are testing for. Another issue with workgroup security is that it can add the burden of yet another password for a user and additional responsibilities to the DBA in sorting them out. Therefore, I have structured this chapter to

- Provide you with driving instructions for the different things you need to do (can do) to implement workgroup security.

- Provide a system in which users (and the developer) never have to enter passwords.

- Produce a database in which the user cannot change the design of any object and cannot view the design of forms, reports, macros, and, to a lesser extent, modules.

- Achieve a lot of security and protection without producing a too-complex security design.

- Create a database that is not susceptible to password-cracking software (discussed in Chapter 9).

- Allow you to protect your startup options and, therefore, protect toolbars and menus, the Database window, and other startup options that you don't want your users to tamper with.

- Set up a framework for other security measures, such as Access data and query security (discussed in Chapter 10) and operating system security (discussed in Chapter 12).

While we are pursuing these goals, I will introduce the different facets of workgroup security that you have to master to secure your database. I have deliberately structured the information on the end goals of security rather than diverging into fuller descriptions of the technology itself because at the end of the day, once you know that an end goal is worth pursuing, the technology becomes all the much easier to research and understand.

To achieve these security goals, we depend on one overriding principle: "The developer must not provide any of the users with the workgroup security file that is used to secure the database." Once you have set up your own developer workgroup file, you will find that you can reuse it when securing your databases from then on.

The demonstration material for this chapter includes forms and Visual Basic for Applications (VBA) examples, as follows:

- A form to build a secure workgroup file from scratch.

- A form to check and change object ownerships.

- A form to remove a module's permissions that supposedly couldn't be turned off in Access 2000 or later.

 NOTE   To find the demonstration material, open the download database for your version of Access—for example, grMAP97.mdb–and select Chapter 8.

To work through the exercises in this chapter, I suggest that you make a copy of the Northwind database for your experimentation. Do not use your own database or workgroup file until you are certain about what you want to do. Naturally, back up your database by using a .ZIP file or the instructions in Chapter 5 before implementing it. Finally, remember to rejoin your original workgroup when you finish experimenting.

Why Is Developer Workgroup Security So Important?

Once again, I will provide alternative overviews about what's important to the developer, the DBA, and the IT manager. In this section, I will also describe why workgroup security set up in this way is in fact secure and why denying your users access to the developer workgroup file is a good form of defense, and then I will provide a complete list of brief instructions for setting up workgroup security.

Overview for the Developer

I can say without any hesitation that the developer workgroup concept that I discuss in this project has been used in a vast majority of the projects that I have been involved in. In most of those projects, I have only ever secured a few key objects in the database. The impact of this approach is that customers generally need to contact me again when they upgrade Access, and I can maintain ownership rights on the objects that I have perfected over many different projects.

If you are an Access developer, you need a secure workgroup file in your collection of database tools. This chapter shows you how to set one up and then how to use it to secure one or more of your databases. Like all the other Access protection measures that I have covered in the book, there are many varied approaches that you can follow to achieve different security and protection outcomes. On initial scanning of the material in this chapter, the process may appear to be a little complex.

Some of the useful outcomes that you will learn by reading this chapter include

- The simple developer workgroup file concept.

- The VBA code that will rebuild a secure workgroup file from scratch.

- The ability to secure the Access startup options properly.

- The undocumented Access 2000 permissions that will secure modules from being opened from the Database window.

If you follow the developer workgroup strategy that I have described, most of your users will probably never even guess that they are using security in the first place, and that will always be good for maintaining a good rapport with your users and clients.

Overview for the DBA

An Access DBA must be able to understand the basic concepts behind workgroup (user-level) security, as it is the key to managing secure Access databases. The developer workgroup strategy detailed in this chapter gains its security because the users do not have access to the workgroup file that is used to secure the database. In addition, it is simple for users to run because they do not have to log on to use the database.

If the strategy is fully implemented with the appropriate startup options, users will not be able to change or avoid the user interface. If the DBA does not want to implement all these steps, the DBA will appreciate that there are significant and simple security outcomes. Unfortunately, these developer workgroup files do not provide specific security for the data and queries, so the DBA should review additional options in the next few chapters to build on the security that this strategy provides.

Overview for IT Manager

When reviewing this chapter, the IT manager should appreciate the simplicity of the developer workgroup strategy because it will help to ensure that your users will not tamper with or spend time fiddling with corporate database applications. Another key benefit is that this system does not rely on passwords and all the maintenance issues that passwords bring. In addition, you should be aware of these issues:

- If external developers are using workgroup files to create your databases, you need to ensure that you have copies of the workgroup files or understand what parts of the application you do not have access to.

- You should watch for the internal proliferation of workgroup files because they will definitely lead to headaches when they become lost or the users connect to incorrect workgroup files. This strategy assumes that most users will simply use the default workgroup file installed by Access, so you may not run into most of those hassles.

In the next section, I will describe why the material in this chapter can claim to offer security rather than just another protection measure.

Security Rather than Protection

For the first time in the book since the introduction in Chapter 1, I am going to describe how you can secure parts of your database rather than simply protect them. To secure your database, you need to apply Access workgroup security in a certain way. By doing so, these techniques will make your database so secure that only a very competent computer person who has a lot of time on his or her hands could work out how to break into the database objects or database settings.

The rest of us, including yours truly, will just not be able to change the designs of queries and tables or look at the design of forms, reports, or modules. We should not be able to readily use any software to crack the workgroup security that we set up, and we should be able to stop the greatest security threat of all, the Access Import command (discussed in Chapter 9). To crack the database will involve paying considerable amounts of money to companies that have those skills and making a legal declaration that the person has the rights to the information. Alternatively, our would-be hacker could waste days or weeks picking through the content of the database in a text editor. Because the hacker would either have to announce him or herself as a criminal to the world or become very determined, my assessment is that this style of security is pretty good.

 NOTE   I should be using the term "user-level security" rather than "workgroup security" if I was to follow the conventions used in Access help. My problem with "user-level security" is that it becomes complicated to differentiate between Access users and Windows users. The term "user-level security" also obscures the connection with the all-important workgroup file. So I believe that the term workgroup security is more definitive, even if it is not the term generally used in the help file. That this term is more definitive is especially true in relation to this chapter because all users will actually be the anonymous Admin account, and thus the term becomes a complication in itself.

Getting your workgroup security properly set up is vital if you are looking for really good security for your data. Workgroup security, properly applied to a front-end database, will deny the user access to the database window or the VBA projects, making it very hard for someone to guess the location of the back-end database. When these techniques are combined with good operating system security, ordinary users of your database will not be able to browse the folders to copy your databases or import the objects into another database.

Denial Is a Good Form of Defense

Those of you who are familiar with Access workgroup security will probably start throwing your hands in the air and wondering how a system can be safe if it allows anyone to open the database. The answer is that a number of companies have cracked the encrypted Access workgroup file, so you need to build systems in which the administration and the objects in a database are controlled by a workgroup file that is not available to the database users. To do this, you first must build a developer workgroup file that is never distributed to your users. If you set up that workgroup file correctly, you can add a number of very useful security measures to the database without introducing user accounts to the workgroup file. Once you have done this, you can then take a number of approaches, including securing your database files, by using the operating system or producing a second workgroup file that does not include the administrator's information.

In the next section, I will show you the different steps that you can take to secure your database with workgroup security.

The Access Workgroup Security Driving Instructions

Before I launch into the details of developer workgroup security, I am going to outline all the different tasks that you can do to apply workgroup security to your database. Because workgroup security requires a different approach for different tasks such as user interface security or data security, the information has been divided into different chapters. This list shows what you can do rather than offer discussions on the issues surrounding the tasks. While reviewing this list, remember that you may want to skip a number of steps by using the User-Level Security wizard. Even if you use all the steps, you really should work through the chapters to understand the issues so that you implement a secure model.

Chapter 8: Developing Workgroup Security

You really must follow most of the steps in this chapter if you are looking for security.

1. Create a workgroup file.

2. Add a password for the Admin account.

3. Add a new user, which will be your Developer account.

4. Add your Developer account to the Admins group.

5. Remove the Admin account from the Admins group.

6. Secure just a few objects by using the Developer account to mark your territory.

7. Transfer ownership of the database and all its objects to the Developer account.

8. For the Admin account and Users group, change permissions as follows:

   • Clear the Administer and Exclusive database permissions.

   • Clear Read Design, Modify Design, and Administer permissions for forms, reports, and macros.

   • Clear Modify Design and Administer permissions for tables and queries.

- For modules in Access 97, clear all permissions. For Access 2000 or later, use the `frmProtectModule` form that I have provided to remove the permissions for the modules.

Chapter 9: Security Concerns, Encryption, and Database Passwords

Use these protection measures where appropriate, but be aware of their flaws.

- Encrypt the database.

- Use a database password.

Chapter 10: Securing Data

Securing data requires you to build on the previous workgroup security, as follows:

- Remove the Open/Run permission for the database for the Users group and the Admin account.

- Create a new group of users and add some users to that group.

- Give that group account appropriate permissions to access your data and objects.

- Create a shortcut file to open the database with the appropriate workgroup.

- In Access 2000 or later, use the User-Level Security wizard to undertake most of steps outlined in the preceding sections ("Chapter 8: Developing Workgroup Security" and "Chapter 9: Security Concerns, Encryption, and Database Passwords").

- Use the Access 97 Security wizard to create a secure database by using most of the steps in the section "Chapter 8: Developing Workgroup Security."

- Add one of the PID authentication techniques to protect your workgroup file.

- Distribute data outside the company network very prudently, because security is not easy to control.

- Use Read with Owner Permissions (RWOP) queries for protecting data.

Chapter 11: Object Protection and Security Measures

Here are some other measures that you can undertake to protect the objects in your database.

- Create a developer workgroup file with the User-Level Security wizard.

- Protect linked tables with remote queries.

- Protect queries design by using RWOP queries.

- Protect forms and reports by opening them with special VBA code.

- In Access 2000 or later, use VBA project passwords.

- Use data access pages with workgroup security.

- Secure forms, reports and VBA code by using the MDE format.

- Hide queries in encrypted MDE-format databases.

Chapter 12: Protecting and Securing Your Database with the Operating System

Although the operating system has nothing to do with workgroup security, many of the permission strategies that workgroup security provides can be provided by the operating system. If you take the time to combine both methods, you will be well on your way to having a very secure Access back-end database and a quite a secure front-end database.

Now I will introduce you to the developer workgroup file strategy and, in the process, explain some of the essentials of Access workgroup security.

The Developer Workgroup File Strategy `Access 97 or later`

As I researched this book, I had to wrestle with the question, "Is it possible to secure an Access security database?" On the positive side, it seems that even the most modest security such as startup options seems to be enough to deter users from straying into the parts of Access that we have decided that they shouldn't be. On the negative side, I came across issues like the fact that Access workgroup and password protection clearly have not been improved much over the years, which has allowed companies and individuals that want to profit from understanding the format of Access databases to create password-cracking software and sell database recovery and security consulting services (discussed in Chapter 9). Another obvious problem is that a lot of people seemed to be confused by workgroup security, which you can verify any day of the week by visiting the Microsoft Access security newsgroup at `http://communities.microsoft.com/newsgroups/`.

So, should we persist with adding security to the database or should we just shrug our shoulders and hope that the database gets upgraded to an enterprise level database such as SQL Server? The answer is yes, it is worth persisting, and in the next few chapters, I will show you how you can tackle the password crackers and Access flaws head-on. In the process, I hope to make it easy enough for you to understand what you need to do and to decide whether it is worth doing. The first critical step that you cannot avoid is that you need to implement workgroup security so that users cannot get their hands on the workgroup file that secures the database. I have called this the developer workgroup strategy, and I encourage you to walk through the steps with sample databases so you can understand the basic concepts.

 User Story *Workgroup security was all too hard, which equaled fewer dollars. I personally stayed away from workgroup security for two or three years because I thought it was a little complex. I even came up with a strategy for convincing my clients to put security off until phase two of Access projects in the hope that the problem would go away. It was only when I realized that I was probably limiting my income by not understanding workgroup security that I finally got into it. And guess what—it's not rocket science!*

So, how do you get started with workgroup security? Guess what—you already have. Whenever you open an Access database, the first thing that happens is that the Access Jet engine opens a workgroup file. If no one has modified the workgroup file, Access then logs on by using Admin, a workgroup user account. This Admin account (like all other Access user accounts) has a security identifier (SID) that is passed to the Access database. From then on, the Access Jet engine uses that SID to define ownership of new objects and to verify your permissions for all objects in the database. What is important to remember is that the SID for the Admin account is always the same, no matter which version of Access you are using or which computer you are starting Access from. For this reason, I will now refer to this account as "the anonymous Admin user" to emphasize its universality.

You are going to use the universal SID of the anonymous Admin account in two ways when securing the database. First, you must secure the objects and the interface in such a way as to ensure that no account other than the developer can modify how your database works. Second, you will allow any users to log on anonymously to your database by using the Admin account and the interface that you provide. Because most users will probably log on to the database through their default workgroup file, they will be logging on by using the anonymous Admin account. This approach removes all the headaches of passwords from the DBA and stops those silly user habits, such as writing down the password and sticking it on the monitor and telling friends that they can log on with their account.

Let's review this basic concept in a diagram, because you are going to use this simple process to secure your databases. In Figure 8-1, you can see that the developer workgroup strategy allows two types of users to log on to the (network) database. The users open the database and log on through the default workgroup file (system.mdw) on their own PC. Because these workgroup files haven't been modified, the user logs on by using the Admin account. The developer though will log on through the developer workgroup file (developer.mdw) using either a developer account or the Admin account to test the database as a user. The developer can also use the original system.mdw file on his or her computer to further test end-user security.

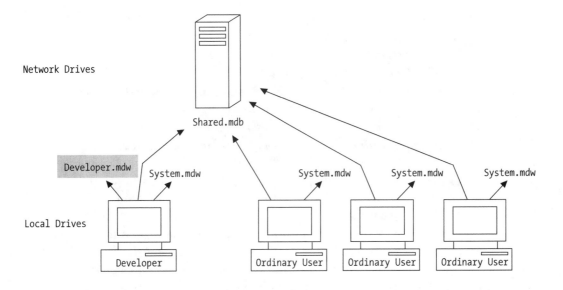

Figure 8-1. The design for the developer workgroup strategy.

The specific features of the default system.mdw workgroup file include the following:

- Every workgroup file has an Admin account. This account has the same security identifiers, regardless of which computer generates the workgroup file.

- Every workgroup file has a Users group account. This group account has the same security identifiers, regardless of which computer generates the workgroup file. All Access users are members of the Users group, and this group cannot be deleted.

- Unless you specify otherwise, Access will open a workgroup file that it creates the first time you use it. Even if you delete this file, Access will create a new default workgroup file in its place.

- If you do not specify a password for the Admin account, the workgroup file opens automatically.

- Because this file is on the local drive, performance will be good and network traffic will be limited to the database.

 NOTE I'll repeat this fundamental concept: Everyone will log on as Admin unless you do something about it. Logging on as Admin requires no work on the part of the user.

What Is a Workgroup File?

A workgroup file contains a list of user names and passwords and a list of groups. Both the users and groups will have a special identifier (SID) that is created by combining the personal identifier (PID) that you enter at the time that you create the user account and the user name. All this information is stored in a workgroup file that is actually an encrypted Access database. Included in the workgroup file will be the Admin account and the Users group. Both the Admin account and the Users group have identical SIDs for every installation of Access on the planet.

Which Workgroup File? Which User?

From the moment that you start working with workgroup file security, you need to know two things before you make any changes:

- Which workgroup file did I use to open the database?

- Which user account did I log on under?

You can find the answers to these questions through VBA code in the Immediate window (open by pressing CTRL+G) or by adding code similar to the following to an Access form or procedure:

```
MsgBox "My current workgroup file is " & SysCmd(acSysCmdGetWorkgroupFile)
```

or

```
MsgBox "My current workgroup file is " & DBEngine.SystemDB
```

My favorite code, which I generally type straight into the Immediate window ("13" here being the constant acSysCmdGetWorkgroupFile), is

```
? SysCmd(13)
```

To find the user account that you logged on as, use the CurrentUser property of the Application object, as follows:

```
MsgBox "My current user account is " & Application.CurrentUser
```

Alternatively, type the following into the Immediate window:

```
? CurrentUser
```

 TIP If you are using Access 97, try choosing Tools ➤ Security ➤ User-Level Security Wizard. This dialog provides both the user and the workgroup files.

Another thing that I find myself looking for is the location of all the workgroup files on my computer or our network. Take it from me—you and your company do not want to have too many such files. To take a look, open Windows Explorer and search for all files that have a file type of *.MDW.

The Workgroup File Database

Each workgroup information file contains an MSysAccounts table that stores all user and group account names, encrypted user passwords, and SIDs. If you are curious about workgroup files, use Access to open one by using the file type of `*.MDW`. After the special database is opened, choose Tools ➤ Options and select the View tab. Now select the System Objects check box. Have a look at both the tables and queries in the database. The queries may prove useful in determining the status of users and groups.

Preparing Your Developer Workgroup File

The first thing that you need to understand before preparing and changing workgroup files is finding the program that allows you to do it. Believe me, this step was tricky until Access 2002 came along. Anyway, the following sections describe the steps for finding the Workgroup Administrator programs.

The Workgroup Administrator for Access 97 and 2000

For Access 97 and 2000, search for a shortcut file in Windows Explorer called `MS Access Workgroup Administrator.lnk`. In Access 97, this shortcut points to a stand-alone program called `WRKGADM.EXE`, which will probably be in the `C:\WINDOWS\system32\` directory. In Access 2000, this shortcut points to a file that is also called `WRKGADM.EXE`, and you will probably find this in the `\Office\1033\` subdirectory in the Access 2000 installation folder. Once you have found the shortcut file, drop a copy of the shortcut file onto your desktop or onto the Windows Start menu because it is likely that you will use it a lot.

The Workgroup Administrator for Access 2002 or Later

For Access 2002 and 2003, you will find the Workgroup Administrator conveniently accessible by choosing Tools ➤ Security ➤ Workgroup Administrator (as shown in Figure 8-2). You do not have to have a database open for this option to appear. In these versions of Access, the Workgroup Administrator is part of the Access executable and thus will be subject to your menu management practices (discussed in Chapter 7). Access 2002 and later are the only versions that allow you to change workgroups while you are using Access.

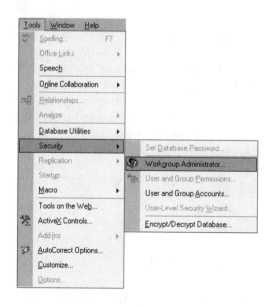

Figure 8-2. Finding the workgroup administrator in the Security submenu in Access 2002 and Access 2003.

Creating and Joining Workgroup Administration Files

Once you start the Workgroup Administrator, you will encounter the dialog shown in Figure 8-3. In this case, I am using the Access 97 Workgroup Administrator, and the currently selected (default) workgroup file on my computer is shown.

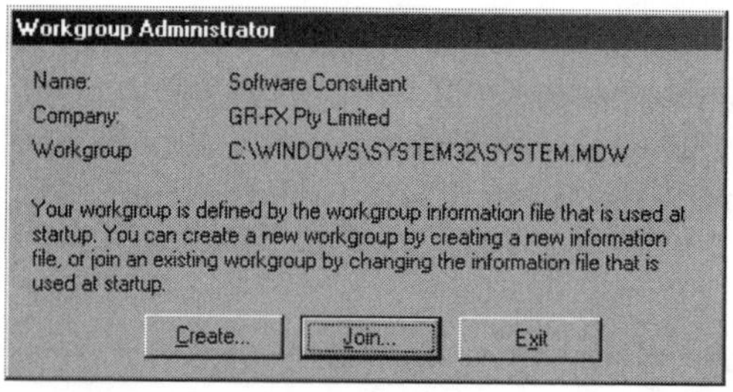

Figure 8-3. The first dialog that appears when you run the Workgroup Administrator.

Joining an Existing Workgroup File

If you want to join another workgroup file, click the Join button in the Work-group Administrator dialog, shown in Figure 8-3. This action takes you to a second dialog. Click the Browse button to navigate to the new workgroup file, click OK a couple of times, and you will return to the dialog shown in Figure 8-3. This dialog then shows what workgroup file you will use the next time you join Access. In Access 2002 or later, when you click Exit, Access will actually change the workgroup file immediately. In Access 97 or 2000, you have to close Access to open the new default workgroup file.

NOTE   Another way to join a workgroup file is to use shortcut files, which allows you to join to a different workgroup temporarily, as you open the database. This workgroup file association only lasts for the current Access session. Shortcut files are discussed in detail in Chapter 10.

Creating a Workgroup File

If you intend to create a new workgroup file, it is a good idea to write down the name and location of the current workgroup file so that you can rejoin it later. To create a new workgroup file, click the Create button in the Workgroup Administrator dialog. The Workgroup Owner Information dialog opens, shown in Figure 8-4. In this dialog, you need to enter your name, organization, and a special workgroup identifier. Then you need to write these details down in a very safe place because you will need the information in these three fields to re-create the workgroup file. I personally like to cut and paste the information into a Word document as well, just in case I get the upper- and lowercases wrong. Taking a picture of the screen by pressing ALT+PRINT SCREEN and pasting it into the Word document is also a good idea. For this book, I have used the following details:

Name: Real World
Organization: Microsoft Access Database
Workgroup ID: Protect and Secure

Workgroup Owner Information

The new workgroup information file is identified by the name, organization, and case-sensitive workgroup ID you specify.

Use the name and organization information below, or enter a different name or organization. If you want to ensure that your workgroup is unique, also enter a unique workgroup ID of up to 20 numbers or letters.

Name:	Real World
Organization:	Microsoft Access Database
Workgroup ID:	Protect and Secure

[OK]   [Cancel]

Figure 8-4. The developer workgroup setup information.

NOTE   To help you with the exercises in this book, I have set up a table in Appendix A with all the identifiers and passwords that you will need. If you like, you can also enter your own information in that same table, maybe including password hints, so that you don't have to write down the exact security information. That way, whenever you forget a password or a PID, you can always refer to the back of this book.

Now save the workgroup security file into a location that will be safe from prying eyes. Remember that the whole point of this file is to keep it secure from your database users. Also, please do not save the file as system.mdw, or you will get the new file confused with the default file on all computers. When these steps are complete, you will have joined that new workgroup.

No Logon Dialog—What Sort of Security Is This?

Now, if you close Access and open it again with a database of your own choosing, you will notice that the database just opens. That's because one of the first things that Access does when it uses a workgroup file is check whether the Admin account has a password. Because this workgroup file is new, the password is blank, so Access opens the database by using the Admin user. Therefore, the first thing that you need to do with this new workgroup file is add a password to the Admin account. To do this, choose Tools ➤ Security ➤ User and Group Accounts. Make sure that the current user is Admin, and select the Change Logon Password tab as shown in Figure 8-5. Leave the Old Password field blank and type the new password into the New Password and Verify fields. I suggest that you make this password very easy to remember, because you will only be using it for testing purposes. Now close Access and open the database again.

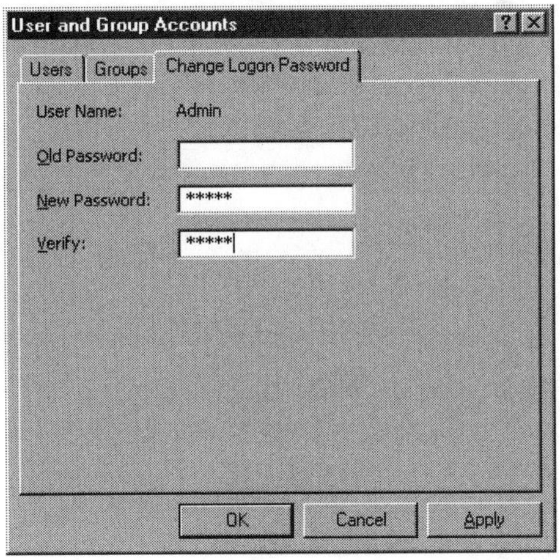

Figure 8-5. Inserting a new Admin user password.

Once you start Access again, enter your user name and password into the Logon dialog that will appear. In Access 97, this dialog appears as soon as Access starts. In Access 2000 and later, you will find that the Logon dialog appears when you are actually opening a database. Once you have successfully logged on, you will continue with this user and workgroup until you close Access again.

Setting Up the Developer User Account

Now that you have your own workgroup file, you must undertake a few basic tasks to start to secure the workgroup file.

Adding a New User

The first thing that you need to do is add a developer user account:

1. Choose Tools ➤ Security ➤ User and Group Accounts.

2. The User and Group Accounts dialog appears, as shown in Figure 8-6. Click the New button in the User area.

3. In the next dialog, enter the user's name (Developer) and a personal identifier (RealWorldDeveloper). Click OK.

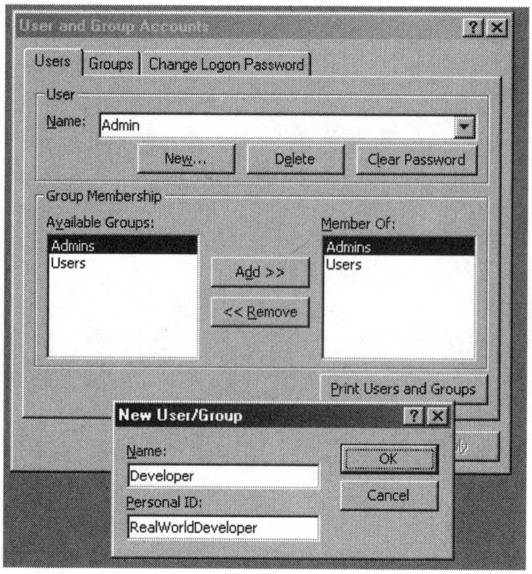

Figure 8-6. Adding a new user, called Developer.

The name of the new user will appear in the User drop-down list of the User and Group Accounts dialog shown in Figure 8-6. Also in the User and Group Accounts dialog in the Group Membership area, you will find that the new user has been made a member of the Users group. That's it. You now have your user. Shut down and open Access, and this time, log on as your new user (Developer). Because you have not added a password, you will not need to enter one. And because you are *not* going to distribute your developer workgroup file, having no password will prove to be a good little time-saver.

CAUTION   Write down both the user name and personal ID for this account because you will need this information to re-create the user.

Now that you have logged on, try choosing Tools ➤ Security ➤ User and Group Accounts again, and you will find that Access has worked out that the new account (Developer) is not a member of the Admins group. In addition, you will find that the new account does not have access to the New, Delete, and Clear Password buttons (as shown in Figure 8-7). The only thing that you can do with this user is change passwords and print lists of users and groups. These attributes are exactly what we are looking for in our anonymous Admin user. The next two steps in the process show you how to swap the administrator permissions from the anonymous Admin user account to the new Developer account.

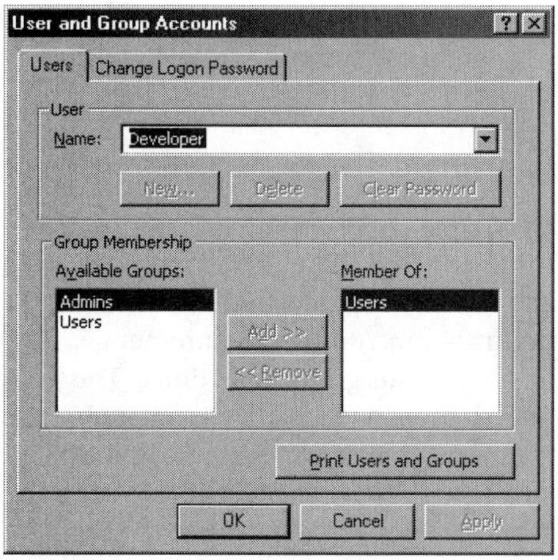

Figure 8-7. A user who doesn't belong to the Admins group.

NOTE   When you are looking at the object permissions for Groups, do not confuse the anonymous Admin user with the Admins (administrators) group.

NOTE   In Chapter 11, I show you how you can prepare a developer workgroup file by using the User-Level Security wizard.

Making Your New User an Administrator

To secure the workgroup:

1. Close and start Access and log on as the Admin user.

2. Open the User and Group Accounts dialog. Choose the new user (Developer) in the User Name drop-down list.

3. In the Available Groups list, choose Admins, then click Add.

The new Developer account can now add and delete user accounts and groups and arrange users into groups whenever they are joined to this workgroup file.

The Admins Group

The Admins group account is unique to each workgroup information file. By default, the Admin user belongs to the Admins group. Another requirement is that at least one user must be a member of the Admins group at all times. The Admins group is created from the owner information when the file is created. The Admins group in the default workgroup file on your computer is created with the company name and user name provided when you install Access. You can find out your company and user name by choosing Help ➤ About Microsoft Access.

Removing Administrator Permissions from the Admin Account

To make the workgroup safer, you should revoke administrator privileges from the Admin account:

1. Select the Admin account in the User Name drop-down list (see Figure 8-8).

2. Select Admins in the Member Of list box.

3. Click Remove to transfer the Admins group from the Member Of list to the Available Groups list (as shown in Figure 8-8).

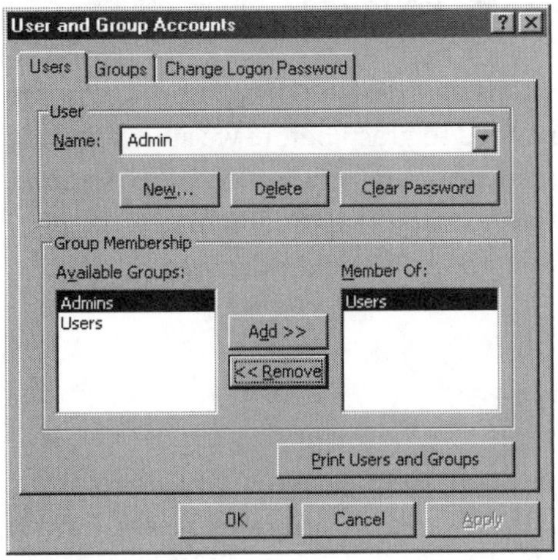

Figure 8-8. *Removing the Admins group from the Member Of list box.*

The Admin User Ends Up in the Users Group

After completing these steps, the Admin account is still a member of the Users group, another important anonymous entity that is common to all databases. This Users group account, which is controlled by the Jet database engine, will always hold all the users in the workgroup. This Users group uses security identifiers that are identical across all workgroups, and the group cannot be deleted, which means that any object permissions that are granted to the Users group apply to any Access user, including the anonymous Admin account. Importantly, this account by default has full permissions on all newly created objects. Given these parameters, it is obvious that the Users group must be managed carefully if you are going to produce a secure database.

Now, if you close Access and log on again as Admin, you will find that the Admin account cannot make any changes, apart from changing its own password. You now have a workgroup file with which you can apply some security to your database. Finally, you may find it a good idea to burn your developer workgroup file onto a CD-ROM for even more backup.

TIP If you feel a little apprehensive about building and saving a developer workgroup file, use the instructions from this section to re-create the file. That way, you can tell your boss how to re-create the workgroup file if something goes wrong.

The Developer Workgroup File Is Ready

Thus far in the book, we have covered the steps to produce a developer workgroup file—the most important concept that you need to grasp before we start securing the database is understanding where your security information ends up. So far in this chapter, I have discussed changes only to the workgroup file. From now on, our security discussions will involve both the workgroup file and the database itself.

Reflecting over a Cup of Coffee

Now is a good time to take a break and have a cup of coffee. While you are relaxing, reflect on the fact that you have made changes only to the workgroup file and haven't actually done anything with your database. It is also a good time to remember that every person is an anonymous Admin user and member of the Users group, which stops only if they join another workgroup file and log on by using another user account.

To make it easier to understand whether I am working on the workgroup file or the database permissions that we will cover soon, I like to modify the titles for the built-in user and security menu commands. The process that we have been using thus far (choosing Tools ➤ Security ➤ User and Group Accounts) only changes the workgroup file. Therefore, I change the command title to "User and Group Accounts...WORKGROUP" (as shown in Figure 8-9) by using the following steps:

1. Right-click a toolbar and choose Customize.

2. When the Customize Toolbars dialog appears, choose Tools ➤ Security ➤ User and Group Accounts.

3. Right-click the "User and Group Accounts" command and choose Rename.

4. Change the name to include "... WORKGROUP," then click Close. (See Chapter 7 for more instructions.)

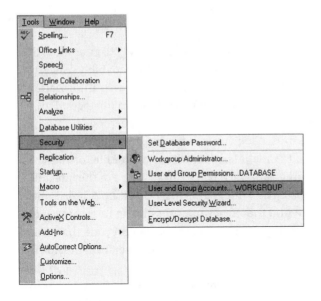

Figure 8-9. Renamed user and security commands

Apart from helping me remember what I am working on, this new name acts as a visual reminder that I need to make sure that I am using the correct workgroup. The second command (Tools ➤ Security ➤ User and Group Permissions), which is located above the Workgroup command, changes only database permissions and database object permissions. I change this command to "User and Group Permissions... DATABASE." These permissions apply to workgroup Users and Groups, and soon I will describe how they work.

 TIP   Always know what account you are using and what workgroup file you are using before making security changes.

Before I discuss database ownership and permissions, I am going to digress into some VBA code that you can use to generate a developer workgroup file from scratch.

Building a Workgroup File in Code

While I was writing this chapter, I became very keen to find a way to guarantee that programmers could re-create the developer workgroup file. This capability concerned me because Microsoft recommends that you write down the owner information, user names, and PIDs. Because over the years I personally seem to be good at keeping electronic files and conversely seem to be useless at keeping and finding paper, creating a workgroup file from code appealed to me. In addition, because Access's workgroup security design precludes upgrades to a later file format, it would be better to create the workgroup file again from software in the latest file format. Therefore, when I was looking into integrating the Workgroup Administrator into Access 2002, I was excited to find that it was now possible to re-create a workgroup file from within Access. This discovery led me to write VBA code that would re-create the developer workgroup file and remove the Admin user from the Admins group. You will find this VBA code in a form called `frmDevelopersWorkgroup` in the `grMap2002.mdb` database. Developers may find this automation of the workgroup file creation to be very useful after reading the PID authentication concept in Chapter 10.

On the `frmDevelopersWorkgroup` form illustrated in Figure 8-10, you will find two buttons. To use the form, click button 1 to generate a workgroup file that will then be your default workgroup file. You then have to close and reopen Access, and this time you will be logged on automatically as the Admin user. Clicking button 2 on this form, which will work only if you joined this new workgroup file, then adds a password for the Admin user account, adds the Developer user account, and removes the Admin user from the Admins administration group. I encourage you to read the VBA code first before running the procedure. In particular, review the constants at the top of the module and the procedures, as these will be your security identifiers. Another thing to be aware of in Access 2002 or later is your default file format (found by choosing Tools ➤ Options ➤ Advanced tab), which defines the file format of your workgroup security file. Naturally, if your intended audience is Access 2002/2003 users, I advise you to go with the later version because it will preclude 2000 users from ever opening the workgroup file.

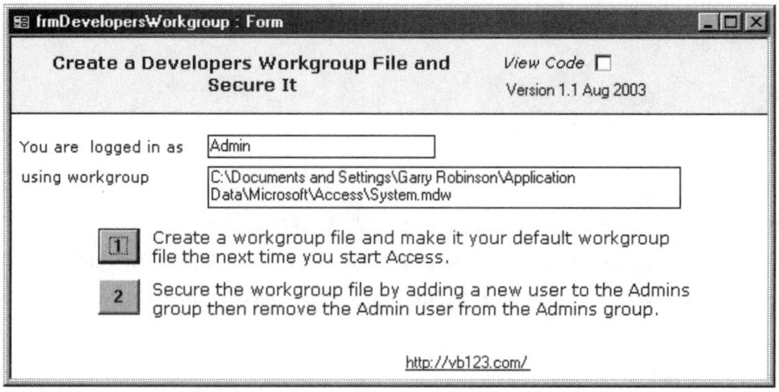

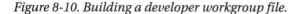

Figure 8-10. Building a developer workgroup file.

This discussion brings us to the specifics of the VBA code under button 1. Initially, a number of constants are declared, including the location of the workgroup file as a module constant common to both procedures. Then you will need to confirm the creation of the workgroup file and its Access file format (2000 or 2002/2003). Then, if all seems okay, the CreateNewWorkgroupFile and SetDefaultWorkgroupFile methods create the workgroup file by using the security details defined by the constants.

```
Option Compare Database
Option Explicit

Const SECUREWRK = "C:\developer.mdw"

Private Sub cmdDevelopWrkGrp_Click()

On Error GoTo err_cmdDevelopWrkGrp

' This code makes a workgroup by using the Access 2002 default file format.

Const FORMATMENU = "See menu (Options > Advanced > Default File format)"
Const WRKGRPNAME = "Real World"
Const WRKGRPCOMPANY = "Microsoft Access Database"
Const WRKGRPID = "Protect and Secure"
Const ACC2K = 9
Dim strFileFormat As String, intCreateWrk
```

```
If Application.GetOption("Default File Format") = ACC2K Then
    strFileFormat = "Access 2000"
Else
    strFileFormat = "Access 2002/2003"
End If


intCreateWrk = MsgBox("Would you like to create the " & SECUREWRK & _
                      " workgroup file in " & strFileFormat & " file format", _
                      vbYesNo, "Create and point to a new workgroup file")

If intCreateWrk = vbYes Then
    Application.CreateNewWorkgroupFile SECUREWRK, WRKGRPNAME, _
                                WRKGRPCOMPANY, WRKGRPID, False

    Application.SetDefaultWorkgroupFile SECUREWRK
    MsgBox "Next time you start Access, you will be using the " & _
            SECUREWRK & " workgroup file." & vbCrLf & vbCrLf & _
            "To secure the Workgroup file, restart Access " & _
            ", Open this form again and click on button 2."

    ' Disable button 2 because you need to start Access with the new workgroup.
    cmdSecureWrkGrp.Enabled = False

Else
    MsgBox "If you want to change the file format,  " & FORMATMENU
End If

Exit_cmdDevelopWrkGrp:
    Exit Sub

err_cmdDevelopWrkGrp:
    Select Case Err.Number
      Case Else
        MsgBox "Error No. " & Err.Number & " -> " & Err.Description
    End Select
    Resume Exit_cmdDevelopWrkGrp
End Sub
```

CAUTION If you have run this procedure, you will join the new workgroup file. Do not forget to rejoin your old workgroup file. See the section "Preparing Your Development Workgroup File" earlier in this chapter for information on how to rejoin your old workgroup file.

At this stage, you will close and reopen Access so that you can log on (automatically) as the anonymous Admin user in the new workgroup file. Now we'll use some special SQL commands that Jet 4.0 (Access 2000) introduced. The purpose of these commands is to create a new user, make the user an administrator, set the Admin password, and remove the Admin user from the Admins group. These special SQL commands—Create User, Add User xxx To Group, Drop User xxx From Group, and Alter User xxx Password—are not available from the normal query window. Instead, you must use the Execute method of the ADO Connection object to run the SQL commands. I particularly like this approach because the VBA code is easy to read. It is also possible to do the same thing by using the DAO library. Yet another approach is the ADOX security library, but this falls down because you cannot specify the user's PID when creating the accounts. Instead, a random PID is generated for you, which makes rebuilding the workgroup impossible. One trick that I worked out by trial and error was using the Null qualifier (which acts as a blank password) in the SQL Alter User admin Password command string. This qualifier resolves the automatic logon into the workgroup by removing the blank password for the Admin account. To complete the VBA code, I have used the RunCommand method to launch the Users and Group Accounts dialog directly from the code. You can verify that the workgroup file is secure by verifying that the Admin account doesn't belong to the Admins group and that the Developer account does belong to the Admins group.

NOTE The following code will also work in Access 2000, but you will need a new workgroup file before starting. Create one by using the manual instructions for the Workgroup Administrator executable as described earlier in the section "The Workgroup Administrator for Access 97 and 2000."

```
Private Sub cmdSecureWrkGrp_Click()
' Secure the workgroup file to be used with the preceding module
' or in Access 2000, by using a newly created workgroup file.

' This subroutine requires a reference to the
' Microsoft ActiveX Data Objects 2.1 library (or later).

Const SECUREUSER = "Developer"
Const SECUREPWD = "Developer"
Const SECUREPID = "RealWorldDeveloper"

Dim cnn As ADODB.Connection

On Error GoTo err_cmdSecureWrkGrp

If SysCmd(acSysCmdGetWorkgroupFile) = SECUREWRK Then
    Set cnn = CurrentProject.Connection

    ' No error handling because the users may already exist or belong to the group.
    On Error Resume Next
    cnn.Execute "create user " & SECUREUSER & " " & SECUREPWD & " " & SECUREPID
    cnn.Execute "add user " & SECUREUSER & " to Users"
    cnn.Execute "add user " & SECUREUSER & " to Admins"
    cnn.Execute "drop user Admin from Admins"
    On Error GoTo 0

    ' Add a password to the Admin account so that you are forced to log on.
    cnn.Execute "alter user admin password " & SECUREPWD & " null;"
    Set cnn = Nothing

    MsgBox "You have created a new user with adminstration rights called " & _
            SECUREUSER & " with a password of " & SECUREPWD & " and a PID of " & _
            SECUREPID & vbCrLf & vbCrLf & ". The Admin account also has " & _
            "the same password and now has been removed from the Admins group", _
            vbInformation, "You Now Will See The Workgroup Users and Groups " & _
            "Dialog Form"
    RunCommand acCmdUserAndGroupAccounts
Else
    MsgBox "You have not logged into the " & SECUREWRK & " workgroup file yet", _
            vbInformation, "No Action Taken"
End If
```

```
Exit_cmdSecureWrkGrp:
  Exit Sub


err_cmdSecureWrkGrp:
   Select Case Err.Number
      Case vbObjectError + 999
         ' To see line immediately after the error line, press CTRL+BREAK,
         ' drag yellow arrow to Resume Next, then prses F8 key.
         Resume Next
      Case Else
         MsgBox "Error No. " & Err.Number & " -> " & Err.Description
   End Select

   Resume Exit_cmdSecureWrkGrpEnd Sub
End Sub
```

So what are we going to do with this VBA code? I suggest that once you are
happy with your security accounts and groups you create a database with this
form in it, modify the workgroup security constants, and use this code as your
documentation. Now you can use this code to regenerate the workgroup file in
Access 2000 file format (using Access 2002) and any later version. You can also
provide your clients with your version of this code so that they can re-create the
workgroup file if you happen to step in front of the proverbial bus.

Securing Your Database with Your Developer Workgroup File

Now that you have a suitable developer workgroup file, you are at the stage where
you are ready to start securing parts of your database. The initial security techniques that I will describe will achieve most of the security that developers are
interested in. If you want to secure the actual data in the database itself, you will
need to work through some other technical issues to achieve the holy grail of a
secure database. Initially, though, I will show you how you can achieve a lot of
good protection and some object security by changing some permissions on just
one (or a few) objects in your database. Thereafter, our target audience, the anonymous Admin user and the Users group (explained earlier in the chapter) will not
be able to change or look at the design of the object, import those objects, or
upgrade the databases to newer versions of Access. This is my favorite and simple
Access security strategy that I stumbled onto in my early days of shareware
development.

One Secure Object Marks a Developer's Territory

To change permissions for just one object (form or report) in your database, you first need a user account with administer permission over that object (and hopefully all others as well). The steps to achieve this protection follow:

1. Join the developer workgroup file (called Developer.mdw) as described in the "Preparing Your Developer Workgroup File" section earlier in the chapter.

2. Select the database that you are going to secure (I use a copy of Northwind in these examples).

3. Log on to the developer's account (which we earlier named Developer). If you are already using Access, double check that you are using the correct workgroup file and user account.

4. Open the database container and select a form or report to protect. In this case, I will select the first form in the Northwind database, called Categories.

5. Choose Tools ➤ Security ➤ User and Group Permissions.

6. Select Admin in the User/Groups Name list. Clear the Read Design check box in the Permissions area. This action also clears the Modify Design and Administer check boxes. Now click Apply.

7. Choose the Groups option. A dialog appears, asking if you want to assign the permissions now. Click Yes.

8. Select Users in the User/Groups Name list.

9. Clear the Read Design check box in the Permissions area, as shown in Figure 8-11. Now click Apply.

10. Finally, change the ownership of the object to the Developer account to make sure that the anonymous Admin user cannot modify this object. To do this, select the Change Owner tab. Now choose the correct object type (form or report) and choose the object. Then select your secure user (Developer) from the New Owner drop-down list, as shown in Figure 8-12.

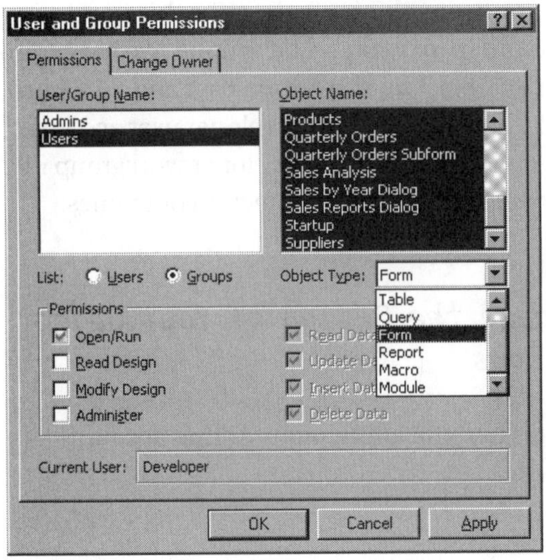

Figure 8-11. Clearing the Read Design check box in the Permissions area.

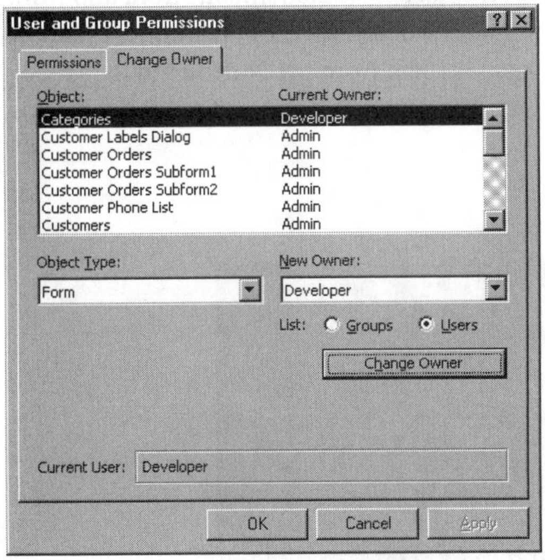

Figure 8-12. Changing the ownership of the form to the Developer.

 TIP You can always check your user account in the Current User field at the bottom of the User and Group Permissions dialog.

That concludes the process of securing an object. To describe this important process in a different way, here is a summary of what we have done. We have minimized the necessary permissions on an object for the Admin user and the Users group and changed the ownership of the object to your Developer user account. Now, unless the user can log on to or re-create the same developer workgroup file, you will achieve the following worthwhile security and protection outcomes.

Stopping Anyone from Reading the Design of Your Object and Changing Its Permissions

The obvious benefit of these changes is that the anonymous Admin account cannot open the object in design mode.

Stopping Anyone from Importing the Object into Another Database

Removing read design permissions from an object prevents someone from importing the object into another database. To try out this deterrence, open another database and import (the already secured) Categories form from the Northwind database with which we have been experimenting. When you do, you will receive the error message shown in Figure 8-13.

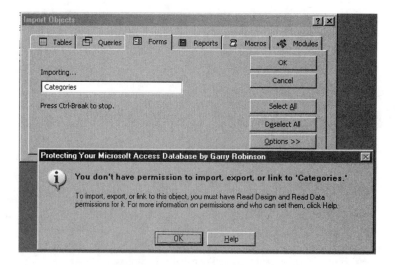

Figure 8-13. The error message issued when an object cannot be imported into another database.

Stopping Anyone from Upgrading the Database to a Later Version of Access

Whenever you open an Access database in a later version of Access, Access will assess the permissions of all the objects in the database. If Access finds that the current user has read design permissions for all the objects in the database (and passes other requirements as well), the user can upgrade the database to a later version of the database. If Access doesn't find that the user is able to convert the database, a warning message appears, as shown in Figure 8-14.

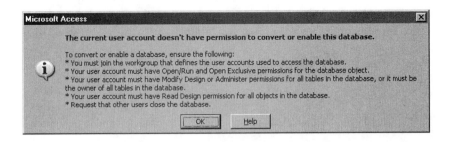

Figure 8-14. A warning message that appears when the user account cannot convert a database.

User Story *This particular result of securing an object has proved profitable to me over the years when the occasional user has wandered off to another employer with the database. When that user arrives, they find that the new employer has a later version of Access, making it impossible to run the database the user depended on. One such user relocated from central Australia to West Africa and, after opening the software, found that he was blocked. If he had looked hard enough, he would have found that he could have imported all the important objects into another database because in this case, I had not protected any object of importance.*

The other way in which this result proves useful is when clients themselves upgrade Access. At this stage, I receive a call and a little bit of work to upgrade and test the software, and I have a chance to reestablish contact after long periods of maintenance-free running. A good analogy is that securing just one object is a bit like designing a refrigerator so that it starts to break down after seven years.

Stopping Users from Opening Access 97 Databases in Access 2000 or Later

One feature of multiversion compatibility with Access is the Open Database option (shown in Figure 8-15) that allows Access 2000 or later to open Access 97 databases without converting the database. This seemingly useful option is not without its pitfalls, however, because the first time that someone opens the database this way, the database expands without warning because Access adds extra compatibility information to the database. As an example, the Access 97 Northwind database expands from 1.5MB to 2.2MB. Not even the unsupported \decompile shortcut switch will retrieve the space. But because you're interested in protecting your database, not having the appropriate permissions will stop the anonymous Admin account from opening the database by using a later version of Access.

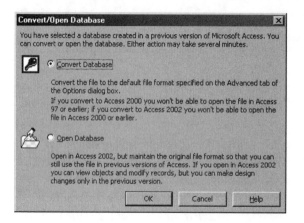

Figure 8-15. The Convert/Open Database message, which appears when you open a database with a later version of Access.

That concludes the descriptions of the considerable benefits that result from removing the object permissions from the anonymous Admin account and Users group. In the next section of this chapter, I describe how to transfer the ownership of all the objects in the database to the new Developer account.

Transferring Ownership of the Database and All Its Objects

As I mentioned in the last section, ownership of objects in the database is important because owners can reset permissions on their objects. To make sure that the Developer user has full control of the objects in the database, that user needs to own all the objects. You can assign objects on the Change Owner tab in the Group and Users Permissions dialog. As a built-in Access security precaution, you cannot change database ownership through that interface or through VBA code. To get around this issue, you have to make a new database and import all the objects into that database. The steps for that action follow:

1. Log on to your new workgroup by using the Developer user account.

2. Check that you actually are using the Developer workgroup file and Developer user account. For details on how to check, see the earlier sections "Which Workgroup File? Which User?" and "Joining an Existing Workgroup File."

3. If you are using Access 2002 or later, check that you are creating the database in the required file format by choosing Tools ➤ Options ➤ Advanced ➤ Default File Format. This setting usually depends on whether your clients use Access 2000 or Access 2002/2003.

4. Choose File ➤ New Database.

5. Create a new blank database.

6. Choose File ➤ Get External Data ➤ Import.

7. Find the database on which you want to change ownership.

8. Select the Tables, Queries, Forms, Reports, Macros, and Modules tabs, then select all the objects for each one. Also remember to click the Options button and select the Menus and Toolbars and the Import/ Export Specs check boxes, and click OK. All the objects will now be imported into the blank database.

9. Now choose Tools ➤ Security ➤ User and Group Permissions and check that the owner of all the objects is now the Developer user.

NOTE   To import a database, you must have Read Design permission for all its objects and Open/Run permission for the database. To import tables, you must also have Read Data permission. If you have permissions for some objects but not others, Access imports only the objects for which you have permission. When an error occurs, Access will issue an error message for each object it cannot import.

The most important ownership issue that is resolved by importing the database is the ownership of the database itself. Generally, when you first start developing an Access database, you will create the database by using the anonymous Admin account. As you can see from the disabled Change Owner button shown in Figure 8-16, you cannot transfer the ownership of the database by using the Change Owner tab. One issue to be aware of with database ownership is that the owner/creator of the database can always open the database, which is why you do not want the default Admin account to own the database. Another reason is that changing ownership of a database means that people who are not database owners cannot encrypt or decrypt the database. Find out more about database encryption in Chapter 9.

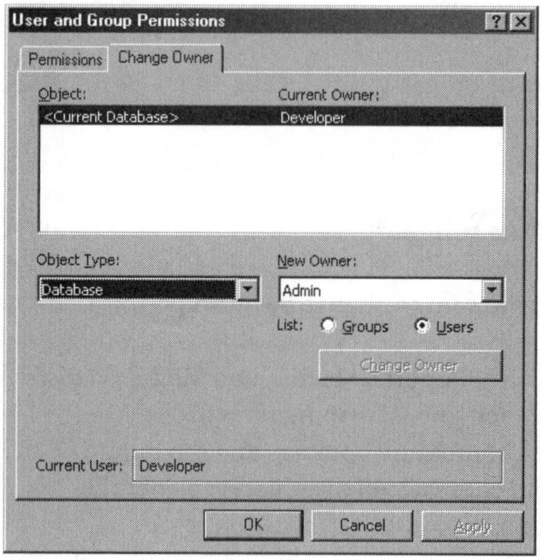

Figure 8-16. The Change Owner tab shows that the Developer is the owner of the database.

In the next section, we will look at how we can maintain object ownership over the long term, as it is likely that a number of people could create objects in a database where anyone can gain access to the database window.

Maintaining Object Ownership and Change of Ownership

Once you have transferred ownership by importing all the objects into a blank database, you probably should not concern yourself with object ownership for a while. When you do, you may find that you have a problem with mixed ownership. In addition, you may wonder how good your permissions (covered in the next section) are at stopping the anonymous Admin account from reversing the ownership changes. To help you with these issues, I have developed an Access form called frmCheckandChangeOwnership (shown in Figure 8-17).

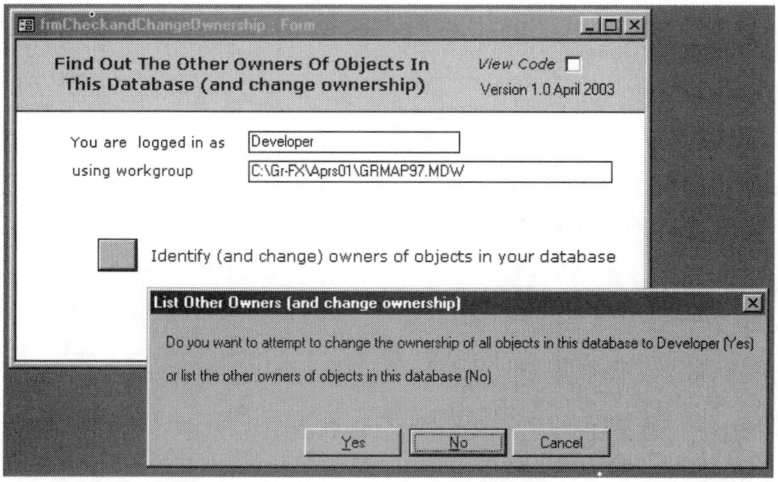

Figure 8-17. The frmCheckandChangeOwnership *demonstration form.*

The purpose of this form is to check and list ownership of all the objects (database, tables, forms, and so on) in your database. The output of this software, demonstrated as follows, displays in the Immediate window (which you can open by pressing CTRL+G). The software will also change the ownership of the object to the current user, if required.

```
>>> Start Of List of Other Owners of Objects @ 9:20:59 AM

--- DATABASES  Container---

    AccessLayout  ... admin
    MSysDb  ... admin
    SummaryInfo  ... admin
    UserDefined  ... admin

--- FORMS  Container---

    Categories  ... admin
    Customer Labels Dialog  ... admin
    Startup  ... admin
    Suppliers  ... admin

--- MODULES  Container---

    Startup  ... admin
    Utility Functions  ... admin

--- RELATIONSHIPS  Container---

    {1F8E2C3D-2471-4FFE-8F53-7DAD3224ADC8}  ... admin
    {2B241988-7600-49E9-9686-A12B933079BA}  ... admin

--- REPORTS  Container---

    Alphabetical List of Products  ... admin
    Catalog  ... admin
    Summary of Sales by Quarter  ... admin
    Summary of Sales by Year  ... admin

--- SCRIPTS  Container---

    Customer Labels Dialog  ... admin
    Sample Autokeys  ... admin
    Suppliers  ... admin

--- SYSREL  Container---

--- TABLES  Container---
```

```
Order Details Extended   ... admin
Order Subtotals  ... admin
Orders    ... admin
Product Sales for 1995   ... admin
Products   ... admin
Ten Most Expensive Products  ... admin
```

`<<< End of List of Other Owners of Objects 9:20:59 AM`

To produce this output and change ownership, if required, I have used the Microsoft DAO library, which allows the code to list all objects that are not owned by the current user account. To produce this output, the VBA code iterates through all the document collections. If you are interested in how the ownership is changed, look through the code that follows for the line that includes doc.Owner. The VBA code that produces this output follows:

```
Private Sub cmdFindOwners_Click()

' Find all the owners of the database objects.
' If requested, change the ownership of foreign objects to
' the current user.

' This subroutine requires a reference to the
' Microsoft DAO 3.6 or 3.51 library.

On Error GoTo err_cmdFindOwners

Dim dbs As DAO.Database, cnt As DAO.Container, doc As DAO.Document
Dim objName As String, strDocName As String, strCurrUser
Dim i As Integer, intChangeUser As Integer

Dim strDocOwner As String

strCurrUser = CurrentUser

intChangeUser = MsgBox("Do you want to attempt to change the ownership of " & _
                  "all objects in this database to " & strCurrUser & _
                  " (Yes)" & vbCrLf & vbCrLf & "or list the other " & _
                  "owners of objects in this database (No)", _
                  vbYesNoCancel + vbDefaultButton2, _
                  "List Other Owners (and change ownership)")
```

```
    If intChangeUser <> vbCancel Then
        Debug.Print vbCrLf & ">>> Start Of List Of Other Owners Of Objects @ " & Time
        Set dbs = CurrentDb()
        For Each cnt In dbs.Containers
            ' Cycle through all the containers.
            Debug.Print vbCrLf & "--- " & UCase(cnt.Name) & "  Container---" & vbCrLf

            For Each doc In cnt.Documents

                If intChangeUser = vbYes Then
                    ' Change the owner of this document to the current owner.
                    ' Will occur only if current user has appropriate permissions.

                    On Error Resume Next
                    doc.Owner = strCurrUser
                    On Error GoTo err_cmdFindOwners
                End If
                strDocOwner = doc.Owner
                If strDocOwner <> "Engine" And _
                    LCase(strDocOwner) <> LCase(strCurrUser) Then

                    ' Only look at nonsystem objects that are not owned by this user.
                    strDocName = doc.Name
                    Debug.Print "    " & strDocName & Chr(9) & " ... " & strDocOwner
                End If
            Next doc
        Next cnt

        ' Open the debug window.
        ' Warning: Databases with large numbers of objects may have their lists trimmed.
        Debug.Print vbCrLf & "<<< End of List Of Other Owners Of Objects " & Time
        RunCommand acCmdDebugWindow
    End If

Exit_cmdFindOwners:
    On Error Resume Next

    Set doc = Nothing
    Set cnt = Nothing
    Set dbs = Nothing

    Exit Sub
```

```
err_cmdFindOwners:
    Select Case Err.Number          ' Problems with unload process
        Case vbObjectError + 999
            ' To see line immediately after the error line, press CTRL+BREAK,
            ' drag yellow arrow to Resume Next, then press F8.
            Resume Next
        Case Else
            MsgBox "Error No. " & Err.Number & " -> " & Err.Description
    End Select

    Resume Exit_cmdFindOwners
End Sub
```

This form will also prove useful when you have completed the next section of the chapter on permissions, because you may want to test that the Admin account cannot regain permissions for objects because they are the owner of the objects. To undertake this test, take a copy of the database, import the frmCheckandChangeOwnership form into the database, and run this code. If this form can change the ownership of an object back to the anonymous Admin account, you will need to check your permissions.

Now that we have seen how to view, manipulate, and test ownership by using automated techniques, the next stage in the path to securing your database involves assigning and removing database permissions.

Setting Database Permissions

It is important to realize when allocating and removing permissions that the database itself is classified as an object and has its own very important permissions. The database object name is MSysDb, and this section describes the outcomes from removing those permissions.

If you go to the User and Group Permissions dialog and select the Object Type drop-down list, you will find that the first option in the list is Database (as shown in Figure 8-18). Intentionally or not, the list box almost conceals the word Database above Tables, the second item in the list. Now we will see what happens when you remove each of the permissions in this dialog.

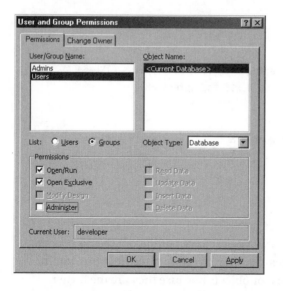

Figure 8-18. The User and Group Permissions dialog.

Clearing Administer Permission

When you clear the Administer check box for a user account (**Admin**) or a group (**Users**), that account will not be allowed to

- Change any permission for the Database object, as shown in Figure 8-18.

- Change the database startup options as shown in Figure 8-19 and discussed in detail in the section "Preventing End Users from Changing the Startup Properties" in Chapter 2.

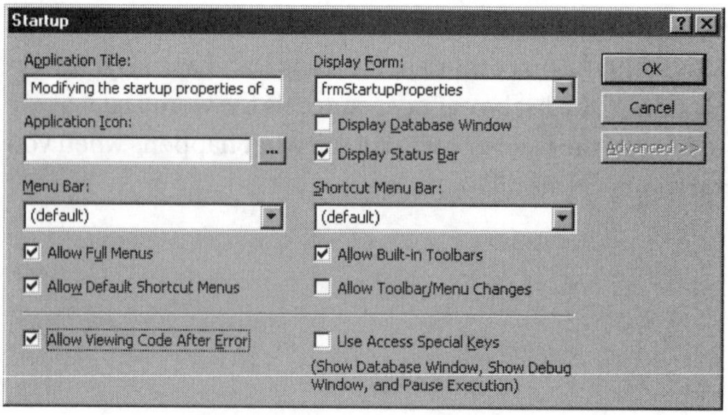

Figure 8-19. Database Administer permission stops users from changing the startup options on this dialog.

- Add or modify the database password (see Chapter 9).

- Convert the database into a replicated design master. Links to further resources on this topic can be found in the section "Further Reading" later in this chapter.

More on Securing the Startup Options

If workgroup security has been defined for your database, you can prevent users from changing the settings in the Startup dialog by making sure they haven't been granted Administer permission for the database. When you test these changes with an account that has the Administer permission removed, the startup properties will seem to change. When you return to view the startup properties, however, you will find that the changes that you made were not accepted.

It is important to be aware that all users can change the startup options if a special setting for a startup option called the Data Definition Language is set to False. This setting is explained in detail in the section "Preventing End Users from Changing the Startup Properties" in Chapter 2. In addition, bear in mind that the startup options are not transferred when you import all or any of the objects from one database into another. For more information on these startup options, see Chapter 2.

Clearing Open Exclusive Permission

If you remove open exclusive permission for an account, that account will not be allowed to open the database in exclusive mode. In Access 97, if the account tries to open the database in exclusive mode, the database will not open.

In Access 2000 and later, no error message is issued and the database opens in shared mode instead. Then comes a wonderful protection measure—the account user cannot save any form, report, macro, or module opened in design view back to the database, which means that users who belong to groups (such as the Users group) who do not have Open Exclusive permission for a database cannot alter any of those objects in the database. Removing this permission resolves two great headaches for the DBA: the software cannot be changed and the database cannot be opened by someone in exclusive mode, thereby stopping all other people from opening the database at all.

Clearing Open/Run Permission

Clearing the Open/Run permission for the Users group (and Admin user) results in a very secure database. No one who uses the anonymous Admin user account will be able to open the database, link to the tables in the database, or import any objects from the database, which means that you will need a workgroup file with an account that has Open/Run permission for the database. We will employ this option in Chapter 10, but for the moment, our whole strategy is to allow the anonymous (Admin) account to access the database, so this permission is not very relevant.

Testing the Database Permissions

To test your database permissions against the anonymous Admin account, you generally can use any workgroup file other than your developer workgroup and log on as the Admin user. Sometimes, though, you may have made alterations to the groups of which the Admin user is a member. To be perfectly sure, you can do the following test:

1. Create a brand-new workgroup by using the steps in the section "Preparing Your Developer Workgroup File." Call it something like AdminTest.mdw.

2. Join that workgroup file.

3. Open the database that you want to test. As long as no user name dialog appears, you will be using the anonymous Admin account.

4. Test the Administer, Open Exclusive, and Open/Run permissions for the database.

5. Rejoin your normal workgroup file.

Removing All Permissions from the Admin User

When you transfer ownership by importing objects into a database by using your Developer user account, the anonymous Admin user is unlikely to have any individual user permissions for objects in the database. Anyway, it is important that you check for and remove all the permissions now so that you don't get caught out at a later date. To do check for and remove these permissions:

1. Log on to your Developer workgroup (as Developer).

2. Choose Tools ➤ Security ➤ User and Group Permissions.

3. Make sure that you select Users for the List option box and Admin in the User/Group Name list (shown in Figure 8-20).

4. Manually work through all the object types (by using the Object Type drop-down list) and remove all permissions from the Admin account. To do this step quickly for forms, you will need to select <New Forms> in the Object Name box and then press SHIFT while you select the last item in the list.

5. Clear all the check boxes under Permissions and then click Apply. It is important to note that by selecting <New Objects> at the top of each list, you are stopping the Admin user from doing things with new objects that you create with the Developer account.

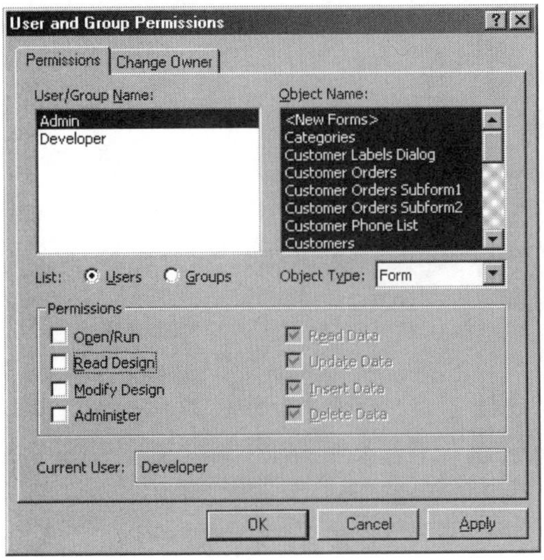

Figure 8-20. Clearing all permissions for all objects for the Admin user.

 TIP   If you use the AutoExec macro to start your database, it will be important to secure it. This rule particularly applies if you are using user surveillance techniques such as those described in Chapter 6.

Using Permissions to Tame the Users Group

Earlier in the chapter when I covered how to make a developer workgroup file, I showed how the Admin user belonged to the Users group on every computer. As this is exactly the setup that we are catering to in the developer workgroup strategy, you need to remove permissions from the Users group. The permissions that need to be changed vary between object types, as shown in this list:

- For forms, reports, and macros, clear the Read Design, Modify Design, and Administer permissions check boxes (shown in Figure 8-21).

Figure 8-21. Removing permissions for objects owned by the Users group.

- For tables and queries, clear the Modify Design and Administer permissions check boxes.

- For modules in Access 97, clear all Permissions check boxes. Unfortunately, this security was removed in Access 2000 and was replaced by VBA passwords (see Chapter 9). Thankfully, you can simulate this effect by using VBA code, which I will demonstrate later in the section "Module Permissions Are Back."

TIP   When changing permissions on an object, it is easier to select the object in the Database window and then switch to the User and Group Permissions dialog.

More on Tables and Query Permissions

When securing tables and queries for the anonymous Admin account as a member of the anonymous Users group, the Modify Design and Administer permissions check boxes should be cleared (as shown in Figure 8-22). The exception to this rule is for linked tables in the front end of split databases, where it is best that you leave full permissions on the linked table because the linked table inherits the permissions from the back-end database. Therefore, you may as well manage the permissions in the back-end database.

Figure 8-22. The minimum permissions that should be applied to the Users group.

Conceptually, the Read Design permission is a bit of a problem because it allows users and groups with that permission to view the design of either the table or the query. This capability is not quite as big a problem as it appears at first glance, however, because

- That user cannot actually change the design of those objects.

- Tables and queries can be well protected through the startup properties discussed in Chapter 2, such as database window, special keys, and allow bypass. You can further protect these startup properties by using workgroup security to remove the Database Administer property (discussed in this chapter).

- You can use the With Owner permission in queries (as discussed in Chapter 11) to secure your query and table designs.

The problem that I have with the Read Design permission is that the data and queries are still vulnerable to importing the data into another database. You may consider using additional workgroup security, as discussed in Chapter 10, to secure your data. In Chapter 11, I show you how you can use With Owner permission in queries to secure your query and table design.

Module Permissions Are Back

It was unfortunate in Access 2000 that the changes to the Visual Basic project meant that the User and Group Permissions dialog no longer allowed you to remove module permissions from the Database window. In Access 97, you could set these permissions as shown in Figure 8-23, and it was a protection measure that I had used since Access 2. Admittedly, it isn't foolproof, but it does deter the ordinary programming snoop.

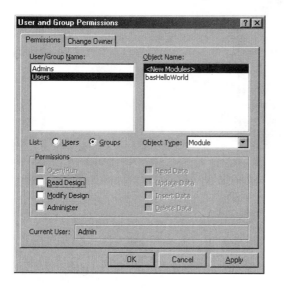

Figure 8-23. Removing design permission from a module in Access 97.

One day when I was upgrading my Graf-FX shareware program from Access 97 to Access 2000, I noticed that the permissions that were supposed to have been abolished by the latest version were actually still prohibiting the anonymous Admin user from opening the modules. After some investigation into DAO permissions, I found that backward compatibility meant that you could still protect your modules from being opened in design mode from the Database window (see Figure 8-24).

Figure 8-24. The user account that does not have the permissions will receive this error message.

The following steps show how the VBA code in the frmProtectModule download form will protect a module:

1. Make sure that you are joined to the Developer workgroup and logged on as the Developer account.

2. Import the frmProtectModule form into your database.

3. Create and save a module called basHelloWorld.

4. Click the only button on the frmProtectModule form.

5. Close Access.

6. Open the database and log on as the anonymous Admin user.

7. Try to open the basHelloWorld module; you should receive an error like that shown in Figure 8-24.

The VBA code that will protect a module follows. Note that I have set up the code to remove all permissions on the object for both the anonymous Admin user and the Users group.

```
Private Sub cmdProtectModules_Click()
' Protect a module in this database from the Admin user
' or the Users group from opening it it in design view.

' This subroutine requires a reference to
' Microsoft DAO 3.6 or 3.51 library.

Const MYMODULE = "basHelloWorld"
On Error GoTo err_cmdProtectModules
```

```
Dim dbs As DAO.Database, cnt As DAO.Container, doc As DAO.Document

Set dbs = CurrentDb
Set doc = dbs.Containers("modules").Documents(MYMODULE)
doc.UserName = "Admin"
' Remove all design permissions from module for the Admin account.
' You can restore it later by using "= dbSecFullAccess."
doc.Permissions = dbSecNoAccess

' Remove all design permissions from module for the Users account.
doc.UserName = "Users"
doc.Permissions = dbSecNoAccess

MsgBox "Permissions for " & MYMODULE & " and Account/Group " & _
        doc.UserName & " are = " & doc.Permissions

cmdProtectModules_exit:
    Set doc = Nothing
    Set dbs = Nothing
    Exit Sub

err_cmdProtectModules:
    GoTo cmdProtectModules_exit

End Sub
```

Naturally, there is a caveat with this approach that says that if the user can open the Visual Basic project, the user can view this code by using the VB Project Explorer. Though that is true, removing this permission stops anyone from opening the module directly from the Database window in the first place, and that will be a major deterrent to alteration and code theft. It will also stop people from importing the module into another database, which is also a useful deterrent.

Further Reading

As you might expect, there is never enough information when it comes to powerful products like Access. To assist you with further investigations, I have put together a Web page with links to Web sites and articles on the issues relating to the material in this chapter. The first three of these links discuss issues relating to the developer workgroup strategy.

- A paper by Microsoft on securing your database without asking the user to log on.

- The highly referenced Access security FAQ paper.

- Mary Chipman's article in Access/VB SQL Advisor, "Is Database Security an Oxymoron?"

The remainder of the reading is related Microsoft documentation.

- A useful paper on many aspects of Access security by Frank Rice, this book's technical editor.

- How to use ADO with Visual Basic or VBA code with databases that are protected by Access passwords and workgroups.

- Find all the specifics about owners, groups, SIDs, and the Admins group.

- A short but definitive article by Microsoft on how to secure a database, including permissions for newly created objects.

- Workgroup security explained in detail by Microsoft.

- How to upgrade DAO to ADO, containing a lot of detail about what library to use for what security aspect.

- Programming user security with VBA code.

- A Microsoft article on the "No permission to convert database" message, which contains insight into some upgrade protection ideas I detailed in this chapter.

- Database security and replicated databases.

- More details on the Admin account, the Admins group, and the Users group.

You can find the further reading Web page for this chapter in the Downloads section of the Apress Web site (http://www.apress.com) or at http://www.vb123.com/map/adm.htm.

Apart from those online links, you can review the Access security in the Contents section of the Access help file. In Access 97, look for "Securing a Database," and in Access 2000 or later, look for "Administering and Securing an Access File," as shown in Figure 8-25.

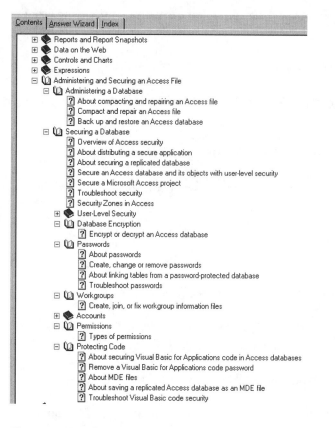

Figure 8-25. Help in Access 2002.

Finally, to find out about the different types of permissions for the different types of objects, search on "permissions" in Access help.

Reflecting on This Chapter

The strategy for this chapter was to adopt a simple model for using Access workgroup security and then to explain how to implement it. The developer workgroup strategy that I settled on is significant in that it doesn't require passwords to use it, it is relatively easy to understand, and it achieves a number of significant security results, including the following:

- Stopping users from viewing forms, reports, and macros in design mode. The open exclusive database permission further assists in this regard.

- Stopping users from changing the design of queries and tables.

- Stopping users from changing the startup options.

- Removing the ability for users to upgrade and view databases in later versions of Access.

- Stopping users from importing secured objects into another database.

All these outcomes are significant for developers who want their Access databases to behave like software produced from compiled languages, such as Visual Basic, within a security framework that you can trust.

Once you manage to work this model into your database, it is important to take a break and let the database settle down. There are many directions to take from here, and it is best to wait for the user pressures to dictate what the next best thing is to invest your software dollars in. As I have said, this model is flawed in that anyone who can find the database will be able to see the data through the user interface. They will not be able to change the interface, however, and there are many ways for you to protect your data, including the following:

- Implementing your own internal security system to stop users from viewing particular data.

- Setting up a front-end database in separate location from a hard-to-find back-end database.

- Using the operating system to restrict usage based on operating system names and groups.

The other flaw is that the VBA code is quite vulnerable if you don't protect your startup options; verify that your menus and toolbars don't provide entry to the VBA environment through buttons, such as the form and report design mode buttons; or use the special module permissions code that I have provided.

Finally, remember when working with workgroup file security that you must know which workgroup you joined and what user you logged on as before you do anything. The number of times that this author has made that mistake seems like a good enough reason to warn the readers.

What's Next?

In the next chapter, we will explore some of the other built-in Access security techniques like encryption and database passwords. The real-world issues that password crackers have brought to these options will taint these discussions. In addition, if you already use or want to take your workgroup security further, you will need to read in more detail about the problems with the workgroup files so that you can appreciate why I have to advocate the developer workgroup strategy in this chapter and the PID authentication strategy in Chapter 10.

CHAPTER 9

Security Concerns, Encryption, and Database Passwords

THIS CHAPTER DESCRIBES how you can use database encryption and database passwords to protect your database. More importantly, it discusses security issues relating to these techniques and to importing objects and the workgroup file. Fortunately, if you use these protection measures in certain ways, you will reduce the likelihood of security breaches. This chapter details these different approaches so that you can maximize your protection.

Before I embark on the detail, bear in mind that some Access security concerns come about because the product's popularity has built a viable market for companies skilled in breaking security. These concerns are partially due to U.S. government rules on exporting encryption technology, but more likely, they indicate that Microsoft has not invested enough resources in securing Access databases. Personally, I am no more perturbed by some of the issues that I have read about concerning flaws in the Access security model than I am about the security in my office. I have safe, locked windows, a back-to-base security alarm, a double-bolted front door, and the office is in a good neighborhood. Soon I will be thinking about a security guard or a big dog with a deep growl. See what I mean? We must stop somewhere, and this chapter helps draw a line in the sand so that you know the best way to protect your database.

While I was writing this chapter, I was tempted to discuss some alternative techniques that allow Access security measures to be thwarted. In the end, I decided to be deliberately vague on security issues that didn't involve freely available software that you can easily and cheaply purchase on the Internet. The result is that this chapter provides you with a path to avoid pitfalls and better protect your database but does not provide a user guide for those unscrupulous people who want to delve into your intellectual property and information.

The demonstration material for this chapter includes an Access 2002 form that will launch a password-protected database without the user knowing either the location of the database or the password. To find the demonstration form, open either the grMAP2002.mdb or the grMap2003.mdb download database and choose Chapter 9.

What Is It That We Should Be Concerned About?

Microsoft Access has a number of flaws that have made parts of its security defenses easy to breach. Before proceeding with those discussions, here are some of the positive things that you can do to make sure that you can minimize the effect of those flaws:

- You can use workgroup security to stop people from importing objects from your database into a blank database.

- If you are using database encryption, make sure that you are using it in tandem with workgroup security, or you will find that the encryption is virtually useless.

- You can use database encryption in tandem with email attachment size limits to stop users from emailing large databases.

- You can open a password-protected database by using automation in Access 2002 or later.

Now I will summarize how these technologies and the security issues that surround them are relevant to the IT manager, the DBA, and the developer.

Overview for the IT Manager

If you are an IT manager and your developer has told you that he has secured your database, you naturally would want to believe him. Unfortunately, you should be concerned with some significant issues, including the following:

- If your database relies on database passwords or workgroup files where the developer and the users share the same workgroup file, then password retrieval software negates the effectiveness of that security.

- If the security of your database relies on the users being sheltered from the objects and data by a specially designed user interface, then you must protect the database from the Access Import menu command.

Conversely, IT managers can rest a little bit easier because the flip side of the password retrieval software is that it will allow you to recover database, workgroup, and VBA Project passwords if the people that add that sort of protection go walkabout.

Overview for the DBA and the Developer

DBAs and developers need to be concerned with all the issues relevant to the IT manager, as listed previously. You also need to check whether your database is encrypted without cause, which will affect both the performance of your database and the compaction of the database into archives. You may also want to have your users log on to a password-protected database through automation so as not to disclose the database password or the location of the database.

Developers should be aware that the VBA Project password is also susceptible to password retrieval software, but in my opinion, this protection is worth persevering with if you are delivering your software in MDB format and you need protection rather than the security offered by the MDE format (discussed in Chapter 11).

Are Password Retrieval Programs All Bad?

One fundamental theme of this chapter is that the prevalence of password retrieval software reduces the security of your Access application. Another important issue with this style of software is that it allows users of the software to attempt to break your Access security provisions anonymously.

A far more likely scenario is that you or your users will forget or change a password and will start to view these programs in a much better light. My discussions with staff at password retrieval companies leads me to form a view that these organizations are making a lot more money from legitimate companies that need to unlock files than they would ever hope to make from people who want to crack passwords for illegitimate gains. Now, before you get totally excited that these programs will be the end of all your password woes, remember that they will not be able to rebuild a lost workgroup file for you.

Now I will explain why the biggest security issue in Access is actually a built-in menu command that allows you to short-circuit many of the simple and popular protection measures.

Importing Objects from Other Databases

The number-one security concern for an Access database is the Import menu command. Importing is a double-edged sword when it comes to security. When securing your database, you need to import all the objects into a new database to change ownership. Conversely, any database that you have protected with measures such as startup options and menus is completely vulnerable if someone imports all the objects into a blank database.

So, what are the main problems exposed with importing?

- The startup options, such as Show Database Window, Allow Bypass Key, and Menus Protection, are not transferred.

- Ownership of all objects will change to the current workgroup user.

- If objects are hidden, they may not be transferred unless you choose the Show Hidden Objects option (Tools ➤ Options ➤ View). This issue can cause problems if the imports are used for legitimate purposes.

- Database options (discussed in Chapter 3) are not transferred, so some of the protection measures will be lost.

Now that we have established that importing is a problem, you may want to use some of the following measures to protect against it:

- Operating system permissions will stop people from using the importing option on a database where a Windows user account cannot read the contents of the folder (see Chapter 12).

- Hiding objects in the Database window is one way to fool the importer. If you want to use this approach, it is better to hide a small number of important objects so that the protection measure is less noticeable. Hiding all the tables, for instance, will be obvious. You may want to turn tables into system tables, as discussed in Chapter 3.

- Workgroup security is the secure way of protecting forms, reports, and macros from importing. To set this security, you should either use the developer workgroup strategy discussed in Chapter 8 or the Access user-level security wizard discussed in Chapter 10.

- Review the module protection measures described in Chapter 8.

- Compiling the database into MDE format will completely secure forms, reports, and modules from being imported. See Chapter 11 for more details.

- To secure tables, you need to implement the workgroup security discussed in Chapter 10. If you need to deny access to the table or query design, use the developer strategy described in Chapter 8. Then implement the Read with Owner Access permission queries, described in Chapter 11.

- If you have permission from the IT manager or DBA, you can disable built-in menu items by using the strategy outlined in Chapter 7. This action can include turning off the Import menu command.

- Install a runtime version of Access on computers where there is little need for Access's development features. This action will hide the Import menu command (discussed in Chapter 7).

- You can move queries to SQL strings and store them in Form and Report properties and VBA code to make them more secure. If you use the same SQL string more than once, be careful how you do it.

When you have digested that long list of protection measures, the next topic that you need to contemplate is that of database encryption.

Database Encryption

You may find this a little odd, but the most important thing to know about Access database encryption is to ascertain whether or not your database is encrypted. An encrypted database costs you in terms of performance and compression of backups and file transfers. Therefore, it is something that you may want to avoid. If you are unsure about the state of encryption of your database, add your database to a compressed format file such as a .ZIP file. If it remains virtually the same size, then you have an encrypted database. If you think that it couldn't happen to you, be aware that anyone may have used the encryption command in Access without your knowledge. Also, bear in mind that you will never know if you have an encrypted database unless you test for it.

Now that the author's unusual and important encryption issue is out in the open, why did Microsoft introduce encryption to Access databases? The reason given is that they want to make the file hard to read in another tool such as a text editor. After looking through a number of normal databases in a text editor, I have concluded that encryption will make it impossible to read the small text strings and numbers that are easy to find by scrolling through the normal database in an editor.

In general, the average user would be hard-pressed to assemble anything substantial from viewing an unencrypted database. Of course, the layout of normal databases will not confuse people who are dedicated to extracting the information, but I don't consider that one of the bigger Access security issues. The main problem with the Access file format is that there are companies that can decipher appropriate parts of the file format and extract your information. For these organizations, the weak encryption method employed by Access is not an issue.

CAUTION   Do not open your important databases in an editor, especially Microsoft Word, as it may render the database useless. If you want to look at it, make a copy first.

If you have not added any workgroup security to your database, you may want to use database encryption to stop the database from being compressed (by a factor of five times or more) into a .ZIP format and transferred by email or onto a disk. If you intend to use encryption to make a database harder to read, you must invest some effort into workgroup security. Chapters 8 and 10 will provide you with enough material to protect your database this way.

How Do You Encrypt/Decrypt a Database?

Start encrypting and decrypting a database by choosing Tools ➤ Security ➤ Encrypt/Decrypt Database, as shown in Figure 9-1.

Figure 9-1. Encrypting/decrypting a database from the Tools menu.

In all versions of Access, if you don't already have a database open, you will first be prompted to select a database. The File dialog will tell you whether you are encrypting or decrypting the database. Be careful to ensure that you are actually making the change that you want and not reversing it back. In Access 2000 or later, if you have a database open, the File dialog will select the current database and then inform you whether you are encrypting or decrypting the database. You can deduce from this information whether the database is encrypted or decrypted.

Before you encrypt or decrypt a database, you must be the owner of the database. This detail is important because, unless you have joined an alternative workgroup such as a developer workgroup file (discussed in Chapter 8), you will probably have created the database by using the anonymous Admin account. If that is the case, then any other person can use that Admin account to reverse the encryption. To verify that ownership will protect your database from being encrypted or decrypted, choose Tools ➤ Security ➤ User and Group Permissions and verify that the Admin account is not the owner of the database (shown in Figure 9-2).

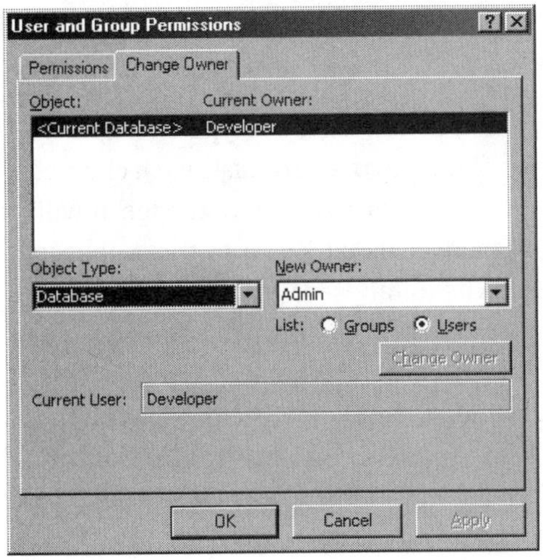

Figure 9-2. Verifying the ownership of the database.

If a workgroup user is not the owner of the database, that user will see a message, such as that shown in Figure 9-3, when they try to change the encryption.

Figure 9-3. Message that appears when you cannot encrypt and decrypt a database.

To change ownership, follow the guidelines in Chapter 8. It is also interesting to note that the Access help instructions discuss exclusive ownership permissions as being important. This statement is incorrect, because only the database owner can decrypt a database. So remember, if the developer workgroup file is not distributed, then your users can never decrypt the database. In addition, users cannot encrypt it either, which will keep the performance at optimum levels.

To encrypt a database regularly, you can use the following VBA DAO command:

```
DBEngine.CompactDatabase "C:\north.mdb", "C:\northEncr.mdb", , dbEncrypt
```

You do not need to add a reference to the DBEngine object in Access 2000 or later because Access maintains a secret reference to that object. Otherwise, you can use the CompactDatabase method of the Microsoft Jet Replication Object in Access 2000 or later.

How Does Encryption Work?

In simple terms, Access opens the database and looks for an encryption flag. If it finds it, then just before Access writes a page of data to the hard disk, each character is encrypted to another character. When Access reads an encrypted page, it will first decrypt the page and then process the page as usual. As far as the database user is concerned, it doesn't matter whether the database is encrypted. Notably, the size of the database does not change after encryption; only the performance suffers.

Microsoft has this to say about the encryption technology: *Microsoft Access uses an RC4 encryption algorithm with a 32-bit key from RSA Data Security Incorporated. If you are creating an international application, this algorithm is acceptable for export outside of the United States (according to United States export laws) because the key is less than 40 bits. When you encrypt a database, all objects (tables, forms, queries, indexes, and so on) are affected because encryption is implemented at the page-level and not at the data-level. Microsoft Access encrypts a database in 2K (kilobyte) pages, regardless of the data stored in a page. Each encrypted page is assigned a unique 32-bit key.*[1]

That said, a number of companies have cracked Access encryption. Fortunately, these companies, as of mid-2003, do not seem to market this software to the public and instead use the software to help clients rebuild damaged databases.

---

1. "ACC: How Microsoft Access Uses Encryption." Microsoft Knowledge Base Article No. 140406, May 2003.

What Are the Disadvantages of Encryption to the User?

The biggest disadvantage is that the database is slower (by 15 percent, according to Access help) as the encrypted pages take time to decrypt. The other disadvantage is that you can't use compression utilities, such as .ZIP, on the database file. This limitation has repercussions for developers because any database larger than a few megabytes might be difficult to transfer over the Internet. DBAs may also be concerned because the encrypted databases may clog your backups if you are relying on compression.

Under What Circumstances Is Encryption Recommended?

If you have a large database and you have some control over the maximum size that your staff can email, encryption would stop staff from transferring the database to their home or to a third party. Of course, CD-ROM burners and other devices would negate the effectiveness of this approach.

The only other reason that I would use encryption would be to make single words of great importance hard to read. Examples of these would be terms such as credit (card), password, salary, commission, and the SQL text of queries. You can test this practice yourself by editing a *copy* of your database and looking to see whether you can make sense of the information that is stored with those terms.

 NOTE   The Access User-Level Security wizard (discussed in Chapter 10) automatically encrypts your database as part of the security process.

If you want to stop people from emailing a small database, you could add a dummy table and fill it with 50,000 records to swell the size of the database.

In summary, if you have implemented workgroup security and protected the user interface, encrypting the database will improve your security. Unfortunately, it is going to come at a cost in performance and compression of backups.

Workgroup Security Files

The effectiveness of the Access workgroup (user-level) security hinges on the security of the workgroup file itself. As I explained in Chapter 8, workgroup security is relatively strong if the developer can ensure that the workgroup file is not released to the users. Unfortunately, the fundamental strategy behind the workgroup security system is that users and developers all share the same workgroup file. This noble strategy has lived on in many books, the Internet, and Access help files for most of the last decade. Unfortunately, in the last few years, that strategy has been compromised because a number of organizations have truly cracked the structure of the workgroup file. To understand this issue, let me first explain the basic structure of the workgroup file.

What Is a Workgroup File?

A workgroup file is an encrypted Access database (see the preceding section) that contains a table of user accounts, passwords, and groups (called MSysAccounts) and a table of which users belong to which group (called MSysGroups). Both the users and groups will have a unique special identifier (SID) that is created from a workgroup identifier and a personal identifier (PID) that you enter at the time that you create the user account. To see the user accounts and groups tables for a developer workgroup file (discussed in Chapter 8), have a look a Figure 9-4. Here you will see that the information is stored in a simple design that has the SID and passwords encrypted. In this database, the Developer account belongs to both the Admins and the Users groups, whereas the Admin account only belongs to the Users group. To understand this data structure further, bear in mind that groups are stored in the MSysAccounts table and that the SIDs are the common data key between that table and the MSysGroups table.

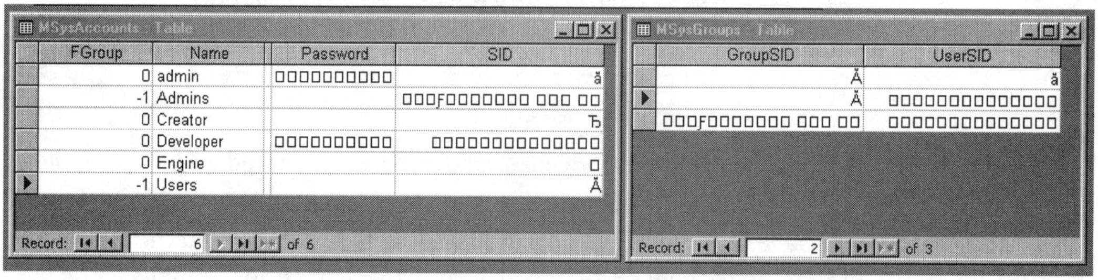

Figure 9-4. The Accounts and Groups tables from a workgroup file.

The Cracks in the Workgroup File

It really doesn't take a lot of guessing to realize that if the Access workgroup file uses a weak encryption algorithm, someone will one day work out how to extract the passwords from the file. To test this theory, I made a simple search on the

Internet and discovered a number of software programs that claim to be able to read workgroup files and database passwords (discussed later in the chapter). Having tried a number of these products, I can tell you that they can read workgroup files and retrieve the passwords for all the user accounts in a few seconds. Figure 9-5 shows the output from one of these programs.

```
Recovering password for the file:
C:\Secured.mdw

Detected Access 2000 system database

Users by Group
------------------------
Admins
  Garry
Users
  admin
  Backup
  Garry
  Reader
  Sean
Backup Operators
  Backup
Full Data Users
Full Permissions
New Data Users
Project Designers
Read-Only Users
  Reader
  Sean
Update Data Users

Users' passwords
------------------------
  admin password: [D2uHJ0D2Bt2ve] (no brackets) <Copy>
  Garry password: [Garry 1231_33] (no brackets) <Copy>
  Backup password: [Operator 1255X] (no brackets) <Copy>
  Sean password: [dkdk20Hdkd 33] (no brackets) <Copy>
  Reader password: [Dkdk222 XXXccc] (no brackets) <Copy>
```

Figure 9-5. A password recovery program, which retrieves complex workgroup passwords instantly.

So in summary, the workgroup file is small, a weak algorithm protects it, and even a novice hacker can open the file as a database and view enough of the contents to verify the supposed contents of the file.

So What Do We Do About Workgroup Security Flaws?

The best solution would be if Microsoft were to support a highly secure workgroup file. Unfortunately, Access 2003 is now on the streets, and there is no sign of any improvements to workgroup files. Therefore, we need an alternative strategy, and it will come from one or more of the following techniques:

- Never release the workgroup files with the developer details to your users (Chapter 8).

- Do your best to conceal the location of the workgroup files from your users.

- Use the operating system to secure the folders and workgroup files from unwanted users.

Otherwise, you can just share the workgroup files between administrators and different levels of users and hope that they don't go looking for a password retrieval program to extract the passwords. If this option is going to be your strategy, make sure that you first enforce passwords for all accounts and second that the passwords are at least eight characters long, because the password retrieval programs provide the first few characters of the user account in the trial version. These unlicensed programs will always identify an account with no password, which is a pity because having no password is a useful time saver.

Database Passwords

Setting up a single password that controls who can open a database is easy compared to other Access protection and security measures. Once a database password is set, all users must enter that password to open the database.

Unfortunately, database passwords have some problems, such as:

- It is another password for all users to remember.

- All users have to be informed of the new password if it changes.

- Passwords waste time and add to general technological stress.

- If someone knows the database password, that person can take the database to another location and the password will remain the same.

- Password retrieval programs can be used by anyone who has access to your database.

There are ways that you can stop the user from having to enter a database password. These methods involve using the OpenCurrentDatabase method in Access 2002, linked tables, and programming by using either the DAO or ADO libraries. I discuss these useful alternatives later on, but first I will show you how to set up a password.

Adding a Database Password to Your Database

To add a password, you first need to open the database in exclusive mode. Choose File ➤ Open, find the file, and for Access 2000 or later, choose Open Exclusive from the list of Open options (as shown in Figure 9-6). In Access 97, select the Exclusive check box before clicking the Open button.

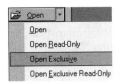

Figure 9-6. Opening the database in Exclusive mode to add a database password.

Now choose Tools ➤ Security ➤ Set Database Password, as shown in Figure 9-7.

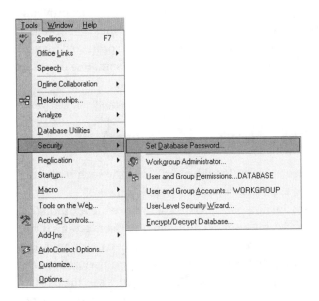

Figure 9-7. Setting the database password.

Enter and confirm the password in the next dialog. I suggest that you use a strong password that should include a combination of upper- and lowercase alphanumeric characters and nonalphanumeric characters. This combination will make it a little harder for someone to guess the password manually. Whatever you do, make sure that you use a password of eight characters or more because the unlicensed version of the password retrieval programs will reveal the first few characters of a password.

CAUTION   Due to the poor encryption used in Access database passwords, never use the same password you use for important things like your online bank account.

How Is a Database Password Implemented?

The database password is always stored (in an encrypted form) in the same location in the header of the database file. This is one reason why the passwords have proved so easy to crack. It is worth knowing that if a database header becomes corrupted, Access might erroneously report the database as being password protected instead of being corrupted. Corruption like this regularly occurs when someone opens and saves the database by using Microsoft Word or a text editor.

Protect the Password with Workgroup Security

Any user who knows the database password and has access to the security menu can remove or even add a database password, as shown in Figure 9-8.

To stop users from changing the database password, remove the Administer permission from the anonymous Admin user account and the Users group. If you have changed the ownership of the database to someone other than the anonymous Admin account, you will only need to remove the Administer permission from the Users group (as shown in Figure 9-9). Fortunately, if a password is set, the user must know the password to remove it and change it. This action will stop a user from jumping onto a machine where the database is open and removing the password.

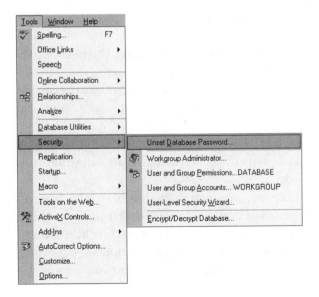

Figure 9-8. The change database password command.

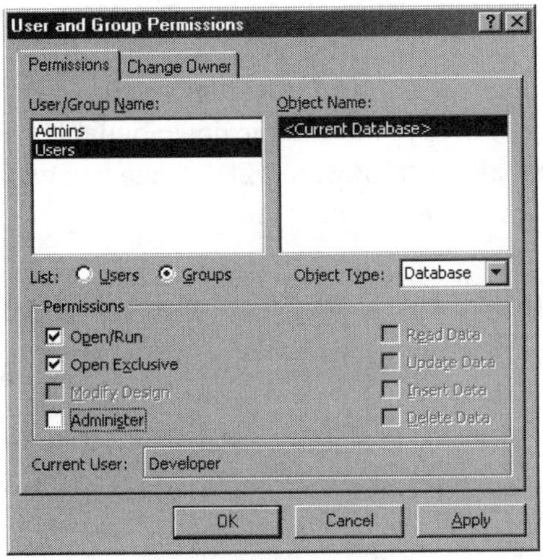

Figure 9-9. Removing Administer permission from the Users group.

Database Passwords and Linked Tables

To link a table in a back-end database that is password-protected, you must supply the correct password. Once you supply the correct password, Access stores the password with the information that defines the link to the table. When a user opens the linked table, Access uses the stored password to open the database where the table is stored. If someone changes the password in the back-end database, the next time that someone opens the front-end database, the link will fail. In this instance, you need to delete and re-create the linked table, because the built-in linked table manager will not work.

Access stores the database password information for the linked table in an unencrypted form. In my view, this is not such a big deal, because the user does not have to know the database password to use the table. In this scenario, if the user were smart enough to work out that the link to the table included a password, the user would probably be smart enough to find a password retrieval program.

Opening a Database with a Password in Access 2002

One problem with database passwords is the fact that users know both the password and the location of the database. In Access 2002, a new argument was added to the OpenCurrentDatabase method that allows you to use the Automation command to open a password-protected database. If you were to include the downloadable form frmLaunchPassword in a separate database, this software will discretely open your password-secured database, as shown in the following VBA code:

```
Private Sub cmdDBPassword_Click()
Dim appAccess As Access.Application
Const DBPATH = "C:\data\dbpwdishello.mdb"
Const DBPWD = "hello"


On Error GoTo cmdDBPassword_error

    ' Create new instance of Access.
    Set appAccess = CreateObject("Access.Application")

    ' Open database in Access window.
    appAccess.OpenCurrentDatabase DBPATH, False, DBPWD
```

```
cmdDBPassword_exit:
    ' Remove comment from following line when code is working
    ' to close the database that this form resides in.
    ' DoCmd.Quit acQuitSaveAll

    Exit Sub

cmdDBPassword_error:
    MsgBox "Problem opening database. Please inform your database administrator", _
            vbCritical, "Database Could Not Be Opened"
    GoTo cmdDBPassword_exit
End Sub
```

To make this code work for your database, import the `frmLaunchPassword` form into a blank Access 2002 database and make it your startup form. Now, change the constants at the top of the VBA procedure to suit your database and password. Finally, convert the database into MDE format (discussed in Chapter 11) to protect the code and the database password. You are now ready to deliver this database as the application that your users open. Now the database location and password should always be a mystery to your users.

 TIP   If you use this technique to launch your database, the most recently used (MRU) list does not reveal the location of the database. You can use the `OpenCurrentDatabase` method in Access 97 and 2000, but you cannot use the database password argument.

Better Situations in Which to Use a Database Password

Database passwords provide a modest deterrent for all the honest people in the world, but they really are not very secure. Consider these situations if you're contemplating using a password:

- On databases used by three or fewer people, where there are other people from whom you need to protect the database.

- To protect a back-end database that is interfaced by a front-end database that has linked tables.

- To protect a database that you emailed to a third party. At least that way, if the third party saves the database to the hard drive, another person at that location will not open it easily. Remember that in that case, the other person probably will not know the value of the information, so the password should be sufficient to stop further investigation or interest. In this scenario, you might also want to rename the database to deter users from opening it because a database such as `Info1.mdb` will be far less appealing than a database called `Salaries.mdb`.

- As an alternative to opening the database and entering the password, you can use ADO and DAO to make a connection to the database. With that connection, you can use a recordset to extract the information to another database or program to display. For this procedure, you will probably need to use the `OpenDatabase` method for DAO connections or the `Jet OLEDB:Database Password` property in the `ADODB.Connection` object. For more on this topic, see the section "Further Reading" at the end of this chapter for a link to an article that I wrote on using ADO database passwords.

Personally, I like the approach of starting the database by using the `OpenCurrentDatabase` method or using linked tables for some front-end databases. Otherwise, the user is stuck with the bothersome password dialog, and you must assess the modest risk that the database will end up in enemy hands. If, after reading this section on database passwords, you are not sure about database passwords, you may want to try a form based on the following idea.

An Alternative for Back-End Databases

Rather than use a database password on your back-end databases, why not set up a simple form with a warning message to tell people that they do not have the permission to enter this database? You may even like to set up your own password on the form as described in "How to Create a Password-Protected Form or Report," Microsoft Knowledge Base Article No. 209871. If the user does not have the password, then use the following VBA code to close the database.

```
DoCmd.Quit
```

You will need to use workgroup security to protect this form, as described in Chapter 8. Also, remember to protect all other avenues into the database such as startup options and protected menus. Now I will briefly discuss the viability of VBA project passwords.

VBA Project Passwords

VBA passwords are also susceptible to password retrieval software, but they are worth keeping as a safeguard because they do protect the VBA project from a number of directions. In particular, it will provide a good deterrent to users from opening the VBA project if your database isn't fully protected by startup options and menus. The VBA passwords are discussed further in Chapter 11.

Further Reading

As you might expect, not all the useful information related to these topics could make it into the chapter. To assist you with further investigations, I have put together a Web page with links to Web sites and articles on the issues relating to the material in this chapter. This page includes

- More information about Access database encryption in Microsoft Knowledge Base Article No. 140406.

- How to add passwords to forms and reports.

- A number of relevant news group threads on the security of encrypted files.

- How to use ADO with Visual Basic or VBA code with databases that are protected by Access passwords and workgroup security.

You can find the further reading Web page for this chapter in the Downloads section of the Apress Web site (http://www.apress.com) or at the following address: http://www.vb123.com/map/pwd.htm.

So What Are the Best Access Security Strategies?

This chapter has thrown a few negative thoughts onto different parts of the Access security framework. To help clear your mind in readiness for the next chapter, here is a summary of the best security techniques that you can adopt. I have put together this list by considering the issues raised in this chapter plus other concerns that I uncovered that I deliberately did not reveal.

- Access security cannot be unraveled easily unless the users have access to the appropriate workgroup file. The exception to this rule is if the user sends the database to a company that specializes in these security-cracking activities. The likelihood of such a company getting access to your database is probably small, as most small-time villains like to work anonymously.

- Hiding the location of the database and workgroup files is very worthwhile.

- Operating system security should form an integral part of protecting both the database and the workgroup file.

- Use ADO with Visual Basic or VBA code on databases that are protected by Access passwords and workgroups.

- I did not see any indication that anyone can reconstruct VBA code from a compiled MDE database (discussed in Chapter 11). There are some concerns for forms and reports in this format, but they do not extend to the VBA code behind the form.

The rest of your security strategy involves working through all the different parts of Access and plugging the gaps. In this case, always concentrate on the important objects and data and then worry about the rest of the database.

Reflecting on This Chapter

In this chapter, we have seen that Microsoft Access protection and security is vulnerable on a number of fronts, including importing, passwords, workgroup security, and incorrectly used encryption. The importing option is a built-in threat, while the password retrieval programs leave all the Access passwords vulnerable. Thankfully, there are measures that you can take to reduce or remove these weaknesses, including using Access workgroup security and hiding the location and password of the password-protected database and the workgroup files.

What's Next?

In the next chapter, we are going to look at how we can best secure data in our databases by building on the developer workgroup strategy discussed in Chapter 8 and incorporating security for different groups of users. We are also going to make sure that we minimize the possibility that password retrieval software will reveal data secured by workgroups with different levels of access. Once the fundamentals of securing data are explained, I will then expand on such topics as using the User-Level Security wizard to set up workgroup security rapidly and using owner permission queries to hide table and query designs, fields, and subgroup data for different user groups.

Securing Data with Workgroup Security

PROTECTING AND SECURING your data is a matter of balancing software technology and people processes. If you trust the people who use your database, then data protection is a straightforward computer process. If you cannot afford to trust your users, you have to make it as difficult as you can for users to thwart your security and protection measures, but at the same time make it as easy as possible to use your database. This chapter takes you through the conventional ways of protecting your data with workgroup (user-level) security and then outlines a new technique that allows you to use Windows Security to secure your Access database. Finally, I offer advice to anyone who is contemplating distributing important Access data outside the company network.

The technical aspects covered in the chapter follow:

- How to modify your workgroup file so others can log on and use the database.

- How to use shortcut files to open secured databases.

- How to protect your Access shortcuts in Windows 2000 and Windows XP.

- The issues that arise from sharing workgroup files.

- How to use the security wizard to protect and secure your database.

- How you can use a new technique that I have called anonymous Windows authentication to transfer the security authentication and protection to Windows XP and Windows 2000 security.

- How you can use dual workgroups to allow users access to databases without ever having access to the developer account details.

The demonstration material for this chapter includes a form to open the Access database with shortcut commands so that you can hide the location of the database or workgroup file.

NOTE   To find the demonstration material, open the download database for your version of Access—for example, grMAP2002.mdb— and select Chapter 10. Before running any samples that involve data, you may need to relink the tables to the Northwind database on your computer.

What Do I Need to Know About Securing My Data?

Once again, I will provide alternative overviews about what's important to the developer, the DBA, and the IT manager. When you are working through the chapter, bear in mind that though the focus of the material is on data and tables, you can apply many lessons to the other objects in an Access database.

Overview for the DBA and Developer

The information outlined in this chapter principally deals with Access tables, and therefore the material applies equally to both the DBA and the developer. If you have followed the popular model of splitting the database, you will be dealing with the back-end database.

   The processes outlined show you how to use shortcut files to open your database, how to add a user group account to your developer workgroup file, and how to use the security wizard to implement workgroup security. Most importantly, you need to understand the PID authentication model, and you should consider either the anonymous Windows authentication model or the dual workgroup model as a way of protecting your database from password-cracking software. In the process of using the anonymous Windows authentication model, you will also be removing the need for Access users to use additional passwords to open the database.

More for the Developer

If you want a secure database that only one or two people are going to use, read the section "Stopping Anyone Else from Opening the Database" later in this chapter.

   If you are distributing your database outside your company network and want to protect the data or the software, you must understand the anonymous Windows authentication model and Read with Owner Permission (RWOP) queries, which will go some way to protecting your database from intrusion.

Overview for the IT Manager

Once your company starts adopting workgroup security for Access databases, you are going to need to ensure the following:

- You have a copy of the workgroup file used to secure the database.

- You have the Group account name and personal ID (PID) of the different Groups used in the permission schemes of the database.

- If you are using user names with passwords, you need to inform the database users of your company's rules for protecting passwords.

- If you are protecting more than one database with workgroup security, you need to think about sharing the development workgroup file and Group account names to ensure uniformity across the databases.

- If you are unsure of the type of workgroup security used for protecting your databases, you should audit your databases.

For more on these issues, read the sections "Trusting Your Users by Adopting the Same Workgroup" and "Time for Reflection" later in this chapter. Another issue that you should consider is how the workgroup files are distributed to users; this issue is discussed in the section "Securing Data with PID Authentication." Finally, you should ponder the rather frank discussions in the section "Protecting Data Outside the Company Network" near the end of the chapter.

Some Thoughts Before We Start

Whatever you do to secure your database, keep your security systems documented and hidden from the users.

Before spending too much time securing a whole database, do an upfront analysis of what you want to protect, and you may find that your concerns may not be for the entire database but for one or two fields in a table.

Terminology Used Throughout the Chapter

In this chapter, I found the need to refer often to a special group of users who are confusingly called the "Users group." Naturally, this term could easily be confused with the regular users, so I have taken the liberty of describing the Users group as the "ubiquitous Users group." Once again, I have called the Admin user the "anonymous Admin user," and I also refer to the term user-level security as "workgroup security" to reduce potential confusion.

Trusting Your Workgroup File to Other Users

The developer workgroup model of Access security that I described in Chapter 8 involved securing your database so that the anonymous Admin user could use your user interface to view and modify the data. This model is good because it forces users to use the application interface that has been set up for them. The problem is that the data is open to anyone who has access to the database files.

The next progression from that model is to add a new Group account to the workgroup file and give that Group permission to edit or read data in the database. This process uses Access workgroup security in the way that Microsoft planned it.

By deciding to share the workgroup file, you have to decide whether you can trust the other persons who share the workgroup file. I am no psychologist, but because most people like to do the right thing, this model of sharing the workgroup files with other users will protect your data in most cases. In my experience, people first try to find a way around Access security when they start searching for an easier and quicker way to do their job. For a flexible environment like Access, the developer and DBA should certainly understand that point of view.

Anyway, this section of the chapter concentrates on how to use the security menu commands to remove permissions from the anonymous Admin account and the ubiquitous Users group. This setup means that these accounts either do not have permission to do anything with the data or have limited rights to the database, such as read-only permission.

Changing Ownership from the Anonymous Account

In Chapter 8, I explained that object ownership is a critical part of the security process, because any workgroup account that owns an object can reinstate permissions to use that object. This rule applies even if the account has been removed from the Admins (administrator) group. Even though I didn't discuss tables in detail before, exactly the same principle applies to tables. Therefore, we must first change the ownership of tables to the Developer account before embarking on the other steps to protect the database.

So that we can focus our attention throughout the chapter on data, the first thing we need to do is make a database with only tables in it. As a result of this process, the Developer account should own all the tables in the database. You should practice this demonstration on copies of files until you are comfortable with the techniques. Now I will show you how to make the demonstration database.

1. Make a copy of the Northwind database and save it in a temporary directory.

2. Make the Developer workgroup file your security file. For details on this procedure, see the section "Preparing Your Developer Workgroup File" in Chapter 8.

3. Log on as Developer. If you followed the exercises in Chapter 8, your password probably will be "Developer."

4. Use the Database Splitter wizard to create a data-only database (which I will call Northwind_be.mdb). Alternatively, create a new database through the Developer account and import all the tables into that database.

When this process is complete, the Developer account should own all the tables. To verify, choose Tools ➤ Security ➤ User and Group Permissions, and then select the Change Owner tab (shown in Figure 10-1). Tables are the default object type for this tab, so verifying ownership is easy. What you should be concerned with is that the Admin account doesn't own any tables. While you are on this tab, select Database on the Owner Type dropdown form and make sure that the anonymous Admin account doesn't own the database.

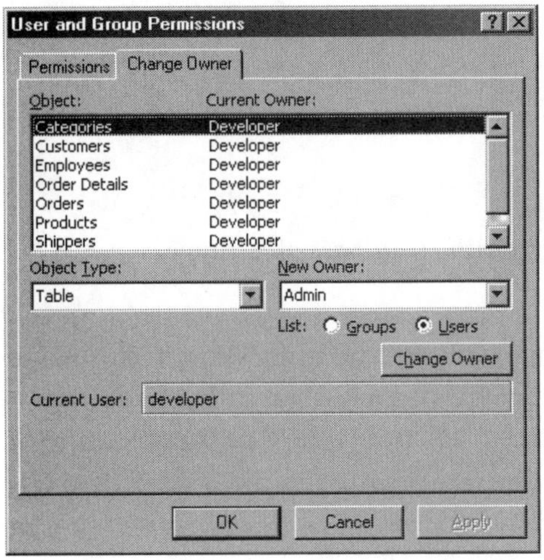

Figure 10-1. Making sure that the Developer account owns all the tables.

Now that the Developer account owns all the tables, you can protect those tables from the anonymous Admin account by removing all database permissions.

Stopping Anyone Else from Opening the Database

In Chapter 8, I said, "Clearing the Open/Run permission for the Users group (and Admin user) results in a very secure database. No one who uses the anonymous Admin user account will be able to open the database, link to the tables in the database, or import any objects from the database, which means that you will need a workgroup file with an account that has Open/Run permission for the database."

Therefore, protecting your data and database requires that you do no more than choose Tools ➤ Security ➤ User and Group Permissions, select Database from the Object Type field (as shown in Figure 10-2), and clear the Open/Run permission check box for the Admins account and the Users group account.

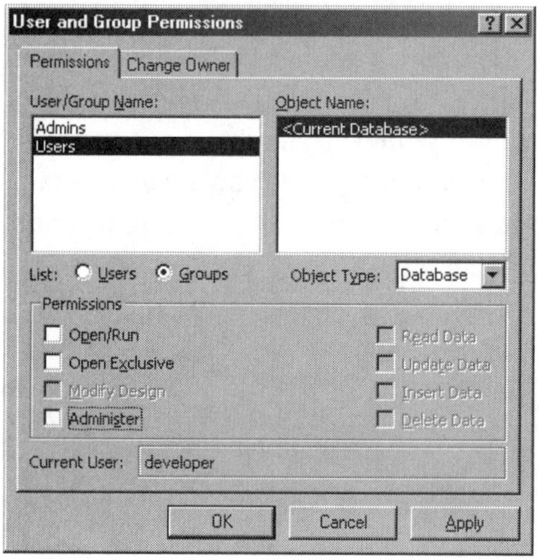

Figure 10-2. Removing all the permissions for the Database object type.

When the anonymous Admin account or any other account without permission attempts to open the database, the account will be locked out with the message shown in Figure 10-3. This lockout applies equally to anyone who tries to link to or import to this database.

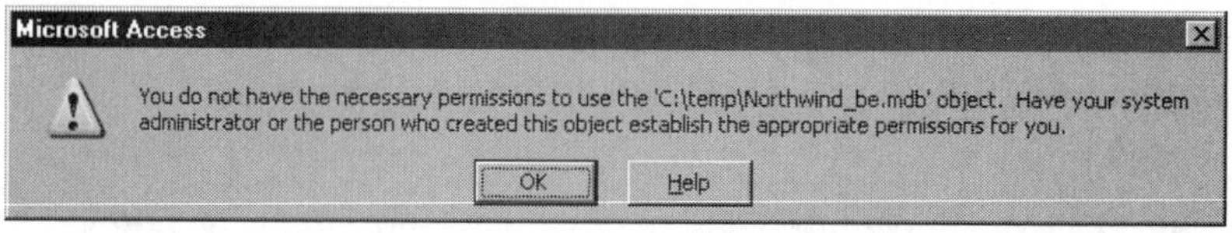

Figure 10-3. The message that results from completely removing the database object permissions.

Removing these permissions is a terrific and easy way to stop any other users from opening the database, and if you are only interested in using the database yourself or with one or two other users, then this approach will secure your data. If you like simplicity, you can even use the Developer account in the workgroup file to log on, modify data, and produce reports. Later on in the chapter, I will show you how you can use shortcut files to open this database. You can use this method of protection for both combined and split (front-end and back-end) databases. To guarantee security, though, you must ensure that you keep the developer workgroup file in a secure folder.

NOTE Whenever you add a user account to a workgroup file, Access (specifically, the Jet engine) automatically adds the account to the ubiquitous Users group. Because the Users group has the same SID for all versions of Access and because you can never remove a user account from the Users group, you have to be very careful with the permissions assigned to the ubiquitous Users group.

Protecting Individual Tables

If you want the anonymous Admin user to have some authority to change data in your database, you need to review the permissions on the tables in your database. This section describes how you can vary the permissions on individual tables. Before starting this process, you first have to verify that the Admin account doesn't have any permissions for any of the tables. To do this, choose Tools ➤ Security ➤ User and Group Permissions, and see whether the Admin account has permissions on any tables (as shown in Figure 10-4). If it does, clear all the permissions check boxes for all the tables in the database. If you have imported your tables (and other objects) correctly into another database by using the Developer account, Admin should not actually have any individual permissions for any objects. If you cleared the Open/Run permission check box from the Users group as described in the last section of this chapter, you will need to select the Open/Run check box again, otherwise removing or adding these table permissions will not have any effect.

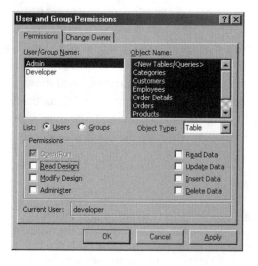

Figure 10-4. Checking whether all permissions have been removed for the Admin account.

Because the default permission structure grants permissions to the ubiquitous Users group for all new objects, it is very likely that the User group will have full permissions for all objects in the database. Obviously, you may want to review these permissions if you are going to protect your database. In Figure 10-5, I have removed all permissions for some of the tables for the Users group. Because the Admin account is always a member of this group, this step is very important for securing your tables. You should also remove permissions from the <New Tables/Queries> object if you want to protect any tables that you may create in this database in the future.

TIP To change the permission on more than one object, you can select more than one object by pressing CTRL as you select each object in the object list. To select a continuous range of objects, select the first object, press SHIFT, and then select the last object.

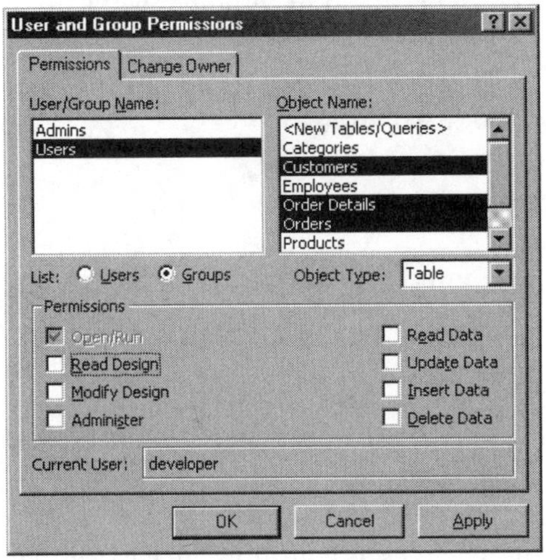

Figure 10-5. Removing permissions from some tables for the Users group.

Now, if you want to test your security, join your default workgroup by using the workgroup administrator or, in Access 2002 or later, by choosing Tools ➤ Security ➤ Workgroup Administrator. Now you will find that the Admin account will not be able to open any secured table and will receive an error, as shown in Figure 10-6. Naturally, you may want to test all secured tables with the Admin account.

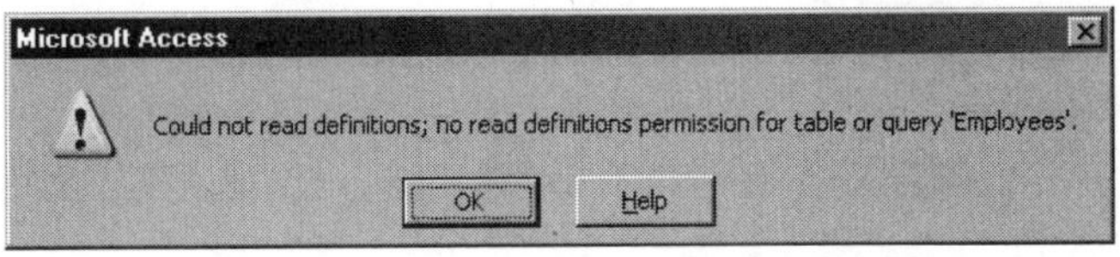

Figure 10-6. Error message that indicates that the Admin account can no longer open the table.

Allowing Ubiquitous Users Read-Only Rights to Data

My favored data security setup, especially in the early stage of projects, is to allow users with the anonymous Admin account to have read-only access to the tables in a database. I like this arrangement for a number of reasons, including:

- Users who want to run reports or view data can do so without logging on to a workgroup.

- There is less administration of workgroup accounts.

- The casual user will not be able to change data.

- Some users and managers feel more comfortable with read-only access so that they cannot do any damage!

- I personally lose less sleep worrying about whether critical data can be recovered when I know that I can always get read-only access to the tables in a database.

The steps to configure permissions on the tables as read-only are very similar to the instructions for removing permissions described in the previous section. The only difference is that you need to select the Read Data check box. In Figure 10-7, I have given read-only permission to the Users group for all the tables. Note that when you select the Read Data check box, Access automatically selects the Read Design check box for you.

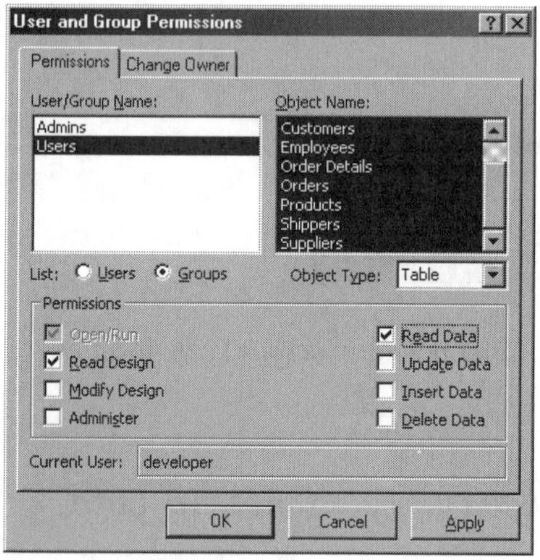

Figure 10-7. Setting read-only permission for all tables for the Users group.

Now we find that whenever someone's software connects anonymously to the database, be it as a front-end database or any other product, that person will not be able to change any data in the database.

TIP If you want to identify whether a table is read-only, look at the record selector control at the bottom of the table's datasheet. When a table is read-only, the new record selector (identified by a triangle and an asterisk [*]) appears unavailable, as shown in Figure 10-8.

		Order ID	Customer	Employee	Order Date	Required Date
▶	⊞	10248	Wilman Kala	Buchanan, Steven	04-Jul-1996	01-Aug-1996
	⊞	10249	Tradição Hipermercados	Suyama, Michael	05-Jul-1996	16-Aug-1996
	⊞	10250	Hanari Carnes	Peacock, Margaret	08-Jul-1996	05-Aug-1996
	⊞	10251	Victuailles en stock	Leverling, Janet	08-Jul-1996	05-Aug-1996
	⊞	10252	Suprêmes délices	Peacock, Margaret	09-Jul-1996	06-Aug-1996
	⊞	10253	Hanari Carnes	Leverling, Janet	10-Jul-1996	24-Jul-1996
	⊞	10254	Chop-suey Chinese	Buchanan, Steven	11-Jul-1996	08-Aug-1996
	⊞	10255	Richter Supermarkt	Dodsworth, Anne	12-Jul-1996	09-Aug-1996

Record: ◄◄ ◄ 1 ► ►► ►* of 830

Figure 10-8. A table, query, or form in read-only mode.

Form-Based Read-Only Mode

If you decide that you would like to grant read-only access (for anonymous Admin users) to your data but do not want to change permissions on the tables, you can use a basic alternative, as follows. When you open an Access form by using VBA code, you can use the read-only argument for certain users. In the following example, I have used the CurrentUser method to test whether the workgroup user is Admin. If it is, I open the form in read-only mode. This approach is suited to some homegrown security systems and works nicely in a function such as the user logging functions described in Chapter 6.

```
If Application.CurrentUser = "admin" Then
   DoCmd.OpenForm "frmMyForm", , , , acFormReadOnly
Else
   DoCmd.OpenForm "frmMyForm"
End If
```

In the next section, I explain how you can adapt your workgroup for trusted users by allowing a special Group account that can modify data but not objects in the database.

Trusting Your Users by Adopting the Same Workgroup File

Access 97 or later

Once you have decided that you don't want everyone on your network to have access to your database, the easiest Access security technique is to add a user or two to your workgroup file. This action means that, for the first time, you have to start trusting your database users. The approach that you will probably want to take in this case is to provide these designated users with the authority to edit your data and use the interface that you have designed for your database. You need to have a level of trust in your users because, by exposing the workgroup security file, your users could install password-cracking software to find your Developer account's user name and password.

Irrespective of what you think about the protection provided by this approach, it is a good idea to learn how to set up a new user and add it to a Group account. To do so, follow these steps:

1. Make a copy of the database and save it in a temporary directory. In this case, we are using the Northwind database.

2. Follow the steps in the previous section to protect the database against the anonymous Admin workgroup account.

3. Back up your developer workgroup file that we created in Chapter 8.

4. Join this developer workgroup file by using the workgroup administrator. Remember to recover the back-up workgroup file if you don't like the changes that you make in this section.

5. Now log on to the workgroup file by using the Developer account.

NOTE If you are already in the database and you want to make changes to the workgroup security, it is always a good idea to test which workgroup and workgroup account you are in by using the CurrentUser and SysCmd(13) functions in the Immediate window (explained in Chapter 8).

Now choose Tools ➤ Security ➤ User and Group Accounts to add a new User account. In this case, you want to add a User account that will edit the data in the database. Call this account the Editor account, as shown in Figure 10-9. Whenever you create a new account, you also have to give the account a personal ID (PID). For this book, I have used a PID of Real World Editor. Please make sure that you record the details of the account, either by writing down the information or by capturing a screen print of the New User/Group dialog and saving it as a file. If you forget or lose these entries, you cannot recover them.

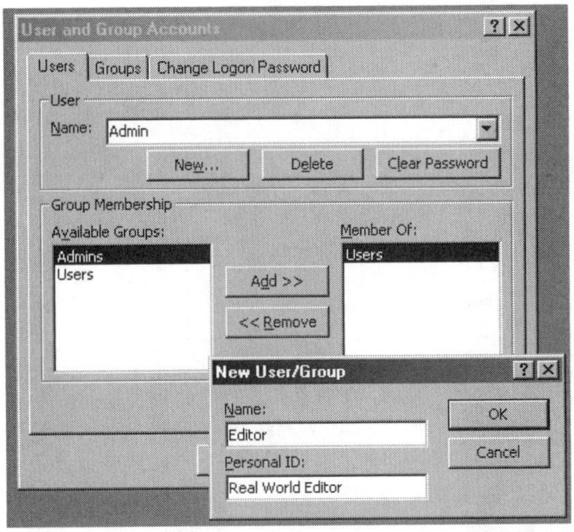

Figure 10-9. Making a new account that will be used to edit data.

Once you have added the account, remember to use the Change Logon Password tab to add a password for the account.

NOTE   Permissions on queries, forms, reports, data access pages, and macros are covered in Chapter 11.

Creating Our New Group of Users

The next step in adding a new user to a database involves creating a Group account and adding the user to it. The group that I want to add will, in this case, have full access to all the data in the database. For simplicity of instruction, I will use the same name for the group as the equivalent permissions scheme used by the User-Level Security wizard (discussed later).

To create a new users group, choose Tools ➤ Security ➤ User and Group Accounts and select the Groups tab, as shown in Figure 10-10. Now click the New button and add the name of your group (Full Data Users) and a PID (Real World Full Data). Remember to write these names down because you will need them to reconstruct the workgroup file or to implement one of the PID authentication strategies that I will outline later in this chapter. When you have added the new Group account, return to the Users tab for the next step.

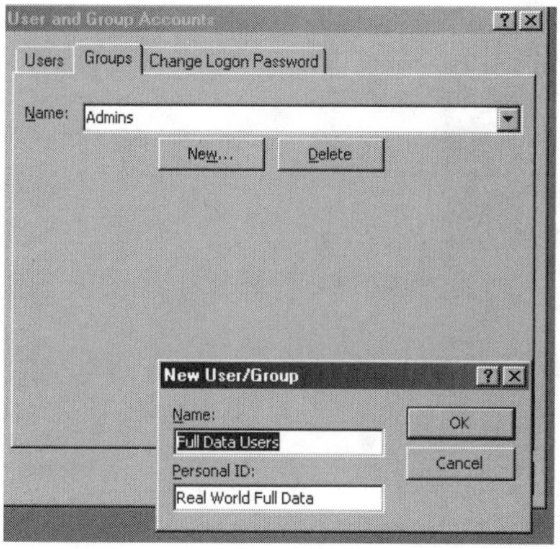

Figure 10-10. Adding a new users group to the database.

To complete the setting up of a Group account, you need to make the appropriate account (Editor) a member of the Group (Full Data Users). Now select the Editor user from the Name drop-down list and move the Full Data Users account over to the Member Of list box (as shown in Figure 10-11) by using the Add button.

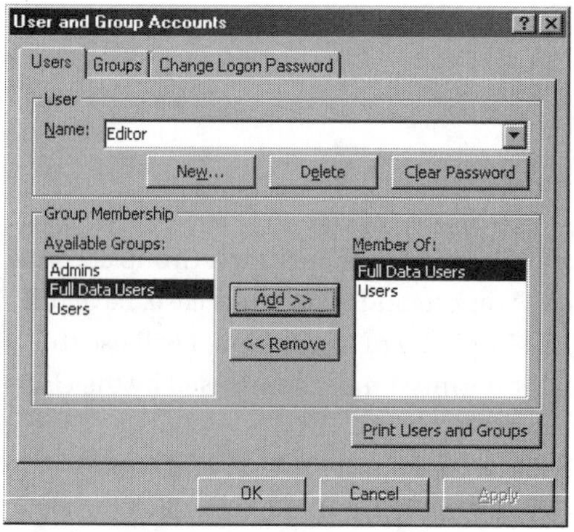

Figure 10-11. Adding the Editor user to the Full Data Users group.

Giving the Group Account Permissions to Access Our Data

To add data-related permissions, choose Tools ➤ Security ➤ User and Group Permissions. Now select Full Data Users from the Groups drop-down list (shown in Figure 10-12). Next, select all the tables for which you want to provide permissions, including, probably, the <New Tables/Queries> value. Selecting this value means that you will not need to remember to select permissions for each table as you add it to the database. Now select all the data editing permissions (the Read Data, Update Data, Insert Data, Delete Data, and Read Design check boxes). There is no need to select Modify Design or Administer, because this user should not need to change your table designs. Now click Apply, and the Group will be granted the permissions.

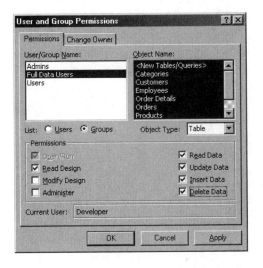

Figure 10-12. Granting full data permissions to the Full Data Users group.

Now you should log on to the database with the new account (Editor) that is a member of this workgroup (Full Data Users) to test that your new permissions are working. If you are as fallible as I am, you will need to take your time setting up your security. I habitually forget to select the correct User/Group name before I apply the permissions, which usually means making changes to the first item in the User/Groups list, which is usually one of the big A accounts, Admin or Admins, and usually results in me getting the big C for confusion.

Can Other Objects Override Table Permissions?

When I first started describing how to use permissions on tables to protect data, I split the Northwind application into front and back ends to separate the application from the data. Then I proceeded to secure the database by denying access to the tables for the ubiquitous Users group. Finally, I added a new users group that had permissions to edit data. If you have also been trying out the examples, you will have seen that this work has secured the data in the tables so that only someone using the account from the correct workgroup will actually have the authority to change (or even view) the data.

But does this mean that the data is protected when you use other objects in the database? To test, join your default workgroup file and log on to the Northwind front-end database. Here you will find that you will be able to see and edit the objects in the front end of the Northwind database. When you go to open a form, such as the Categories form, however, you will find that the anonymous Admin account that you logged on as does not have the appropriate permissions to view or modify the data, and you'll get an error message (shown in Figure 10-13).

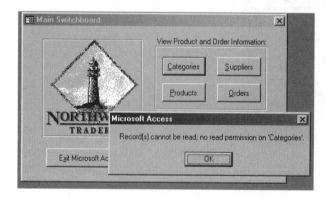

Figure 10-13. No permission to open the Categories form due to read data permissions.

Therefore, if you are only concerned about protecting your data and not too worried about protecting your user interface, you may find that the instructions thus far are sufficient for your database. Either way, you should read on because the discussions on shortcut files and PID authentication will make you more efficient and protect your data as well.

Opening Databases with Shortcut Files Access 97 or later

If our world were simple, there would be only one database to open and protect. In this world, we could install Access on an end user's computer and use the workgroup administrator to join to a workgroup file. We could then train users to open Access and select the first database on the most recently used list, and DBAs would have a relatively simple time of it. Of course, the world isn't that simple, as most Access sites have many Access databases and sometimes more than one workgroup security file for each user. This section of the chapter shows you how to use special commands in shortcut files to circumvent these issues. It also shows a more secure way of using Access VBA code to open databases that are protected by workgroups, or even those that aren't.

Irrespective of your current development and users' workgroup arrangements, it is a good idea to understand how to use shortcut files to start Access because they will provide you with a quick way to open your database with a workgroup file. Unfortunately, if you don't get on top of the quick and simple ways to switch workgroups and databases, you will forever be gnashing your teeth when you or your users open a database while connected to the wrong workgroup file.

Using shortcut files is good because people only join the workgroup for the session. If you combine this measure with menu-specific startup options, protected menus, and toolbars (see Chapter 7), users will not as easily be able to open the back-end database by using the workgroup file. The shortcut file helps protect the back-end database because users have to close Access and, hence, lose their association with the workgroup file. In the Access help guide, shortcut commands are referred to as startup command-line options. Access has quite a number of these options, but for the purposes of protecting the database, the ones that I will cover follow:

/wrkgrp. Starts Access by using the specified workgroup information file.

/user. Starts Access by using the specified user name.

/pwd. Starts Access by using the specified password.

Creating a Shortcut File

If you want to create a shortcut file, you must first include the path to the Access executable on your computer. The way that I like to do this is to find the Access executable (MSAccess.exe), which is generally located in the Program Files folder on your computer. Now right-click the MSAccess.exe executable and choose Send To ➤ Desktop (Create Shortcut). (The sample demonstrated in Figure 10-14 is from Windows XP.) Now switch to your Desktop, which you can do quickly by pressing the Windows key and the D key together.

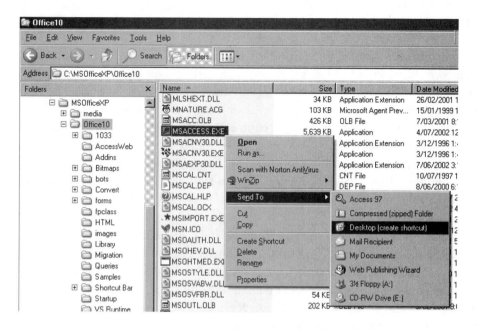

Figure 10-14. Right-clicking the Access executable to send a shortcut to the desktop.

To customize the shortcut on the Desktop, right-click it and choose Properties, as shown in Figure 10-15. The first item that you want to add to the target line is the full path to the database, which should occur directly after the path to the executable.

Once the shortcut to the database works, you can start adding the command-line options. To demonstrate, I will show you a command line that will open a copy of the Northwind back-end database with a workgroup file and the Editor user (described in the section "Trusting Your Users by Adopting the Same Workgroup"). You should organize these commands together in the shortcut's target field. As you can see, after each argument is entered, you need to leave a single space before putting the required entry in the line. These shortcuts can be a bit cumbersome to build and test, so you should add each item one at a time.

```
C:\MSOfficeXP\Office10\MSACCESS.EXE c:\data\Northwind_be.mdb
/wrkgrp c:\developer.mdw /user editor
```

NOTE   If a workgroup file or database is in a folder that has spaces in the name, you will need to enclose the path to the file in double quotes.

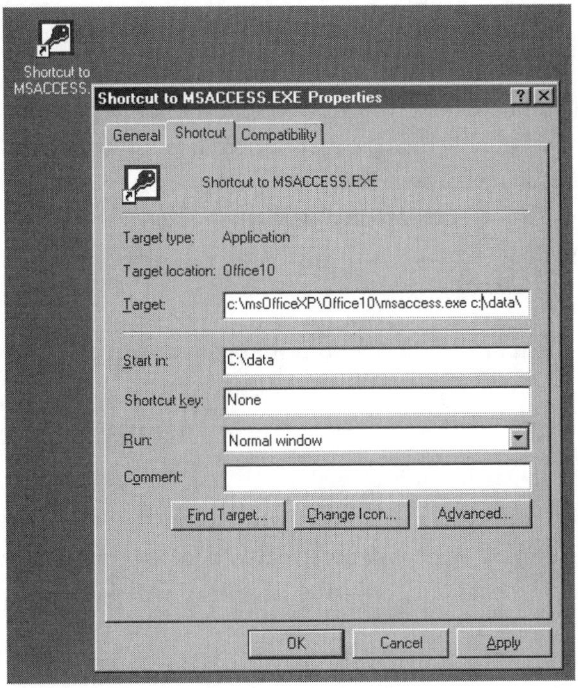

Figure 10-15. Modifying the target line of the shortcut by right-clicking the shortcut file.

Another thing that I like to do at sites where multiple users use the same computer is to enter the name of the user account that has the least permissions as part of the path. That way, even if the user may have found out the password of a higher-level account, the interface may persuade them to use the lower-level account anyway.

Shortcut Files Identify the Location of Files

The problem with shortcut files is that they expose both the location of the database and the location of the workgroup file. This visibility means that any user who has even a small amount of computer knowledge will be able to read the target line of a shortcut file. Therefore, if you don't take steps to protect the database folder (discussed in Chapter 12), these locations can be useful to someone who's trying to copy the database or workgroup file.

Secure (Personal) Shortcut Files

In Windows 2000 or Windows XP, it is possible to store your Desktop shortcuts in either a shared folder or in a personal folder. If you store the shortcut in a personal folder, those shortcuts will not be available to any other limited users of your computer or any other users of the local area network.

In essence, you can keep your shortcuts safe in a personal folder, such as

```
C:\Documents and Settings\Your Name\Desktop
```

where the folder \Your Name\ is the name of the account that you log on to. If your shortcut is kept in the folder

```
C:\Documents and Settings\All Users\Desktop
```

then your shortcut will be shared among all the users of your computer.

Therefore, I recommend that if you want your personal folders to be very safe, you use the personal folders and protect your computer accounts with passwords and time-outs.

Unfortunately, storing shortcut files in personal folders still does not provide much protection from the actual user of the shortcut file, because that user can still gain access to the target text string in the shortcut file. Windows XP security and how it relates to Access is described in more detail later in this chapter.

Creating a Secure Shortcut File

Though starting Access by using shortcut files is quick and easy and offers a temporary connection to the workgroup file, shortcut files are not encrypted. Any person who has any computer awareness can therefore view the properties of the shortcut file to reveal the location of both the workgroup file and the database itself. As I explained in the previous chapter, the location of your workgroup file can be a security issue if your users are not fully trustworthy.

 TIP If you really want good security, combine the shortcut file method with the protected folders operating system instructions in Chapter 12, and you can make it very difficult for users to copy your databases.

To help you get around the problems caused by the shortcut files' target being visible, I have written some VBA code that uses the startup command-line directly from a form in another Access database. This approach, when used in a compiled MDE database (explained in the next chapter), will hide the location of the files.

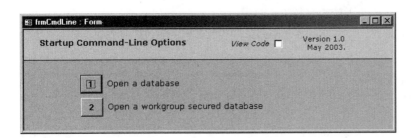

Figure 10-16. The frmCmdLine *form, which allows you to mimic shortcut files securely.*

In the first VBA code example from the form frmCmdLine (shown in Figure 10-16), I demonstrate how to open the Northwind database directly from another database. To make this work on your computer, you need to change the FILENAME constant that points to the location of your database. The other part of the command-line string that you need is the location of the executable so that you can start Access, which you can is retrieve by using the SysCmd method. To launch Access, I use the VBA Shell method to open a new version of Access with a command line. This new version looks exactly like the target line property of the shortcut file when you look at the
strShell string in the Immediate window.

```
Private Sub cmdDBOpen_Click()
' Open a database.

Const ACCESSEXE = "msaccess.exe"
Const FILENAME = "C:\data\Northwind_be.mdb"

Dim strFilePath As String, varAppID As Variant, strShell As String

On Error GoTo err_cmdDBOpen
strFilePath = SysCmd(acSysCmdAccessDir)
```

```
If Len(Dir(FILENAME)) > 0 Then
   ' Create the text target path and use Chr(34) to add inverted commas.
   strShell = strFilePath & ACCESSEXE & " " & Chr(34) & FILENAME & Chr(34)
   varAppID = Shell(strShell, vbNormalFocus)
Else
  MsgBox "Problem Opening Your Application. Contact your DBA", vbCritical, _
         "Database Is Out of Action"
End If

' Reinstate the following line once you have finished testing.
' DoCmd.Quit acQuitSaveAll
exit_cmdDBOpen:
   Exit Sub

err_cmdDBOpen:
   Select Case Err.Number
      Case Else
         MsgBox "Error No. " & Err.Number & " -> " & Err.Description, vbCritical
   End Select
   Resume exit_cmdDBOpen
End Sub
```

In the second, slightly more complicated, example (see button 2 on the form frmCmdLine), I demonstrate how you can open a database with a workgroup file and a workgroup user and password. Because this information may be sensitive, I recommend that you compile the database into MDE format. This example is an extension of that used in example one, in which the workgroup file, User account, and User password are also included in the strShell command line string.

```
Private Sub cmdWrkOpen_Click()
' Open a workgroup-secured database.
' Open a database.

Const ACCESSEXE = "msaccess.exe"
Const FILENAME = "C:\data\Northwind_be.mdb"
Const SECUREWRK = "C:\developer.mdw"
Const SECUREUSER = "Developer"
Const SECUREPWD = "Developer"

Dim strFilePath As String, varAppID As Variant, strShell As String

On Error GoTo err_cmdWrkOpen
strFilePath = SysCmd(acSysCmdAccessDir)
```

```
If Len(Dir(FILENAME)) > 0 And Len(Dir(SECUREWRK)) > 0 Then
    ' Open the database while using Chr(34) to add inverted commas.
    strShell = strFilePath & ACCESSEXE & " " & FILENAME & _
              "/WRKGRP " & Chr(34) & SECUREWRK & Chr(34) & _
              "/USER " & Chr(34) & SECUREUSER & Chr(34) & _
              "/PWD " & Chr(34) & SECUREPWD & Chr(34)
    varAppID = Shell(strShell, vbNormalFocus)
Else
    MsgBox "Problem Opening Your Application. Contact Your DBA", vbCritical, _
           "Database Is Out of Action"
End If

' Reinstate the following line once you have finished testing.
' DoCmd.Quit acQuitSaveAll
exit_cmdWrkOpen:
    Exit Sub

err_cmdWrkOpen:
    Select Case Err.Number
        Case Else
            MsgBox "Error No. " & Err.Number & " -> " & Err.Description, vbCritical
    End Select
    Resume exit_cmdWrkOpen
End Sub
```

Now I will describe the other shortcut command-line switches that you can use to start Access plus offer some other advice on shortcuts.

Another Way to Switch Workgroups and User Accounts

When you work on multiple databases in different versions of Access like I do, even shortcuts can become a bit unwieldy. To counter this, I wrote a program called the Access Workbench to handle these circumstances in a more versatile way. If you look in Appendix B, you can find out how to download and register for a free version of this program.

Other Issues to Consider with Shortcut Files

You can use other helpful command-line switches in a shortcut file to open an Access database. All these switches, which will work with workgroup user name and password commands for secured databases, include:

/ro. Opens the specified database in read-only mode.

/compact. Works out to be the easiest way to compact a database if you are not actually in the database.

/repair. In Access 97, repairs the database. In later versions of Access, repairs and compact are combined, so this option is superfluous.

/x. Starts Access and runs a macro that is specified after the switch. This switch provides an alternative to using the AutoExec macro to start the database.

/cmd. Allows you to specify additional parameters that are used when you open the database.

Finally, here is some advice to the person who installs Access on your company networks: Always install Access and/or Office in the same directory on every computer in your company if you can, because it will make your shortcut files easier to maintain. It is also better to have a different directory name for each version of Office, irrespective of whether there is only one version of Office on the computer. The location of each of these versions of Access and Office should be consistent across your company computers.

Now I will introduce some background material for you to consider before we launch headlong into more complex data protection and security measures.

Time for Reflection

We are now at a stage where you have a way to make your database protected in either read-only mode or totally secured from the anonymous Admin user and the ubiquitous Users group. You also know how to allow another person to manage data in your databases without being able to change objects, if that's how you want to play the game.

At this stage in the development lifecycle of an Access database, I like to recommend to the client that we watch to see how the application develops before proceeding with any more security enhancements. I have been involved in many Access development exercises, and I have found that unless you start adding the security late in the project, you tend to waste both the developer's and the DBA's time by repeating work. By holding out on security, testing will not take as long and you will be far wiser as to how people will use your application. Probably the best approach is to implement other, simpler protection systems like startup options, menu control, and operating system security before embarking on a full implementation of workgroup security. By introducing security later in the development cycle, users will be more comfortable with the application. At that time, your database and user base will have grown to the extent that you will be ready to invest more time in data security. In the meantime, here are some background issues to reflect on.

Organize Your Users in Groups

Ever since the early days of computing, the model of organizing users into groups and then assigning permissions to the groups has been prominent. Access workgroup security has been built to use this approach, and I highly recommend that you use groups for managing permissions for data and objects because it is far easier to manage than assigning permissions for individual users. The processes that you would use to add a new person to a workgroup-protected database sums up why this method works well.

- Establish object permissions for the Group accounts. This information is stored in the database and is completely independent of the workgroup file itself.

- If a person needs access to a database, you can add that user's account to the workgroup and then add that account to a user group.

- If that person needs different permissions, you will remove the account from the first user group and assign the account to another user group.

- When that person leaves the company or the department, you will remove their account from the workgroup file, which automatically deletes the user account from any group that he or she belongs to.

- Meanwhile, the object permissions that you have set up for those user groups in the database remain the same.

This is a good management model for Access databases, irrespective of whether they are developed on-site or off-site. It works well because you can manage the accounts in the workgroup file on-site and set up the group permissions on objects in front-end databases anywhere.

The only time that I advocate adding permissions for a single user is for the Developer account. In this case, adding permissions for a single account makes reconciliation between ownership and developer permissions a little easier to conceptualize, as ownership is assigned by the user account rather than by a user group. Of course, if more than one person is developing the database, granting permissions to the Admins group is a good idea.

Employee Security Considerations

Another important security consideration are the employees of your company and how they handle issues that can directly or indirectly affect your database. I have been at a number of client sites where all the good intentions of security seem to come to naught because of the way people use the systems. First, remember that good old genie in the bottle, the password. Access passwords, because they are specific to a computer system and aren't tied to more personal material such as email or documents, seem to be treated with too little respect.

Another prevalent Access-related security issue that I have noticed seems to be when people hand over a password to another person so that person can get on with a job that isn't officially their responsibility. For example, some data is missing on the daily report. The data-entry person is working on some other urgent task when someone enquires about the missing data entry. In this case, the data-entry person passes on his password to the enquirer so that she can complete the data entry. At this stage, the integrity of the system is compromised, and the person who passed on his password should actually change his password. But he doesn't!

How can this sort of issue be addressed? First of all, the users of important parts of the system need to be informed of their obligations to protect user names and passwords. Second, a system of regularly changing passwords needs to be enforced. Another approach that I advocate is that the developer and the DBA need to make time to observe how users are interacting with the database because such observation may lead to insights as to how better to design and protect the user interface and data.

 NOTE   If you think that you have a problem with users trading passwords and workgroup accounts, have a look at the user logging software in Chapter 6.

So, if you are thinking of heading down the path of passwords and secure users, please make sure that the software users understand their security obligations. You should also regularly review security issues that occur because managing security is yet another adventure in the process of maintaining ever-changing databases.

Investigate Operating System Security as an Alternative

You may now be at a point where you are sharing the developer workgroup file with users, so you might consider it more appropriate to work on operating system security as the next step that you take to protect your database. Operating system security is discussed at length in Chapter 12. Anyone who already has a workgroup-secured database or is considering using the User-Level Security wizard (discussed in the next section) is at the stage where you need to decide which direction to head next.

Beware of Falling Through the Cracks

If you remember from the last chapter on security concerns, allowing more than one person to use your workgroup file exposes your database to password-cracking software. Therefore, as we move further into workgroup security, it is important to reflect that it is not difficult for anyone who has access to a workgroup file to find out a password to an account that has more permissions. So, as we move on to allocating permissions to different groups of users, please temper your enthusiasm for workgroup security with the knowledge of the relative ease that password-cracking software can be obtained. To counter this issue, once you have completed the section on security wizards, I will describe a system, which I have labeled PID authentication, that will make it a lot harder for users to break into other work-group accounts with different permissions.

Security Wizards

If you want to secure your database and data with workgroup security, there is no better way to make wholesale changes than with the User-Level Security wizard in Access 2000 or later. This very well-crafted wizard will undertake a lot of complex tasks for you. If you are using Access 97, the wizard does not set up any particular Group accounts and requires more setup time and testing after it finishes. Nevertheless, when running either of the wizards, I suggest that you wait until a good portion of the application is completed before implementing detailed workgroup security.

Access 2000 (or Later) User-Level Security Wizard

This wizard adds Users and Groups to the workgroup file and then offers you a number of permission schemes that you can apply to the database that you are going to protect. To demonstrate how the security wizard works, I will show you how to secure data in a back-end version of the Northwind database. The purpose of this demonstration will be to:

- Secure the tables in that database so that members of the ubiquitous Users group (Admin user) can have read-only access to all the tables in the database.

- Add a new Group account that will allow permission to insert and change data but will not allow changes to any objects in the database.

To do this demonstration, I am going to use a copy of the Northwind database that has been split into a back end that contains only tables and an existing developer workgroup file as described in Chapter 8. This workgroup file should already have the Developer and Admin accounts in it, and, if you have the Editor account (as described earlier), don't worry—the steps are almost identical. If you have never run the security wizard before, it is always a good idea to test the wizard on the copy of your database prior to running it on a live database. The steps to protecting data with this User-Level Security Wizard follow:

1. Join the developer workgroup.

2. Open the database that you want to secure (probably called Northwind_BE.mdb).

3. Open the User-Level Security wizard by choosing Tools ➤ Security ➤ User-Level Security Wizard.

4. On the first page of the wizard, you will be asked whether you want to modify an existing workgroup file or create a new one (as shown in Figure 10-17). In this case, select Modify my current workgroup information file. You are also informed that a backup will be made of your database before the permissions are changed.

5. On the second page of the wizard, a multitab form allows you to select the objects that you want to secure. In most cases, you will be securing all the objects in the database, which is the wizard's default selection. For this example, the wizard selects all the tables, including four New object properties (as shown in Figure 10-18). The permissions on these new objects ensure that you will be covered by the same permission schemes when you create new objects in the database after the wizard is run.

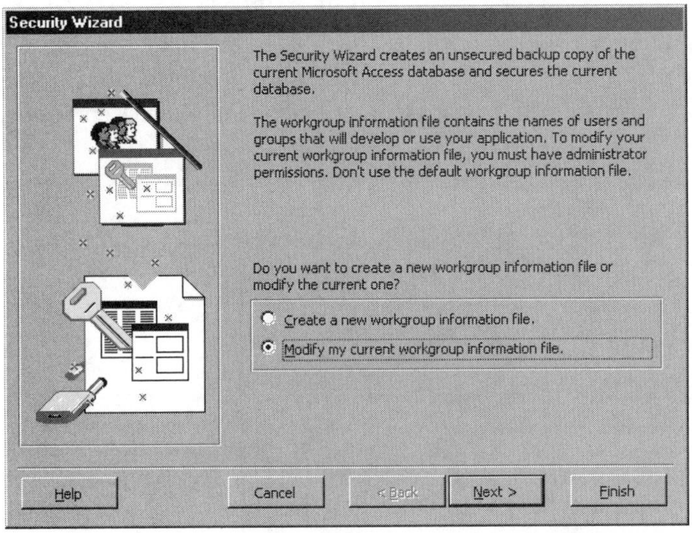

Figure 10-17. Page one of the security wizard, where you can select an existing workgroup file.

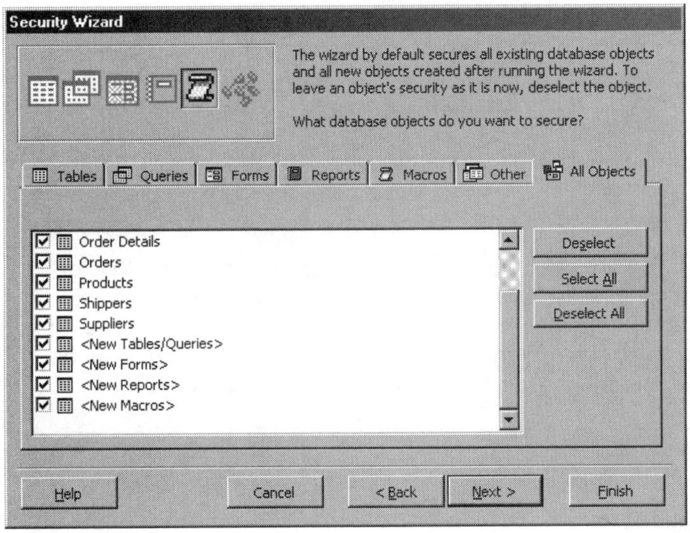

Figure 10-18. Page two of the security wizard, showing the optional selection of objects.

6. The third page (in Figure 10-19) shows this wizard's sophistication. On this page, you can select from a number of very useful permissions schemes to apply to your database. As you select each option, you will see a description of what each scheme does. If you decide to adopt one of the

schemes, choose a meaningful group ID (called a PID in the rest of the Access help guide), because you will use this PID to re-create the Group account later. For this exercise, we are interested in allowing a new class of users to change any data in the database, so select the Full Data Users Group.

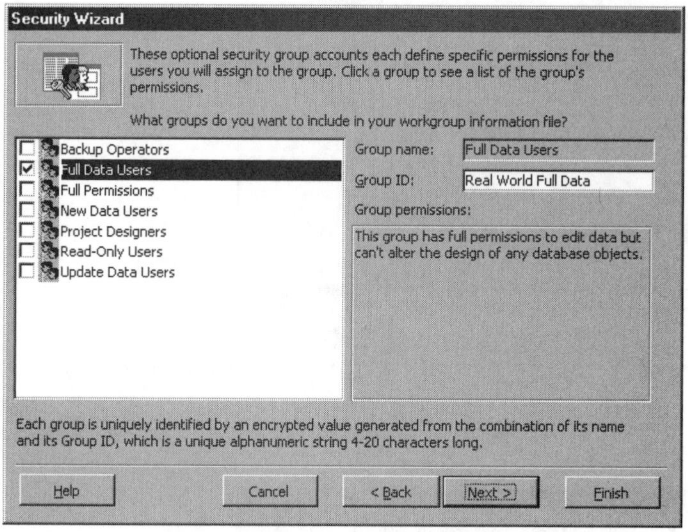

Figure 10-19. Page three of the wizard, which allows you to choose the different permission schemes.

> **CAUTION** If you use the User-Level Security wizard in Access 2000 or later, you have to be aware that the wizard does not allow you to use different names for the Group accounts. Therefore, if you have two different databases with different group account PIDs, you should set up one of them manually, or you will be forever pulling your hair out.

7. The fourth page of the wizard allows you to grant permissions to the ubiquitous Users group (as shown in Figure 10-20). As I explained in Chapter 8, it is possible to have protected Access systems where the users do not have to log on to a workgroup but instead can use the anonymous Admin account to use the database. Of course, if you want protection against the ubiquitous Users group, you should select No, the Users Group Should Not Have Any Permissions. This option locks out all workgroup users who are not a member of a group defined on the third page of this wizard. Also on this page of the wizard, select the Database tab and the Open/Run permission to allow the Users group to open the database.

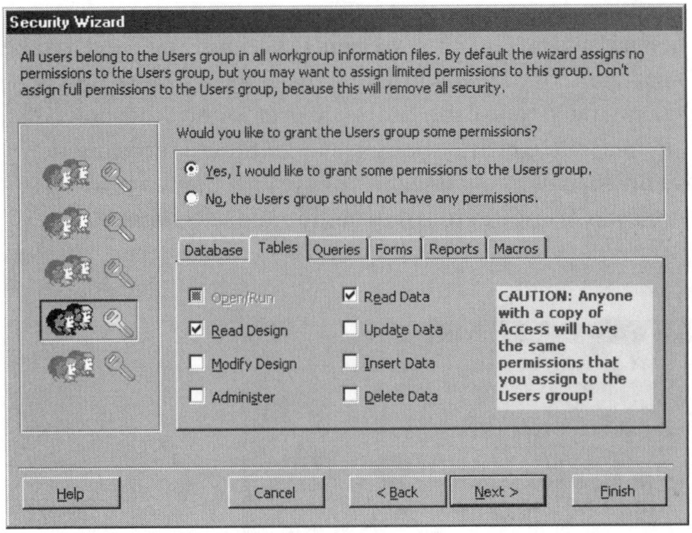

Figure 10-20. Page four of the wizard, which allows you to assign permissions to the Users group.

8. The fifth page of the wizard (in Figure 10-21) allows you to add user accounts to the workgroup file. When you have typed in the new user name, password, and PID, click the "Add This User to the List" button. In this case, I am going to add the identical Editor user that I established earlier in this chapter.

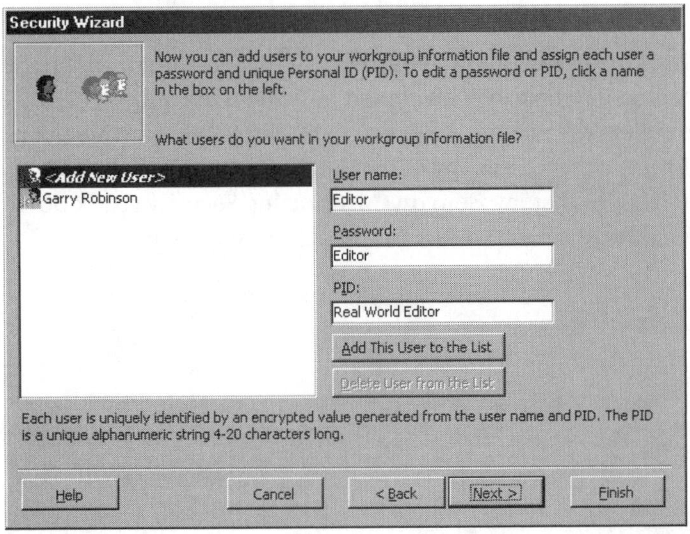

Figure 10-21. Page five of the wizard, which allows you to add additional user accounts, passwords, and PIDs.

9. The sixth page of the wizard (as shown in Figure 10-22) allows you to allocate Groups to Users or, conversely, Users to Groups. You need to take care with this page to ensure that you set up the associations correctly. Remember that you need to use the Group or User Name drop-down list in the center of the form to change your user selections. I recommend, when you have finished defining who belongs where, that you switch to the alternative view of users or groups to verify your selections.

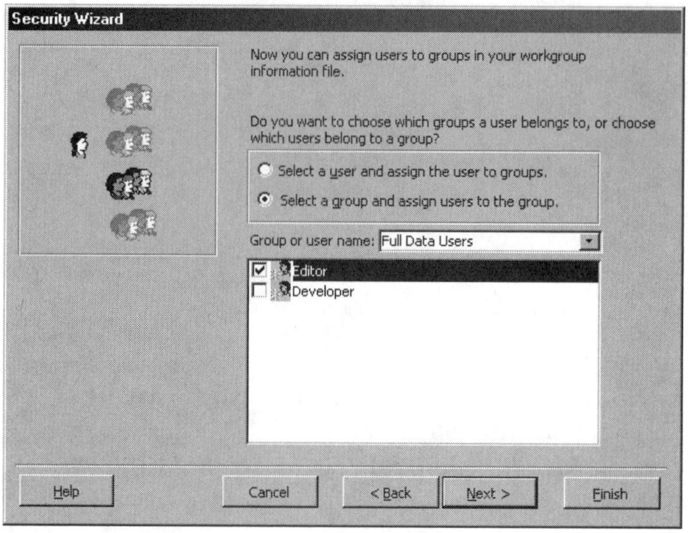

Figure 10-22. Page six of the wizard, which allows you to allocate users to groups.

10. The final page of the wizard allows you to select the location to which the current unsecured database will be copied (as shown in Figure 10-23). When you complete the wizard, you need to be careful about where you leave the (current) unsecured copy of the database. On this page, you should also select the Display Help on Customizing Security check box, which will open the Access help as a good point of reference.

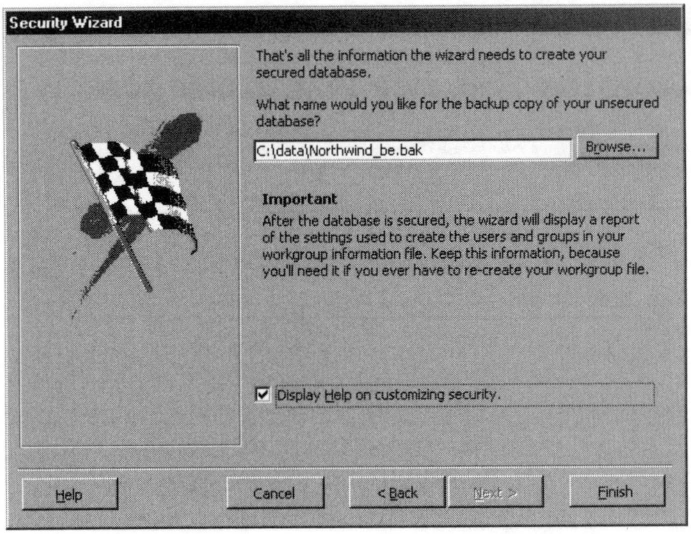

Figure 10-23. Saving the unsecured database in the final page of the wizard.

11. When you click the Finish button on that last page, the wizard will first rename your current database to the backup name and then will create a new encrypted database and import all the objects into it by using your secure User account. When the objects are imported into the new database, the wizard will allocate all the permissions on the objects according to the permissions schemes that you selected. When this task is complete, an Access report appears that details all the changes made to the database. This report (a portion of which is shown in Figure 10-24) will include the workgroup IDs if this is a new workgroup file plus personal IDs for each User and Group account. When this report appears, you should print it or even save it in Microsoft Word format as a password-protected document. Once you have printed it, you will be asked to save the report as an Access snapshot.

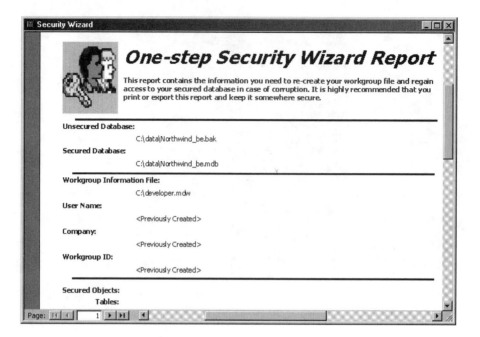

Figure 10-24. A report showing all the security settings and passwords.

Checking Out the Results of the Wizard

Once the wizard has completed its tasks, what has actually happened to the database? The first thing that has happened is that the database is now in an encrypted format. If you are worried about the small items of information in your database, then this may be important to you. Alternatively, if you are confident that your database doesn't offer any little gems to a hacker manned with a Hex editor, then you should contemplate returning the database to an unencrypted format. I explained the vagaries of this database format in more detail in Chapter 9.

To verify what has happened to the workgroup file that you altered, join the workgroup file and then open any database. I know you may have been tempted to say that we should open the secured database, but I want to make a point that the changes that you made to either User or Group accounts only apply to the workgroup file, not to the database itself. Now choose Tools ➤ Security ➤ Users and

Group Accounts, and on the dialog that appears, click the Print Users and Groups button. A report of the workgroup file, as shown in Figure 10-25, will print on your default printer.

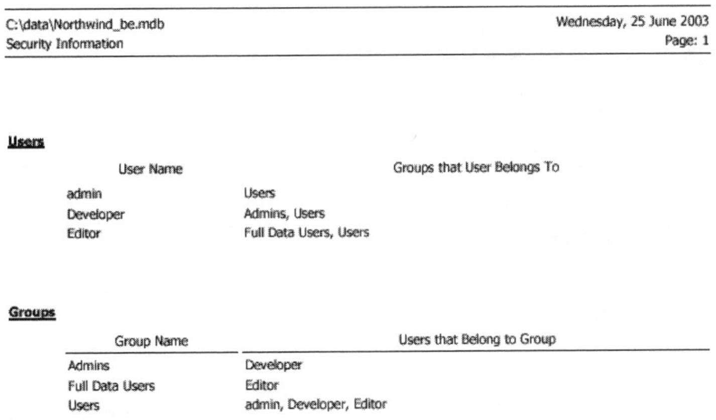

C:\data\Northwind_be.mdb
Security Information

Wednesday, 25 June 2003
Page: 1

Users

User Name	Groups that User Belongs To
admin	Users
Developer	Admins, Users
Editor	Full Data Users, Users

Groups

Group Name	Users that Belong to Group
Admins	Developer
Full Data Users	Editor
Users	admin, Developer, Editor

Figure 10-25. The report of the workgroup file.

TIP   To keep a copy of the Users and Group report, you need to set up a PDF printer driver such as the one that comes with Acrobat Distiller. Make that driver your default printer by using your Windows configuration dialogs, then you can capture the output of the printout to a file.

Now you can open the database that you secured with the wizard and verify the object permissions. First choose Tools ➤ Security ➤ User and Group Permissions, and then look at the permissions for a random selection of objects in the database. If the wizard has done its job properly, all the user accounts, apart from your Developer account, should have no permissions for any objects. Figure 10-26 shows that the new Editor account has no permissions for the Orders table.

Figure 10-26. The Editor should have no permissions for any table.

Finally, we need to review the permissions for the Groups that the wizard has established. To do this, select the Groups option and select Full Data Users, as shown in Figure 10-27. You will see that anyone who is a member of this group will have the ability to change or add any data in this table. This result, of course, is the same that we achieved manually earlier in the chapter (as shown in Figure 10-12), and it is exactly the result we want.

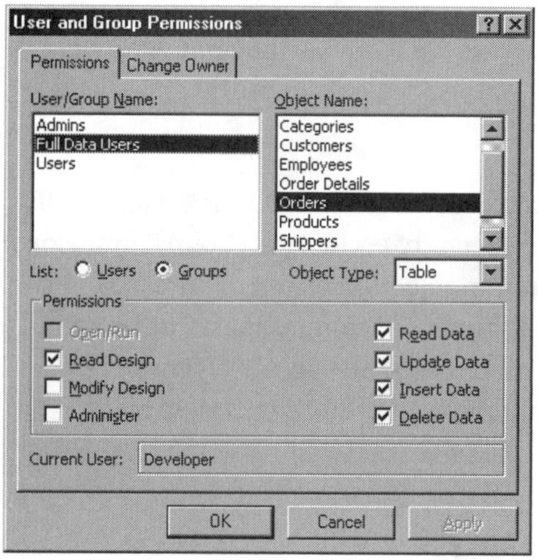

Figure 10-27. The Full Data Users group permissions on tables.

TIP   As a test of your documentation, give the workgroup IDs and PIDs to someone else, and get him or her to rebuild the workgroup file from scratch.

The Access 97 User-Level Security Wizard

Unlike its newer cousins, the Access 97 User-Level Security wizard is a very Spartan affair. In fact, the whole wizard fits on just one page. Used correctly and at the right time in your project, it will accomplish the following:

- Create a new database and export all the objects into it.

- Transfer ownership of all the objects in the new database to the User account that is running the wizard.

- Remove all the permissions from the object types selected on the first page of the wizard (as shown in Figure 10-28) for all but the Admins group (administrators) and the User account that is running the wizard.

- Grant full permissions for all the object types selected on the first page of the wizard to the Admins group and the User account running the wizard.

- Encrypt the database.

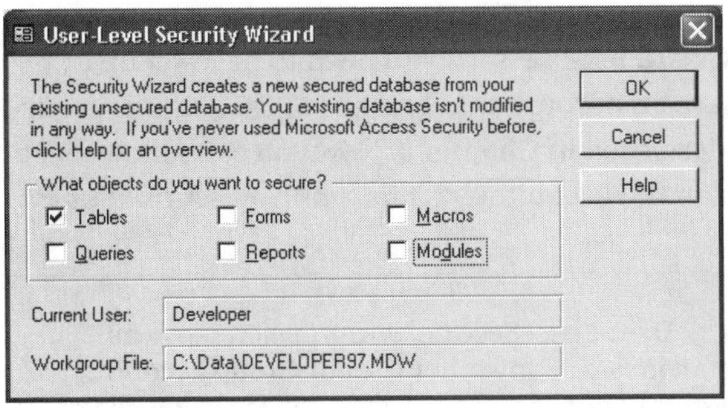

Figure 10-28. The Access 97 User-Level Security wizard.

How Not to Run the Access 97 Wizard

When you start the Access 97 User-Level Security wizard, you first need to make sure at the bottom of the page that you are not logged on as the anonymous Admin account or joined to the default workgroup file. In Figure 10-29, I show you how the security wizard should *not* look when you start it up. In this case, the default Admin account is using the default workgroup file. If you continue past this form by using the Admin account, the wizard will tell you that the database and all its objects will be unsecured because the Admin user will own all the objects in the new database and have full permissions for all object types selected in the wizard. Therefore, if the current user is Admin or the current workgroup file is in Windows' System32 subdirectory, do not bother going any further with this wizard.

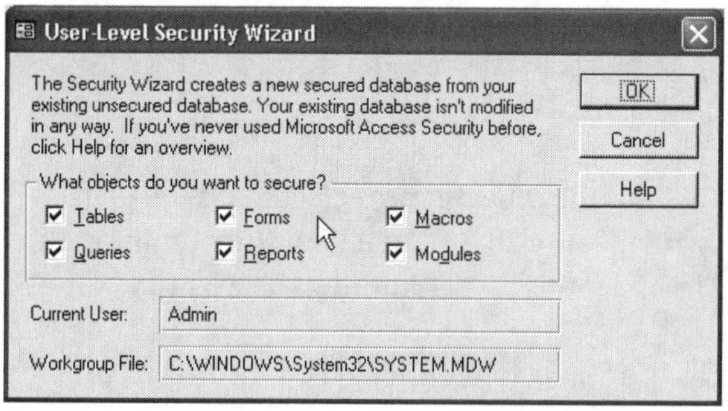

Figure 10-29. The Access 97 Users-Level Security wizard should not look like this.

Running the Access 97 Wizard

To run the User-Level Security wizard in Access 97, you need to have set up a developer workgroup file and have an account that belongs to the Admins group, such as the Developer account described in Chapter 8. Now you can follow these steps to secure your database from the ubiquitous Users group and Admin user.

CAUTION   The Access 97 User-Level Security wizard will remove all permissions granted previously to any other User or Group account. Therefore, this wizard should not be used on any database to which you have already added significant security.

This wizard is good to use when you haven't added any security to the database and want to start the database in a secure state. Once you have run the wizard, you will need to resort to the User and Group Permissions or User and Group Accounts menus to add the rest of your security. That said, the wizard is useful for taking the database from an unsecured state to one in which it is ready for you to add User and Group accounts and to establish permissions for groups of users.

Testing for Flaws After Running the Wizard

Despite this wizard's sophistication and power, a lot happens behind the scenes that really does need testing. As an example, both the Access 97 and 2000 User-Level Security wizards sometimes do not remove the open/run permissions on the Database object. In all cases, you need to test your database by attempting to open the database by using a default workgroup file and the anonymous Admin account. Irrespective of which version of Access you are using, testing the permissions is as important as creating them.

Now we come to the all-important part of the chapter where I tell you how your Access database can be secured rather than just protected for multiple users. To secure it, you must adopt one of the techniques explained in the next section.

Securing Data with PID Authentication

This section of the chapter shows you how to use more than one workgroup file to counteract two of the greatest issues with workgroup security:

- Anyone with access to a workgroup file can use password-cracking software to extract the user accounts and their passwords. We will counter this by restricting the workgroup file that the person uses to one or a minimum number of Group accounts so that the effect of the password-cracking software is minimized.

- Logging on to an Access workgroup account is fraught with many perils, from users forgetting passwords to users passing passwords of different accounts from person to person. We will counter this management problem by transferring the onus of authentication to the more secure authority offered by recent Windows operating systems.

To fix these problems, we are going to adopt modified versions of a technique that Microsoft suggested. This technique is discussed in the Access 2000 help guide under the topic "Set Up More Than One Workgroup to Manage the Same Secure Database," and in the Access Security FAQ "Item 33" ("I Want Users in Other Groups Besides the Admins Group to Be Able to Administer the Database and Add Accounts"). You will find a link for this page in the "Further Reading" section at the end of the chapter.

I have called this technique "PID authentication" because it involves setting up an equivalent Group account name with its unique PID into a different workgroup from that used to assign the permissions in the database. You can also use this technique with User accounts, but that is generally harder to maintain than the Group accounts.

The technique can be summarized as follows:

1. Grant the permissions for objects (tables) to a Group account by using the Developer account in the developer workgroup file (discussed in Chapter 8).

2. In a second workgroup file, add the same Group account and its PID.

3. Make a User account a member of that Group in the second workgroup file.

Now I will show you how you can use this technique to allow a user to log on to a database by using the anonymous Admin account. By combining this approach with the file security offered by the latest Windows operating systems, you can achieve a highly secure authentication of a person. This approach mimics the same Windows authentication system used by SQL Server.

Anonymous Windows Authentication Access 2002 or later

Anonymous Windows Authentication (AWinA) is a secure system that involves the DBA setting up a workgroup file in such a way that the Windows User account can open a secured database without having to log on. To set up this system, you will need a computer running the Windows 2000 or Windows XP operating system and you will need Access 2002 or later. Then, for this technique to work properly and securely, you need to establish Windows User accounts with passwords. Another important criteria is that the disk partition needs to be formatted by using NTFS, a subtlety that I discuss in Chapter 12. Because you want the user to be blissfully unaware of the process, I advise that you make these changes when the user is not watching.

NOTE   I include the following anonymous Windows environment information with the aim of providing information for a developer or small team of developers who uses a peer-to-peer network to manage his or her development. If you work on a domain that uses Windows Server 2000 or later, your users will also use the same Documents and Settings folders but in a number of subtly different ways, the descriptions of which are beyond the scope of this book. Therefore, I suggest that you read this information and then ask your network administrator how these files are managed in your network environment.

The Anonymous Environment

To set up AWinA, open Access 2002/2003 on your end user's computer and confirm that the current workgroup file is the default workgroup file. You can do this by opening any database, switching to the Visual Basic Editor and typing ? syscmd(13) into the Immediate window. If the path includes the Application Data folder like the one below, then you are ready to set up anonymous Windows authentication. The path that I would expect to see would be similar to this one:

```
C:\Documents and Settings\Mr Robinson\Application Data\Microsoft\Access\System.mdw
```

where the Windows User account on my computer is Mr Robinson. This path establishes that you are using a workgroup file that is stored in an area protected to all but the Windows User called Mr Robinson. Now you are in a position to alter this local workgroup file so that Mr Robinson can open the database as a member of the Full Data Users group.

Before we do that, let's confirm that the anonymous Admin account cannot open the database. To do this, log on to your secured database as the anonymous Admin user. If you find that the Admin user either is blocked from opening the secured database or only has the permissions that you intentionally granted to the ubiquitous Users group, then that is good. This situation is what we want all the Windows users on your network to encounter before we start to establish AWinA for a particular Windows User account.

Setting Up AWinA for a Windows User Account

Now I will show you how to modify the user's personal workgroup file so that it has a hidden Group account.

1. Choose Tools ➤ Security ➤ User and Group Accounts.

2. Select the Groups tab (as shown in Figure 10-30) and click the New button.

3. Add a new Group (Full Data Users) by using exactly the same name and PID that you used when securing the database manually or with the User-Level Security wizard, and click OK.

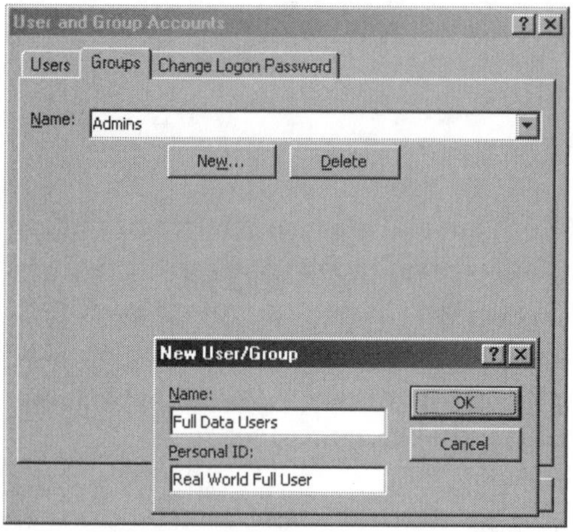

Figure 10-30. Adding a new group account to the end user's default workgroup file.

4. Select the Users tab and make sure that you have selected the Admin user. Now choose Full Data Users in the Available Groups list and click the Add button (as shown in Figure 10-31).

That is all you need to do to set up the User and Group accounts. If you are worried about whether the user will explore this workgroup file, you will want to set the Access startup options (Chapter 2) to turn off the full menus so that the Security command is hard to find. That said, even if outsiders were to process the contents of the workgroup file with password-cracking software, they would discover nothing that would change their permission levels for the database.

Now try this account on your workgroup-secured database, and you will find that it works perfectly for the permissions that you have set up for the Group that you just added. Because the Admin account doesn't have a password, there's no reason to log on to a workgroup, because it happens automatically for Admin users who have no passwords.

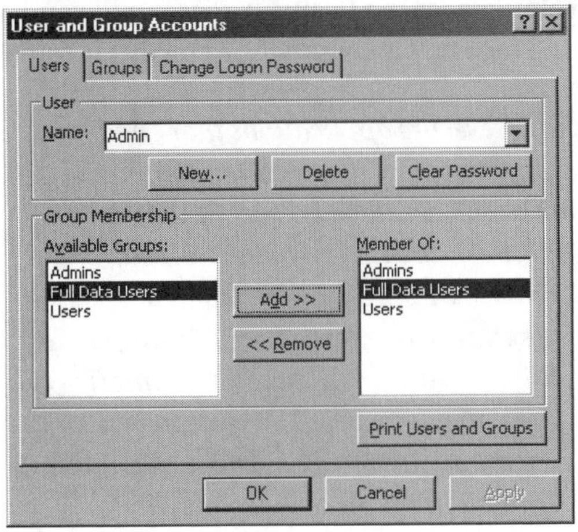

Figure 10-31. Adding the Admin account to the group.

Bingo: Simple, Secure Access

When I first worked out that I could secure a database with AWinA, I was flabbergasted. Here I was after many months into research on Access security, and the best method of security that I could devise for data was to allocate permissions by using the Admin account from a workgroup file with no security at all. The reason I was fooled was that I had always been under the misapprehension that in some way a Group account SID was constructed by using the PID of the workgroup itself. I never actually considered that permissions to the objects in a secure database could be granted to any old user who joined an authorized group in any old workgroup file. Anyway, you can, and after careful consideration, I believe that AWinA is the best combination of security for Access data and simplicity for the user.

To understand why this happens, let me review the Access security model. Access uses SIDs to check users' permissions. Each database has a table called MSysACEs that keeps permissions information for all the objects in the database. Before a user account uses a database object, the Access Jet engine scans the MSysACEs table by using the current user SID and the SIDs of the groups that the user belongs to, to see if the action is allowed.

But where do these SIDs come from? Group account SIDs are generated from the group account name and the personal identifier when the group is established. They are not created from any information in the workgroup file. This means that creating a group account in any workgroup with the same PID will give you the same permissions that the equivalent group account had in the original workgroup file. Exactly the same principle applies to a workgroup user account, which means that you can re-create your Developer account in any workgroup file and the permissions that the account had in the secured database will be exactly the same.

 User Story *One of the first secure applications that I had to write was a land rights system built for a mining company using an Informix database. I developed a very functional and neat Informix 4GL interface that ran on text-based terminals. Everyone who required access to the application had first to log on to UNIX by using an individual account. The Informix security implementation involved granting permission to each UNIX account to insert, update, and delete data for each table in the database. Therefore, when a person started the Informix 4GL application, the database engine would check that the UNIX account had permissions on the table before any changes were allowed. This was a great system to administer because the user only ever had to log on to UNIX and the database security would take its cue from the UNIX account name. This type of security interface is far friendlier to users than a system like the Access workgroup security system, where logon details are required for each user and each database. I like Anonymous Windows Authentication for this reason—it emulates this process.*

Returning to Anonymous Windows Authentication

So why do PIDs and all that other technical stuff make a local workgroup file with a hidden group account so effective? Because if it is used in the correct way in a version of Windows 2000 or Windows XP Home or Professional, it can be protected by Windows security itself. That is, if the user logs on through a valid secure Windows account, the following points are true:

- Windows passwords and screen-saver passwords (discussed in Chapter 12) will help to protect the Access session and the data that is left exposed by an unattended computer.

- The workgroup file is protected in a folder that only the Windows User account or the computer's administrator can access.

- The actual workgroup file itself is quite hard for an ordinary user to find because it is kept deep in a hidden folder.

- If a person were to take the database and the workgroup file off-site, that person would only have the same permissions that they had on-site.

- If the person didn't realize that there was a workgroup file, he or she could take the database off-site and then find that they had no permissions to do anything. This scenario is quite likely when the Admin account doesn't have a password and the user doesn't get a logon prompt.

Of course, this assurance comes with one big caveat. Everyone must log on to his or her own Windows account on the computer and the concept of the walkup computer that anyone can use with no permissions must be forgotten. The same can also be said about Windows accounts in a domain, and I encourage you to discuss with your system administrator how the Windows server manages the \documents and settings\ folders.

When a person leaves the company, you must take care to remove the Windows User account from the computer(s) that that person logged on to. Obviously, if you are using Windows Server, you need to remove the account from the active directory. Also, you must make it clear from the onset that computer accounts are not for sharing.

Now I will show you how the Windows User account ensures that you have a secure workgroup file.

The Secure Personal Workgroup File

In Windows 2000 and Windows XP, every Windows User account (see Figure 10-32) has personal secured folders that other users of the computer and the network cannot access.

Figure 10-32. Multiple users on a single Windows XP home computer.

As it happens, Microsoft Access 2002 and 2003 store their default workgroup files in these same secure personal folders, which allows you to use the Windows User security to your own advantage. In Figure 10-33, I have opened the folder where these versions of Access store the default workgroup file. As you can see, the path to this file is quite long, and, with the file being stored in a hidden Windows folder, it will be quite hard for the Windows User account owner to find the file.

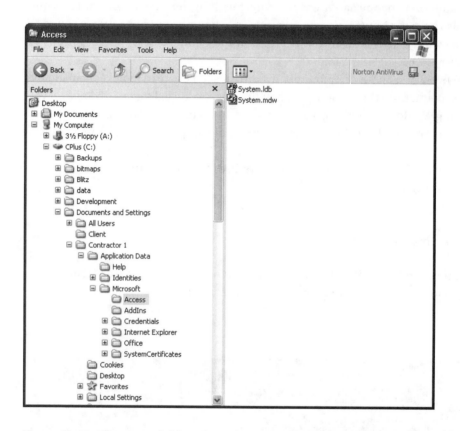

Figure 10-33. The secure folder where the Access default workgroup file is stored.

Now, if another limited Windows User account tries to look at the files in someone else's personal folders, that account won't be allowed access (as shown in Figure 10-34).

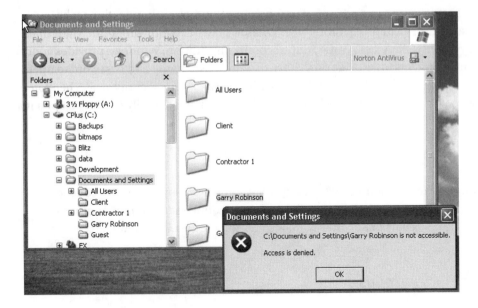

Figure 10-34. Other limited accounts cannot look at your personal files.

Anonymous Windows Authentication Pro   (Access 97 or later)

If you are using Access 97 or later, you can set up a workgroup file in the user's personal folders. You can then use a more secure version of the previous technique by creating a new workgroup file in the Windows personal folders and then opening the database by using a shortcut that also opens the workgroup file. The command line for this process would look similar to this one (all in one line):

```
C:\Program Files\Microsoft Office\msaccess.exe c:\data\northwind..mdb  /wrkgrp
   "C:\Documents and Settings\Contractor 1\Application
   Data\Microsoft\Access\system.mdw"
```

Once you have established the workgroup file, you can then add the group account and join the anonymous Admin account to the group account to start using the AWinA system. This version of AWinA is better because the user has only temporary access to the workgroup file. Subsequently, permissions are revoked if the user opens the secured database without using the shortcut file or joining the workgroup file.

In summary, I like both of the anonymous Window authentication techniques because users will protect their own Windows User account with more vigor than they would their Access workgroup accounts. In addition, Windows provides good security, and because users don't have to enter a user name and password to open the database, they will probably be blissfully unaware of any security at all. Therefore, if they were to steal a secured database, they would not actually be able to open it.

The Developer's Challenge

By using the instructions for adding Groups and Users by using VBA code in Chapter 8, you could add the AWinA Group account and then join Admin to that group as part of an automated installation process for a new user.

Dual Workgroups

Dual workgroups are another variation of the technique that involves adding a Group to an alternative workgroup that I have called PID Authentication. This variation works as follows:

1. A new workgroup file is set up with a different workgroup ID.

2. A new administrator account is set up and added to the Admins group.

3. The anonymous Admin user is removed from the Admins group.

4. The new administrator then sets up the group accounts by using the same name and PID as the original workgroup file that was used to secure the database.

5. Each user account is added to the group account just as if it were a member of the original workgroup.

You can read more about this process in the Access 2000 (or later) help under the topic "Set Up More Than One Workgroup to Manage the Same Secure Database" or in the Access Security FAQ "Item 33."

Things to Watch for in PID Authentication

When setting up AWinA or dual workgroups, there are a number of things to be aware of:

- The developer account must own all the objects in the database.

- The anonymous Admin account must have no permissions or own any objects.

- The ubiquitous Users group should have no permissions unless you specifically want any Access user to have that permission.

- No groups should have Administrator permissions on any objects in the database.

- Keep your developer workgroup file hidden.

- Developers should have a secure copy of the workgroup and secure documentation of the name and PID of the workgroup. DBAs and IT managers should pester the developer for the same information or you'll risk losing the workgroup security information.

- If you are using the AWinA system with Windows XP or Windows 2000, you must use NTFS for your hard drive partitions. If you use FAT32, all users will have access to all files on your hard drive, regardless of their account type (Administrator or Limited/Restricted).

Now we will see what you can do to protect databases that you want to distribute to other people or companies, or even make available for download from the Internet.

Protecting Data Outside the Company Network

As soon as you distribute your database, you lose some of the important trump cards, such as disguising the location of the database and workgroup files and control over your environment. You also present users with the time and opportunity to try any tricks that they want. To better understand this reality, I have included an email from a person who was interested in protecting a database and my response.

User Story *It's a typical user predicament. The email said, "I stumbled upon your* vb123.com *site thanks to a Google search, and I wonder if you could answer this question.*

"I have a back-end/front-end application that I would like to distribute, but I need to protect the back-end data so that it is accessible (readable, maybe modifiable) only via front-end forms, but not extractable. I wondered if this is practical, and, if so, what are your suggestions? Also, have you any thoughts about including an individual encryption algorithm on some of the fields themselves?"

I replied, "Only distribute what you want your users to see and no more. Keeping the full design of the database from the end users is one way of guaranteeing the secrecy of important data. For example, do not distribute the names and addresses of people, or better still, only distribute consolidated information such as total number of people in each suburb.

"Securing a database that you want to send to people around the world is probably the hardest thing that you could do. The MDE format will secure the VBA code and do a good job of protecting the reports and forms. The queries and tables can be secured to a reasonable level with user-level security and RWOP queries. There are a number of organizations that can unravel this security, but the catch is that the would-be thief would have to sign a legal document and pay a hefty fee for the job. Thankfully, software cannot currently be purchased or downloaded to do this for you. One thing that you will want to do is keep the developer workgroup file from your users at all costs.

"To take this a step further, a simple encryption of some key fields like you mentioned would probably suffice. This measure, combined with Access user-level security, would probably make it expensive to decipher, but some companies will do anything for a fee. Access is too popular and has been around too long to be bullet-proof. I would think long and hard about getting too carried away by it all."

Distributing Your Data in Some Other Form

A good way to make your data safer is to adopt alternative ways of distributing it. In this case, Access provides many distribution alternatives, such as:

- Send users snapshots or PDF versions of reports.

- Save your reports to Excel or Word (*.RTF format) if the output is suitable.

- Distribute your information through email by using Microsoft Outlook Automation.

- Create remote systems based on XML data that you export from Access 2002 or later.

- Create Excel spreadsheets that summarize the information and allow users access to manipulate only the data that is relevant to them. I have been involved in a number of projects in which the end users simply view and manipulate data that is transferred through Excel Automation.

- Install a third-party reporting system, such as Crystal Reports or SSW Reporter, to provide an alternative way to view the information.

- Include your database on the Web and use Web-based technologies to secure and interface the data.

Now I will show you how to hide part of your data from your (remote) users.

Read with Owner Permission Queries

One way to restrict what a remote user account sees in an important table would be to use a particular query type called a Read with Owner Permissions (RWOP) query. This type of query allows a user account that has no permissions to view or change data by inheriting the permissions of the owner of the query. For example, if the owner of a table has read design permission and a user account does not, a RWOP query will allow the user to read columns from a table.

When you are protecting data, especially remote data, RWOP queries are very useful because the user will see only some of the fields in a protected table. Another use is to allow the user to see a consolidated view of data (group by query). To illustrate this view, let's make a query where the anonymous user can see only the total number of orders per region but cannot see the orders table itself.

1. Log on to a copy of the Northwind database by using the Developer account.

2. Remove the read permissions from the ubiquitous Users group for the Orders table.

3. Create a query that returns only the table or query columns or calculated fields that you want the users to see.

4. When you have set up the query, choose View ➤ Query Properties.

5. Select the field Run Permissions from the list and choose Owner's, as shown in Figure 10-35.

6. Save the query.

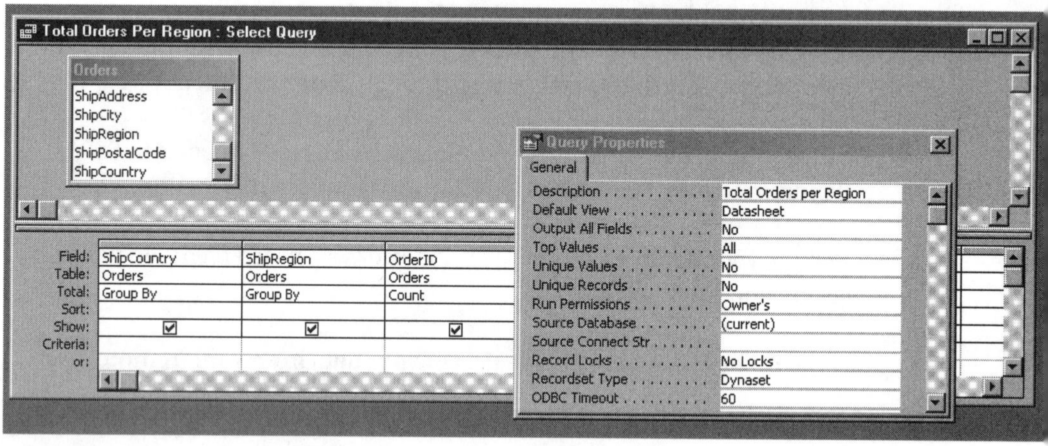

Figure 10-35. The design view of a RWOP query, showing the Run Permissions properties.

The SQL for the RWOP query will look like the following:

```
SELECT ShipCountry, ShipRegion, Count(OrderID) AS TotalOrders
FROM Orders
GROUP BY ShipCountry, ShipRegion
WITH OWNERACCESS OPTION;
```

Though I do see the merits in the occasional RWOP query, I would rather the data weren't distributed at all, because you just cannot be too sure when the information goes off-site. In addition, there is a security issue (that I will be intentionally vague about) with the output from RWOP queries that makes them less than secure when it comes to protecting data. In the next chapter, I will show you how RWOP queries will keep your query designs secret.

Legal Stuff

If your data is valuable, you really should consider making the recipient of the information sign a nondisclosure agreement, which will probably inhibit theft as much as any other security procedure. Of course, if you are distributing the data as a download on the Internet, do not actually expect anyone to read it, even if it is legally binding.

Server-Based Databases

One good approach to securing your data is to transfer the data and relationship rules to a server-based database such as SQL Server, Informix, or Oracle. Before you do that, remember that though Access provides good prototyping development for server databases, it is also useful as a tool to decide whether a database is going to survive. Using Access in this way is interesting because when most databases start off, they are terribly important to the people who are pushing the concept. The reality, though, is that a good percentage of databases waste away after a year or so because they were based on a business model that really wasn't as important as was first thought. In this case, using Access as your initial database is a terrific way to decide whether the database is actually worth upgrading to a more expensive server database environment.

Server-based databases generally are more secure than Access databases by virtue of the fact that users cannot copy the database and take it home with them. However, to put off your security because you think that you might upgrade to a server-based database at some stage is not protecting your data in the meantime. Also, if the supposed complexity of Access security puts you off, don't in any way believe that it is going to get any easier when you adopt a server-based solution. In fact, I remember reading one statistic that showed that a very high proportion of SQL Server-based databases being hosted on the Internet were vulnerable because the system administrator account (sa) did not have any password at all.

 NOTE In Appendix C, you can review the reasons why you would want to migrate Access to SQL Server. The information in the chapter, though specific to SQL Server, also provides valuable insight into the reasons for and against migrating to any server-based database.

Remember, if Access is what you have and what you understand, upgrading to SQL Server to make your database more secure is like upgrading your house to a complex (all bells and whistles) security system. Most of the time the alarm is going to go off as you enter the bathroom in the middle of the night, and you are just going to wish that you hadn't bothered.

Further Reading

As you might expect, there is never enough information when it comes to powerful products like Access. To assist you with further investigations, I have put together a Web page with links to Web sites and articles on the issues relating to the material in this chapter. This page includes:

- A useful paper from Visa Card International that provides many terrific checklists for creating good office, human, and computer security.

- The highly referenced Access security FAQ white paper.

- Mary Chipman's article, "Is Database Security an Oxymoron?" in Access-VB-SQL Advisor magazine web site.

- How to use ADO with Visual Basic or VBA for Access passwords and workgroups.

- Various Microsoft book chapters on security that have been published on the Web.

- Discussions on shortcut files and startup commands.

- Papers on running the User-Level Security wizard.

- Windows authentication security in SQL Server.

- A link to SSW Access Reporter.NET.

- Various other links, book references, and article references.

You can find the further reading Web page for this chapter in the Downloads section of the Apress Web site at `http://www.apress.com` or at the following address: `http://www.vb123.com/map/dat.htm`.

Reflecting on This Chapter

If you have read the chapter from start to finish, you might think that securing your data was quite time consuming. Well, actually, it really doesn't take all that much time—it's just explaining it that takes the time! So what are some of the things that we learned from the chapter?

- You must use Access workgroup security to secure your data.

- You can easily make a database very secure for one or two people.

- Shortcut files join you temporarily to a workgroup file.

- You can hide the location of a workgroup file and database by using VBA code.

- Once you start sharing your database, you need to keep your developer workgroup file hidden from your users.

- The User-Level Security wizard is a useful tool for securing your database.

- You need to organize your table permissions by using group accounts.

- Group accounts can be added to any workgroup file.

- RWOP queries allow you to display some data from a secure table to users who do not have permissions.

- If you want to distribute secure Access data, restrict what you send to people.

Finally, my favorite topic from the chapter is the anonymous Windows authentication method, which allows you to use a workgroup in the secure private folders of Windows XP or Windows 2000 with group accounts to produce a simple and secure way of allowing users to log on to the database.

What's Next?

In the next chapter, we will explore a gold-plated security method plus a few additional tricks to distract that database snoop whom we spend so much time worrying about. Some of the techniques that we will cover:

- Compiling a version of our database into MDE format to provide the best possible security for the programmable parts of the application.

- Disguising our queries behind forms and even using queries to remove linked tables from our databases.

- Making our forms and reports launch as objects so that the forms cannot be placed in design mode.

- Discussing the User-Level Security wizard and how it affects other objects.

We're in the home stretch for Access protection and security, and a few of these topics are just additional and interesting padlocks for a well-locked database.

Object Protection and Security Measures

PROTECTING AND SECURING the objects in your database are best handled by workgroup (user-level) security or by converting the database into MDE format. To that end, I discuss and review these important topics in more detail in this chapter. As usual, Access's flexibility means that there are more issues related to protecting objects that are worth exploring. Bearing these issues in mind, I have put together an eclectic mix of additional protection and security measures that will supplement or act as an alternative to workgroup security and the MDE database format. The material presented in the chapter will help you to

- Review workgroup object permissions and create the developer workgroup file by demonstrating the User-Level Security wizard.

- Hide links to other databases or files.

- Secure the design of your queries.

- Protect forms and reports from being opened in design mode in an unsecured database.

- Show you how to use workgroup security with data access pages.

- Discuss Access data project security.

- Give more details on the MDE database format.

The download material for this chapter includes forms and Visual Basic for Application (VBA) examples that will

- Stop anyone from opening a form or report in design mode.

- Open a form in such a way that VBA code hides the form's record source.

- Convert the current database to MDE format.

NOTE To find the demonstration material, open the download database for your version of Access (for example, grMAP2002.mdb) and select Chapter 11. Before running any samples that involve data, you may need to relink the tables to the Northwind database on your computer.

Have I Done Enough to Protect the Objects in My Database?

This chapter is one fundamentally for developers, even though there are some topics that may be relevant to DBAs and IT managers. Nevertheless, I will once again provide alternate overviews about what's important to the developer, the DBA, and the IT manager.

Overview for the Developer

If you are a developer, then you should enjoy the different solutions presented in this chapter. The solutions described will aid in protecting all the object types in the database, and they include concepts that are applicable to other topics.

- A refresher course on securing objects and producing a developer workgroup file by using the User-Level Security wizard.

- A special query, called a remote query, that can replace linked tables.

- Using RWOP (Run with Owner Permissions) queries to protect the design of your queries.

- Hiding queries in code.

- Protecting the forms and reports in your database by using them as class objects.

- Adding passwords to the VBA project.

- Discussions on code cracking and VBA project passwords.

- Using data access pages with workgroup file-protected databases.

- Access data project protection.

- Detailed discussions on the MDE format.

As you can see, a number of developer goodies are in the chapter, and I suggest that you adopt the technologies at a gentle pace in case they don't suit the way you and your users like to work.

Overview for the DBA and the IT Manager

In the beginning of this chapter, I once again demonstrate the User-Level Security wizard. In particular, this section includes a rundown on the permissions that you should give to users of your databases to protect your objects. In addition, you will find useful information on the VBA project password and its fallibility to password-cracking software, plus the full story on the MDE database format. You may also gain from reading about data access pages (DAP), an Internet-based option that may provide a useful and cheap alternative for users who require limited access to the database.

A Workgroup Security Refresher

Before we start looking at the developer goodies, we first need to prepare a secure Northwind database, which will provide a perfect opportunity for a refresher course on workgroup security. We will first re-create our developer workgroup file and then secure a copy of the Northwind database to use later on in the chapter. In Chapter 8, I demonstrated how to make a developer workgroup file by using the conventional security commands. This time around, I will use the User-Level Security wizard, making the file as a by-product, which will demonstrate that you can produce an identical developer workgroup file by using both techniques. When we have finished running the wizard, I will review the correct object permissions that you should assign to your database users.

Before I demonstrate the wizard again, I should point out that you can find all the workgroup file and personal identifiers (PIDs) that we have been using in the book in Appendix A. If you feel like saving your own workgroup information, I have set up the tables in Appendix A so that you can enter your own workgroup information details, user and group names, and PIDs.

The Developer Workgroup File and Security Revisited

Access 2000 or later

To reproduce a workgroup file and secure the database, I will walk you through the User-Level Security wizard.

1. Go to the Northwind samples directory and copy the Northwind.mdb file and all the HTML files (*.HTM) to a temporary folder. In my examples, I will use the C:\data\ folder.

2. Open the Northwind database in the temporary folder and choose Tools ➤ Security ➤ User-Level Security Wizard.

3. On the first page of the wizard, select Create a New Workgroup Information File, and then click Next.

4. Enter the same workgroup information (as shown in Figure 11-1) that we used in the developer workgroup file creation exercise from Chapter 8. Be careful here, because the field order in the wizard is not the same as that displayed when you create a new workgroup file by using the workgroup administrator. Because this is a demonstration, you should select the I Want to Create a Shortcut to Open My Secured Database option at the bottom of the wizard. Then click Next.

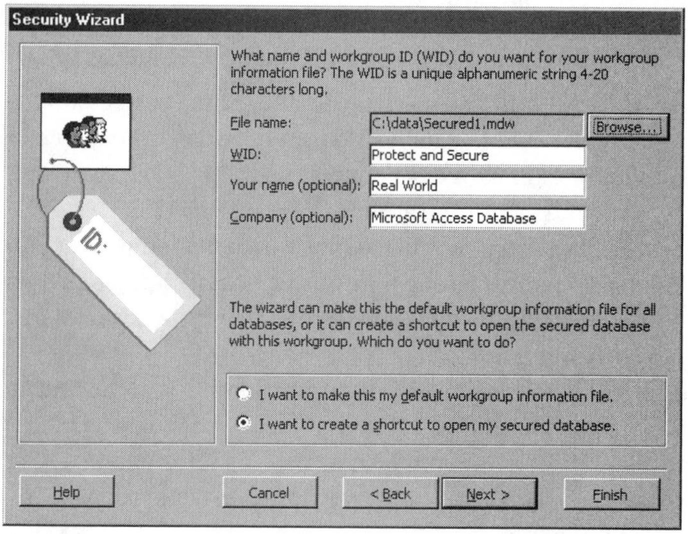

Figure 11-1. Entering the developer workgroup information into the wizard fields.

5. Select all options on the third page of the wizard and click Next.

6. Select the Full Data Users permissions scheme on the fourth page of the wizard. Now enter "Real World Full Data" for the PID. At this stage, you could also select any other permission scheme that you are interested in experimenting with. Once you've selected the permission schemes, click Next.

7. On the fifth page, select the No, the Users Group Should Not Have Any Permissions option. This option will remove all permissions for the entire ubiquitous Users group, of which the anonymous Admin account is a member. Click Next.

8. On the sixth page, add two new users called "Developer" (with "RealWorldDeveloper" as the PID) and "Editor" (with "Real World Editor" as the PID). Remember to click the Add This User to the List button. Click Next.

9. On the seventh page, you will find, in the drop-down list, the two users that you set up plus a special user account that was set up automatically with the same name as your Windows user account. Add the developer account to the Admins group and the editor account to the Full Data Users group. Finally, remove the Windows user account from the Admins group.

10. On the eighth page, the final page, enter the name for the backup of the currently unsecured database, and then click Finish.

11. Check that the workgroup, users, and groups all have the correct PIDs by looking at the report produced by the wizard.

12. Open the database by using the shortcut file that the wizard placed on the Desktop, and log on with the Developer account.

Now you will have a developer workgroup file that is identical to the one that we created in Chapter 8, and the database will have set up the appropriate permission schemes for you. Remember not to distribute the same workgroup file to your users.

Now we will look at the permissions that the User-Level Security wizard established for the Editor account, as these will explain what we need to do for all the objects.

Workgroup Permissions that Protect Your Objects

Now that you have logged on to the database by using a Developer account, you should be ready to start checking the permissions. Of course, if you are unsure exactly which account you logged on as, open the Immediate window in the Visual Basic Editor and check the workgroup file by typing the following:

```
? Syscmd(13)
```

Once you have confirmed that the workgroup file is okay, choose Tools ➤ Security ➤ User and Group Permissions. To confirm that you are using the correct account, look for the account name at the bottom of the dialog. Now I will show you the minimum permissions that are necessary for Groups accounts to use your objects.

Table Permissions for Users

In a nutshell, what you have to do is clear the Modify Design and Administer permissions on all tables for all User and Group accounts that aren't specifically developers or administrators. If you need more information on table permissions, read Chapter 10.

Query Permissions for Users

First, you need to verify the permissions on your queries by selecting the Groups option on the Permissions tab on the User and Group Permissions dialog, and then select Query from the Object Type drop-down list. Now choose the group Full Data Users for all queries. Read Design should be the only design permission selected (as shown in Figure 11-2). The data permissions on the right-hand side will vary according to what permission scheme you selected in the User-Level Security wizard. Considering the work that developers sometimes put into queries, it is a pity that users can always see the query designs. I will discuss how to combat this capability later on in this chapter.

In a nutshell, what you have to do is clear the Modify Design and Administer permissions on all queries for all User and Group accounts that aren't specifically developers or administrators.

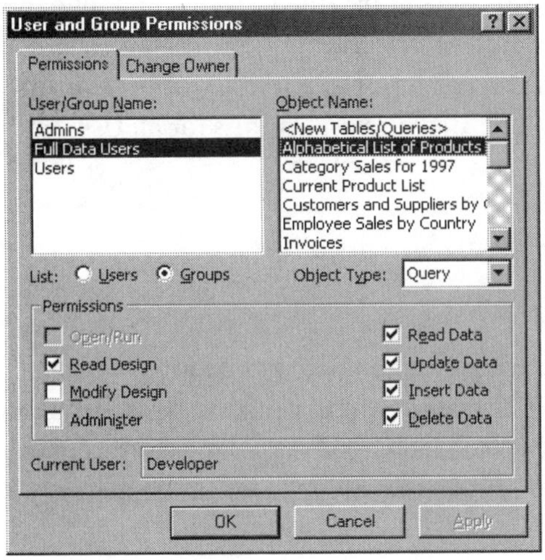

Figure 11-2. All users requireRead Design permission for queries.

Form, Report, and Macro Permissions for Users

Because the permissions that you want to allocate to your users are the same for forms, reports, and macros, let's look at form permissions. On the Permissions tab of the User and Group Permissions dialog, select the Groups option, select the Form object type, and then select any form. If you select the Full Data Users group (as shown in Figure 11-3), you will find that the form only has Open/Run permission.

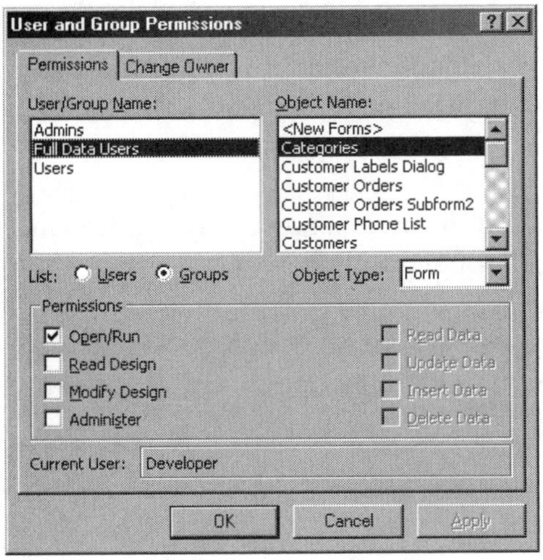

Figure 11-3. The Open/Run permission for forms.

Unless you actually want a user or group of users to be able to view or change the design of a form, report, or macro, Open/Run should be the only permission assigned.

In a nutshell, what you have to do for forms, reports, and macros is clear the Read Design, Modify Design, and Administer permission options for all User and Group accounts.

Module Permissions for Users

For modules in Access 97, clear all permissions for all User and Group accounts that aren't specifically developers or administrators. Unfortunately, Microsoft removed this security in Access 2000 and replaced it with VBA passwords (discussed later on in this chapter). Thankfully, you can simulate the Access 97 protection by using the DAO library, and you can find out all about that in Chapter 8.

Other Permissions Issues

Finally, here are some other permission issues that you need to consider while securing your database with workgroup security:

- You should review the permissions for Users accounts. For example, to review permissions for forms, go to the Permissions tab on the User and Group Permissions dialog, select the Users option, select the Form object type, and then review the permission on all the users. If you ran the User-Level Security wizard, you should find that none of them has permissions on that or any other form or report.

- You may want to give the Developer account permission for all objects. I prefer this option when I am the only developer on a database because it is easier to manage than using the Admins group.

- Remember that ownership is critical, as owners can reset any permission, even if they are not members of the Admins group.

- When you are looking at the object permissions for Groups, do not get the anonymous Admin user and the Admins (administrators) group mixed up.

Remember to *test* your actual user accounts when you have finished, and don't forget to *test, test, test* the anonymous Admin account. Now I will show you a neat way to avoid having linked tables in a database.

Protecting Linked Tables' Paths with Remote Queries

`Access 97 or later`

The best ways to protect and secure individual linked tables are by using the Hidden property (see Chapter 3) and by using workgroup security on tables in the back-end database. If you want to disguise your linked tables, consider trying the following remote query technique.

One of the more interesting ways to protect against people opening or importing directly from a linked table (see Chapter 4) in a front-end database is to replace your link with a remote query. These queries work by including a direct reference to the back-end database in the SQL of the query itself. To illustrate this process, have a look at the following SQL code of a query that will retrieve the Orders table from a remote Northwind database. The SQL extension that allows this query to work is the IN clause that follows the FROM Table clause in the query.

```
SELECT Orders.* FROM Orders
  IN 'C:\Program Files\Microsoft Office\Office 10\samples\Northwind.mdb';
```

To start experimenting with remote queries yourself, try the following:

1. Open any database, select the Database window, and choose the Queries object type.

2. Create a new query in design view and do not select any tables.

3. Choose View ➤ Properties.

4. Type the full path to the Northwind database in the Source Database field on the Query Properties dialog (as shown in Figure 11-4). The default term (current) in the property line refers to this database.

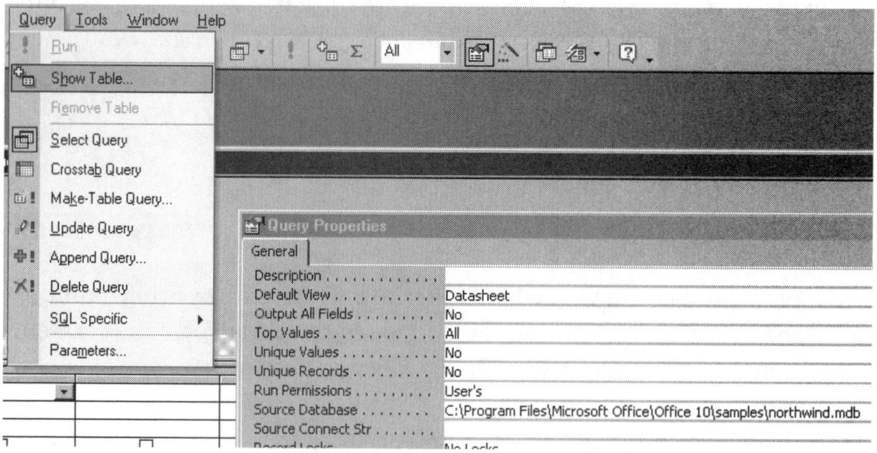

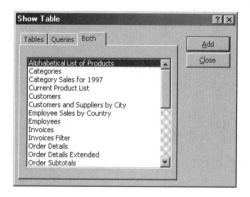

Figure 11-4. Entering the full path to a database in the Source Database field.

5. Choose Query ➤ Show Table, and you will now have a full list of all the tables and queries that are in the source database (as shown in Figure 11-5). You should find this same button on your Query Design toolbar.

Figure 11-5. A list of tables and queries in the source database.

6. Choose the Orders table and drag the appropriate fields down to the grid.

7. The query will now work as though you had actually opened the Northwind database itself.

Now that you have seen how you can write a remote query to remove a linked table from your database, how are remote queries actually a protection measure?

- You can use a remote query to remove a number (or all) of your important linked tables so that they do not appear in the Tables tab in the Database window or in the Tables list when they're imported from another database.

- Because developers and users rarely use remote queries, they offer a subtle way to hide the location of your back-end database(s).

- They let you secretly link to a second database.

- Because front-end queries can refer directly to queries in the back-end database, you can move queries to the back-end database. This action, which is something that linked tables cannot do, will stop the duplication of queries when more than one front-end database uses the same query.

- You can store the remote query in either VBA code or a form's `RecordSource` property, making it much harder for someone to locate the back-end database.

One interesting extension to remote queries is that you can use them on Microsoft Excel data, text files, SQL Server tables and any other data source to which Access can link. I have used the Excel extension in a number of my production databases with success.

Using Remote Queries in Normal Development

Where I use remote queries the most in ordinary applications is when I need to get or put some data into a database that is not the normal back-end database. If you were to add a link to a second back-end database, you would have to be very careful which tables you or your DBA users choose when you run the standard Access Linked Table Manager. If tables are selected that appear in more than one database, the Linked Table Manager will refresh the links one at a time and ask for the location of those links one at a time. This process can be very confusing for the DBA (and a certain Australian software developer). If you, too, want to experience this confusion, follow these steps:

1. Open Access and create a new blank database.

2. Link to two tables in two separate back-end databases by choosing File ➤ Get External Data ➤ Linked Tables, making a total of four links.

3. Start the Linked Table Manager in Access 2000 or later by choosing Tools ➤ Database Utilities ➤ Linked Table Manager. In Access 97, choose Tools ➤ Add-Ins ➤ Linked Table.

4. Select the Always Prompt for a New Location check box and select all the linked tables.

5. Click OK.

Now you will need to point individually to the correct back-end database for each and every table in the database. Naturally, in databases that have more than 10 different linked tables spread across two or more back-end databases, this process can get a little tedious. This particular trait of the linked table manager doesn't surface unless you link to more than one database.

How I generally approach external file issues like this is by storing the external database in the same relative folder path as the software database; that is, a sub-directory. Then, just before the query is run, I modify the remote path by using VBA code to suit the relative directory. This method works particularly well for spreadsheets and temporary databases.

Remote Queries May Require Additional VBA Coding

This manual design of remote queries is terrific when you are on-site, but you must be aware that there's no add-in like the Linked Table Manager to manage these database paths. If you want to read more on this topic, see the section "Further Reading" at the end of the chapter for information on how to reach a link to an article that I wrote on remote queries.

Protecting Your Query Design

The more common ways to protect and secure your query design (from being changed) are done through the Hidden property (see Chapter 3) and by using workgroup security (see Chapter 8 and this chapter). If you want to hide the design of the queries, consider trying the different techniques outlined in the following sections.

Protect Your Query by Using RWOP Queries

In Chapter 10, I described how a certain type of query, called a Read with Owner Permission (RWOP), would allow a workgroup User account that had no permissions on a table or query access to any fields included in the RWOP query. What I didn't explain, though, was that RWOP queries provide very good protection for the design of a query itself. To demonstrate this protection, we need to remove permissions granted to the Full Data Users group from a query in the Northwind database that we secured earlier in the chapter. Then we will set up a RWOP query that actually returns all the information that the Full Data Users group can no longer view directly, which means that the Editor user, as a member of the Full Data Users group, will never find out the design of this query. Here are the detailed steps:

1. Use the Developer account to log on to the secured Northwind database.

2. Remove all permissions for the ubiquitous Users group for the Invoices query (as shown in Figure 11-6). If any permissions exist for the query, then you need to review permissions for all objects, as something may have gone astray with the User-Level Security wizard.

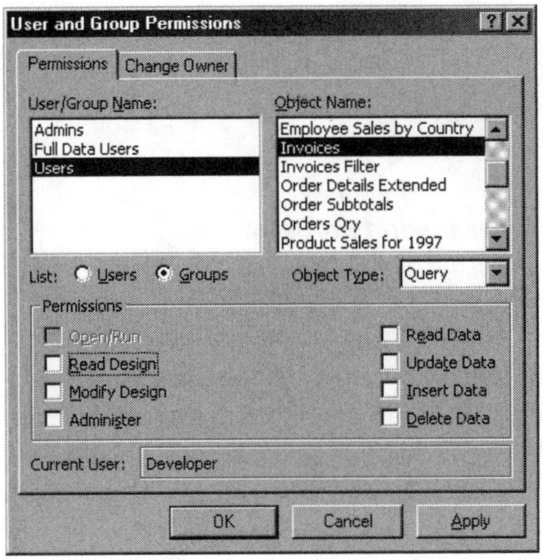

Figure 11-6. Removing all permissions for the Invoices query for the Users group.

3. Select the Full Data Users group for the Invoices query and clear all permissions.

4. Select the anonymous Admin user for the Invoices query and clear all permissions.

5. Create a new query that returns all information from the Invoices query by using the following SQL code:

```
select * from invoices
```

6. While you have the query in design mode, choose View ➤ Properties.

7. Select the Run Permissions property and choose Owners, as shown in Figure 11-7.

8. Save the query with a name of `Invoices RWOP`.

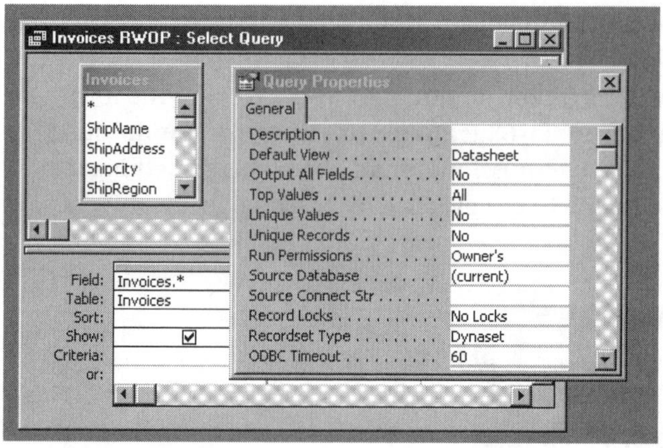

Figure 11-7. Choosing Owners as the query permission property.

Now close Access, log on as the Editor account, and try to open the Invoices query. You should get a No Read Definitions error, whether you want to open the query or view it in design mode. When you open the Invoices RWOP query, however, the Editor account will be able to see all the data. Voila—you have protected the design of your query from your users.

Hiding Your Query (Design) in Forms and VBA Code

You can make some of your queries visible to fewer people by storing the design in a form or in a module. The biggest benefit here is that there is far less chance that the average user will accidentally change your query if you are not using workgroup security. You can use these places to store your queries:

- In the `RecordSource` property of a form or a report.

- By saving the SQL code of the query in VBA code as a string variable and assigning the `RecordSource` property of a form or a report when opening the form.

- In VBA code rather than in the Database window, if you are using the DAO and ADO `RecordSet` property.

Remember that if you store your query in VBA code, you should consider using both a VBA project password and module protection in the Database window (described in Chapter 8). Of course, workgroup security on your form will also make the VBA code and the `RecordSource` property harder to find, as will the appropriate startup options (see Chapter 2).

 TIP Though it makes sense to hide the queries in VBA code and the `RecordSource` property, do not store the same query twice in different places. If you have to, store the SQL in a function and call the function to return the value.

Encrypting a Database to Obscure the SQL in Queries

In both of the query protection issues I've described in this chapter, you need to be aware that a query's SQL is small and readily distinguishable when viewing a normal decrypted database in a text editor. If you are totally serious about hiding the query's design, you may want to encrypt the database by choosing Tools ➤ Security ➤ Encrypt/Decrypt Database or by using the protected folder strategy discussed in Chapter 12. This option also applies to the MDE format as described at the end of the chapter.

Now I will show you a neat trick that will turn off the Design View button for forms and reports. As you read that material, you should gain an insight into the virtues of class objects.

Protecting Forms by Using VBA Code

The best ways to protect and secure the design of individual forms are to compile the database into MDE format (see the section "The MDE Database Format Revisited" in this chapter), to use the `Hidden` property (see Chapter 3), and to use workgroup security (see Chapter 8 and the section "A Workgroup Security Refresher" earlier in this chapter). If you are not sure about using the MDE format, consider using the following programming technique to stop people from opening your forms in design view.

With the release of Access 97, Access forms became a much more versatile class object. By exploiting this object technology, we can open Access forms in a different way so that the users cannot use the Design View commands. To demonstrate how this process works, I have set up a simple form (called frmClassy) that opens another form as a class object. This process works because you can open the form by creating a new instance of the form class, albeit an invisible one. When the Visible property of the form class object is set to True, the form appears just like an ordinary form, with one exception: the Design View command on the menu and toolbars is disabled. You can see the disabled design button in two places by looking at Figure 11-8.

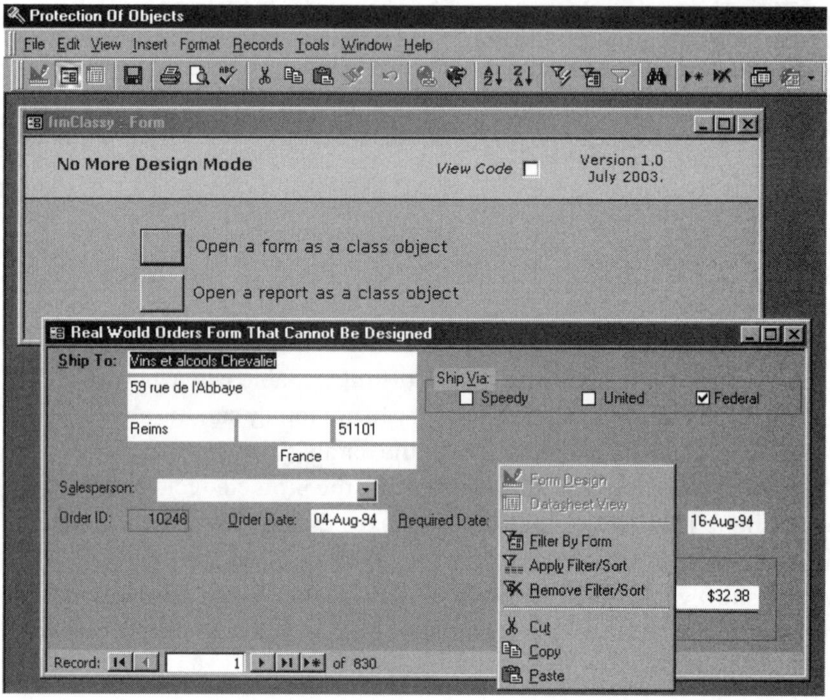

Figure 11-8. A form opened as a class object cannot be put in design mode.

Some VBA code that illustrates this process is stored in a module called basOpenProtected in the demonstration database. As you can see in the following subroutine, the first thing that has to happen is that a specific form class object (called clsFrmOrders) must be declared and instantiated. Once this happens, you can manipulate all the methods and properties of the form. Then, in the important last step in the code, you make the form visible. I personally use form properties and methods when setting up interfaces to be more intuitive for my clients.

```
Sub ProtectOrdersForm()
' Open the Orders form as a class object to protect it from
' being opened in design mode.

' If you include this code in a form module, the form below
' will be closed when the form that opens it closes.
On Error GoTo ProtectOrdersForm_error

Static clsFrmOrders As Form_frmOrders
Set clsFrmOrders = New Form_frmOrders

With clsFrmOrders
    .Caption = "Real World Orders Form That Cannot Be Designed"
    .Detail.BackColor = vbGreen
    .Visible = True
End With

ProtectOrdersForm_exit:
    Exit Sub

ProtectOrdersForm_error:
    MsgBox "Error number " & Err.Number & " ... " & Err.Description
    GoTo ProtectOrdersForm_exit

End Sub
```

Now, you may be wondering why I had to place this code in a module and not in the more logical place, in the code behind the form. It has to do with a behavior of the form class object, called scope. When you open a form by using code in a module, you have to declare the new form object as a static variable. Because you use a static variable, the form class remains in scope even when the subroutine has completed running. An example of the Static statement follows:

```
Static frmOrders As Form_frmOrders
```

Now, you should be aware that the form class behavior changes according to where you place the Static statement. If you declare the same static variable in the code behind a form, the second form will close if the form that holds the static variable is closed. Because you would generally want to avoid this behavior, I recommend that you call a subroutine in a separate module, as follows:

```
Private Sub cmdOpenClassyForm_Click()
' Open a form as a class object, thus protecting it.
' This subroutine should appear in a module except when you
' want the instance of the form class to close when this form closes.

Call ProtectOrdersForm
End Sub
```

If this "scope behavior" stuff doesn't make sense, try experimenting with the basOpenProtected module. When that works, copy the code module and place it in the Click event of a new command button on a form. Then press the new button to open the form class, and close the form with the new button.

Before finishing this topic, I will give you some other things to contemplate when using forms as class modules:

- You need to have the Has Module property of the form set to Yes for the form to be available as a class module.

- You need to ensure that you have adequate error handling code in your forms, or a bug can send the user into the VBA code debugger.

- You can actually open multiple versions of the form, but you will need to keep an array of form objects.

If you want to read more on this topic, see the "Further Reading" section at the end of this chapter for information on how to reach a link to an article that I wrote on scope behavior for the *Smart Access* magazine.

Watch Out for Cut and Pasted Datasheets

One great thing about Access forms is that you can readily switch between the single record view to the spreadsheet-like datasheet view. Though this power is terrific, you need to be aware that the datasheet and continuous form views make it very easy for the end user to cut and paste all the records in a form into a product like Microsoft Excel or Word. If your intention was never to provide the user with this facility, then make sure that you turn off the form's Allow Datasheet View property.

Protecting Reports by Using VBA Code

The best ways to protect and secure individual report designs are to compile the database in MDE format (see the section "The MDE Database Format Revisited" in this chapter), to use the Hidden property (see Chapter 3), and to use workgroup security (Chapter 8 and the section "A Workgroup Security Refresher" earlier in this chapter). If you are not sure about the MDE format, consider using the following programming technique to stop people from opening the report in design view.

Just like with forms in the previous section, you can also open reports as class modules to protect them from being opened in design mode. The VBA code to do this is very similar to that demonstrated for a form class, and you can find the subroutine in the basOpenProtected module and the code that calls that subroutine in the form frmClassy. The code follows.

```
Sub ProtectOrdersReport()

' Open the Orders report as a class object to protect it from
' being opened in design mode.

' If you include this code in a form module, the report below
' will be closed when the form that opens it closes.
On Error GoTo ProtectOrdersReport_error

Static clsRptOrders As Report_rptOrders
Set clsRptOrders = New Report_rptOrders

With clsRptOrders
    .Caption = "Real World Orders Report That Cannot Be Designed"
    .Visible = True
End With

ProtectOrdersReport_exit:
    Exit Sub

ProtectOrdersReport_error:
    MsgBox "Error number " & Err.Number & " ... " & Err.Description
    GoTo ProtectOrdersReport_exit

End Sub
```

That code provides just about all the additional security techniques that you can use for reports. Now we will review the protection that is available for macros.

Protecting Macros by Using VBA Code

The only ways to protect individual macros are to use the Hidden property (Chapter 3) or to use workgroup security (Chapter 8 and the section the section "A Workgroup Security Refresher" earlier in this chapter). If you are not using workgroup security to protect macros, your only option is to convert them to VBA code, which you can do by following these steps:

1. Open the Database window and select Macros so that you can see all the macros.

2. Select the macro that you want to convert.

3. Right-click the macro and choose Save As.

4. Choose Module.

Please note that the MDE database format does not protect macros. Now I will show you how you can protect your VBA code.

Protecting VBA Code by Using a Password

The best ways to protect and secure your Modules and VBA code are to compile the database into MDE format (see the section "The MDE Database Format Revisited" in this chapter), to use the Hidden property (Chapter 3), and to use workgroup security in Access 97 (see Chapter 8). If you are not sure about the MDE format, consider using the VBA project password to protect your VBA code.

As I discussed in Chapter 8, it is possible to lock your modules by using workgroup security and DAO commands so that people cannot open the module directly from the Database window. In Access 97, this method provided to be good security for your code, but with the advent of Access 2000, the separation of the database from the Visual Basic Environment (VBE) meant that the code was far more accessible. Microsoft's solution for this issue was to allow you to place a password on the VBA project.

To add a password to your VBA project, follow these steps:

1. Open your database and switch to the VBE (by pressing ALT+F11).

2. Choose Tools ➤ *ProjectName* Properties.

3. Select the Protection tab, shown in Figure 11-9.

4. Select the Lock Project for Viewing check box and fill in the password fields. Remember to write down the password somewhere safe. Click OK.

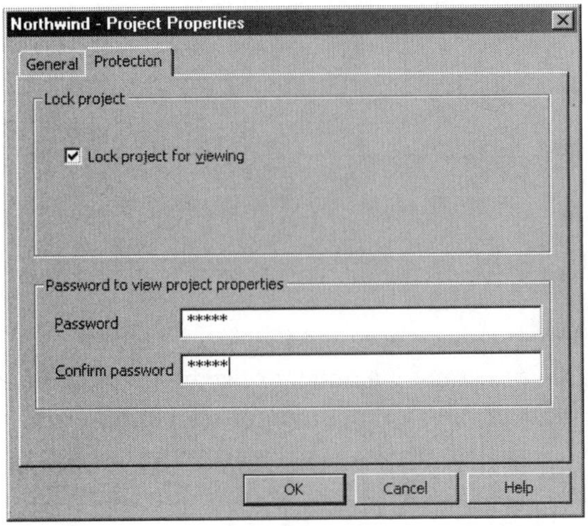

Figure 11-9. Protecting the VBA project by a password.

From now on, the first time that anyone wants to view VBA code after opening the database, he or she will be asked to enter the password. This protection also applies to the VBA code for any form or report. If you find entering this password irritating, you can clear the Lock Project for Viewing check box to allow anyone to open the VBE, as though a password weren't entered. That way, when you release the database, you can select the check box again and the same password will protect the VBA project.

Unfortunately, the Password Crackers Are at It Again

If you are starting to feel comfortable about the protection offered by your VBA code password, hop off your horse because the code crackers have sorted out this one as well. In Figure 11-10, I demonstrate one of the tools from which it took just a second or so to recover the VBA password from an encrypted database. As a result, I would use the VBA password as a deterrent and generally would apply it only when I was about to post my front-end database to the live environment. That said, because the VBA password does not hinder your users, the password will deter most intruders and is certainly better than no password at all. Therefore, if you have a lot of code to protect, consider using this password.

Recovering password for the file:
C:\...y Robinson\My Documents\vbsecuretestencrypt.mdb

Detected Access 2000 database

Loading database...
VBA Project password: **[TYH]** (no brackets) <Copy>

Figure 11-10. Password-cracking software figures out your VBA project password.

Other Code Protection Options

If you "just must" protect your code and cannot use the MDE format for the complete front-end database, you have to step up a notch or two in the difficulty stakes. The first option is to move some of the modules to another database and then produce an MDE library. Another alternative is to create an ActiveX object or a COM add-in. You can then reference those objects from your within your VBA environment. See the "Further Reading" section at the end of this chapter for information on how to reach links to continue to read on these topics.

 User Story *Why not sell your source code? If you are worried about whether someone will use your software to produce an alternative product, consider this approach, which I stumbled on with my graphical data mining shareware. One day when I was considering options for selling my software, I decided to heed the advice of a number of programmers who had asked for the source code of the database. Given that sales weren't going to keep me in cappuccino, I decided to charge for the source code as an extra. This option soon improved the sales and let prospective buyers know that they wouldn't be hung out to dry if my company stopped supporting the software. This approach also had the benefit of letting potential thieves know that they would also have to sell the source code that they modified and thereby reduce their chances of profiting from their misdemeanors. An example of a popular Access vendor that has taken this "open source" approach is Database Creations.*

Using Data Access Pages
with Workgroup Security

Access 2000 or later

One approach that I recommend to protect your database is denying all but the most important users any direct access to the database. Once you do that, you have to find another way for these users to access the database, and for that task I suggest that you try an Internet technology called data access pages (DAP). This less-than-popular technology works by using ADO and some software objects that are installed with Access 2000 or later. The principal difference between DAP and most Internet technologies you may have dealt with is that it works with software on the client computer rather than on the host to interact with the Access database. DAPs are useful for interactive reporting, interactive cube analysis and charting, and simpler data entry and management.

NOTE   If you have never paid much attention to DAP, you should have a look at the samples that come with the Northwind database. In particular, have a look at how the reports work, because they are quite interactive and offer a different style of solution to the conventional Access report.

Earlier in the chapter, in the section "The Developer Workgroup File and Security Revisited," I described how to use the User-Level Security wizard to secure the Northwind database. In that list of instructions, I asked you to copy the HTML (*.HTM) files from the Samples directory to the temporary directory in which you are experimenting. You will now need these HTML files, because they are your data access pages. Inside the DAP HTML, you will find the instructions to connect to your database and open the appropriate DAP objects. You may also want to copy the *.BMP files from the sample directory if you want to see images on the Employees DAP. Now I will show you how to convert your DAPs to the workgroup-secured database.

1. Open the database by using your developer workgroup file and Developer account. The User-Level Security wizard probably left a shortcut on your desktop so that you can open the correct workgroup file.

2. Find the Pages object type in the Database window and choose a page, such as Employees. Open it, and you will find that your links no longer exist or that the data provider will not work. Fix the link by finding the employees.htm in the directory with your sample database.

3. To fix the problem that you are having with the data provider, open your DAP in design view. Ignore the "Can't Find" warning that comes up, because you can't do anything about it.

4. Choose View ➤ Properties and then edit the connection string. The Data Link Properties dialog appears, as shown in Figure 11-11. Alternatively, you can click the Page Connection Properties button at the top of the Field List pane.

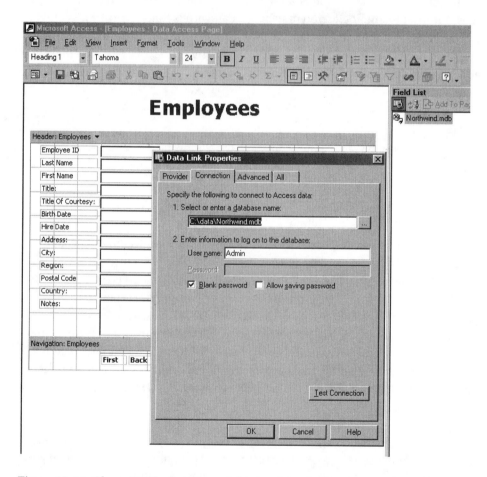

Figure 11-11. Changing the location of the database in the Data Link Properties dialog.

5. Now connect the DAP page the mischievous way, by saving the user name and its password in the HTML of the DAP page. To complete the roguish connection, type the Developer account and password into the User Name and Password fields and select the Allow Saving Password check box.

6. Choose the All tab and edit the Jet OLEDB:System Database property. Type in the name and path to the system database, as shown in Figure 11-12.

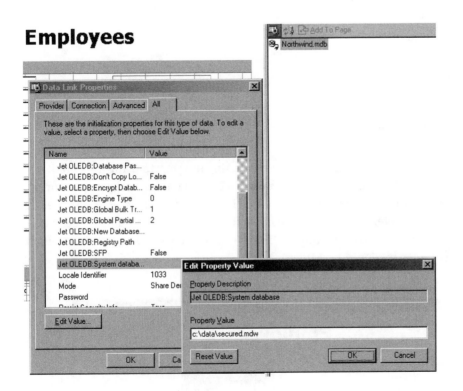

Figure 11-12. Changing the System Database property to point to the workgroup file.

7. Click OK in all the dialog boxes and click Yes to save the password in an unencrypted format.

You should now have a full list of tables and fields in the Field List pane, as shown in Figure 11-13.

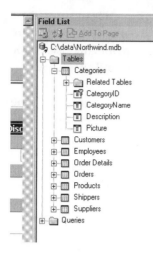

Figure 11-13. The Field Pane, showing all tables.

That concludes the discussion on converting the DAP to using a secured database. Well, sort of! What we have now is a DAP that uses workgroup security with a password embedded in an unsecured HTML text file. This working page will provide a good reference point as we move to a better model and will speed your development. For the record, the DAP that we have been working on is a data entry page (as shown in Figure 11-14).

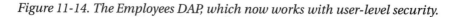

Figure 11-14. The Employees DAP, which now works with user-level security.

If we were to poke around in the HTML of the DAP, we would find that the user name and password are stored in plain text in the body of the HTML. This is a security breach that you clearly want to avoid. To fix this matter, open your DAP in design mode and remove the password. Now, when someone opens the DAP, he or she will encounter a password dialog like that shown in Figure 11-15. Once you have tested your page inside Access, you need to test it by using Internet Explorer.

Figure 11-15. When users open a data access page, they will need to enter a user name and password to view it.

Other DAP Protection Issues

Because each DAP is stand-alone, you must be organized when managing your DAPs. To help you set up your DAPs for your users, here are some things to consider:

- Place the workgroup file in a network folder by using a path that will be the same for everyone.

- Ensure that your developer account is not in the workgroup file that the DAP uses.

- Consider setting up a workgroup file with only one group account in it to limit susceptibility to password-cracking software.

- Access doesn't provide workgroup security for the links stored in the Pages tab of the Database window.

- Consider using operating system security to place read-only permissions on the HTML files.

- You cannot develop in different versions of Access for DAP. If you have Access 2002, you will render the DAPs unworkable in Access 2000 if you edit them.

- Make sure that you are using workgroup files and databases that are created with the same version format; that is, both 2002 or both 2000.

- When the security wizard runs, it doesn't change the security of your DAP files.

Now I will discuss some of the protection and security issues that relate to Access Data Projects.

Access Data Projects

Access 2000 or later

Access Data Projects (ADP) are a new incarnation of Access databases that have been designed to work with SQL Server or MSDE databases, a cut-down version of SQL Server. Because they are not the most popular choice for Access users, even after being out for three years, I have restricted the material in this book to a summary of views expressed in Access help, the MSDN Web site, and newsgroups on ADP protection and security, as follows:

- Use the startup options on the Tools menu to protect your database, just as you would an Access MDB database. The instructions are also available in VBA code if you search for "startup options" in the VBE.

- You can turn off the AllowByPass option by using VBA code, as follows:

```
CurrentProject.Properties.Add "AllowBypassKey", False
```

- Compile the Access Data Project into ADE format just as if you were creating an MDE-format database from an MDB database. This action will provide gold standard security for your forms, reports, and modules.

- Establish security within SQL Server to protect database diagrams, tables, views, and stored procedures.

Of course, as for its older brother the MDB format, you'll need to ponder some protection issues for Access Data Projects, such as:

- You cannot protect the startup options by using workgroup security. The lack of workgroup security makes the ADP startup options more vulnerable than the MDB startup options because programmers can change the options by using VBA code.

- No workgroup security is built into ADP, so you will have no way of protecting different parts of your application, as you would in an MDB database.

- Do not assume because your data is in SQL Server format that it is safe, because it isn't. You will need to invest resources in establishing and maintaining the SQL Server security.

- A number of Internet group postings indicated that ADP projects suffer from vulnerabilities from importing from another ADP project.

My recommendations for ADPs are that you

- Use SQL Server security for the data.

- Compile the ADP database into ADE format to protect the forms, reports, and code.

- Set up the operating system-protected folders by using the concepts that I outline in Chapter 12.

Third-Party Access Data Project Protection Solution

Though I haven't made a point of discussing third-party solutions to security issues in the book, a prominent Access development company called Database Creations sells a tool for managing security at the user level in an ADP. You will find a link to this company's Web site in the "Further Reading" section of this chapter.

The MDE Database Format Revisited   Access 97 or later

As I said in Chapter 1, the MDE format is the only gold standard security that Access provides, and it is dead easy to use. All you have to do is choose Tools ➤ Database Utilities ➤ Make MDE, and you are done. But what special things does the MDE format do for your database to make it so secure?

- All forms, reports, and modules are permanently locked so that they cannot be opened in design mode. For once in Access, there are no exceptions or workarounds—these objects are locked.

- All the VBA code is compiled and saved in PCode format (an explanation follows).

- All the VBA code is then removed from the database.

- There is no development environment, so the user cannot use the Project Explorer, the Intermediate window, or the Object Browser to find out more about the application.

- The PCode, forms, and reports remain static and can never be changed.

- The PCode is quite secure because software cannot translate it back to useful VBA Code.

But What Is PCode?

PCode is an interpretation of your beloved VBA code that has been transferred into a computer-independent and very machine-ready language of bytes, memory locations, pointers, and English text. Once it is in this machine format, the Access PCode interpreter will then send instructions to the Access application so that it interacts correctly with the Windows operating system. Access always requires PCode for the current VBA code that it is processing. If the current code module is uncompiled, Access will compile and create PCode for it. And finally, because the MDE format is always compiled, Access never wastes time recompiling code.

When an MDE Database Is Applicable

If you are interested in the concept of the MDE format and are not sure whether it will work for you, my first recommendation is try it out on a database that you use regularly. When you change to the MDE format, you will encounter issues similar to those when you work with a programming language such as Visual Basic 6. You first write some code, you compile it, and then you deliver it for use. The user only ever sees the final product, and you maintain the code in a safe location.

But at what sort of database environments should you be aiming your MDE database?

- The MDE file format is suited to front-end databases or database wizards.

- The MDE format is relevant in situations where you distribute the Access application to many clients or where the database is available as a download from the Internet. I personally have been using the MDE format for shipping trial versions of my data mining shareware since 1997.

NOTE The process of saving a database as an *.MDE file compiles all modules and compacts the destination database, so there is no need to perform these steps before saving a database as an *.MDE file.

Problems with the MDE Database Format

Though I am generally bullish about the security of the MDE format, there are a number of things to be aware of, such as:

- The MDE format is unsuitable when a database is used as a back-end database or as a standalone database. In this case, upgrades of software require you to transfer all the data into a new database.

- If you only have the *.MDE file and don't have the MDB database, then no one can restore your code for you. This issue can be a big problem for the IT manager if you thought you purchased source code; and if it happens to the developer, stick your head under a pillow and scream loudly.

- The MDE format provides no protection for tables, queries, macros, relationships, database properties, and startup options.

- If you have a bug in the MDE database, you will need good error handling code to work out the problem.

- The MDB format can be too restrictive if your users or your VBA code needs to create new forms and reports in the database.

- If you are using Access 2002/2003 to develop an Access 2000 database, you cannot create an Access 2000 MDE.

- Backups and versions of software are more important when you're working with MDEs, because you do not have the dual live and development MDB situation anymore.

- Password-cracking programs can still detect database passwords just as easily as before, and because the workgroup file remains the same, it is just as vulnerable. Only VBA code is secure because there is none to crack.

- You cannot add or delete references to object libraries or databases by using the References command on the Tools menu.

Now we will look at how workgroup security interacts with MDE databases.

Workgroup Security

Workgroup security works the same for the MDE format as it does for the MDB format, except that the Administer and Modify Design permissions do not apply to forms and reports. One thing that you need to be aware of if you want to convert the database to the MDE format is that your workgroup user account will need the following permissions:

- Open/Run and Open Exclusive permissions for the database itself.

- Modify Design or Administer permission for any tables in the database, or you must be the owner of any tables in the database.

- Read Design permission for all objects in the database.

To conclude this section, I will repeat myself by reminding you that workgroup security is the only way to secure individual tables in an MDE database.

Database Password

Database passwords work the same on MDE-format files as on MDB files. In both cases, you will need to open the database in exclusive mode to set or clear the password.

Hiding Queries in MDE Databases

Early in the chapter, I described how you could save queries as SQL text strings and store them in the RecordSource property of a form or report or in VBA code to make them more secure. Move your queries from the Database window and save them in the RecordSource property of a form or a report. This action is especially pertinent when you are using the MDE format, because it will do a very good job of protecting the query. Of course, if you can save the SQL of the query in SQL in the VBA code, it will be very secure.

Using Forms in MDE Databases

Access forms in MDE databases are very secure in most ways because you can never open them in design view and you can never get to the code. Nevertheless, a clever programmer can find out things like the RecordSource of a form or report, and maybe even the RecordSource of a data-aware control, such as a drop-down list. Of course, once someone discovers a query, that person can run it from an unprotected Database window. If you don't want this to occur, you should manipulate the properties and methods of the form by using code in another form or module and add the RecordSource to the form in this code. In this instance, the (unbound) form in design mode does not have a value in the RecordSource property until the software sets it. For those of you who are just looking for interesting code, you may enjoy the flexibility offered by using an Access form as a class module.

```
Private Sub cmdOpenUnbound_Click()

' Open a form, manipulate some of the form's properties, and then
' add the (secret) RecordSource to the form.

DoCmd.OpenForm "frmOrdersUnbound"
With Form_frmOrdersUnbound
    .AllowEdits = True
    .RecordSelectors = False
    .NavigationButtons = True
    .Caption = "Real World Demonstration"
    .RecordSource = "select top 5 * from Orders order by OrderDate, Freight desc"
End With

End Sub
```

You can find the code for this example in the frmOpenUnbound form in the demonstration database. Now I will show you how to create an MDE database using VBA code.

Creating an MDE Database Automatically

While writing this chapter, I had discussions with another Access developer about what he does before he sends a new version of his Anesthetics database. He explained that he creates an .MDE file, adds a version number to the database, clears a few startup options, and then packs the resulting file into a *.ZIP file.

Though it is beyond the scope of the book to explain all those steps, I thought it would be worthwhile to put an example together that automated the MDE creation process. You will find this example in the demonstration database in a form called frmConvertToMDE. The following code from that form illustrates how to automate the menu commands required to create an *.MDE file. In this example, I have added some additional checks to see whether the file exists and whether it is actually an MDE-format database.

NOTE   The frmConvertToMDE form in this example requires an unsecured Northwind database.

```
Private Sub cmdDBtoMDE_Click()

' Compile the current database into MDE format.

' This form requires a reference to
' Microsoft DAO 3.6 or 3.51 library.

Dim strMdeName As String
Dim OKtoMake As Boolean
Dim intMakeMDE As Integer
Dim wrkJet As Workspace
Dim dbs As Database
Dim accApp As Access.Application

Const MDBFILE = "C:\Data\Northwind.mdb"
Const FILENOTFOUND = 3024
Const MAKEMDE = 603

On Error GoTo err_cmdDBtoMDE

strMdeName = left(MDBFILE, Len(MDBFILE) - 4) & ".mde"

' Create a Jet workspace object by using the anonymous Admin user
' You will need to change the user name and password if the
' database is secured with a workgroup.
Set wrkJet = CreateWorkspace("", "admin", "", dbUseJet)

On Error Resume Next
Set dbs = wrkJet.OpenDatabase(strMdeName, True)

If Err.Number = FILENOTFOUND Then
   OKtoMake = True

ElseIf Err.Number = 0 Then
   On Error GoTo err_cmdDBtoMDE
```

```
' Let's find whether the file is actually an MDE-format file.
If IsItMDE(dbs) = True Then

    intMakeMDE = MsgBox("The MDE format database " & strMdeName & _
                    " already exists" & vbCrLf & _
                    "Would you like to overwrite it?", _
                    vbYesNo + vbDefaultButton2, "Overwrite MDE database")
    If intMakeMDE = vbYes Then
        ' Confirmation means that the database will be deleted.

        dbs.CLOSE
        wrkJet.CLOSE
        OKtoMake = True
    End If
Else
    MsgBox "This file is not an MDE database"

End If


Else
    ' Problem opening the database in exclusive mode.
    MsgBox "Error No. " & Err.Number & " -> " & Err.Description, vbCritical, _
        "Problem opening the database in exclusive mode"
    GoTo exit_cmdDBtoMDE

End If

' Now procede to making the MDE-format file by using
' a secret action of the SysCmd method.

If OKtoMake Then

    Set accApp = New Access.Application
    ' Use an undocumented constant of the syscmd function.
    accApp.SysCmd MAKEMDE, MDBFILE, strMdeName

    If Len(Dir(strMdeName)) > 0 Then
        MsgBox strMdeName & "file has been created"
    Else
        MsgBox "There seems to have been a problem creating the MDE file. " & _
            "You should open your database and see that it compiles " & _
            "and then try a manual build of the MDE database from the " & _
            "Database Utilities Menu", vbCritical, "Problem creating MDE File"
    End If
```

```
     Else
        MsgBox "MDE file creation was canceled"
     End If

  exit_cmdDBtoMDE:
     Set wrkJet = Nothing
     Set dbs = Nothing
     Set accApp = Nothing

     Exit Sub

  err_cmdDBtoMDE:
     Select Case Err.Number
        Case Else
           MsgBox "Error No. " & Err.Number & " -> " & Err.Description, vbCritical
     End Select
     Resume exit_cmdDBtoMDE

  End Sub
```

Just in case you missed it, the magical command that actually makes the .MDE file is the SysCmd function. In this case, it uses an undocumented number (603) that I have stored in the constant MAKEMDE. Now I will show you the VBA function that checks whether the database is actually an MDE database. To do this, I test the MDE property in the database and, if it is set to the string value of "T", then the database is MDE.

```
Function IsItMDE(dbs As Object) As Boolean
   ' Software to test whether the database is in MDE format.

   Dim strMDE As String
   On Error Resume Next
   strMDE = dbs.Properties("MDE")
   If Err = 0 And strMDE = "T" Then
      'This is an MDE database.
      IsItMDE = True
   Else
      IsItMDE = False
   End If

End Function
```

To wrap up the discussions on MDE files, I have to mention that MDE format databases actually come in two formats, encrypted and normal. This information came as a bit of surprise to me because I never came across any literature on the topic.

Encrypting MDE Databases

The final word on MDE databases must be devoted to the subject of database encryption. As I mentioned in Chapter 9, it is possible to protect a database by encrypting it. This protection feature will definitely hide the contents of a database from someone who is keen enough to snoop around by using a text editor, but as I said, it is worthwhile to consider whether the benefits outweigh the penalties. Surprisingly, the same arguments for and against apply to an MDE database as to an MDB database, with the exception that the VBA code is not visible. Even in the MDE database, I have no trouble identifying the SQL of queries even if they are embedded in code. Once again, you have to decide whether this is really a concern because you will pay a price in terms of performance and the inability to compress the database.

If you decide that you would like an encrypted `*.MDE` file, your best course of action is to encrypt the MDB database, and then, when you make the conversion, the `*.MDE` file will also be encrypted.

Further Reading

As you might expect, there is never enough information when it comes to powerful products like Access. To assist you with further investigations, I have put together a Web page with links to the Microsoft Web site, my articles, other articles, and newsgroup postings on the material in this chapter. This page includes the following:

- How to set up and maintain remote queries and the `In Database` clause.

- How to use RWOP queries.

- Programming with forms as class module.

- Adding database tools to Excel spreadsheets.

- Setting permissions on objects by using the ADO Extensions library (ADOX).

- Creating secure data access pages (DAP).

- Deploying DAP over the Internet.

- Two- and three-tier DAP and preventing malicious scripts.

- Deploying DAPs on the Internet or your intranet.

- Programmatically changing the connection string property of DAP pages.

- Using FrontPage and DAP.

- How to store DAP passwords in a cookie.

- Interesting reading on Access Data Project security.

- Documentation on MDE libraries and references.

- Database Creations provides a solution for managing ADP security.

- A good explanation about MDE databases and PCode.

- How to save your database as an MDE or project as an `*.ADE` file.

- Discussions on workgroup security and MDE files.

- If you have a database that needs a very simple protection mechanism, try the software at Peter De Baets's Web site.

- Various other links, book references, and article references.

You can find the further reading Web page for this chapter in the Downloads section of the Apress Web site (`http://www.apress.com`) or at `http://www.vb123.com/map/mde.htm`.

Reflecting on This Chapter

Securing and protecting a Microsoft Access database is like heading out to sea in a rusty boat: you initially need to fill all the big holes in the hull so that you stop sinking. Once those important tasks are completed, you keep plugging the holes until you can turn the bilge pump off. Naturally, some big storms may await over the horizon, water may still keep coming in over the side, and you may find more holes in the hull as time goes on. In other words, you have to be forever vigilant.

In this chapter, you found out that workgroup security and the MDE format are two big plugs that fill the security holes. After that, if you just keep working along with all the other tricks, you will happily sail across the ocean without needing to turn on the pumps too often.

What's Next?

In the next chapter, I think it is high time that I showed you how to protect your database by using the operating system, which is a good way to stop any cyclones from sinking the ship, metaphorically speaking.

CHAPTER 12

Protecting and Securing Your Database with the Operating System

A MICROSOFT ACCESS SYSTEM IS a collection of files: a workgroup file, a front-end database, a back-end database and a locking database. This chapter tells you why and how you can use a modern operating system to protect and secure this file collection. If you are not the person who can actually make the changes to the system, I have deliberately set up this chapter so that you can show your system administrator how it works on your own computer. Regardless of who sets up the operating system security, you will end up with databases that only a select group of Windows users can access. If you want to go one step further, the instruction material will show you how to make it difficult for that select group of users to copy any of the files that make up your database collection.

If you are wondering how applicable this information may be to you, consider this scenario. You are running a small company with 15 people. These people all share the same Windows server on your network. You have a database that holds important customer details in it, and you have now decided that you would like only five staff to make changes to that data and another two staff to administer the database. What will you do? Read on, because this chapter will demonstrate how folder permissions will restrict usage of your Access database to the seven Windows accounts, and it will show you how the two administrators can also have the required permissions to do all the necessary administration tasks.

There is no download material for this chapter—rather, I've included a series of step-by-step demonstrations of how you might set up operating system security by using the Windows 2000 Professional operating system. You'll also find supplementary information on how you might undertake the same task by using Windows XP Professional. You can find a full description of the steps you need to take to set up Windows XP security together with the code download, but I've also included hints on how Windows XP differs from Windows 2000 within the chapter. The operating systems to which this information is applicable include Windows XP Professional, Windows 2000 Professional, Windows 2000 Server, and Windows 2003 Server. The only instructions that are applicable to Windows XP Home are those that describe how to use Windows XP Home to gain permission to use a protected folder on another computer in a peer-to-peer network.

Why Is Operating System Security Important for My Database?

These next sections summarize how these technologies and the security issues that surround them are relevant to the IT manager, the DBA, and the developer. Because this is the final chapter, I also have included a combined introduction on a number of other topics so that everyone can be informed about the other issues that can influence your database's security.

Overview for the DBA and the Developer

This is one chapter in the book where the DBA may feel more comfortable than the developer when it comes to Access security. In this chapter, I will demonstrate all the steps necessary to establish appropriate operating system security for your database:

- To establish folder permissions to restrict who uses your database.

- To establish folder permissions so that users who have permission to use the database will find it very hard to copy either your database(s) or workgroup files as complete files. These instructions will also make it hard for users to locate the database so that they can export objects and data into another database.

- To use the same folder permissions to make it very hard for password-cracking software to analyze the workgroup files and deduce the user names and passwords in those files. Because users will also find it difficult to copy these files, this technique greatly reduces the problems posed by this software.

The purpose of these demonstrations is to help you undertake proof-of-concepts testing before you demonstrate the ideas to a system administrator. If you just happen to be that system administrator, you should find that the information readily adapts to your Windows server environment. If you are an Access developer who works from home or on a small peer-to-peer network, you can actually undertake this testing on your computers and then incorporate this knowledge into your portfolio of skills. In the end, these operating system strategies will greatly improve the level of your database security.

Overview for the IT Manager

When it comes to protecting important Access databases with the operating system, the question is more one of why shouldn't we be doing this rather than why should we. In the section "Proof-of-Concept Operating System Security," you will see how to set up permissions for a folder so that only members of an operating systems permission group (called Access Editors in this chapter) will be able to open the database or any other file in that folder. If you really want to protect your database with the operating system, the section "The Access Protected Folder Strategy" will show you how to stop users from listing contents of the database folders and, subsequently, copying their contents.

If your system administrator sets up these permissions for a database folder, any new users of your computer systems (or domain for bigger sites) will have to be added to the Access Editors group as part of an additional step. If I were the IT manager, I would rather worry about giving additional permissions to a user rather than lose sleep worrying about whether that user had found and opened an important Access database.

For both of these approaches, you will find a discussion, "Testing the Permissions," toward the end of each section that will show you what happens when this security is set up.

Wrap Up for All Readers

Because this is the final chapter in this book, I will address a number of other related issues that you should be aware of. Having an understanding of what these issues are will allow you to promote a more secure environment for the database that you are trying to protect. These discussions include

- The security implication of installing front-end databases on client computers' local drives.

- Why you cannot set permissions on individual database files.

- An overview of why NTFS (new technology file system) hard drive partitions are important.

- Why you might consider screen saver passwords.

- An overview on how to set up Windows XP clients properly.

- A comparison of the differences between Windows XP Home and Windows XP Professional operating systems.

- A checklist of other security-related issues that you need to be concerned about.

Overview of Applicable Operating System Security

Access 97 or later

Access is a software development and database system that is pretty well operating-system independent. I know that because I develop and test Access 97 to Access 2003 on machines that run Windows 95 to Windows XP for clients who run all flavors of networks and desktops. Because of this operating system independence, it is easy to neglect the operating system as a strategy in the protection of your databases. Conversely, if you are involved with SQL Server or the like, you would be far more aware of the operating system on the server and, in particular, the use of user accounts to validate your database users' credentials. Regardless of your knowledge, this chapter will provide you with demonstrations that will show you how and why you might protect the folders where the database files are, thereby protecting your database.

So, how do we establish this security? If you have Windows XP Pro or Windows 2000 Professional, you have an operating system that will allow you to create different Windows accounts and apply permissions to different groups just like the administrator of large company networks.

So that the majority of readers can test this information, I've made the demonstration for a single computer. When that test is complete, I will show you how to apply the same permission techniques to a peer-to-peer network. With that information under your belt, you can chat to your systems administrator about what needs to be set up on the server to protect the database file collection.

 NOTE   You may notice some interesting similarities between operating system security and workgroup security as you read this chapter. In particular, watch for the preferred practice of allocating permissions to groups rather than users.

Do not be alarmed at the number of pages devoted to using this technology. Once you get the hang of it, you will be able to do the whole setup in less than a morning, especially if you work through the samples with your system administrator.

 CAUTION   Operating system security on its own is not the complete answer; rather it is only one of the many layers of defense that you need to place in the way of your would-be database scoundrel. If you set up operating systems security, you also need to put in place many of the other security systems discussed in this book to support it. Return to the Chapter 1 driving instructions to see what protection to apply for different situations.

What You Need to Know to Talk to Your System Administrator

Because this book is targeted to an audience of Access specialists rather than to system administrators, the material in this chapter caters to an audience that has a wide variety of experience with Windows 2000, Windows XP Professional, or Windows Server 2003 data security. I provide an overview of three different permissions groups into which you will need to divide your database users. As far as this description is concerned, we are going to be protecting a folder whose primary purpose is holding the database. This folder will hold a front-end database and a back-end database, the .LDB files created when users open the databases, and the workgroup file when the database is shared between users. Though there are many ways to slice and dice your operating system permission groups, I believe that the best protection strategy that operating system security offers is to use the following three users permission groups. It's important to remember that if a person is not a member of these groups, that person won't be able to open any files in the database folder.

The Access Editors Group

Access editors are all those users who are going to make changes to data, changes to objects in the database, or even just need read-only permission for the database. The folder permission scheme should allow members of this group to create, read, and write to a file in that folder, as these are the permissions necessary to run a database. When I discuss the Access protected folder strategy, I will revoke some permissions granted to this group so that you can make it extremely hard for this group to copy your databases.

The Access DBA Group

The persons who are going to administer the group are going to need permission to see all the files in the directory and have all the permissions that are allocated to the Access Editors Group. You need to use this group only if you adopt the Access protected folder strategy.

The Administrator

This person makes the permission changes for the server and for the local computers when they are secured. If you can help it, try not to use the administrator account for any task other than for administration of the computer. There is nothing new about this account—it is on every Windows 2000 or Windows XP computer.

Configuring These Folder Permissions

When you are dealing with operating system security for Windows 2000, Windows XP, and Windows 2003 Server, you are dealing with two styles of networks, as follows.

Peer-to-Peer Network

In a peer-to-peer network, a group of networked computers share resources, such as files, printers, and scanners. All computers in the workgroup can share resources as equals, without a dedicated server. Each computer in the network maintains a local security database, which contains a list of user accounts and resource security information that is specific to that computer. Included in that security database is security information to allow other computers to use the current computers' resources.

Windows Server Domain

The Windows Server domain is a collection of computers as defined by the administrator of a Windows Server network that share a common directory database (active directory). A domain has a unique name and provides access to the centralized user accounts and group accounts that the domain administrator maintains. Each domain has its own security policies and security relationships with other domains and represents a single security boundary of a Windows 2000 computer network.

An important part of the domain to Access security is the domain roaming profile. When a person logs on to a domain, Windows copies the document and setting files (or personal profile, as it can be known) to a local computer. If this is the process by which your server manages person profiles, you need to be aware of the permissions on the local machine if people are storing important information in their own personal folders. You should discuss how this works with your system administrator.

 CAUTION   Peer-to-peer folder permission will not work on a hard drive that has been partitioned as a FAT volume. If your file server is old, you may benefit from the information on NTFS volumes later in the chapter.

Applying the Permissions

When securing information with the operating system, there are three levels at which you can apply these permissions:

- The Share level, which is a top-level directory that is established so that members of a workgroup can share a drive or a folder and its subfolders. You will always need to set up a network share before you apply any of the more powerful permission structures.

- The Folder level, which allows you to share folders and the files in them. It is possible to nest different permissions structures within subfolders of a parent folder.

- The File level, which allows you to apply permissions to individual files. This form of protection is generally not encouraged because it can be difficult to maintain the permissions. You can read more on this topic in the section "Why You Can't Set Permissions on Individual Files."

Now that you have had a brief overview of where you can apply operating system security, let's have a look at a real-world example of how to set up operating system security. Once armed with this knowledge, you will be able to convey to your systems administrator the practical requirements for protecting an Access database.

Proof-of-Concept Operating System Security

Over the new few pages, I am going to illustrate how you can establish operating system security for your Access databases and associated files on computers that are running either Windows 2000 Professional or Windows XP Professional. Quite a lot of steps are involved in this exercise, and for the target audience—Access developers and DBAs who may have all levels of skills—the examples will include many graphics so that you can visualize what to do. Remember that the main purpose of these examples is to help you become familiar enough with the underlying concepts of folder permissions. Once you have grasped those concepts, you will be able to demonstrate the viability of this technique to a system (Windows server) administrator. You will also have the knowledge to test anything that they set up for you. For some of you who have small networks that do not use a Windows server computer—such as small teams of developers—you may well be able to use the concepts directly on your databases.

For these illustrations, I will use Windows 2000 Professional, but the same concepts apply to Windows XP Professional. On this computer, which I will call the peer-to-peer server, you will need to have an NTFS-formatted drive (covered later in the chapter) for this demonstration to work. To establish the correct folder permissions, do the following:

1. Prepare a database folder to hold the database and related files.

2. Set up a network share so that other computers can use the folder.

3. Set up the Windows user accounts that will use the database.

4. Set up a Windows user group to hold the Windows Users that will use the database.

5. Add the users to the users group.

6. Set the permissions on the database folder.

7. Assign your network accounts to the Database Editors user group.

The security, once established, will be able to be tested by using a client computer running either of these professional operating systems or Windows XP Home edition. For now, it's time to strap yourself into your chair and start working through the demonstrations.

Preparing Databases in a Protected Folder

The first stage of the exercise is preparing a folder that will hold the database files that we want to protect. We have been working in a folder called \data\ previously in the book, so let us use that as the basis for our protected folder. Follow these steps:

1. Log on in as Administrator on your Windows 2000/XP computer.

2. On an NTFS-formatted drive, create a folder called \data\. Instructions in section "The All-Important NTFS Format" will follow later in the chapter.

3. Create a subfolder called \data\Protect\.

4. Add a copy of the Northwind database to that subfolder.

5. Split that database into a front end and a back end by using the Database Splitter wizard (see Chapter 4). Save the back-end database into the same \data\Protect\ folder.

The next step involves setting up a network share. This is a folder and all its associated sub folders that will be available to computers on your network

Setting Up a Network Share

Setting up a network share, or "simple file sharing," as it is sometimes called, is a straightforward process. Before you start on your network share, you should ensure that you have already implemented a firewall. The built-in Internet connection firewall on Windows XP will do for starters, though you may need to research others like ZoneAlarm later. Otherwise, you will need to be very particular about the file permissions in your shared folders because you are potentially exposing your data to the real world. The steps to create a network share on a Windows 2000 Professional computer follow:

1. Right-click the \data\ folder and choose Sharing (or in Windows XP, Sharing and Security), as shown in Figure 12-1.

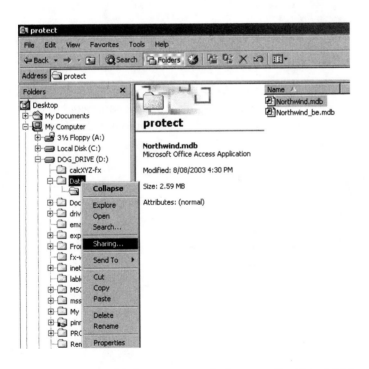

Figure 12-1. Establishing a network share on the /data/ folder.

2. Enter the details for the network share (which I have called Databases), as shown in Figure 12-2. Click OK.

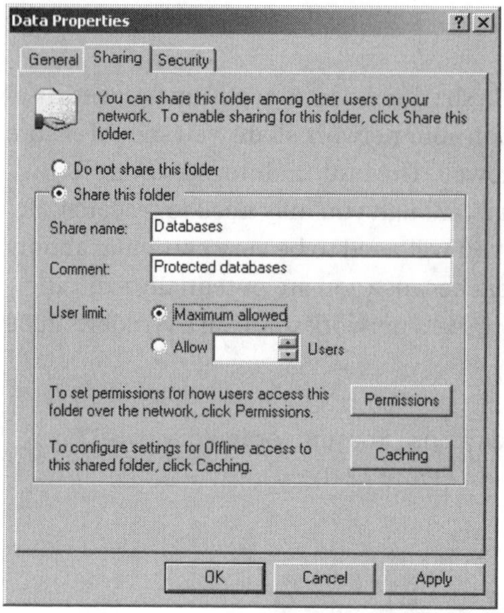

Figure 12-2. Entering the details for the network share.

3. You now have set up a network share that other people connected to your workgroup can use. You can see the share called Databases that I have created in Figure 12-3.

Figure 12-3. The network share, now set up and available to be referenced in the Address bar.

Hiding Your Network Share

If you want your network share to be invisible on the network, you can enter a share name with a dollar sign at the end. If I wanted to set up our example as hidden, I would call it Databases$. From then on, I would reference it as \\Databases$\.

Setting Up a User Account

Now you need to set up a user account on the peer-to-peer server that will be allowed to open and edit information in the database. To set one up, follow these steps:

1. Open the Windows Control Panel by clicking the Start button and choosing Settings.

2. Double-click Users and Passwords (in Windows XP, User Accounts).

3. In the Users and Passwords dialog, shown in Figure 12-4, click Add to add a new user.

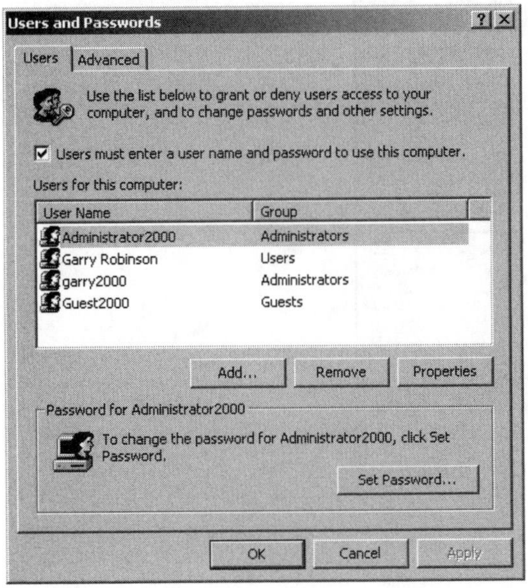

Figure 12-4. Adding new users in the Users and Passwords dialog.

NOTE   In Windows XP, click Create a New Account to start a wizard that lets you specify the name and type of the new account.

4. Enter a user name and description. Throughout this chapter, I will use Editor2000 as the account that is allowed to edit the database. Click Next.

5. Enter a password and confirm it.

NOTE   This option doesn't exist at this stage of the wizard in Windows XP, because you need to create the account first, then set its password.

6. Add the user as a restricted user (as shown in Figure 12-5). Windows XP documentation refers to this as a Limited User. This option adds the user to the Users group and does not allow the user to install software on this computer, which is what we want at this stage.

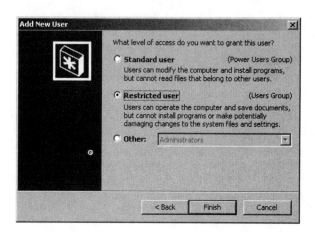

Figure 12-5. Selecting the Restricted User option.

7. Click Finish.

The Users and Passwords dialog now reappears, and you will find that the account that you just set up (Editor2000) will be a member of the Users group (as shown in Figure 12-6).

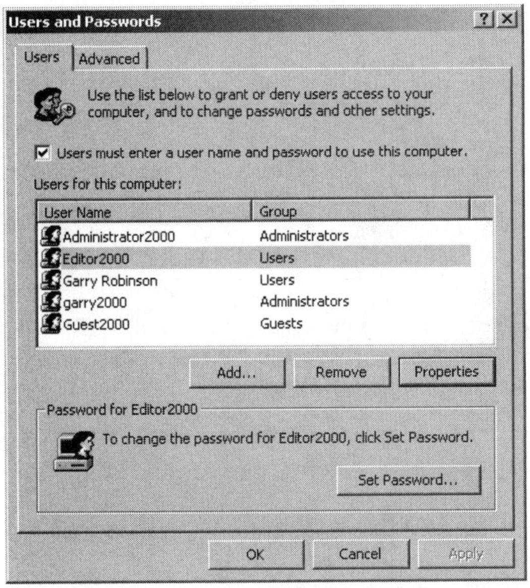

Users and Passwords ? X

Users | Advanced |

Use the list below to grant or deny users access to your computer, and to change passwords and other settings.

☑ Users must enter a user name and password to use this computer.

Users for this computer:

User Name	Group
Administrator2000	Administrators
Editor2000	Users
Garry Robinson	Users
garry2000	Administrators
Guest2000	Guests

Add... | Remove | Properties

Password for Editor2000

To change the password for Editor2000, click Set Password.

Set Password...

OK | Cancel | Apply

Figure 12-6. The new account, which is now a member of the Users group.

NOTE   To see the new account in Windows XP, choose Start ➤ Programs ➤ Administrative Tools ➤ Computer Management. Select Local Users and Groups under System Tools to see the Users and Groups dialog. Select Groups, and a list of the groups on your computer will appear in the right pane. If you double-click the Users group in this pane, a list of the members of this group will appear, including the Editor2000 user.

NOTE   If you're using Windows XP, you still need to set the password. To do so, click the newly created account in User Accounts from the Control Panel and select Create a Password. This action allows you to enter a password for the user as well as a hint in case the user forgets his or her password.

Setting Up a New Access Editors Group

Now we need to add the new account Editor2000 to a special group of users who will be allowed to edit information in the database. Because this group probably doesn't exist yet, we first need to create the User group that will hold a list of our database users' accounts. Before starting, make sure that you are still able to see the Users and Passwords dialog illustrated in Figure 12-6. Now you are ready to create the Users group, as follows:

1. Select the Advanced tab and click the Advanced button to open the Users and Groups dialog.

 NOTE In Windows XP, choose Start ➤ Programs ➤ Administrative Tools ➤ Computer Management. Select Local Users and Groups under System Tools to see the Users and Groups dialog.

2. To set up a new group, right-click Groups (as shown in Figure 12-7) and choose New Group.

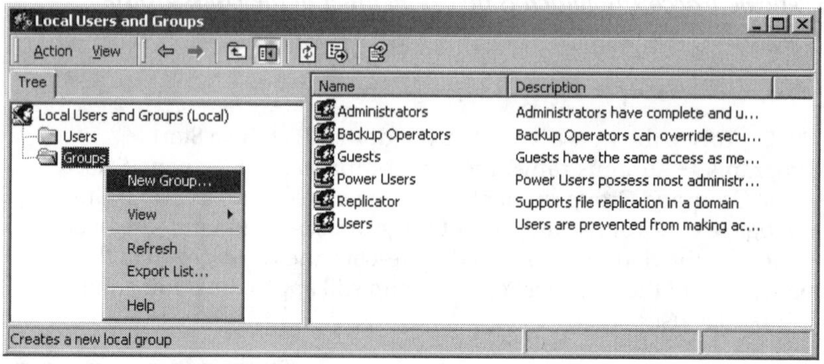

Local Users and Groups	
Action View	⇐ ⇒

Tree	Name	Description
Local Users and Groups (Local)	Administrators	Administrators have complete and u...
─ Users	Backup Operators	Backup Operators can override secu...
─ Groups	Guests	Guests have the same access as me...
New Group...	Power Users	Power Users possess most administr...
View ▶	Replicator	Supports file replication in a domain
Refresh	Users	Users are prevented from making ac...
Export List...		
Help		

Creates a new local group

Figure 12-7. The first stage in adding a new group of users.

3. Enter the details for the new group in the New Group dialog. I will use the group name *Access Editors* throughout the chapter.

4. Click Create to add the group.

5. Click Close to return to the Local Users and Groups dialog (shown before in Figure 12-7).

Adding the Users to the Group

At this stage, the Local Users and Groups dialog should now be visible. In the next stage, we need to add one or more users to the Access Editors group, as follows:

1. Select Groups (as shown in Figure 12-8) and then select Access Editors in the list of groups.

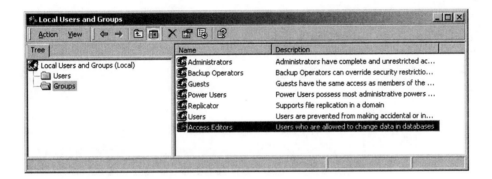

Figure 12-8. Viewing all the groups on your computer.

2. Choose Action ➤ Properties. You can also open the Properties dialog by right-clicking Access Editors and choosing Properties.

3. Add all the users that are going to belong to the group by clicking Add on the Access Editors Properties dialog. Now, find the names of the users in Select Users dialog, and click Add to make that account join the Access Editors group, as shown with the Editor2000 account in Figure 12-9.

NOTE In Windows XP, enter the name of the group (Editor2000) into the Select Users dialog, then click the Check Names button to ensure that you've typed the name of a valid user.

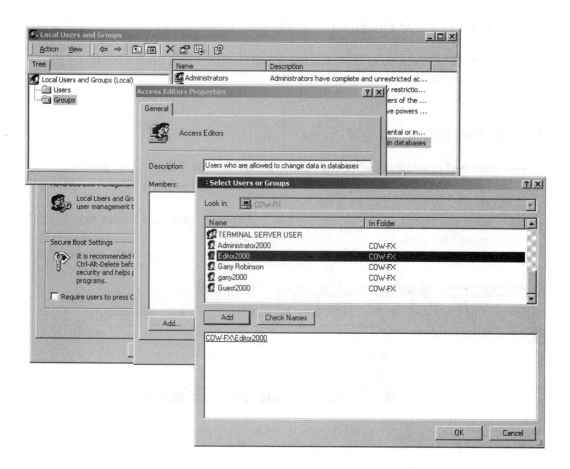

Figure 12-9. Adding user accounts to the Group that will edit your databases.

4. Click OK when you have completed adding all the users.

You will now return to the Local Users and Groups dialog, where you can explore the properties of the Editor2000 account, as shown in Figure 12-10. As you can see, this new account is now a member of both the Users and the Access Editors group. If you have followed the other chapters on Access workgroups, you will notice the similarity between the Users group in Access and the Users group in Windows 2000/XP. Just what we needed, more shared terminology!

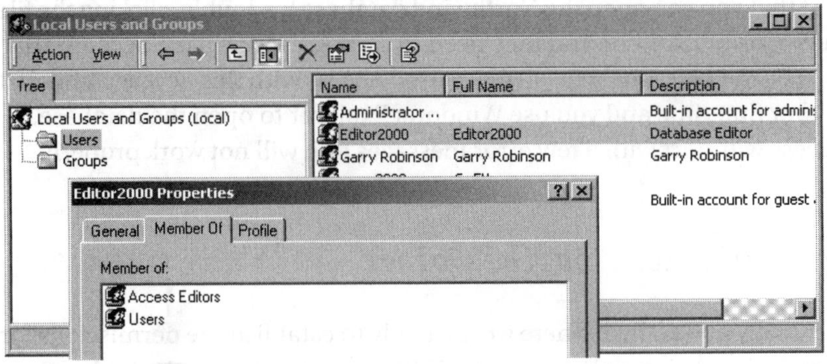

Figure 12-10. *The new User account is now a member of two groups.*

Testing the New Windows Account

It is a good time now to test whether your new user account actually works and also to see what permissions it has for the network share. To do this, follow these instructions on your peer-to-peer server:

1. Close both the Users and Passwords dialogs and log off the Administrator account.

2. Log on to the new user account (Editor2000).

3. Because we haven't yet set up any special permissions on the folders, the Editor2000 account should be able to open the Northwind database in the \data\Protect\ folder by browsing to it in Windows Explorer.

4. Because we are going to use this \data\ folder as a network shared folder, you can use the official name of \\ComputerName\Databases\ to locate the folder, where *ComputerName* is the name of your computer and Databases is the name of the network share. Type this name into the Address bar of Windows Explorer, as shown in Figure 12-11.

Figure 12-11. *Typing the path to the Network share into the Address bar.*

5. Test that you can open the Northwind database by double-clicking the file in Windows Explorer. You may need to start Access by itself because this may be the first time that you have used Access with this new account. If it is your first time and you use Windows Explorer to open the database, Access will start with a few error messages and will not work properly.

Setting Permissions on the Folder

Now we are finally at the stage where we are ready to establish the permissions for the database folder so that only our Access Editors group can use the folder. To complete this process, follow these steps:

1. Log on again through the Administrator account on your peer-to-peer server; we are now going to apply permissions to the folder.

2. Open Windows Explorer and find the Protect subfolder within the new Database network share by using the path \data\Protect\. Right-click that Protect subfolder and choose Properties, as shown in Figure 12-12.

Figure 12-12. Choosing properties to change permissions on a folder.

3. Select the Security tab.

NOTE The Security tab may not appear in Windows XP. To ensure that it does appear, choose Tools ➤ Folder Options in Windows Explorer, then select the View tab. Ensure that the Use Simple File Sharing (Recommended) check box in the Advanced Settings list is cleared.

4. Select the Everyone group at the top of the dialog. (See the following note for Windows XP instructions.)

5. Clear the Allow Inheritable Permissions from Parent to Propagate to This Object check box (shown in Figure 12-13). This action immediately opens another dialog, which asks if you want to see the permissions currently applied to the Everyone group to be inherited by this folder. Because we want only fully authenticated users to use this folder, click Remove.

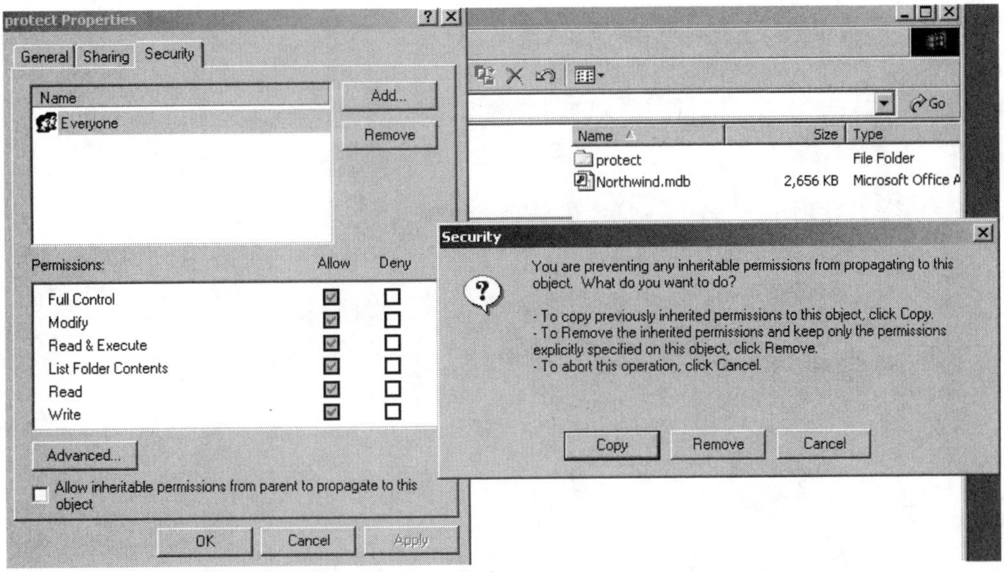

Figure 12-13. Removing permission from the Everyone group.

NOTE Permissions aren't granted to the Everyone group by default in Windows XP; however, we do want to remove permissions for the Users group. To do this, select Users in the Group or User names drop-down list, and then click Advanced. Clear the Inherit from Parent... check box on the Permissions tab, then click Remove in the Security dialog as in Windows 2000. Finally, click OK to close the Advanced Security Settings dialog. You will be shown a warning that says that no one will now be able to access the folder. We're going to rectify this straightaway, so accept the changes.

6. Now we need to add two groups to the permissions for this folder: the Administrators group for this computer and the Access Editors group that we established earlier. In Figure 12-14, I have already added these groups to the Permissions list by first selecting each group and then clicking Add.

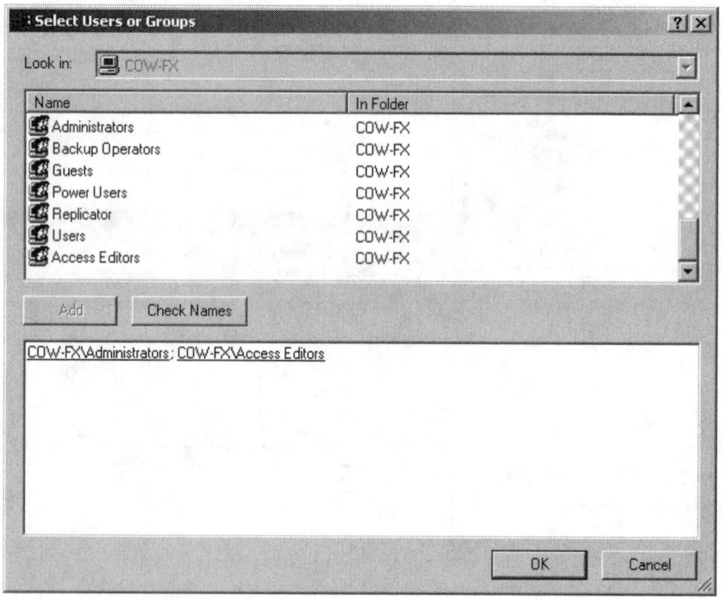

Name	In Folder
Administrators	COW-FX
Backup Operators	COW-FX
Guests	COW-FX
Power Users	COW-FX
Replicator	COW-FX
Users	COW-FX
Access Editors	COW-FX

Select Users or Groups

Look in: COW-FX

Add   Check Names

COW-FX\Administrators ; COW-FX\Access Editors

OK   Cancel

Figure 12-14. Adding the two groups to the permissions for this folder.

NOTE In Windows XP, simply type the names of the groups you want to grant permissions to (Administrators and Access Editors) in the field, separated by a semicolon. You can then click Check Names to ensure that you entered valid user or group names.

7. After you have added the second group, click OK to return to Folder Permissions dialog.

8. Now we need to establish the correct permissions for the Access Editors group so that members of that group can read, edit, and delete any data or file in the Protect subfolder. On the Security tab on the Protect folder Properties dialog, which you can open by right-clicking the folder, select all the permissions except Full (as shown in Figure 12-15).

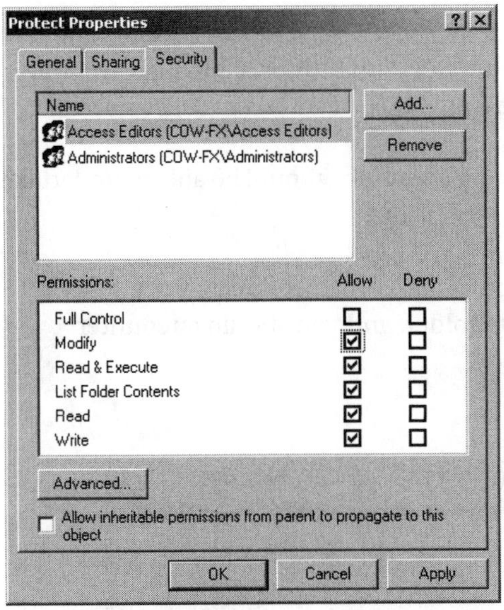

Figure 12-15. The file and folder permissions.

9. We also need to establish the correct permissions for the Administrators group (of this peer-to-peer server) so that that they can read, edit, and delete any data or file in the Protect subfolder. Select Administrators in the name list and select the Full Control check box. That's all the permissions we need to establish at this stage.

NOTE You must log off for the folder permissions to take effect.

Testing the Permissions

Let's test that all the permissions for the \\ComputerName\Databases\Protect\ folder have been set up correctly. To do this, you need to try out the permissions for user accounts that belong to different groups.

- Try out a member of the Access Editors group (Editor2000). This account should be able to use the front-end database (Northwind.mdb) as normal.

- The administrator of the peer-to-peer computer should be able to undertake all tasks in the folder as normal.

- If your peer-to-peer server is part of a local area network, try the \\ComputerName\Databases\Protect\ folder, and you should encounter the error shown in Figure 12-16.

Figure 12-16. The error that appears when a user account cannot open a folder.

- If you only have one computer, log on as the administrator of the peer-to-peer computer and create a new restricted/limited Windows account. Do not add this account to any groups. Now test whether that new account can open the Protect folder. It should also encounter the same error as shown in Figure 12-16.

If you cannot open the folder when trying out the third or fourth test, that's perfect because you now have a folder that only members of the Access Editors group and Administrators of the peer-to-peer server can use.

Assigning Your Network Account to the Database Editors Group

As I was alluding to in the previous sections, you can establish what amounts to quite powerful operating system protection for your database by using a Windows peer-to-peer network. If this happens to be the situation under which your database operates, you can easily make any other computers on your network a client to your peer-to-peer server. If that is the case, you will probably be keen to join that client computer to the Access Editors group on the peer-to-peer server that we set up in the last section. In the following instructions, I will show you how to do this:

1. Make sure that your account is set up on the client computer and that it has a password. It is prerequisite of Windows peer-to-peer networking that the peer-to-peer server knows both its password and the account password for the client computer.

2. On the server computer, log on as the Administrator and choose Control Panel ➤ Users and Passwords.

3. On the Users tab, click Add.

4. Enter the user name information for the user on the Add New User dialog (as shown in Figure 12-17). In this case, the name of the user must be the same as that on the client computer. Click Next (I called it Contractor 1).

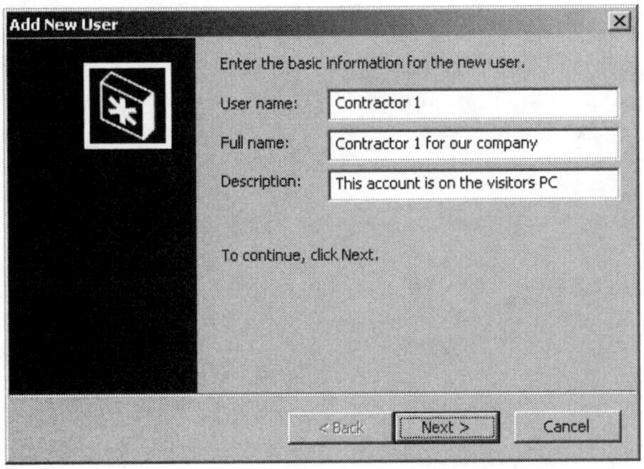

Figure 12-17. Setting up an equivalent user account on the peer-to-peer server.

5. Enter and confirm the password by using exactly the same password as on the client machine (as shown in Figure 12-18).

Add New User

Type and confirm a password for this user.

Password: *********

Confirm password: *********

To continue, click Next.

< Back   Next >   Cancel

Figure 12-18. Entering and confirming the password on the peer-to-peer server.

NOTE In this environment, regularly changing account passwords is not encouraged because the network administration can become onerous. This condition especially applies when you are getting close to the peer-to-peer network limit of 10 computers.

6. When selecting your account type, you can either add the account as a restricted user and then join it to the Access Editors group later or just add it directly to the Access Editors group as I have done in Figure 12-19.

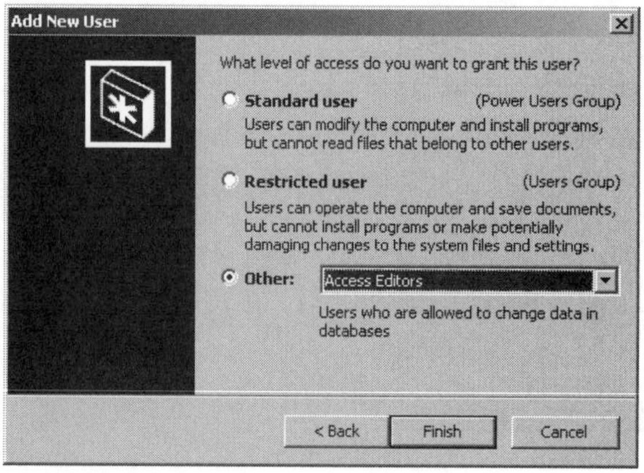

Add New User

What level of access do you want to grant this user?

○ **Standard user**   (Power Users Group)
Users can modify the computer and install programs, but cannot read files that belong to other users.

○ **Restricted user**   (Users Group)
Users can operate the computer and save documents, but cannot install programs or make potentially damaging changes to the system files and settings.

⦿ **Other:** Access Editors ▾
Users who are allowed to change data in databases

< Back   Finish   Cancel

Figure 12-19. Joining this new user to the Access Editors group.

NOTE   The Other option isn't available for Windows XP if you create the account with the User Accounts wizard from the Control Panel. Instead, you need to create a limited user account and then add it to the group later by using the Computer Management snap-in. Alternatively, you can simply create the account through Computer Management instead of the wizard.

7. Now click Finish, close any open security dialogs, and log off both the server and the client computers.

8. On the client computer, log on by using the account that you just set up.

9. Go to the \\ComputerName\Database\ network share and try to open the \Protect\ subfolder, and you should find that you have access to that folder. You now have rights to that folder as a member of the Access Editors account. In fact, you have rights to that entire computer, according to the permissions of the Group accounts that you are a member of on the server computer.

That completes the material that shows you how to set up the appropriate permissions for users who are authorized to open your database. You can now do the following:

- Add a new user to the Access Editors users group, which will allow that account to open the database.

- Remove any user account from the Access Editors users group so that user will not be able to open the database.

- Remove the account from the server, and you will automatically remove that account from any groups that it is a member of.

Now I will show you how you can build on these folder permissions considerably by protecting your database folder from your Access Editors group.

The Access Protected Folder Strategy

I am now going to show you how you can set up folder permissions in the Windows operating system so that users will not be able to browse the folder and subfolders where the database is located. This strategy will make it very difficult for users to copy the database to their local folders, to a CD-ROM, or any other place. It will also stop them from importing objects from the database into another database. I call this the Access protected folder strategy.

The first part of the strategy involves setting up a new group of Windows users (called the Access DBA group in this chapter) that will be allowed to manage the files in a database folder. In essence, these permissions are exactly the same as those we set up for the Access Editors group before. The second and most important part of the strategy will be a revised permission scheme for the Access Editors group, discussed in the last section. This time though, we are going to deny the Access Editors group the ability to list the files in a folder.

Setting Up a New Access DBA Group

Stage one of Access protected folder strategy involves setting up a new Windows permission group that will manage the database. We need this new Windows group because a number of Access administration functions require you to list the contents of a folder. To set up this group (which I am calling the Access DBA group), follow these instructions:

1. Make sure that you have set up and tested the Access Editors group and the related folder permissions as detailed in the section "Proof-of-Concept Operating System Security" in this chapter.

2. Log on as the Administrator on the peer-to-peer server.

3. Set up a new group called the Access DBA group by using the same instructions as for the Access Editors group. See the section "Setting Up a New Access Editors Group" earlier in the chapter.

4. Add the appropriate Windows account(s) to the Members Of list for the Access DBA group.

5. Give the Access DBA group the same permissions to the protected database folder (`\\ComputerName\Databases\Protect\`) that we gave to the Access Editors group.

6. To test the new group folder permissions, log on as one of the members of the Access DBA group.

7. Test that a member of the Access DBA group can browse the \Protect\ folder: open the database, compact the database, create a small text file, and delete that text file in the folder.

NOTE   This group is not essential if the DBA of the Access database is also the administrator of the computer. This case is unlikely in larger organizations, and even for smaller organizations, it is probably best if the administrator's role and the DBA's role were kept separate because it is a good idea to limit the time that the administrator is using a server to server administrator tasks only. This practice is good because it reduces the chances of viruses and mistakes affecting the server.

Now we are going to modify the permission scheme for the Access Editors group so that members of that group will not be able to browse the protected folder.

Denying Users the Ability to List the Contents of a Folder

Stage two of the Access protected folder strategy requires that we make some modifications to the permissions that the Access Editors have on the protected database folder (\\ComputerName\Database\Protect\). To make these modifications, we need to delve into the Windows advanced permissions for the Access Editors group:

1. Make sure that you have set up and tested the Access Editors group and the related folder permissions as detailed in the section "Proof-of-Concept Operating System Security" in this chapter.

2. In Windows Explorer, right-click the \Database\Protect\ folder to display the folder's Properties dialog.

3. Select the Access Editors group in the group name list and make sure that the properties are set up like those shown in Figure 12-20.

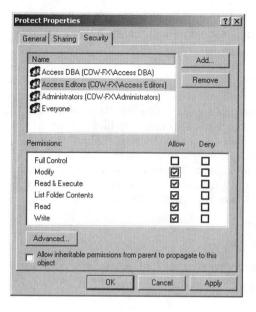

Figure 12-20. Modifying folder permissions for the Access Editors group.

 NOTE At this stage, you may want to remove the Modify permission (shown in Figure 12-20) because this permission allows members of the Access Editors group to delete files in the folder. In some Access situations, this capability may be a good idea, and in some, it may not. The users in this group need this permission because Access automatically deletes the .LDB file when the last user closes the database. Naturally, this action won't happen if the permission to delete a file is removed. Deleting the .LDB file improves performance when determining which other users have locks. Personally, I would keep the Modify permission selected unless you can work out another way to delete the .LDB file when it is not being used. See more information on this topic in the "Further Reading" section.

4. Click Advanced, as shown before in Figure 12-20, so that we can look at the advanced permissions.

5. On the Access Control Settings dialog that appears (shown in Figure 12-21), we need to add a second permission for the Access Editors group. Make sure that you have selected the Allow Access Editors entry in the permissions entry list, and then click Add.

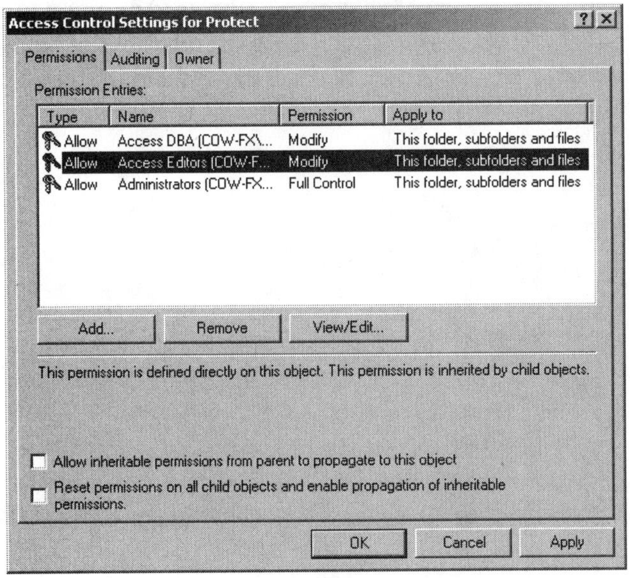

Access Control Settings for Protect

Permissions | Auditing | Owner

Permission Entries:

Type	Name	Permission	Apply to
Allow	Access DBA (COW-FX\...	Modify	This folder, subfolders and files
Allow	Access Editors (COW-F...	Modify	This folder, subfolders and files
Allow	Administrators (COW-FX...	Full Control	This folder, subfolders and files

Add... | Remove | View/Edit...

This permission is defined directly on this object. This permission is inherited by child objects.

☐ Allow inheritable permissions from parent to propagate to this object

☐ Reset permissions on all child objects and enable propagation of inheritable permissions.

OK | Cancel | Apply

Figure 12-21. The Access control settings for the folder.

6. Once again, choose the Access Editors group in the Select User or Group dialog (shown in Figure 12-22) and click OK.

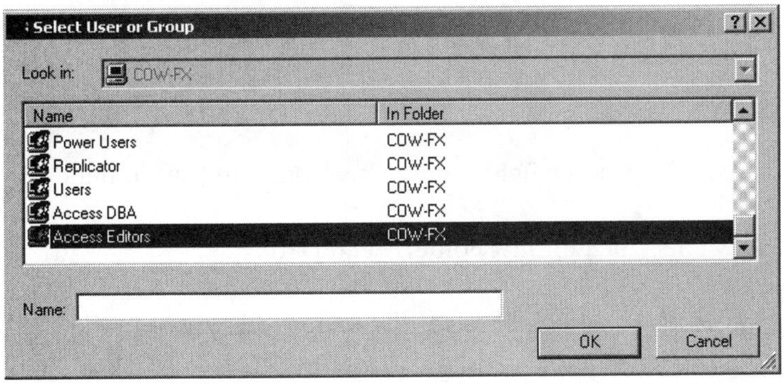

Select User or Group

Look in: 🖳 COW-FX

Name	In Folder
Power Users	COW-FX
Replicator	COW-FX
Users	COW-FX
Access DBA	COW-FX
Access Editors	COW-FX

Name:

OK | Cancel

Figure 12-22. Selecting a user or group.

NOTE In Windows XP, type the name of the user or group, then, optionally, click Check Names.

7. The Permission Entry dialog appears; it has all the advanced permissions for the folder. Figure 12-23 shows this dialog and the appropriate permissions for the folder already selected. Nevertheless, I will detail them in steps 8 and 9.

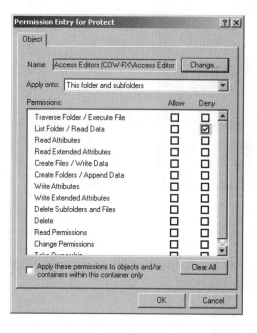

Figure 12-23. Selections required to stop a group from browsing the contents of a folder.

8. From Apply Onto drop-down field, select This Folder and subfolders.

9. Select the Deny check box for List Folder/Read Data.

10. Click OK, and the list of permissions for the folder will appear in the Access Control Settings dialog as shown in Figure 12-24. Notice that the Deny permission is now at the top of the Permissions Entries list.

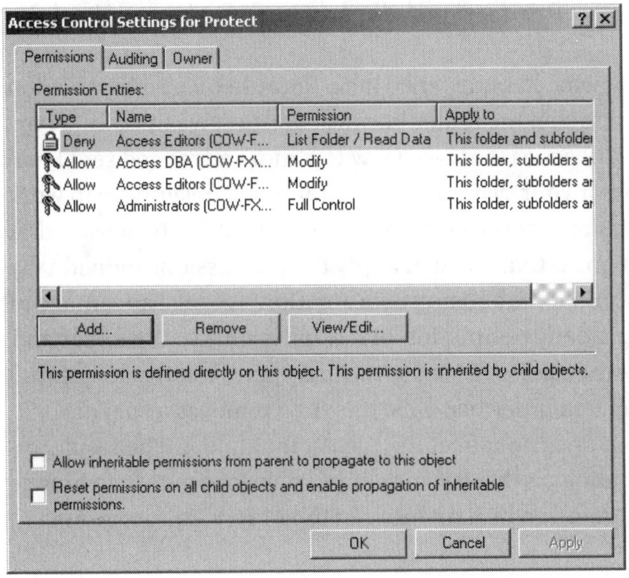

Figure 12-24. The Access Editors now have a new deny permissions entry.

11. When you click OK on the Access Control Settings dialog, a message box appears, telling you that deny permissions take priority over allow permissions, as shown in Figure 12-25. You will need to click Yes to confirm those changes.

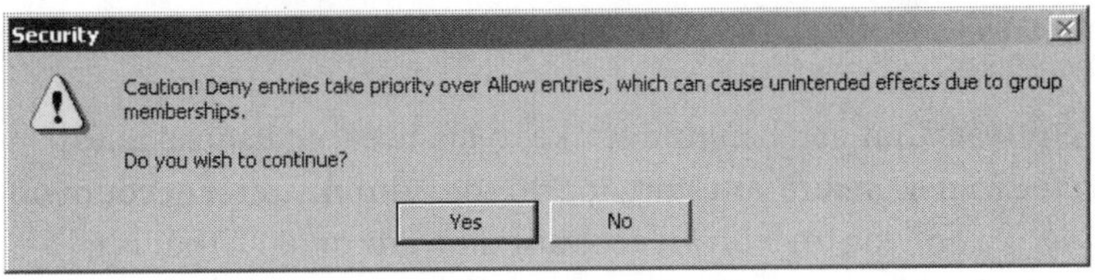

Figure 12-25. Confirming that the deny permission is going to take priority.

That's what it takes to stop someone from listing the contents of a folder. Now I will describe what we have done here.

How Does This Access Protected Folder Strategy Work?

It's a good time to think about what has happened here. Because we need permission to read and write to files in a folder, the folder permissions that we initially set up (shown earlier in Figure 12-20) act as a simple view to a more advanced set of permissions. In most cases, you or your system administrator will never have to work with these advanced permissions (shown earlier in Figure 12-23). The reason that we need advanced permissions is that you can apply the permissions individually to the files, the folder, the subfolders, and any combination. We take advantage of this capability by setting up a deny permission that applies only to the folder and subfolder and not to the files themselves. Because the deny permission takes priority over the already-established folder permissions, this then removes a specific permission for the folder but does not affect the files in that folder. The result, all that most of us really care about, is that it is now impossible for a person to browse that folder if that person happens to be a member of the Access Editors group.

NOTE Importing and linking is substantially more difficult to do for people who do not have list file permissions.

Testing the Permissions

After working your way through all these steps, you will be eager to test that your database user will be unable to browse your protected folder. Following are a number of different tests that you can undertake to ensure that users cannot browse the protected folder. Before you start, log off the Administrator account on the peer-to-peer server and log on with an account (like Editor2000) that is a member of the Access Editors group. Here are the different tests:

- Open Access and choose File ➤ Open. Now browse to the \\ComputerName\ Database\Protect\ folder and try to open either of the databases. When you get to the folder, you will encounter the error message shown in Figure 12-26.

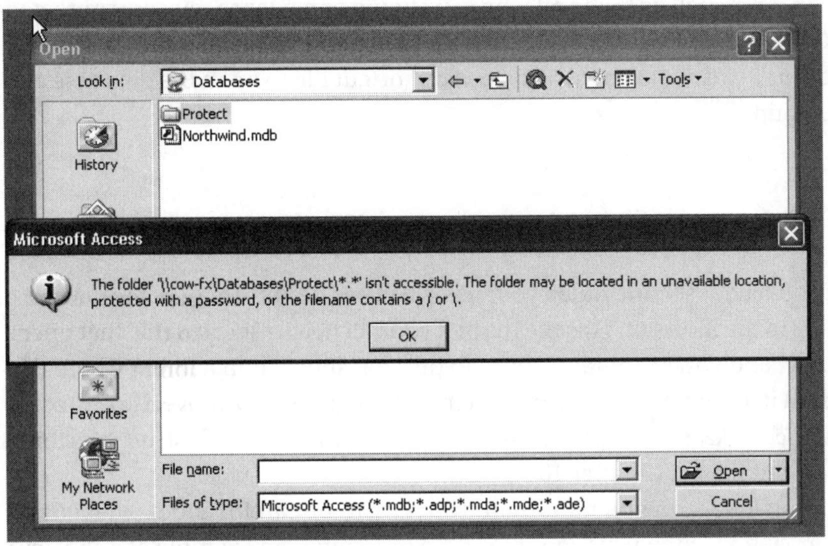

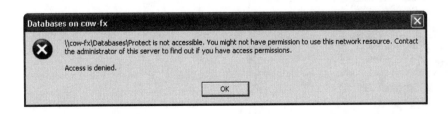

Figure 12-26. The error received when browsing to a folder that has no listing permission.

- Open another Access database and then try to import tables from the back-end database into it. You will find that you cannot locate the database in the folder.

- Open Windows Explorer and try to look at the files in the folder. When you do, you will get the error message shown in Figure 12-27. Naturally, this stumbling block makes it very hard to copy a database.

Databases on cow-fx   [X]

❌ \\cow-fx\Databases\Protect is not accessible. You might not have permission to use this network resource. Contact the administrator of this server to find out if you have access permissions.

Access is denied.

[OK]

Figure 12-27. You cannot browse the folder.

That, in a nutshell, is how and why you should consider the Access protected folders strategy. Before you start discussing these new processes with the system administrator, I will explain why you need a shortcut file to open the database and how to set it up.

You Will Need a Shortcut File

Now that you have a secure folder, your users will not be able to open the database by browsing to the file itself. This means that you will need a shortcut file that opens the database, and you are going to have to put that shortcut in a folder where the user can find it. I suggest that you place it in the folder directly above the protected folder (\\ComputerName\Database\). You will find comprehensive instructions for Access shortcut files in Chapter 10.

When you are setting up a shortcut, you have to be careful about what goes into the Target line (shown in Figure 12-28). Following is an example of a shortcut that works on the network share that I set up on our network:

```
C:\MSOfficeXP\Office10\MSACCESS.EXE "\\cow-fx\Databases\Protect\Northwind.mdb"
```

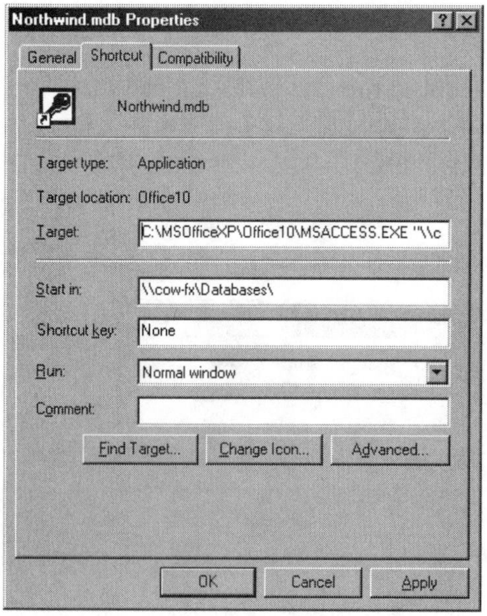

Figure 12-28. A shortcut file that points to a database in a protected folder.

There are a couple of things to understand about the Target line in the shortcut file that are particular to protected folders:

- You must put the full path to the Access executable at the start of the line. If you don't, then the shortcut will try to look at the contents of the protected folder and the shortcut will not work. If your computers have different locations for the Access executables, then you will need to place the shortcuts on the users' desktops.

- You need to enter the path to the database that includes the network share, rather than a local path. You only need to use inverted commas if there are spaces in the path to the database location.

If you want to add another layer of security, you can also hide the location of the front-end database by concealing the path to the database in an .MDE file, as discussed in the section "Creating a Secure Shortcut File" the Chapter 10.

As you probably already know, anyone who can read the shortcut file will be able to find the location of the front-end database. Of course, that person will need to be a member of the Access Editors group to copy the database, but a protected folder makes getting access a difficult task. More importantly, we can make sure that users will have a devil of a time opening the back-end database by setting up the following protection measures on the front-end database:

- Turn off the startup options (Chapter 2).

- Protect the menus (Chapter 7).

- Set up and secure a database by using a developer workgroup file (Chapter 8).

NOTE   It is possible to apply read-only permissions to shortcut files, but as a rule, most systems administrators would not apply permissions at the file level because of the maintenance required.

Another useful benefit of the Access protected folder strategy is that you can save your backups (described in Chapter 5) to a subfolder protected by the Access protected folder strategy. Because the Access Editor group cannot list the contents of subfolders, it is unlikely that a user from that group will be able to find out what backup files (tables or data) are in those folders.

Other Permission-Related Topics

I will briefly explain a number of other issues to complete the discussions of the Access protected folder strategy.

Setting Up a Read-Only Group

I investigated the possibility of also including a demonstration of using the operating system for read-only Access database permissions. This option worked out to be far more difficult than it needed to be, due to complications with the deny permissions and the need for yet another Windows permission group. If you want to offer this protection, it is probably better to switch completely to a read-only folder rather than try to combine it with the Access protected folder strategy that I outlined in this chapter. Otherwise, you can approach read-only security by using alternative shortcut files that include a read-only command line option. It is also possible to set up simpler read-only folder permissions, but this method would allow that group to copy the database. I would rather that people can't copy the database than have read-only permissions on the files. Anyway, you can always use Access workgroup security to manage the read-only permissions for the database (Chapter 10).

Bundling All Related Databases in the Same Folder

If one group of users uses the same network share, then you can place a number of Access databases in the same folder that the same Access Editors group uses. That way you will save a lot of time as compared to setting up and managing the permissions for different folders for different databases. The downside of this method is that granting permission for a user to use one database is actually granting permission for the user to use all the databases in the folder.

Client-Based Access Front Ends

A popular method of distributing Access databases is to install the front-end databases on the client computer. If you are intending to use operating system security on your database, you should be careful with this approach because you will significantly reduce the quality of the operating system security. If you still want to go ahead and install the front-end database on the client, be aware that you are going to make it harder to protect the location of the back-end database. Also, because you will have databases scattered across a number of machines, any changes to the front-end security will rely on all the databases being updated.

I personally am not in favor of this approach, because networks and file servers have improved a lot in the last few years, negating the performance reason for using this approach.

Why You Can't Set Permissions on Individual Files

When you compact an Access file that's located on a volume that uses the NTFS file system, Access removes the existing file and replaces it with the compacted file. It then applies the default file permissions to the new file, which may not be the original permission that you established for the database file. On a more general note, if a file is copied between a single NTFS volume or copied and moved between NTFS volumes, NTFS treats it as a new file. As a new file, it takes on permissions of the parent folder, and any existing permissions will be lost.

In the next section, I will discuss the importance of using NTFS for your hard drives.

The All-Important NTFS Format

Windows 2000 and Windows XP support three formats of file systems: FAT, FAT32, and NTFS. FAT and FAT32 are file systems used by the Windows 95, 98, and ME operating systems to organize and manage files. The file allocation table (FAT) is a data structure that Windows creates when you format a drive partition (which I will call a volume from now on) by using the FAT or FAT32 file systems. Windows stores information about each file in the FAT so that it can retrieve the file later. NTFS is an advanced file system written specifically for Windows NT, the original source of Windows 2000 and Windows XP. It provides, according to Microsoft, performance, security, reliability, and advanced features not found in any version of FAT. For the purposes of this book, we are interested in the advanced NTFS features, such as file and folder permissions and, to a lesser extent, file encryption.

The reasons why we are interested in NTFS volumes instead of FAT volumes follow:

- On a NTFS drive, if you grant read/write permissions for a user group for a folder like \\wg1\myfiles\, you will then be able to vary permissions for that same group for a subfolder, like \\wg1\myfiles\dbase\. On a FAT volume, you cannot vary permissions for subfolders.

- To protect a database by storing it in the personal profile areas of the Documents and Settings folders, you need to use NTFS because on a FAT32 volume, any user of the computer can read any other user's personal information.

- Windows XP and 2000 will provide protection for important folders such as the top level of the C: drive, the Windows folder (all the system files), and the Program Files folder.

- To share a volume between a new operating system and a Windows 98 or ME operating system, you will need to use a FAT volume because those older operating systems do not support NTFS.

- With Fat32 volumes, lower level folder network shares inherit the permissions from higher up the folder tree, which thereby renders any additional protection on the folder worthless unless you upgrade to NTFS.

 CAUTION   Never set up a network share for a complete C: drive or any drive that has the operating system on it. Windows XP and 2000 will probably cover you for this issue, but not if you are running a FAT32-formatted drive.

Finding Out Whether Your Drive Partition Uses NTFS

To use NTFS, you will need to be using Windows XP or Windows 2000 because Windows ME or Windows 98 only supports volumes formatted with FAT or FAT32. To find out whether your drive partition uses NTFS:

1. Open Windows Explorer or double-click My Computer on your desktop.

2. Find and right-click the Drive Volume, such as C: or D: drive.

3. Choose Properties.

4. You will find the file system in the General tab.

Converting from FAT Volumes to NTFS

To convert a file from FAT to NTFS, you should search your Windows 2000 or Windows XP help for NTFS. You will find the help that you need under the topic

"To convert a volume to NTFS from the command prompt." You can also find this information at the following address:

```
http://www.microsoft.com/windowsxp/pro/using/itpro/managing/convertfat.asp
```

It goes without saying that you should make sure that you have your backups in order before you convert the volume.

Protecting Against Unattended Computers

One security concern for a database in an environment where trusting users is not an option is what to do when a person authorized to use a protected database leaves his or her computer for half an hour. In this section, I discuss a possible solution and give an overview of another related problem, the recent document list.

Screen Saver Password Security

Screen saver password security is a solution for unattended computers, and you can find it on your Windows desktop. To set a screen saver password:

1. Click Start and choose Settings ➤ Control Panel.

2. Double-click the Display icon.

3. Select the Screen Saver tab.

4. Select a screen saver from the Screen Saver drop-down list. To save the environment a little, stay clear of the fancy 3D pipes and text boxes, which consume more resources.

5. In Windows 2000, select the Password Protected check box (see Figure 12-29) or in Windows XP, select the On Resume, Display Welcome Screen check box.

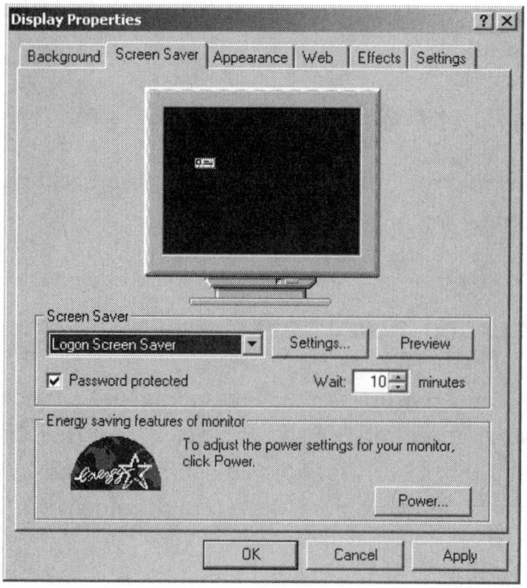

Display Properties ? X

Background | Screen Saver | Appearance | Web | Effects | Settings |

Screen Saver
Logon Screen Saver ▼   Settings...   Preview

☑ Password protected   Wait: 10 minutes

Energy saving features of monitor
To adjust the power settings for your monitor, click Power.
Power...

OK   Cancel   Apply

Figure 12-29. Setting up password protection on your logon screen saver.

If you think that screen saver password security is a good idea and you belong to a Windows domain, ask your systems administration whether he or she can set up a protected screen saver policy so that all domain users who use your database are automatically covered by this protection.

TIP If you are leaving your Windows XP computer for a few minutes, try pressing ⊞ +L, which will send you to the Switch user window, immediately password-protecting your account.

Recent Documents List

As I have mentioned on a number of occasions in this book, keeping the location of the database secret is one of the more important parts of your database protection strategies. Therefore, you need to be aware that the recent documents list, very easily found from the Start button, reveals the document path to anyone who could sit in front of your computer while you disappear to a meeting or make yourself a cup of coffee.

Unfortunately, every time you open Access, the recent documents list in Windows will change. Therefore, anyone could use this list to find the documents path. Fortunately, this recent documents list is stored in the personal settings folders \documents and settings\, which means that it is safe from users who prowl around the operating system.

NOTE If you want temporary protection from prying eyes while you're at a meeting, you can search your Windows help for "clear documents," which will provide you with information on how to empty and manage the recent documents list.

Issues of Relevance in Windows XP

As time goes by, more and more Access database users are going to consider or will upgrade to Windows XP operating systems. To assist your important decision, I have compiled a checklist of how to set up a secure Windows XP computer plus a list of the differences between Windows XP Home and Windows XP Professional.

Setting Up a Secure Windows XP Computer

When you purchase or upgrade a computer to Windows XP operating system, the good news is that the operating system generally offers solid protection. The bad news is that you will probably have to set it up first, because it comes with all the security features turned off. Here are some of the things that you will need to do to secure the Windows XP computer:

- You need to add passwords to secure that the Windows users accounts as the accounts that you add during the installation all come without any passwords. For a secure computer, all accounts should have passwords. Remember to write down the administrator's password or use the password reminder correctly.

- If you are setting up accounts for more than one user account, you should consider using the limited accounts for all but the administrator of the computer.

- If you are sharing your computer with other local users, it is important that you ensure that you use an NTFS volume. The alternative, FAT, is far less secure because all the personal profiles, Windows, and program folders are unsecured for anyone using the computer.

- You should use the firewall that comes as standard with Windows XP. If you can, you should upgrade to products that have more robust firewalls, such as Norton or McAfee or, even better, the product most lauded at the time I wrote this book, ZoneAlarm.

- Ensure that you have antivirus software installed and that it is continually up to date with the latest virus definition files.

Therefore, if you are working on a Windows XP machine where security is obviously a little lax, a morning's work will have you plugging a big hole in your security. If a system administrator manages your computer, you should discuss how to secure your XP computer because your organization may have a different way of doing things.

Comparing XP Operating Systems

If you are developing or using Access databases, which of the two Windows XP operating systems is the best? To answer that question, you first need to consider these situations:

- If you are using the Windows Server and you need to connect to a domain, you must have Windows XP Professional.

- If you are buying a new computer, Microsoft tends to offer much better prices for Windows XP Professional on a new computer. Microsoft also tends to offer quite steep prices to upgrade from Windows XP Home to Windows XP Professional, so your procrastination will cost you money.

- If you are a developer and just happen to have two or three machines, it is always a good idea to have different machines in different configurations. That way, you can understand the client's problems better when they ask you a question or detail a bug.

Now, before we look at the differences between the two operating systems, what do they both have in common that will protect your databases?

- Personalized logon.

- Fast user switching.

- Personal privacy of files, as long as NTFS is used.

- Internet connection firewall.

- Simple sharing through a shared documents folder.

- Network shares.

What is there in Windows XP Professional that might be worth the extra money and the bigger slice of your disk space and computer resources? Here is the list of reasons, and if you want to find out more about these topics, have a look in the "Further Reading" section at the end of the chapter.

- Corporate security: Windows server domain logons.

- Blank password restrictions.

- Folder- and file-level permissions (access control).

- Encrypting file systems—something to consider for laptop systems.

- Certificate services.

- Credential management for Internet passwords.

- Internet connection sharing.

- Software restriction policies.

- Internet protocol security.

- Smart card support.

Of course, if you are running Windows 2000 Professional, you already are on a winner, because Windows 2000 Professional has similar security to Windows XP Professional.

Checklist of Other Security-Related Issues

Database security is all part of a bigger security picture, and it would be remiss of me not to mention some of the other issues that can have some influence on database security. To help you classify those risks, I have divided the list into computer issues and people-specific issues. I will leave it to you, the reader, to prioritize these issues.

Computer and Network Issues

Following is a very brief overview of some of the more important technological issues that are relevant to the readers of this book.

Software Updates

Protecting your computers against a bombardment of Internet-related threats requires constantly updating the programs discussed in this book—Microsoft Windows, Office, and, to a lesser extent, Access. To manage this course of action, Microsoft is putting considerable resources into technology that can deliver the latest Windows and Office security patches. In the "Further Reading" section at the end of the chapter, you will find links that explain how to keep your computer updated. To get information that's even better than that, though, head to http://www.microsoft.com, and you will find that the update links are very prominent on the site.

Antivirus and Spyware

Make sure that your company protects all its computers with antivirus software and antivirus signatures that are fully up to date. You should also consider anti-spyware software to test for programs that try to track user activities.

Firewalls

As very potent viruses like Blaster and SoBig have taught us, all corporate networks require the protection of corporate firewalls and all laptops require personal firewall protection.

TIP   You can deny specific computers on your network any access to your computer by using a personal firewall product like ZoneAlarm. To deny access, make sure that the IP address of that computer is not included in the trusted IP addresses, which gives you a simple but effective way to stop some people from sharing your computer.

Laptop Theft

Laptops are a lot easier to steal, break, or lose than normal computers, and thus, maintaining their security is more of an issue. Be wary of laptop computers that have important databases or copies of important databases.

Backups

Make sure that all computers that have valuable databases on them are fully backed up. Make sure that you test recovery on a regular basis.

Security for Your Building

Security to your buildings is important. Naturally, some of these tools will keep thieves from the premises and your computers: locks, safes, vaults, lighting, alarms, cards, codes, and biometrics.

Regularly Defrag Your Hard Drive

Defragging your hard drive protects against people who might scan a stolen hard drive for deleted but valuable data. The good thing about defragmenting is that it will speed your computer as part of the process.

People Issues

All the following issues probably need to be supported by corporate policies that are regularly brought to the attention of staff via documentation and training.

Home Computer Security

With more and more employees telecommuting from home, you need to be aware of what is happening with your databases. If taking a copy of the database home is inappropriate, your staff need to be aware of your preference.

Healthy Passwords

Explain to your staff the importance of password selection and protection and explain why passwords are important in the first place. If passwords are passed on to other users, their usefulness is greatly diminished.

Acceptable Internet Use

The Internet and email are standard in today's workplace, making inappropriate use of the Internet a bigger concern than ever before. Naturally, you need to ensure that staff understand the company guidelines for Web surfing.

Email Issues

Staff need to understand what is and isn't appropriate for transferring via email. Naturally, databases transferred by email to an outside organization could be something that companies may want to advise against.

Software Piracy

Installing unauthorized software on company computers is something that should be discouraged because it may be infringing software license issues or introducing viruses and spyware software.

Be Vigilant

Occasional discussions with your staff about security will help instill in them a reason to be on the lookout for security issues. If a member of your staff raises a security issue, be sure to follow it up because doing so will encourage them to keep improving security.

Data Piracy

Even though it should be obvious to most staff, you should consider making it clear via appropriate documentation that certain databases and files should remain on-site.

Further Reading

As you might expect, there is other useful information related to these topics that couldn't make it into the chapter. To assist you with further investigations, I have put together a Web page with links to http://www.microsoft.com and other Web sites and articles on the issues relating to the material in this chapter. This page includes the following:

- An interesting article by Microsoft: "The 10 Immutable Laws of Security."

- Comparisons between Windows XP Home and Windows XP Professional security.

- Links to many important resources for the Windows XP Professional operating system.

- Sharing files on Windows XP Home, including hidden shares and firewalls.

- Network file sharing with Windows XP Professional.

- NTFS file security.

- How to set up a Windows XP peer-to-peer network.

- Converting from Fat32 to NTFS volumes.

- Configuring NTFS permissions.

- Discussions on Windows NT workstation security.

- Planning a secure Windows 2003 server environment.

- Why you need delete permissions on a folder for Access .LDB files.

- Setting up read-only access to an Access database.

- Encrypting documents on NTFS volumes.

- Keeping up to date with Windows and Office security patches.

- Adam Cogan's tip on keeping service packs up to date by using Windows 2003 server.

- Using software restriction policies to protect against unauthorized software.

- Credential management for Internet passwords on Windows XP.

- Comprehensive guide by Microsoft to help you protect your computer.

For more information about Window security and NTFS file volumes, type NTFS into Windows XP and Windows 2000 help.

You can find the further reading Web page for this chapter in the Downloads section of the Apress Web site (http://www.apress.com) or at the following address: http://www.vb123.com/map/opr.htm.

Reflecting on This Chapter

In this chapter, I have shown you that one of the best ways to build on your database's security is to apply operating system security, which lets you specify which users can use any of the files in the database folder and subfolders. If you also want the security of knowing that the users will find it very difficult to import the contents of a database or copy the database files themselves, I have demonstrated the Access protected folder strategy. These additional measures, applied with the other Access security and protection measures, will give us a database secured by industry best practice.

In addition to these powerful protection measures, I have also discussed a number of other security issues that Access professionals should understand, including:

- Why NTFS drive volumes are important.

- Why unattended computers are an issue and how to safeguard against it.

- How you can set up a secure Windows XP computer and comparisons between Windows XP Home and Windows XP professional.

- A checklist of computer and network issues to consider.

- A checklist of personnel related issues to consider.

Now, I will discuss my personal favorite part of the book: THE END. It's been amazing to me that there was so much relevant material to consider for a product that some people believe is just a simple data management tool for end users. Nevertheless, if you have come this far in the book, you probably won't need me to tell you that Microsoft Access is a substantial database with a superb developer's toolset. And now, to the conclusion.

Is That the End of the Journey?

Because you have successfully navigated your way to the end of my book, you will probably ask yourself the question, "Is that the end of the journey?" My counsel is that you should embrace protection and security of your database and all that goes with it. For example, you should take time to convince the key stakeholders of your databases that there is merit in security and that investment in security is far more preferable to no investment at all. Another important attitude to take is to aim to resolve security issues by using legitimate means, rather than to compromise your security by adding cute little workarounds. Finally, there is just one more thing to be said about security and protection: always stay ahead of the game by keeping your skills up to date.

I'm a great believer in luck, and I find the harder I work, the more I have of it.

—Thomas Jefferson (1743-1826)

So thanks for reading my book and, as these final words are put to paper two weeks after the birth of my second son, let me tell you that life can be quite a satisfying journey.

APPENDIX A

Specific Access Security Information

IN CHAPTERS 8, 10, AND 11, I referred to specific workgroup information that you would need to work through the examples yourself. This appendix provides you with that specific Access security information.

The second purpose of this appendix is to provide you with a handy place to write down your own Access security information, because we all know what a challenge it is to manage your security information. To this purpose, I have set up a number of tables with lots of blank space so that you can enter your own information.

The security information tables that I have included in this appendix follow:

- The workgroup file security information used in this book.

- The workgroup file User and Group accounts security information used in this book.

- Your own workgroup file security information.

- Your own workgroup file User and Group accounts security information.

- Your own database and VBA project passwords.

If there were any likelihood that someone else would borrow your book, I would encourage you to enter a hint to help you remember the security information or password so that that person doesn't get your secret information. When deciding on your hint, try to make it a word or a phrase that is vague enough so that nobody else can guess your information but clear enough that it will remind you of it exactly. Your other alternative to lending this book is to ask that someone else to purchase his or her own copy of this book. That is clearly a security practice that I would encourage wholeheartedly.

CAUTION   When entering security information and passwords into the tables, remember that uppercase, lowercase, and spaces are important.

Table A-1. The workgroup file security information used in this book.

Owner Info	Security Details
File Name	C:\data\developer.mdw
Name	Real World
Organization	Microsoft Access database
Workgroup ID	Protect and Secure
MDW Format	97/2000/2002
Purpose	Developer workgroup file

Table A-2. The workgroup file User and Group Accounts used in this book.

User/Group	Type	PID or PID Hint	Your Password or Hint
Developer	U	RealWorldDeveloper	Developer
Editor	U	Real World Editor	
Backup Operators	G	Real World Backup	
Full Data Users	G	Real World Full Data	
Full Permissions	G	Real World Full Perm	
New Data Users	G	Real World New Data	
Project Designers	G	Real World Project	
Read-Only Users	G	Real World Read-Only	
Update Data Users	G	Real World Update	
	U/G		
	U/G		

Table A-2. The workgroup file User and Group Accounts used in this book. (Continued)

User/Group	Type	PID or PID Hint	Your Password or Hint
	U/G		
	U/G		
	U/G		
	U/G		
	U/G		
	U/G		
	U/G		
	U/G		
	U/G		

Table A-3. Your own workgroup file security information.

Owner Info	Security Details or Hint
File Name	
Name	
Organization	
Workgroup ID	
MDW Format	97/2000/2002
Purpose	

Table A-4. Your own workgroup file User and Group accounts.

User/Group	Type	PID or PID Hint	Your Password Hint
Backup Operators	G		
Full Data Users	G		
Full Permissions	G		
New Data Users	G		
Project Designers	G		
Read-Only Users	G		
Update Data Users	G		
	U/G		
	U/G		
	U/G		
	U/G		
	U/G		
	U/G		
	U/G		
	U/G		
	U/G		
	U/G		

Table A-5. Your own database and VBA project passwords.

Database Name	Type	Password or Hint
	DB/VBA	
	DB/VBA	
	DB/VBA	
	DB/VBA	
	DB/VBA	
	DB/VBA	
	DB/VBA	
	DB/VBA	
	DB/VBA	
	DB/VBA	
	DB/VBA	

Registering the
Access Workbench

IF YOU HAVE PURCHASED a copy of my book, you are entitled to download and get free registration to the Access Workbench 1.3.4. This entitlement does not extend to newer versions of the software, but at the start of 2003, quite a number of people commented on this version's simplicity and usefulness. If you want to find out how it works, you can review the material in Chapter 6 or view the HTML help file that comes as part of the installation .ZIP file.

You can find out how and where to download the file at the following address:

```
http://www.vb123.com/map/wkb.htm
```

Once you have downloaded the software, you can find out how to install the software by viewing the readme.txt file in the download .ZIP file.

Once you have installed the software, click the Register button on the Startup window. Enter your email address, name, company, and the following registration number exactly as you see it into the registration code input field.

5463-4726-0017

To find out about the latest version of the Workbench and to pay for the upgrade, head to the following address:

```
http://www.vb123.com/workbench/
```

APPENDIX C

Why Migrate from Access to SQL Server?

ONE WAY THAT YOU CAN IMPROVE your Access data security is by migrating your database to a server-based database such as SQL Server, Informix, or Oracle. If you have already migrated a database to an enterprise-quality database product like one of these, you will appreciate that this process is not a trivial task. If you haven't, then let me assure you that it is worthwhile that you understand both the benefits and the pitfalls of such an undertaking long before you take the plunge with some real live data.

To help you make up your mind, Russell Sinclair and the gang at Apress have allowed me to reprint a chapter from Russell's book, *From Access to SQL Server*. In this chapter, you will find out things about Access to SQL Server migration, like:

- Why migrating a database that has been in use for a long period of time is more involved than migrating a brand new database.

- Why big Access tables are an impediment to Access performance. (Remember that Chapter 5 in my book shows you how you can work out your largest tables.)

- SQL Server can process the query on the server and return only the results, thereby freeing network traffic.

- SQL Server handles multi-user issues, such as locking, much better than Access, especially when compared with Access 97.

- Introduction into the differences between Access and SQL Server security, maintenance, and cost.

So, if migrating your database is something that you think you should consider or is something that you have tried and felt like you need more information for the next time, try another of Russell Sinclair's book chapters at http://www.apress.com/ or find the book online at http://www.vb123.com/map/rus.htm. The ISBN is 1-893115-24-0.

Why Migrate?

MIGRATING AN APPLICATION from Access to SQL Server can be a daunting task. Preparation and careful planning is essential to make the transfer of data go smoothly. Before a migration can take place, a complete evaluation of the migration and the reasons behind it must occur. In this appendix, we'll review the different types of migration, the advantages of SQL Server, the reasons to migrate, and the reasons not to migrate. In order to evaluate a migration, you first need to understand exactly what migrating is.

What Is Migrating?

Migrating from Access to SQL Server involves evaluating, categorizing, and moving tables, data, objects, and functionality from an Access application to SQL Server. It also requires that you preserve—and possibly enhance—the functionality available to the user. Migrating is not a simple matter of transferring all of the Access tables to a SQL Server database and then linking the new tables into Access. You must perform a complete analysis of the items being migrated before the migration takes place. This analysis includes evaluating queries, macros, form and report data sources, ADO, DAO, and VBA code, and tables and their properties. You should also determine how your Access objects will scale and whether their implementation should be modified or remain the same in the new system. You should consider the timing of the migration in the lifecycle of the application because it affects how much work has to be done and how that work occurs. The decisions that the analysis helps you make will have a dramatic effect on the methodology you use to migrate your application. Before I get into the specifics of the migration itself, I will examine the different types of migrations that can occur.

Many applications are prototyped in Access because it is much faster to develop a database in Access than in SQL Server. An application is prototyped in Access with the knowledge that the application will be moved to SQL Server before it is rolled out to users. Once potential issues and development changes are finalized based on the prototype, the database is migrated to SQL Server. This type of migration is often one of the easiest to perform because the original design of the application takes into account the fact that the backend RDBMS will be SQL Server. It allows a developer to follow certain practices that can make the migration easier. Also, because the application has not been rolled out to the general user community, there is often little or no data that must be migrated to the server.

As you will see, this eliminates many of the potential issues that are encountered during a migration. In this appendix, I will take an in-depth look at the issues that you need to consider in order to migrate an application to SQL Server.

Migrations sometimes take place shortly after a system is rolled out into a production environment. Developers using Access for the first time or using it in a different way than they normally do, often find that Access does not give them the performance and functionality they need for the successful implementation of their system. Sometimes Access simply does not meet all of the requirements of the application. This can be the result of poor planning, but is just as commonly a result of greater use of the system than was originally anticipated. A migration immediately after implementation is usually one of the hardest migrations to deal with. Confidence in a system that is withdrawn after it is released to users can be very low. This can lead to difficulty dealing with users and management when justifying the migration and the extra development time involved. However, because the original developers are available to support the migration, the planning of the changes can take place very quickly. Less time is spent in "discovery" learning the functionality of the system because the knowledge of the system is still fresh in everyone's minds. The system is already well understood.

By far the most common time for an Access database to be migrated is after the system has been in a production environment for some time. This type of migration can occur for any number of reasons, but the most common reasons are performance and security concern. This type of migration is usually the most difficult to plan and implement for a number of reasons. Often, the original developers are not available to help out in the planning. This means that a significant amount of time is spent in learning how the application works and determining all of the purposes it fulfills. Developers must evaluate the entire application to ensure that none of the components of the system are missed in the migration. This type of migration can also be the most risky. Applications that reach the point where they need to be migrated are often critical applications in a business. If a migration fails or does not meet the new or old requirements for the system, it can end up completely destroying an application unnecessarily.

Because of the problems involved in moving from Access to SQL Server, it is imperative that the person performing the migration has a solid understanding of the Access application that is being migrated as well as the reasons the application should be migrated. In order to understand the reasons behind migrating, you need to take a look at the major differences between Access and SQL Server that cause people to want to upgrade. This will help you to better understand the specific set of problems that can be solved by moving to SQL Server.

Access versus SQL Server

Access and SQL Server are very different systems. SQL Server is a client/server RDBMS, whereas Access is a file-based application. They have very different limitations and work very differently.

Size Constraints

One of the major differences between SQL Server and Access databases is the maximum size of a database. Despite what many people believe, Access databases can support a great deal of data. Access 97 and earlier versions have a documented size limit of 1 gigabyte. In Access 2000, this limit has been increased to 2GB. However, anyone who has experience with a shared Access database over 10MB is well aware of the fact that the larger a database gets, the worse the performance from the Jet engine. This is especially true if the majority of the data is housed in only a few tables. Attempting to retrieve data from one very large table can take a long time. Attempting to retrieve data from multiple large joined tables can take even longer. Needless to say, this is not the desired behavior for an application.

SQL Server can support much larger databases. The maximum size of a single database in SQL Server 6.5 is 1 terabyte. In SQL 7, this has been increased to 1,048,516 terabytes. A terabyte is equal to 1,024GB. Consequently, the limit of a SQL Server database in version 7 is approximately 536 million times larger than the limit of an Access 2000 database.

Recently, some changes were made to SQL Server to optimize its support for what the industry has termed Very Large Databases (VLDBs). These are databases that house millions of records of information. VLDBs can be very difficult to manage without the appropriate RDBMS. If the RDBMS is not designed to handle these types of databases, the methods they use to work with data may cause large degradations in the performance of the application that accesses that database. The definition of this name is somewhat subjective, but it is doubtful that anyone would dispute that VLDBs include databases over 100GB. Microsoft SQL Server can handle these types of databases and even does it well. When a SQL Server VLDB is designed correctly, it can support lots of users without any problems and still respond quickly to requests from other applications.

Transferring Data

SQL Server and Access return data in very different ways. Access must retrieve all of the data in a table to the local computer in order to filter and manipulate the data. SQL Server has the capability to process a request for data, perform any data manipulation on the server, and only return the resulting records to the client application. How the data is handled by an application once it is requested can also differ a great deal between Access and SQL.

When you run a query against a Microsoft Access database, the Jet engine goes out to the database, retrieves the entire contents of the table that the data is requested from, and copies that data locally for the client. The Jet engine then handles this data in local memory to filter it according to the specifics of the request that was generated. When you run a similar query in SQL Server, the server takes the request for data and processes it on the server. The requested data is extracted from the table by the server, and then sent across the network to the client. The client then works locally with the data that was requested.

Due to these differences, more memory is required on the client when using Access than is required with SQL Server. If the Access database resides on a disk drive on a remote computer on the network, the network load is also much higher because more data must travel over the network to the client.

Another major difference between how Access and SQL Server deal with data is how they support cursors. Cursors define where and how data is updated. They can be server-side or client-side. With server-side cursors, a constant connection is held to the database. Any changes to data are immediately transmitted to the server. All indexing of data and changes to data take place on the server. As a result, server-side cursors use the network a great deal. As each change is sent back to the server, sorting of the data and data changes made by other users must be passed back and forth between the client and the server. With client-side cursors, all sorting, updating, and manipulation of data takes place on the client. Once the server has sent the data to the client, it becomes the client's responsibility to handle the data until it is resubmitted to the server in a batch update. The server only tracks the fact that the data is currently being used by another system.

SQL Server 6.5 and 7 fully support client-side and server-side cursors. You can request data from the server, and then completely disconnect from the database once the data has been sent to the client. The application then works with the data locally. You can also maintain your connection to the server and have each update sent to the server as it occurs. On the other hand, the Jet engine does not truly support cursors through DAO. Although it is possible to implement cursor types in ADO, you cannot use the DAO interfaces to implement cursors. When using DAO, the server handles all updates to the data. Sorting changes and updates to the data are transmitted to the client as they occur. Access 2000 offers better support for cursors using ADO, but in Access 97, you cannot bind any objects to data that uses client-side cursors because ADO binding is not supported. Essentially, this means that an Access 97 application must maintain a constant connection to the server. This increases the load on the network as changes are constantly being sent back and forth between the backend database and the client application.

Multi-User Constraints

Anyone who has developed an Access application that is used by more than 10 people concurrently has probably run into the dreaded "record locked by another user" error that is common to multi-user Access databases. This error is a result of how Access locks records and how concurrency is managed.

When a user is updating a record, an RDBMS locks that record or the table the record resides in, so that other users cannot make modifications to it. This prevents multiple users from being able to update the same record at the same time. Access's record locking locks not only the record that is being edited, but also some of the other records physically stored close to it. As a result, two users may not be able to add records at the same time. Access locking information is stored in an .LDB file that is kept in the same directory as the database that is being used. This file is created when a user connects to the database and is deleted once the last connected user leaves the database. The locking that is implemented by Access in this file tends to have a number of problems when many concurrent users are accessing the database. This can create a severe limitation to an application when the user base starts to increase. SQL Server handles locking considerably better than Access. SQL Server can handle thousands of concurrent users, all accessing the same data. Of course, they can't all be updating the same information at the same time, but the potential to have a large user community sharing data is there. Access can have a large community too—as long as users don't all show up at the same time.

Implementation of the security model is much different in Access than in SQL Server. In Access, all security information is kept in the system.mdw file. This file contains all of the user IDs, groups, and passwords for each defined user on the system. In order to connect to a database using customized logon information, users must have access to a copy of the version of this file that was used to develop the application. If this file is lost or damaged and proper documentation on it is not kept, a database can become completely inaccessible. Also, in order to implement security on the database, either a new version of this file must be created or all permissions must be explicitly removed from all objects for the default user "Admin." The Admin user ID is common to all Microsoft Access systems and if the permissions for this user are not properly removed, anyone with a clean copy of Access can open the database and modify it. The security administrator must remove these implicit permissions, which can be a long and tedious process.

SQL Server security is implemented locally to the system. All user and group information is stored in the master database on the server, so there is no conflict with different versions of the security implementation. Security is also set to the highest possible level by default: Only the system administrators have access to all databases, for instance. User permissions must be assigned as needed and are not given explicitly. The default admin user, "sa," can have his or her password changed for the entire server, so that users cannot access the server where the change occurred using the "sa" logon from their own server. This prevents unauthorized access to the database at a level that Access cannot even come close to.

Maintenance and Administration

Administration in Access may seem rather simple. However, there are some maintenance tasks that must be done to a database in order to ensure the optimal performance of the system. When using Access, each database must be repaired and compacted on a regular basis. Repairing rebuilds the indexes in the database, and compacting clears out any empty space or deleted objects in the file. Repairing and compacting can prevent the database from becoming corrupted by high volume usage or improper application shutdown. Databases should also be backed up on a regular basis as a precaution against unexpected events, such as hard disk failures or accidental deletion. Each of these Access maintenance functions must be run separately for each database either manually or by using a third-party tool that comes at an extra cost. And, there is no facility in Access that records this activity. There is no central administration point for all Access databases on a computer, and there is no common way to schedule these tasks to occur at times when users are unlikely to be in the system. When fatal errors, such as a corrupted database, are encountered, the only way for administrators to know about the problem is when users contact them. This notification is inefficient and can become a problem if the support staff is not around to take the call.

SQL Server administration and maintenance is run through stored procedures included as system utilities or through SQL Server Agent/SQL Executive. Maintenance for all databases on a server is performed through one entry point and is therefore centralized. Rebuilding indexes, removing unused space from databases, checking database integrity, and backing up the database and transaction logs can be done for one or many databases using the tools supplied with SQL Server. Jobs can be scheduled at times when users are not on the system and can even be executed from remote servers. These tools maintain logs of all activities and, if configured to do so, notify users if any of the jobs failed or page someone if a fatal error has occurred on the server. You can even configure the server to email or page someone when an unexpected error occurs during the normal operation of the databases.

Replication

Access has the capability to create databases that replicate their data to other Access databases. This can be quite useful if users outside the normal network require access to information contained in a local database, if you're trying to reduce the number of users on a single MDB, if you're supporting a data ware-house, or for many other reasons. However, replication in Access is not without its problems. Replicated databases that become corrupted are no longer replicable and trying to determine what changes occurred in the database since the last time it was synchronized can be a difficult, if not impossible task. Access replication must also be managed through a separate utility called Replication Manager and can be difficult to administer. Replication Manager does not handle conflicts between the replicas very well and if a replica becomes damaged and needs to be repaired, it will lose its capability to be replicated. Also, you cannot create a database in Access that automatically replicates its data to another RDBMS.

SQL Server replication is much more robust. The replication that SQL Server uses is much more reliable and less prone to conflict errors or outright failure. It can replicate SQL Server data with another database on a separate SQL Server system, with an Access database, with an Oracle database, or with any other ODBC or OLE DB compliant data source. A SQL Server database can, therefore, share some or all of its data with completely different database systems. SQL Server Replication is configured through the same interface that is used to manage the rest of SQL Server's functionality. It can also be managed through system stored procedures or programmatically. In addition, replication can be scheduled through these interfaces and notification of job status can be configured.

Cost

The difference in cost between a purely Access-based application and one that uses SQL Server is considerable.

The costs of the software alone are quite different. A copy of Microsoft Office Developer Edition can be purchased for approximately $1,000. This allows royalty free distribution of the Access runtime engine with your Access application. SQL Server, on the other hand, must be purchased as a separate application and costs approximately $1,500 with five client licenses. Extra licenses must be purchased depending on the number of users that will be accessing the server. These extra licenses cost approximately $100 per additional user and can become very expensive if the number of users who will be accessing the server is sizable. On top of this, there is still the additional cost of the Office Developer Edition (or all users must have a licensed copy of Access) if you want to create an Access database or project to manipulate the data in the SQL Server database.

The hardware requirements for SQL Server are more stringent than the hardware requirements for Access. Access applications rarely require purchasing new hardware because the computers and network that the applications run on usually exist before an application is designed. Users can run Access on the equipment they already use for their word processing and spreadsheet applications. SQL Server, however, is best run on a dedicated server, so that the maximum performance of SQL Server can be extracted. Because servers are not usually purchased and left unused, a new server will almost certainly have to be acquired for SQL Server. For a mission-critical application, the minimum cost of an adequate server is about $3,000.

The cost of development and maintenance of a SQL Server application is also higher than one that is purely designed in Microsoft Access. Often, a professional database administrator (DBA) must be hired. This person must have the knowledge and the experience to maintain the server in optimal condition and to ensure that developers are using best practices when designing the database. If any of the developers is unfamiliar with SQL Server and how it works, there can be extra costs in development trying to get these developers up to speed with a new development environment.

The difference in costs between a SQL Server application and one developed solely in Access can be anywhere from $500 to $50,000.

Reasons to Migrate

Now that we've reviewed the differences between Access and SQL Server, let's discuss the reasons that people migrate their Access applications to SQL Server. Although there are almost as many reasons to migrate as there are Access databases, you should be prepared to justify your reasons for upgrading to yourself as well as others. Making the move with poorly defined reasons can cause you to address the wrong areas for improvement when you plan your upgrade.

Size

Probably the most common reason that people have for migrating an application from Access to SQL Server is the amount of data. Many users notice that the performance of a networked Access application tends to degrade once the database expands to between 10MB to 20MB. This is because Access must constantly deal with the passing of large amounts of data back and forth between the database and the client. When a database reaches 100MB, it can take a very long time to run complicated queries against the data. Despite the absolute 2GB physical limit of the size of a database, performance is usually degraded long before the limit is even approached. This is a very good reason to migrate an application to SQL Server.

Number of Users

Due to Access's problems with multi-user access, SQL Server is often a viable alternative to using Jet engine. Access tends to run into problems with more that 10 concurrent users. SQL Server can handle thousands of concurrent users and can help administer them much better than Access can. If you are building a large system where there are many different types of users, SQL Server can make it easier for administrators and users to add and remove logons with appropriate permissions.

Network Traffic

As previously mentioned, SQL Server reduces the amount of data traffic between the database and the client. If you are planning on running an application over a slow network, it is best to reduce, as much as possible, any traffic on the system. This frees resources for other users. Even if you have a fast network, if Jet engine-based applications are a significant portion of the network's number of requests or packets, then a migration might extend the life of the system.

Response Issues

SQL Server is much faster at working with and returning data across a network than Access is. This is because of the reduced amount of data that must be transferred across the network. If you have a table with hundreds of thousands of records in it, Access has to return the entire contents of the table. SQL Server only returns the requested data, and it will retrieve it faster than Access can. This is because SQL Server can take advantage of the processing capability of the computer on which it resides. The computer that requests the data must do all of the processing of an Access database. The server running SQL Server can also handle all of the indexing and updating of the data, freeing the client to implement the rules required by the business case.

Maintenance and Administration

The centralized administration interfaces provided by SQL Server can be used to justify a migration. They allow one entry point for all activities including the ability to schedule jobs, which can guarantee the state of the database and provide the added security of constant backups. SQL Server also supports rollbacks when the server fails. If SQL Server stops unexpectedly, once it is restarted, it attempts to restore all of its databases to the last known good state. This means that any transactions that were committed before the crash remain in the database. When this occurs in Access, a corrupted database will often have to be recovered from a physical backup if one exists. The data changes that took place since the previous backup are lost. Although this is also possible with SQL Server databases, it is much more likely that the server will be able to recover from the damage and only those changes that were not complete at the time of failure are lost.

Replication

Access does not have the native capability to replicate to other RDBMSs as SQL Server does. If an application needs to retrieve data from multiple systems with a minimum of user intervention or development effort, migrating to SQL Server may be able to solve this issue. For example, SQL Server can be configured to replicate its data to another data source that is used to do reporting on actions within multiple systems. You can also use SQL Server 7 with any OLE DB compliant data source to bring data together into one place. You can replicate external data into SQL Server or replicate SQL Server data to these data sources. The number of OLE DB drivers available is growing and includes such systems as AS/400, Oracle, Sybase, Btrieve, and Informix. Any of these systems can be replication partners with SQL Server using the built-in capabilities of SQL Server. If multi-system replication is a requirement for a system, SQL Server's capabilities can be used to justify a migration.

Reasons Not to Migrate

Just as there are reasons to migrate an application to SQL Server, there are also reasons not to migrate an application. Take a good look at your motivations in migrating the application and make sure they are sound. You should ensure that the migration is necessary (after all, it is a lot of extra work) and that migrating the application will not negatively affect users.

Size

Just as size is a reason to migrate, it is also a reason not to migrate. Access is very good at dealing with small databases. You may find that migrating a database that is less than 10MB is not worth the effort involved. Also, SQL Server has a certain amount of overhead that can degrade the performance of a small database. You will probably find that a small database in Access performs better than the same database on SQL Server because of the index processing that must take place.

Organization of Data

If you are using size to justify your migration, you may also want to take a look at how the database is designed. Running queries against an Access database that has 100 tables, each containing 1,000 records can be very quick. This may seem like a large database, but Access returns the data in much the same way that it would if there was only one table containing 1,000 records. If, however, your database has one table with 1,000,000 records, you can safely assume that this database should be migrated. SQL Server will deal with this database much better than Access will.

User Connectivity

One of the problems with using SQL Server as your database is that users must have constant access to the server. In some applications, this is not possible. If each copy of the application runs separately from each other and has its own data file, you probably should not move the application to SQL Server. Doing so would eliminate the users' ability to work with the application when they are not connected to the network. Although it may be possible to redesign the application so that all users access the same database, it may not be practical. Because the original database was running locally on a user's PC, the original design will probably run much faster because it does not need to engage network resources to work with data.

Cost

Cost is always a major factor in each migration from Access to SQL Server. It is often a very good reason not to migrate an application. There are multiple costs that are incurred in the process of migration and any one or all of them should be considered carefully before a migration takes place.

Migration Considerations

Any migration should be thoroughly analyzed before it takes place to ensure that it is justified and that it will give you the benefits that you expect. Part of this analysis must include your reasons for migrating. The reasons given in this appendix are by no means exhaustive. There are many more reasons that you or your company may need to consider before migrating an application. The reasons may not only need self justification, but may also need to be justified to colleagues and, more likely, a management team. If the migration is not justifiable, the developer should take a second look at the motivation for performing the upgrade. This is not to say that migrating for the sake of migrating is not justified. There is a lot to be gained in learning to migrate an application. And sometimes, the reason to migrate may be the learning itself.

Index

Symbols

A

T

X

XML (eXtensible Markup Language)
recovering data from XML files, 137–38
using Access 2002 XML methods to
export tables, 134–37
using ADO to generate XML files in
Access 2000, 139

Z

.ZIP files, 91, 122–24, 291, 292

forums.apress.com

FOR PROFESSIONALS BY PROFESSIONALS™

JOIN THE APRESS FORUMS AND BE PART OF OUR COMMUNITY. You'll find discussions that cover topics of interest to IT professionals, programmers, and enthusiasts just like you. If you post a query to one of our forums, you can expect that some of the best minds in the business—especially Apress authors, who all write with *The Expert's Voice*™—will chime in to help you. Why not aim to become one of our most valuable participants (MVPs) and win cool stuff? Here's a sampling of what you'll find:

DATABASES

Data drives everything.

Share information, exchange ideas, and discuss any database programming or administration issues.

INTERNET TECHNOLOGIES AND NETWORKING

Try living without plumbing (and eventually IPv6).

Talk about networking topics including protocols, design, administration, wireless, wired, storage, backup, certifications, trends, and new technologies.

JAVA

We've come a long way from the old Oak tree.

Hang out and discuss Java in whatever flavor you choose: J2SE, J2EE, J2ME, Jakarta, and so on.

MAC OS X

All about the Zen of OS X.

OS X is both the present and the future for Mac apps. Make suggestions, offer up ideas, or boast about your new hardware.

OPEN SOURCE

Source code is good; understanding (open) source is better.

Discuss open source technologies and related topics such as PHP, MySQL, Linux, Perl, Apache, Python, and more.

PROGRAMMING/BUSINESS

Unfortunately, it is.

Talk about the Apress line of books that cover software methodology, best practices, and how programmers interact with the "suits."

WEB DEVELOPMENT/DESIGN

Ugly doesn't cut it anymore, and CGI is absurd.

Help is in sight for your site. Find design solutions for your projects and get ideas for building an interactive Web site.

SECURITY

Lots of bad guys out there—the good guys need help.

Discuss computer and network security issues here. Just don't let anyone else know the answers!

TECHNOLOGY IN ACTION

Cool things. Fun things.

It's after hours. It's time to play. Whether you're into LEGO® MINDSTORMS™ or turning an old PC into a DVR, this is where technology turns into fun.

WINDOWS

No defenestration here.

Ask questions about all aspects of Windows programming, get help on Microsoft technologies covered in Apress books, or provide feedback on any Apress Windows book.

HOW TO PARTICIPATE:

Go to the Apress Forums site at **http://forums.apress.com/**.
Click the New User link.